STRANGE TRUTHS IN UNDISCOVERED LANDS

Shelley's Poetic Development and Romantic Geography

The great Romantic poet Percy Bysshe Shelley had a complicated relationship with the British Empire and the culture of colonialism. Considered politically radical and scandalous in Britain, Shelley lived in self-imposed exile and set much of his writing in foreign places. In *Strange Truths in Undiscovered Lands* Nahoko Miyamoto Alvey examines the ways in which Shelley developed a 'Romantic geography' to provide visionary alternatives to an earth devastated by a new type of European colonialism and global expansion.

Intertextually rich, Alvey's work establishes the context in which poems by Shelley and other Romantics were written by presenting relevant histories, travel texts, scientific writings, and archival material, complemented by postcolonial analysis. Unique in its emphasis on the optimistic and positive aspects of Shelley's poetical works, *Strange Truths in Undiscovered Lands* offers a different perspective on Romantic Orientalism, and a new look at how the poet imagined the relationship between the Self and the Other.

Thorough and original, this book will be of interest to Romanticists, postcolonialists, and anyone interested in alternative responses to acts of colonialism and empire.

NAHOKO MIYAMOTO ALVEY is an associate professor in British Section, Area Studies at the University of Tokyo, Komaba.

NAHOKO MIYAMOTO ALVEY

Strange Truths in Undiscovered Lands:

Shelley's Poetic Development and Romantic Geography

UNIVERSITY OF TORONTO PRESS
Toronto Buffalo London

© University of Toronto Press 2009
Toronto Buffalo London
utorontopress.com

Reprinted in paperback 2020

ISBN 978-0-8020-3956-9 (cloth)   ISBN 978-1-4875-2606-1 (paper)

Library and Archives Canada Cataloguing in Publication

Title: Strange truths in undiscovered lands : Shelley's poetic development and romantic geography / Nahoko Miyamoto Alvey.

Names: Alvey, Nahoko Miyamoto, 1961– author.

Identifiers: Canadiana 20200198181 | ISBN 9781487526061 (softcover)

Subjects: LCSH: Shelley, Percy Bysshe, 1792–1822 – Criticism and interpretation. | LCSH: Geography in literature. | LCSH: Geopolitics in literature. | LCSH: Romanticism – Great Britain.

Classification: LCC PR5438 .A59 2020 | DDC 821/.7–dc23

University of Toronto Press acknowledges the financial assistance to its publishing program of the Canada Council for the Arts and the Ontario Arts Council, an agency of the Government of Ontario.

 Canada Council   Conseil des Arts
for the Arts   du Canada

ONTARIO ARTS COUNCIL
CONSEIL DES ARTS DE L'ONTARIO
an Ontario government agency
un organisme du gouvernement de l'Ontario

Funded by the   Financé par le
Government   gouvernement
of Canada   du Canada

*To my husband, James Alvey,
and my parents, Minako and the late Taisuke Miyamoto*

Contents

Acknowledgments ix

List of Abbreviations xi

A Note on Shelley Texts xv

Introduction 3

1 *Queen Mab*: The Female Dreamers and a Pathless Wilderness 19

2 'Alastor': A Solitary Quester and a New Eastern Geography 51

3 'Mont Blanc': The Questioning Traveller and a Visionary Geography of Chamonix 83

4 *Prometheus Unbound*: The Eastern and Western Lovers on the Highest Mountain 109

5 'The Witch of Atlas': The Hybrid Explorer and Shelley's Joyous Challenge 145

Conclusion 181

Notes 195

Bibliography 219

Index 251

Acknowledgments

The writing of this book has not been a solitary effort undertaken in hush of night. On the contrary, many people have contributed, directly and indirectly, and not once but many times, to the making of this book.

My initial thanks go to my first professors, who helped me to understand the language of poetry and the genre of literary criticism, especially Professors Yuichi Takamatsu, Hisaaki Yamanouchi, George Hughes, the late Hiroshi Izubuchi, Kenkichi Kamijima, Kenji Nakamura, and Yoshiyuki Fujikawa of the University of Tokyo. I subsequently benefited from the support, instruction, and comments of the following individuals, to whom I am deeply thankful: Professors Alan Bewell, Jay Macpherson, J.R. de J. Jackson, M.F.N. Dixon, William Keith, and Ronald Tetrault. I am particularly grateful to J.R. de J. Jackson and Jay Macpherson for their enormous intellectual generosity, criticism, and kindness. My greatest debt is to Alan Bewell, who supervised this work in its earliest stage as a doctoral thesis with unfailing kindness and readiness, and with many invaluable comments.

Thanks are also due to those who have provided thoughtful comments, advice, and help, which were fundamental to the completion of this book. I wish to thank Stephen Clark and Kaz Oishi for their insightful and incisive comments on the manuscript. I also wish to thank three anonymous readers for the University of Toronto Press for giving invaluable advice and feedback, and forcing me to broaden the scholarly scope of the book. Thanks to Marco De la Cruz-Heredia for his technical support, and to Miya Itabashi and Haruki Inagaki for their editorial assistance. I am greatly indebted to my editors. At the University of Toronto Press, Jill McConkey provided indispensable assistance, and Barbara Porter helped to see the manuscript to completion with great patience and skill. Charles Anthony Stuart gave scrupulous attention to the manuscript. Mary Newberry provided an excellent index.

I am grateful to the Fukuhara Foundation for the grant in aid which assisted with publication costs. I greatly appreciate the generous support I received from my colleagues and the staff at the Area Studies and the English Language Department of the University of Tokyo, who allowed me to take a sabbatical in the second semester of 2008, and the Department of Communication, Journalism and Marketing of Massey University, New Zealand, in which pleasant environment I was able to complete the book.

On a more personal level I wish to thank Professor Hisaaki Yamanouchi for his continued interest and encouragement. I had the rare good fortune to be taught by him. Without his guidance, I doubt I would ever have crossed the ocean to pursue a degree in English literature. His scholarly integrity, wisdom, generosity, patience, and support meant – and mean – much more than he could possibly know.

Finally, I wish to thank my parents, Minako and the late Taisuke Miyamoto, and my husband, James, whose presence, like the 'shape all light' in Shelley's 'The Triumph of Life,' is unseen but felt throughout this book, and whose warm and loving support is invaluable.

The illustration is reproduced by permission of the Thomas Fisher Rare Book Library of the University of Toronto. Part of chapter 2 appeared in an earlier version as '"Strange Truths in Undiscovered Lands": *Alastor* and a New Eastern Geography' in *Corresponding Powers: Studies in Honour of Professor Hisaaki Yamanouchi*, edited by George Hughes (Cambridge: Brewer, 1997), 63–77, and is reprinted by permission. A much condensed, shorter version of chapter 4 appeared as 'Love as Infection: Hybridity and Multiple Idealisms in *Prometheus Unbound*' in *Poetica* 54 (2001), 71–92, and is reprinted by permission.

Abbreviations

CLSTC *The Collected Letters of Samuel Taylor Coleridge.* Ed. Earl Leslie Griggs. 6 vols. Oxford: Clarendon, 1956–71.

Continuation *Arabian Tales; or, a Continuation of the Arabian Nights Entertainments. Consisting of Stories, Related by the Sultana of the Indies, to Divert Her Husband from the Performance of a Rash Vow. Exhibiting a Most Interesting Picture of the Religion, Laws, Manners, Costumes, Arts, and Literature of the Nations of the East. In Three Volumes. Newly Translated from the Original Arabic into French, by Dom Chaves, a Native Arab, and M. Cazotte, Member of the Academy of Dijon.* 3 vols. Trans. Robert Heron. London: Faulder, 1794.

Correspondence *The Life and Correspondence of Robert Southey.* Ed. Charles Cuthbert Southey. 2nd ed. 6 vols. London: Longman, 1850.

CPPBS *The Complete Poetry of Percy Bysshe Shelley.* Ed. Donald H. Reiman and Neil Fraistat. 2 vols. to date. Baltimore: Johns Hopkins UP, 2000–.

CWPBS *The Complete Works of Percy Bysshe Shelley.* Ed. Roger Ingpen and Walter E. Peck. 10 vols. London: Benn, 1926–30.

EN	*The Esdaile Notebook: A Volume of Early Poems by Percy Bysshe Shelley*. Ed. Kenneth Neill Cameron. New York: Knopf, 1964.
First Discourse	*Discourse on the Sciences and Arts*. Ed. Roger D. Masters and Christopher Kelly. Hanover, NH: UP of New England, 1992. Vol. 2 of *The Collected Writings of Rousseau*. 12 vols. to date. 1990–.
HSWT	Mary Shelley and Percy Bysshe Shelley. *History of a Six Weeks' Tour 1817*. 1817. Ed. Jonathan Wordsworth. Oxford: Woodstock, 1989.
Journals	*Journals of Mary Shelley 1814–1844*. Ed. Paula R. Feldman and Diana Scott-Kilvert. Baltimore: Johns Hopkins UP, 1987.
LBCPW	*Lord Byron: The Complete Poetical Works*. Ed. Jerome J. McGann. 7 vols. Oxford: Clarendon, 1980–93.
Letters	*The Letters of Percy Bysshe Shelley*. Ed. Frederick L. Jones. 2 vols. Oxford: Clarendon, 1964.
LMWS	*The Letters of Mary Wollstonecraft Shelley*. Ed. Betty T. Bennett. 3 vols. Baltimore: Johns Hopkins UP, 1980–8.
Prelude	William Wordsworth. *The Prelude: 1799, 1805, 1850*. Ed. Jonathan Wordsworth, M.H. Abrams, and Stephen Gill. New York: Norton, 1979.
Prose	*The Prose Works of Percy Bysshe Shelley*. Ed. E. B. Murray. 1 vol. to date. Oxford: Clarendon, 1993–.
PS	*The Poems of Shelley*. Ed. Geoffrey Matthews and Kelvin Everest. 2 vols. to date. London: Longman, 1989–.
PWRS	*The Poetical Works of Robert Southey, Collected by Himself*. 10 vols. London: Longman, 1838.

PWWW	*The Poetical Works of William Wordsworth.* Ed. E. de Selincourt and Helen Darbishire. Rev. Helen Darbishire. 5 vols. Oxford: Oxford UP, 1952–9.
Ruins	C.F. Volney. *The Ruins, or, Meditation on the Revolutions of Empire; and The Law of Nature.* Baltimore: Black Classic, 1991.
SC	*Shelley and His Circle 1773–1822.* Carl H. Pforzheimer Library. 10 vols. to date. Cambridge, MA: Harvard UP, 1961– .
Second Discourse	*Discourse on the Origins and Foundations of Inequality among Mens.* Ed. Roger D. Masters and Christopher Kelly. Hanover, NH: UP of New England, 1992. Vol. 3 of *The Collected Writings of Rousseau.* 12 vols. to date. 1990–.
SP&P	*Shelley's Prose and Poetry.* 2nd ed. Ed. Donald H. Reiman and Neil Fraistat. New York: Norton, 2002.
SPW	*Shelley: Poetical Works.* Ed. Thomas Hutchinson. Corr. G.M. Matthews. Oxford: Oxford UP, 1983.
STCPW	*Poetical Works.* Ed. J.C.C. Mays. 3 vols, in 6. The Collected Works of Samuel Taylor Coleridge 16. Princeton, NJ: Princeton UP, 2001.
Triumph	*Shelley's 'The Triumph of Life': A Critical Study.* Ed. Donald H. Reiman. 1965. Rpt. New York: Octagon, 1979.

A Note on Shelley Texts

References to Shelley's poetry and prose are to the Norton Critical edition, edited by Donald H. Reiman and Neil Fraistat (abbreviated as *SP&P*), whenever possible. Poems not in the Norton edition, Shelley's *Notes on Queen Mab*, and Mary Shelley's notes on Shelley's poems are quoted from the Oxford Standard Authors edition, edited by Thomas Hutchinson and corrected by G.M. Matthews (abbreviated as *SPW*). The early poems in *The Esdaile Notebook* are taken from *The Poems of Shelley*, edited by Geoffrey Matthews and Kelvin Everest (abbreviated as *PS*). The prose works written before the Shelleys left England in the spring of 1818 are quoted from the Oxford edition, edited by E.B. Murry (abbreviated as *Prose*), with the exception of Shelley's and Mary's joint work, *History of a Six Weeks' Tour* (abbreviated as *HSWT*), for which I use the facsimile edition by Jonathan Wordsworth. All other prose works are cited from the Julian edition, edited by Roger Ingpen and Walter Peck (abbreviated as *CWPBS*). All dates for Shelley's works are dates of composition. All other dates are dates of publication, unless otherwise stated.

STRANGE TRUTHS IN UNDISCOVERED LANDS

Introduction

At the beginning of *The Prelude*, Wordsworth, echoing the concluding lines of *Paradise Lost* (12.646–7), poses a question many Romantics repeatedly ask: 'What dwelling shall receive me,' when '[t]he earth is all before me'? (*Prelude* 1.11, 15).[1] 'Dream not of other worlds,' the angel Raphael warns Adam (Milton, *Paradise Lost* 8.175), but in the late eighteenth and early nineteenth centuries, various 'other worlds' were appearing from beyond the confines of the known world. The earth that was all before the Romantics was not an uninhabited wilderness. It was crammed with unfamiliar peoples living in various non-European cultures. Moreover, Europeans were starting to develop a complex strategic network of European metropoles and colonial outposts. Already in the *Discours sur l'origine et les fondements de l'inégalité parmi les hommes* (the *Second Discourse* [1755]), Jean-Jacques Rousseau observed the tendency for the earth to be unified by an early form of globalization and imperialism: 'commerce, Voyages, and conquests unite various Peoples more, and their ways of life are constantly brought closer together by frequent communication' (3: 80–1).[2] Edmund Burke in his speech 'Moving his Resolution for Conciliation with the Colonies,' delivered on 22 March 1775, referred to the Spanish Empire as 'extensive and detached' (3: 125).[3] Adam Smith wrote in *An Inquiry into the Nature and Causes of the Wealth of Nations* (1776) that Europeans and capital were moving all over the world: 'capital may wander about from place to place, according as it can either buy cheap or sell dear' (1: 364); '[In Brazil] there are said to be more than six hundred thousand people, either Portugueze or descended from Portugueze, creoles, mulattoes, and a mixed race between Portugueze and Brazilians' (2: 569).

Read side by side with these observations, Wordsworth's question reveals a potentially threatening aspect of the Romantic imagination that appropriates other peoples or places, especially when we remember that the same poet celebrated London as a 'great emporium,' the 'fountain' of the 'destiny' of Great Britain as well as 'of earth itself' (*Prelude* 8.749, 747, 748). It is not just breathless enthusiasm that we hear in his poetry, however. An ambivalence mixed with guilt and anxiety, which he would have felt toward an emergent form of globalization, manifests itself in 'The Brothers' (1800). Transferring the psychologised landscape of Coleridge's 'Rime of the Ancyent Marinere' (1798) back to the contemporary Lake District, Wordsworth focuses on Leonard, who returns to his native place 'with some small wealth / Acquired by traffic 'mid the Indian Isles,' which suggests his engagement in colonial trade in the West Indies (66–7).[4] The local priest, however, unable to recognize him, recounts his only brother's death and the rumour about him the villagers believe: 'When last we heard of him, / He was in slavery among the Moors / Upon the Barbary coast' (316–18). Immediately after the conversation, Leonard exiles himself on the sea as a 'grey-heard Mariner' (435).

Thirty years after Edward Said's seminal *Orientalism* (1978), the complicity of power and literature has become a shared critical language in literary studies, postcolonial studies, and history. The passages quoted above and numerous other Romantic texts have been analysed to produce some excellent scholarship in the critical terrain, which Nigel Leask's *British Romantic Writers and the East: Anxieties of Empire* (1992), together with John Barrell's *The Infection of Thomas De Quincey: A Psychopathology of Imperialism* (1991), brought into the mainstream of Romantic scholarship. While sharing the critical stance with other critics in the study of anxieties of empire, I started this book wondering why these passages awaken a sense of *déjà vu* in us; living in the twenty-first century, we often find ourselves interrogating and experiencing what seems to have been questioned and observed two hundred years ago. Is the term postcolonialism 'prematurely celebratory and obfuscatory' (McClintock 13)? Is it 'far too long now' since colonial discourse analysis, derived from Said's *Orientalism*, assumed that 'identical regimes of power and knowledge organised both the political management of empire and all the varied literature which represent it' (Moore-Gilbert, 'introduction' to *Writing India 1757–1990* 25)? Debbie Lee answers in the affirmative in *Slavery and the Romantic Imagination* (2002); she considers nuanced differences between colonial and literary discourses and elaborates the concept of 'the distanced imagination' by drawing on Adam Smith's sympathetic imagination in his *Theory of Moral Sentiments* (1759), Coleridge's meditation on alterity in *Marginalia*, and Emmanuel Levinas's idea of otherness (3, 29–43). Staying on literary terrain, this book also re-examines why nineteenth-century colonialism is not a thing of the past and what the nature and role of the Romantic imagination is in the making and unmaking of empire in the geopolitical imaginings recorded in the Romantic texts. I will assume the importance of the topic in what follows.

The Subject and Structure of the Book

Strange Truths in Undiscovered Lands: Shelley's Poetic Development and Romantic Geography attempts to investigate the Romantic poets' geopolitical imaginings, which are shaped by actual and imaginary engagement with the earth that is all before them in the formative age of a new type of European colonialism and global expansion. I will explain more about the meaning of 'Romantic geography' shortly but it is essentially an internalized geopolitical space of the Romantics that records the extent to which the poetic imagination stretches itself on the global scale, hand in hand with, or against, the globalizing force, and it breaks 'a hegemonic geometry of centre and periphery that conditions all perceptions of Self and Other' in the European mind (Denis Porter, *Haunted Journeys* 19).

The inner geopolitical space, which responds to the outer political and cultural situations, shows how and where Romantic poets, in tune with or ahead of their time, position themselves in the British Empire's complicity with knowledge and literature. Sometimes it repeats or reinforces the outer hegemony, but sometimes it can defy or even amend or go beyond it, making the embedded mental map of the world different from any formal map of the generally understood sort. The present book concerns the latter kind of mental geography, and calls it a 'Romantic geography.' It is a space where the poetic imagination, in response to the outer world, engages in the visionary making and unmaking of inner geopolitical space, and creates a different geography from the outer ones. When poets resist (in vain) being part of the larger economic and political world system that underwrites ideologies of colonialism and imperialism, this mental space becomes a space of crisis, contestation, and failure. When envisioned by the poetic imagination working against empire and breaking down the 'hegemonic geometry of centre and periphery' (Denis Porter, *Haunted Journeys* 19), however, this space becomes a space of interrogation and inculcation that can offer an opportunity to turn the failure into positive or productive failure. It becomes a space where the self can grow, and refashions itself, whether it is a disempowerment of the Eurocentric self or not.

In order to examine the inner geopolitical space of the Romantic psyche, the present study focuses mainly on Percy Bysshe Shelley's earnest endeavours to provide visionary alternatives to the desolate earth he saw in front of him, devastated by colonialism and global economy. Shelley, who was one of the most versed in contemporary science among British poets, thought that the mind should be 'considerably tinctured with science, and enlarged by cultivation' ('A Refutation of Deism' [1814], *Prose* 120). For Shelley, however, the purpose of educating imagination is significantly different from those early imperialists, whose modes of thinking were based upon the centre-periphery distinction. Shelley wants the poetic imagination to be educated by science and culture in order to 'contemplate itself, not as the centre and model of the Universe, but as one of the infinitely various multitude of beings of which it is actually composed' (*Prose* 120). In this regard, his view of imagination as an agent fostered by science and culture is the exact opposite to ideologies of imperialism and global economy aided by scientific, medical, or militaristic means. As early as 1813, Shelley depicted a prototype of an ideal metropolis that, blessed with 'peace and freedom,' welcomes 'strangers' (*Queen Mab* 2.202, 201). It was only from the 1960s that multiculturalism started to be favourably received, but Shelley's passage can be taken as an early notion of such an open society. This aspect of Shelley has not been investigated until now and requires attention.

Shelley's view of the growing empire of his day can be considered strictly within the context of his times, but I believe that positive sides of his struggle and imaginary leap beyond colonialism, despite negative sides that arise from his complicated and contradictory stance on the British Empire, also have special relevance for the postcolonial age in which we live. Leela Gandhi's definition of postcolonialism as 'a disciplinary project devoted to the academic task of revisiting, remembering, and, crucially interrogating the colonial past' (4) can be applied well to current Romantic scholarship, but it can also be applied to the Romantic writers, who took it as a task of creative imagination to (re)visit, remember, and crucially interrogate the colonial past/present long before their country became an empire on which the sun never sets. This is a painful task because it requires one to face the dire consequences of one's involvement in colonialism, but this is exactly what Shelley had been doing all his life. Two important figures in Romanticism – Prometheus and Rousseau – also do this in his later poems. In *Prometheus Unbound* (1818–20), Prometheus is bound on the Indian Caucasus for an incredibly long number of years to contemplate the results of what he has done as a founder of European civilization, and to remember and relinquish his Curse. In 'The Triumph of Life' (1822), amid the green Apennine, Rousseau is disfigured by voluntarily bathing in the colonial light issued from the centre of Europe and still keeps wondering about the worth of his deeds.

The present study thus has two purposes: to offer a case study of 'Romantic geography' as an early literary attempt to challenge globalization and to reconsider the Shelley canon by scrutinizing Shelley's major works as a developing quest in which the imagination, contemplating itself as one of the 'infinitely various multitude' that constitute the world, discovers and maps 'strange truths in undiscovered lands' in the teeth of globalizing tendencies ('A Refutation of Deism' *Prose* 120; 'Alastor' [1815] 77). Shelley's poetic space is vast, covering East, West, North, and South. The chapters that follow will examine the crucial sites in Shelley's 'Romantic geography' by tracing chronologically Shelley's major poems. Chapter 1 considers the role of marginal places in Wales and in America, on which intersect the European myth of Prometheus, the nationalistic Welsh myth of Madoc, and the obscure Welsh myth of Mab, in *Queen Mab*. Chapter 2 explores the geographical trajectories of a poet's solitary quest to India through the Middle East in 'Alastor.' Chapter 3, on 'Mont Blanc' (1816), deals with Shelley's attempt to recreate Mont Blanc's glacial world in a different way from eighteenth-century British travellers, who turned an unnamed, accused mountain into a celebrated source of international tourism. Chapter 4, taking up India again, investigates negotiations and contagious influences between East and West in *Prometheus Unbound*. Chapter 5 presents an exploration of the African continent by a female hybrid in 'The Witch of Atlas' (1820). The concluding chapter draws a conclusion with Shelley's poetic quest that ends in Europe and the cold northern shore of New Britain (Labrador) in 'The Triumph of Life.' Before turning to the detailed analysis of these poems, I wish to discuss the book's emphasis on the positive sides of

Shelley's Romantic geography, its priority of geography over the self, and its position in Shelley criticism.

Tensions in Shelley's Encounters with Others

Shelley's writings on empire were not entirely consistent. The tensions in his writings on this theme have led to a variety of interpretations of Shelley, typically due to the selection of his works that were analysed. The youthful, idealistic poet of *Queen Mab*, who visualized an idea of an open society and later realized an utopian world in *Prometheus Unbound*, was becoming more and more aware of his involvement with imperialism toward the end of his life. It is true, however, that despite Shelley's open-mindedness and his unfailing criticism of any form of tyranny or imperialism that runs throughout his poetic career, we cannot expect any writer of this period to be fully detached from colonialist attitudes. The extent to which Shelley complies with imperialism and the extent to which his imagination, backed by an astonishing breadth of learning and a sharp critical insight, overcomes the predicaments of Orientalism need to be measured by examining his earlier and his later works, both poetry and prose, and his positive and negative sides.

Shelley's ambivalence toward colonialism and the British Empire is, for example, seen in his literary and political relationship with his close friend, Thomas Love Peacock, who was employed by the East India Company and associated himself with the philosophic radicals like Bentham (Butler, *Peacock Displayed* 178). Peacock maintains the predominance of scientific and economic knowledge over poetry in 'The Four Ages of Poetry' (1820), and, in a private letter to Shelley written at 'India House' on 4 December 1820, separates 'moral, political, and physical science' from poetry, whose audience is no longer among 'the higher class of minds' (8: 218–19).[5] In *A Defence of Poetry*, written as a sharp riposte to Peacock's essay in the spring of 1821, Shelley ascribes to poetry the higher kind of utility, which produces '[p]leasure or good' that is 'durable, universal, and permanent'; political economy, which Shelley bitterly criticizes for 'the abuse of all invention for abridging and combining labour, to the exasperation of the inequality of mankind,' is 'the selfish and calculating principle,' and concerns only the lower kind of utility, giving only 'transitory and particular' pleasure (*SP&P* 528–31). His distinction between higher and lower forms of utility 'anticipates J.S. Mill's subsequent, critical modification of Benthamite philosophy' (Connell 226), but in contrast to Peacock and Bentham, who, according to John Stuart Mill's famous quotation in 'Bentham' (1838), thinks that 'push-pin is as good as poetry' (*Essays on Ethics, Religion and Society* 113),[6] Shelley assigns the task of producing and preserving the 'true utility' to 'Poets or poetical philosophers' (*A Defence of Poetry*, SP&P 529).

While seeking to liberate humankind from 'the selfish and calculating principle' (*SP&P* 531), however, Shelley asked Peacock about a possibility of 'a respectable appointment, of going to India' in October 1821 (*Letters* 2: 361, 361n.5). A part of him was seized by colonial desire, while another part of him believed in the power of liberating imagination throughout his life, trying to educate those who 'burst the chains, / The icy chains of custom' (*Queen Mab* 1.126–7) and to set humans free, including 'those spoilers spoiled' and 'the ribald crowd' ('The Triumph of Life' 235, 136).

Here in the introduction and in the following chapters, Shelley's ambivalence and tensions are discussed, but the positive aspects of Shelley's imaginative making and unmaking of empire are the book's main interest, because, if modern Orientalism originated in the age of Romanticism as Said argues, hints for solutions to the predicaments and problems of Orientalism can also be found in the age. In the advent of globalization and imperialism, European attitudes toward others were torn between fascination and fear, and a sense of superiority and anti-colonial feelings. The British people's sense of superiority and excitement at colonial conquest were disturbed by 'a confusion of nations and peoples promiscuously mixing' (Bewell, *Romanticism and Colonial Disease* 310). It is exactly from this confusion of geographical sense of centre and margin that there emerge new attitudes toward others about which they groped for the words to explain.

One example of this groping is how to define, in a broader social context, love (as opposed to desire) between the self and others when trying to recognize the other as the other and yet to love it as it is. In *Don Juan* (1819–23), Byron attempts to describe the unnameable relationship between Juan and Leila: Juan loves Leila as '[p]atriots (now and then) may love a nation' and she seems to select him 'in place of what her home and friends once *were*,' though they are connected in 'neither clime, time, blood' (10.535, 451, 455).[7] Although Byron's language can become only paradoxical, a number of negatives and contradictions that surround the couple disturb the fixed relationship between the conqueror and the conquered; pieced together, they are about to produce an internal geography that interlocks Europe and non-Europe by love, as a counter to the external universal forms of Europe and non-Europe yoked together by global economics and imperialism.

Byron confesses his inability to 'tell exactly what it was' between these two that made them feel towards each other *'naturally'* (10.419, 452), but Shelley defines these feelings as the 'great secret of morals,' and aligns them with moral, political, and 'scientific and œconomical knowledge' via poetic imagination (*A Defence of Poetry*, *SP&P* 517, 530), trying to forge an alliance between them to form a counter-force against imperialistic and globalizing tendencies. Shelley's famous definitions of love as the 'great secret of morals' and imagination as the 'great instrument of moral good' should be understood in this broader context (*SP&P* 517). Love, defined as 'a going out of our own nature, and an identification of ourselves with the beautiful which exists in thought, action, or person, not our own,' can be extended beyond the political/colonial division, and in a way different from globalization and imperialism, change the geography of the world, creating an alternative space where humans are 'free, uncircumscribed,' 'unclassed, tribeless and nationless' (*SP&P* 517, *Prometheus Unbound* 3.194, 195); as means employed in globalization and colonialism, political economy and the physical sciences 'have enlarged the limits of the empire of man over the external world,' but 'for want of the poetical faculty,' they have 'proportionally circumscribed those of the internal world,' and 'man, having enslaved the elements, remains himself a slave' (*A Defence of Poetry*, *SP&P* 530). Shelley here recalls the famous opening of book 1, chapter 1, of Rousseau's *Social Contract* that epitomizes Rousseau's concepts of human nature and history: 'Man was/is born free, and everywhere he is in chains. One who believes himself the master of others is nonetheless a greater slave than they' (4: 131).

The problems and dark aspects of colonial landscapes that Shelley, Byron, and other Romantics faced are now given more prominence in our time, and we have not solved them yet. I regard this as important and will investigate the positive sides of Shelley's imaginings on empire, that is, his endeavours to recreate the colonial geography and present a Romantic geography in which the self is given an opportunity to grow even under the darkest shade of the anxieties of empire. They offer a model for the postcolonial age all the more because Shelley lived the tensions of imperialism and idealism, as we do, and yet continued attempts to amend by his pen the situation in which man is 'in chains,' believing in the power of poetic imagination that goes 'out of our own nature' and identifies 'ourselves with the beautiful which exists in thought, action, or person, not our own' (*A Defence of Poetry*, SP&P 517).

The Relationship between Geography, Identity, and Hybridity

The importance of the other in the formation of the self has been well recognized in literary studies, but it is worth noting that since Freud's introduction of the unconscious as 'the other scene,' the otherness has been variously theorized as a place; Lacan considers 'the big Other' ('*L'Autre*'), which cannot be assimilated into the ego, as a locus where speech is constituted (Evans 124–5, 132–3). After Said's *Orientalism* associated the subject-object relationship with the relevant geographical identities in the study of literature and imperialism, geography has become an important element in the relationship between the self and others in the dynamics of the external globalizing power and internal poetic imagination, and this book emphasizes geography more than the formation of identity in approaching the Romantic psychic space. There are two reasons for the priority of place over the self; one being theoretical and the other historical. Let me begin the theoretical reason.

Although Lacan's concept of 'the big Other' has no obvious connection to colour, Lacanian psychoanalysis is able to contribute to subtle historical discussions on racial differences (Lane, 'The Psychoanalysis of Race: An Introduction' 15) and has been applied to cultural and literary studies. Alain Grosrichard's *Structure du Sérail: la fiction du despotisme asiatique dans l'occident classique* (1979), which, though written independently and with a different purpose and scope, shares with Said's book the same interests examining Western (mis)representations of Oriental identity, applied Lacanian psychoanalysis to Asian despotism in order to deconstruct French discourse on the East in the seventeenth and eighteenth centuries.[8] In the post-Saidian English-speaking world, Barrell and Leask, influenced by Homi K. Bhabha, have brilliantly proved the applicability of psychoanalysis to the study of anxieties of empire.

While the psychoanalytical method stresses the identity crisis caused by contact with geographical others, other approaches to the relationship between the self and others put more emphasis on the meeting place itself. In *Critical Terrains: French and British Orientalisms* (1991), Lisa Lowe, trying to go beyond the 'ultimately binary frame of opposition' of Orientalism, proposes 'heterotopicality' as *'multiple* sites' where overlapping and shifting articulations emerge from a variety of positions, including class, race, nation, gender, and sexuality (15).[9] Mary Louise Pratt, in *Imperial Eyes: Travel Writing and Transculturation* (1992), explores the 'contact zones' of the geographical frontlines of European colonial projects, where various kinds of 'intractable conflict' occurred between the colonizers and the colonized (6).

The meeting place concerns not only peoples and cultures but also unfamiliar faunae and florae, and geographical strata. Modern theories on otherness – psychoanalytical, philosophical, or postcolonial – deal with humans and power relationships, but otherness in the Romantic period included non-human forms, both organic and inorganic, as seen in Barbara Stafford's *Voyage into Substance: Art, Science, Nature, and the Illustrated Travel Account, 1760–1840* (1984), Onno Oerlemans's *Romanticism and the Materiality of Nature* (2002), and Noah Heringman's *Romantic Rocks, Aesthetic Geology* (2004). Research on the 'other' loci, where the self meets others in human and non-human forms, and where contacts – dialogues, mutualities, negotiations – occur, is still an underdeveloped branch of literary studies, and one worth pursuing. The 'other' places have been mostly treated from a perspective that Sara Suleri condemns as 'an alteritist fallacy,' the 'continued equation between a colonized landscape and the female body' (16). Shelley encounters geographical others in the forms of primeval mountains and cities. By investigating his 'Romantic geography,' the present study endeavours to show that Shelley's new geopolitical imaginings are not conditioned by 'an alteritist fallacy.'

Now I move on to the second reason for giving priority to place over the self, which is historical. As in the Renaissance, the birth of a new cartographic consciousness in the European mind by contact with newly discovered places and peoples was writ large in the poetry and literature of the Romantic period. Figures of travellers, questers, and explorers abound in Romantic poetry, and Romantic quest poems are characterized by frequent and detailed descriptions of natural landscapes that alter the consciousness. If 'the most eccentric feature of the entire culture' of this period that was 'inward turning toward self-discovery' is the society's 'mad[ness] for poetry' (Curran, *Poetic Form and British Romanticism* 15), one of the reasons must be that the poets and society in general were so sensitive to this new type of mental space.

The Romantic poets and most of their metropolitan readers did not have first-hand experiences with the contact zone but either consumed information on distant lands second-hand or experienced the transferred 'contact zones' that were brought back to European centres in the forms of people, goods, specimens, and so on. As their imaginary geographical space attests, though they did not travel worldwide, the Romantic poets were very much global travellers at the textual level, and the forces of globalization can be matched only by the imagination that can scale the globe. Why they were so sensitive to geography is a fruitful line of enquiry and merits special attention, which it has not received to date.

The centre–periphery distinction that was sensed in the Romantic period corresponded to Britain's relationship to much of the globe; Britain and other European powers were dividing the world into what the world-systems theorist Immanuel Wallerstein and his followers call the exploiting 'core' and the exploited 'periphery' within the world economy.[10] The term imperialism was coined in the 1870s (Hobsbawm, *The Age of Empire 1875–1914* 56–60), but John Gallagher and Ronald Robinson have argued that British imperialism was constant, though flexible in forms of political intervention and control according to local circumstances, observing 'a fundamental continuity in British expansion throughout the nineteenth century' (6).[11] The term 'globalization' seems to have arisen in the 1980s when the phenomenon received much attention, but many critics think that manifestations of globalization were experienced much earlier; for example, Wallerstein applies his theory to the period roughly between 1500 and 1850.[12] In the Romantic age, early expressions of what we now call globalization were evident, and an imperial mentality, though as yet nameless, was evolving in response to the process that was about to 'draw everything into itself, to destroy the many synchronous worlds and histories, and incorporate them into the one unilinear, universal, diachronic and tyrannical world history' (Makdisi 184–5). At the same time, however, the ambivalent mixture of enthusiasm for European dominance and anti-colonial feeling, and of fascination with and fear of one's geographical others, does not allow the European psyche to integrate itself but creates the multivocal and motley strata in the European mind. The emergent new type of internalized geopolitical space is thus recognized as the space of otherness, crisis and challenge. Its darker aspects have been examined in the study of anxieties of empire; now it is time to examine its multilayered structure and listen more carefully to different voices embedded in the landscape.

When we began this section, there appeared to be a binary choice between identity and geography. The term 'hybridity,' however, interrelates and blends the two. A key component in my discussion of Romantic geography, 'hybridity,' is a versatile notion that comes out of the long history of interdisciplinary borrowing and fusion, and it is now used differently in many disciplines. I will shortly explain its origins, how I use the term, and its relevance for my book. I will also develop other theoretical concepts; they will be discussed as occasion warrants in later chapters.

Originally a biological term referring to the offspring of two different species, whether plants or animals, the concept of hybridity was much discussed in racial debates in the late nineteenth century and crossed disciplines in the last century, mutating into linguistic hybridity in Bakhtin's work and then cultural hybridity in Bhabha's work. Bhabha, borrowing the term from Bakhtin and modifying it in order to examine an identity crisis in the colonizer caused by mutualities and negotiations across colonial relations, considers hybridity as a counterforce of the other that answers back to the colonial authority and disrupts Europe's sense of superiority over the East.

As Bhabha has cogently shown,[13] the self and others are intrinsically meshed in the hybrid psychic space, disrupting the Saidian binary relationship between the colonizer and the colonized. The imperial mentality, which is shaken by Bhabha's 'hybridity,' however, can hardly 'open itself dialogically to the Other' (Leask, *British Romantic Writers and the East* 2, 135–54). By modifying Bhabha's concept of hybridity, the present book tries to illuminate what has not been foregrounded in the inner geography of the Romantic psyche under the dark shadow of anxieties of empire – how this hybrid space of otherness offers an opportunity for the self to be aware of its complicity with colonialism, and yet to grow and change the colonial relationship between the self and others.

In applying the concept from postcolonial studies to the inner space in the Romantic period, I stress its original scientific and sexual meanings,[14] but I broaden the original concept to encompass the aspects of cultural hybridity that are relevant to the processes of hybridization. Namely, in my discussion of Romantic geography, the term is applied to both the objects (the products of hybridization) and the processes (of mixing, fusing, and hybridizing). I include in the latter a reciprocal process of dialogue by drawing upon Bhabha's definition of hybridity as 'revers[ing] the effects of the colonialist disavowal, so that other "denied" knowledges enter upon the dominant discourse and estrange the basis of its authority' (*The Location of Culture* 114). In Shelley's Romantic geography, hybridity interrelates the self and the inner geopolitical space in ways in which the hybridizing process enables these 'denied knowledges' to be sought after in their unfamiliar forms and recognized as 'strange truths in undiscovered lands' (Shelley, 'Alastor' 77). This internalized space shows, with a critical tool of hybridity, how the poetic psyche, which is aware of its complicity with colonialism, still tries to disentangle power from literary imagination, and alter the centre–periphery hegemony of European geographical imaginings.

Recent Criticism of Shelley on Imperialism

The scholarship on imperialism and culture started with Said's enormously influential *Orientalism*. It has appealed to a wide audience because of its postcolonial relevance and its applicability to other parts of the world; Patrick Brantlinger's *Rule of Darkness: British Literature and Imperialism, 1830–1914* (1988) examined how English literature reifies the hierarchies of racial difference and guided the public image of empire.[15] At the same time, however, Said's theoretical model has been severely criticized by imperial historians, theorists in postcolonial studies, and literary critics, all of whom have been trying to position themselves against Said. The most compelling criticism comes from Bhabha, who analyses the destabilized and fractured psychic space found in colonial relations. Pratt explores the 'contact zones' in faraway regions; Leask analyses the internalized contact zones of Romantic writers in the vast metropolis, which became a global contact zone; and Bewell reconceptualizes Pratt's 'intractable' colonial contact zone to 'include biomedical contact' (*Romanticism and Colonial Disease* 3), suggesting that the diseased colonial landscape can be cured through the dialectical relationship between political-economic development and medical-ecological transformation. John Mackenzie, a leading British historian of imperial culture, criticizes Said for his weak grasp of the historical context in *Orientalism: History, Theory and the Arts* (1995), and Linda Colley argues that Western reactions to Islam 'were never homogenous or monolithic' (*Captives* 102).

The investigation of the complex matrix of poetics, politics, culture, and geography in Shelley's writings has been an important strain of Shelley scholarship since Stuart Curran's *Shelley's Annus Mirabilis: The*

Maturing of an Epic Vision (1975), but in the study of anxieties of empire, Shelley's position has been quite problematic, and therefore to make Shelley a case study of 'Romantic geography' is a challenge. In 'Orientalism' (1994), Marilyn Butler, treating *Queen Mab*, 'Alastor,' *The Revolt of Islam* (1817), *Prometheus Unbound*, and 'The Witch of Atlas,' assigns Shelley to the camp of 'Volney, Grant, Southey, [and] Mill,' not to that of 'Landor, Byron or Moore, who can all sound more simply critical of foreign occupation' (436–47). In *Orientalism in Lord Byron's 'Turkish Tales'* (1995), influenced by Butler and Leask, Abdur Raheem Kidwai praises Byron's unique sympathetic view of the Orient and dismisses Shelley's poems as depicting 'a negative view of the Orient' that is an 'endorsement, as in Southey's, of the colonialism and evangelism of the day' (21). Critics tend to choose 'Alastor' (rather than *Prometheus Unbound*) or the poems of the Middle Eastern setting to find a poetic enthusiasm for imperialism. Makdisi's chapter on Shelley and Byron in *Romantic Imperialism* (1998), based upon the same choice of poems as Kidwai, expresses the standard view of Shelley as deeply committed to colonialism (122–53).

Eleanor J. Harrington-Austin in *Shelley and the Development of English Imperialism: British India and England* (1999) tries to defend Shelley against this tendency in the secondary literature. Examining his later prose works – 'A Philosophical View of Reform' (1819–20) in particular[16] – in relation to British colonization of India and providing good background information, she opposes Makdisi's argument that Shelley considers Eastern peoples as merely 'inferior versions' of Westerners (Makdisi 153), and denies the view of Shelley as a prototype of what Brantlinger calls the Victorian 'reluctant imperialist' (Brantlinger 7). Her conclusion, however, derives from two factors. Shelley's political writings, including 'A Philosophical View of Reform,' which was published in 1920, appeared too late to contribute to Victorian imperialism, and Shelley consistently refused 'all forms of oppression,' whether Eastern or Western, that injure not only 'others' but also 'imperializers themselves' (iii, 281).

Harrington-Austin tries to save Shelley from the image of proto-imperialist, but Shelley was not exempt from colonial desire; the poet, who in January 1819 considered 'Poetry [as] very subordinate to moral & political science' and thought that if he had been well he 'should aspire [to] the latter,' dreamed of getting 'a respectable appointment' in India through the East India Compnay in October 1821 (*Letters* 2: 71, 361, 361n.5). My book attempts to see positive sides of Shelley in a different way from Harrington-Austin's approach by investigating his geopolitical imaginings in his poems that seek to break the hegemonic centre–periphery distinction of the European mind.

Radical rereadings of Shelley have enriched recent Shelley studies, as shown in *The Cambridge Companion to Shelley* (2006), edited by Timothy Morton. My book shares critical concerns with, though with a different emphasis from, Benjamin Colbert's *Shelley's Eye: Travel Writing and Aesthetic Vision* (2005) and Cian Duffy's *Shelley and the Revolutionary Sublime* (2005), in pursuing the interrelated complex triangle of poetics, politics, and culture in Shelley's writings. Colbert reconsiders Shelley's own travel writing and his visionary poems of 'metacultural encounter' as 'negotiat[ing] an alternative cultural space,' arguing that the observing 'eye' of Shelley as an ideal traveller reveals instabilities that arose from the 'post-Napoleonic tensions between Grand Tourism, modern travel, and mass culture' (10, 5). Whereas Colbert is more interested in how Shelley's 'eye' reshapes the language of travel discourse, and in 'valorizing European travel as a foundation for the poet's education' rather than discussing 'his desire to make landscape through poetry a force for renewal and hope' (10, 97), this volume emphasizes Shelley as a global textual traveller and quester whose imagination engages in foreign encounter and visionary improvement of colonial geography. After deconstructionists put so much emphasis on Shelley's repeated failures, reassessment of the role of Romantic idealism has resumed with such works as Cian Duffy's *Shelley and the Revolutionary Sublime*. My study joins this line of enquiry from a different angle, throwing light on his repeated (and often failed) efforts to provide a visionary alternative to a colonial pathogenic space.

In short, my book will investigate the complex social and cultural composition of Shelley's Romantic geography, trace Shelley's global search for visionary improvements of places, and consider the possibilities as well as the limits of his attempts. As part of my critical approach, I will establish the context in which these poems were written by presenting relevant histories, travel texts, scientific writings, and so on. Instead of having literary discourse drowned in the ocean of historical documents, by treating literature as just one among many, however, I will discuss individual works of literature side by side with historical archive material, with some aid from postcolonial critical tools, such as 'hybridity,' though modified in order to apply to early-nineteenth-century phenomena. The close readings of the poems, in turn, highlight the contexts that surround the texts. Three different but related kinds of enquiry are brought out here. The first is to examine the complex cultural dynamics of Shelley's poetical exploration of the world in his 'Romantic geography.' The second is to ground his poetic attempts to provide alternative geographies in the literary and political culture of his time. The third is to consider Shelley's approach toward globalizing tendencies through the lens of postcolonial theories in order to have a better understanding of the predicaments of his age as well as ours.

1 *Queen Mab*: The Female Dreamers and a Pathless Wilderness

1. The City of Destruction and the Wonder of Wales

Shelley had a visionary experience during his solitary wandering in the mountains of Keswick on 23 November 1811, and it reveals some aspects of his Romantic geography. Alone among the 'gigantic mountains piled on each other,' he was absorbed in nature's 'awful waywardness,' displayed in the waterfalls, the 'million shaped clouds tinted by the varying colours of innumerable rainbows,' and a lake 'as smooth and dark as a plain of polished jet' (*Letters* 1: 189). A Wordsworthian poet would have evoked a living spirit in nature per se that would correspond to the poet's heightened imagination in solitude. For Shelley, nature's 'awful waywardness' offered an opportunity to envision how places are physically and socially constructed, that is, how humans are integral to the natural world in moral and social ways. His imagination was 'resistlessly compelled to look back,' seeing in 'this retirement of peace and mountain simplicity,' 'the Pandemonium of druidical imposture, the scene of Roman Pollution, [and] the resting place of the savage denizen of these solitudes with the wolf' (1: 189): 'Still, still further! – strain thy reverted Fancy when no rocks, no lakes no cloud-soaring mountains were here, but a vast populous and licentious city stood in the midst of an immense plain, myriads flocked towards it; London itself scarcely exceeds it in the variety, the extensiveness of [or?] consummateness of its corruption! Perhaps ere Man had lost reason, and lived an happy happy race. – No Tyranny, no Priestcraft, no War. – Adieu to the dazzling picture' (1: 189). The 'dazzling picture' reflects the extraordinary expansion in space and time Europeans were experiencing in the Romantic period, with unprecedented discoveries in new sciences ranging from geology, archaeology, and ethnography to comparative linguistics.[1] Shelley travels far beyond the biblical six thousand years and sees a prosperous city in the abyss of geological time, and the city seems to have been populated with myriad peoples of different origins. Although science had revealed something of the immensity of geological time in the history of the earth, there still remained, in the early decades of the nineteenth century, an implicit faith in the sacred history tradition.[2] Wordsworth's 'strong fancies' see '[n]o appanage of human kind, / Nor hint of man' among Cambrian mountains that 'four thousand years have gazed' ('The Pass of Kirkstone' [1820] 6–7, 20).

This visionary scene shows three important points that suggest the nature of Shelley's imagination and sense of place. First, in the visionary review of the history of a place, nature appears from beginning to end as human habitat. This does not necessarily mean that a city precedes primordial rocks and mountains; it means that nature appears as the environment, as a place of human engagement with the physical world.[3]

Second, located among the lonely mountains in the margin of England, the vast populous city, which is as old as the earth and in which Shelley sees prelapsarian happiness, breaks the centre–periphery distinction dominated by London, which absorbed a continuous influx of displaced people from other parts of Britain and overseas, its commercial network covering the entire kingdom and proceeding to span the whole globe. Baron Dupin, a member of the Institute of France, who visited London from 1816 to 1819 to investigate the reasons for Britain's victory over France, concluded that the practical key to British power was London's centrality: London is simultaneously 'the metropolis of the empire' and the centre of 'the interior, as well as exterior, commerce of England,' which makes the city 'the richest, the most extensive, and the most populous of all the cities of the old world' (2: 2).

Third, all the cities in the vision are of the type of the city of destruction, described by such words as 'Pandemonium' and 'Pollution.' The primordial city occupied by an innocent happy race is also 'licentious.' Its huge size and 'corruption' can be matched by the modern Pandemonium, London, which dominates and fascinates the poetic imagination as the culmination of all great cities in history and legend. The city, evoking the image of 'Hell' (Shelley, 'Peter Bell the Third' [1819] 3.147) or a 'thickening hubbub' that echoes Milton's 'universal hubbub wild' (Wordsworth, *Prelude* 7.227; *Paradise Lost* 2.951), is a 'blank confusion, and a type not false / Of what the mighty city is itself' (*Prelude* 7.696–7). Wordsworth's image of metropolis in sublime confusion, which appears in the 1850 version of *The Prelude*, is quite similar to Shelley's visionary populous city:

> Rise up, thou monstrous ant-hill on the plain
> Of a too busy world! Before me flow,
> Thou endless stream of men and moving things!
> Thy every-day appearance, as it strikes –
> With wonder heightened, or sublimed by awe –
> On strangers, of all ages; the quick dance
> Of colours, lights, and forms; the deafening din.   (7.149–55)

The close association of the image of the sublime city with corruption corresponds to a Rousseauian idea of the destruction of pristine innocence and virtue by the sciences and the arts,[4] and what is interesting in Shelley's vision of a great city is that his visionary city, which knows '[n]o Tyranny, no Priestcraft, no War,' is also paradoxically drawn from images of London (*Letters* 1: 189). To put it another way, although the visionary city has a central position in Shelley's Romantic geography as a model of the pristine flourishing city that counters the modern, corrupt metropolis of London, Shelley has not yet found his ideal city – one that is not a figure of corruption.

Between 1811 and 1813, Shelley was incessantly moving back and forth between London and British peripheries in Wales, Scotland, and Ireland, as if seeking a place where a new ideal image of human habitat could be realized through his imagination.[5] During this period Shelley observed a sharp contrast between scenes of extravagance and misery; while the Prince Regent, later George IV, and aristocrats thrived amid 'plate & balls & tables & kings,' the internal colonies of Wales, Scotland, and Ireland were systematically exploited by the political and commercial centre of Great Britain, and overwhelmed with 'famine-wasted inhabitants' (*Letters* 1: 213).[6]

In 'On Leaving London for Wales,' composed in November 1812, a revolutionary landscape that opposes London appears among the mountains of Wales. While London is a 'miserable city' where 'tyrant's pride' kills 'Freedom's hope and Truth's high Courage,' Wales fosters 'the eternal flame of generous Liberty' and tends human virtues that are impaired in London (1, 2, 4, 18).

> True! Mountain Liberty alone may heal
>   The pain which Custom's obduracies bring,
>   And he who dares in fancy even to steal
>   One draught from Snowdon's ever-sacred spring
> Blots out the unholiest rede of worldly witnessing.   (23–7)

Shelley's 'Mountain Liberty' echoes Milton's 'mountain nymph, sweet Liberty' ('L'Allegro' 36). In a note to this line in the 1785 edition of Milton's selected poems, Thomas Warton introduces a comment by an interpreter that 'the people in mountainous countries have generally preserved their liberties longest, as the Britons formerly in Wales, and the inhabitants in the mountains of Switzerland at this day,' though Warton himself believes that Milton thought of 'the Oreads of the Grecian mythology' (Milton, *Poems upon Several Occasions, English, Italian, and Latin with Translation* 42). From 1798 till 1815 when the Congress of Vienna re-established the country's independence, Switzerland was subjugated by the French. In 'Thought of a Briton on the Subjugation of Switzerland' (1807), Wordsworth deplored that Liberty, although fighting against the 'Tyrant,' was 'driven' from her 'Alpine holds' (5, 7). Coleridge reprinted Wordsworth's poem in *The Friend*, number 18, 21 December 1809, and introduced it as 'the happiest comment' on Milton's 'The *mountain* Nymph, sweet Liberty' (*The Friend* 2: 233).

Shelley's 'Mount Liberty' stands in a long tradition from Milton, but he does not invite Liberty from Switzerland, because what he seeks 'amid thy [Cambria's] rocks to ruin hurled' is 'the weapon' he 'burn[s] to wield' for a 'bloodless victory,' not for a violent revolution ('On Leaving London for Wales' 42, 41, 44). In order to reinforce the association of Liberty with Welsh mountains, Shelley superimposes on Snowdon Mount Helicon rather than the Swiss Alps. The Mountain Liberty, which is slightly feminized through the Miltonic echo and association with the Muses, is embodied as splendid Welsh nature, and is praised as a healer and an inspiration of revolutionary hope to the 'freeborn mind' suffocated by London, where 'the gloom / Of penury mingles with the tyrant's pride' (30,1–2), but Wales's Mount Liberty is injured, too; amid the magnificent landscape is found 'Nature's wound' (54). Cambrian nature heals the poet in her bosom of mountains, and the poetic imagination as an agent for a 'bloodless' weapon is prepared in turn to work to amend both physical and social ills, to heal 'Nature's wound' and to improve political and social conditions (44, 54).

'Nature's wound' is a vague phrase. As Kenneth Neil Cameron writes, the phrase 'does not make sense unless it is taken as a reference to the embankment [at Tremadoc (Tremadog)]' (*EN* 192). A great embankment project by a Whig reformer, William Alexander Madocks, was begun in 1798 and remained incomplete due to lack of funds. In 1812, Shelley was involved with the project as a fund-raiser, visiting London twice in October and November. Amid the splendour of Snowdonia, where immense 'rocks to ruin hurled' were reminiscent of geological upheavals and the prehistoric world ('On Leaving London for Wales' 42),[7] Madocks undertook to improve the physical features of the place and set up an ideal community and environment. Seeing a 'wonder of Wales' – Madocks's grand embankment project and the new town of Tremadoc, built on the recovered land at the mouth of Traeth Mawr (the Great Sand) – Shelley must have felt as if his visionary city in Keswick were coming into being, although on a much smaller scale.[8] The 'wonder of Wales' gives the young poet hope to heal 'Nature's wound' by humanity's reclaiming hand, from which is created a new ideal city that can oppose London as the global centre.

In order to examine the 'weapon' Shelley is seeking in Wales, it will be useful to see Madocks's enterprise and Shelley's active engagement with it briefly.[9] Sir Richard Colt Hoare's 1810 journal of his tour in Caernarvonshire records at length both Madocks's newly founded town of Tremadoc and his ongoing grand reclamations of the whole tract from the ravages of the sea:

> [We] pursued our road over the new road lately cut under the rock by Mr Madocks ... [T]he Traeth Mawr bore the appearance of a most beautiful and extensive lake. The sight of this tract of land caused sensations of pleasure and pain: pleasure in reflecting how many valuable lives will be saved by the abolition of the dangerous passage across the sands and how much land will in future times be brought into cultivation; pain in considering that I viewed this glorious scenery and expanses of water perhaps for the last time ... I was much struck with the new creation I found at Tre Madoc on a spot which I remember to have been houseless: a neat little town, good inn, handsome town hall, shops, church and meeting house. All the work of an individual now engaged in the stupendous and arduous undertaking of excluding Neptune from his extensive dominion over the sands between this place and Pont Aberglaslyn and thereby reclaiming several thousand acres of cultivable land. The

work is in great forwardness and another year will probably decide between Neptune and Ceres. (263–4)

Peacock does not value Madocks's schemes for improvement; in *Headlong Hall* (1816), which depends largely on his experience in North Wales in 1810 and Shelley's *Queen Mab*, he describes with 'regret' the majestic natural scene created by the 'liquid mirror,' which is to be sacrificed by the 'probable utility' of the embankment (1: 74).[10] A traveller or temporary sojourner would miss the picturesque scene set by Treath Mawr: the grandeur of the water that corresponds to the formidable mountains and rocks of Snowdon at the other end. For the local residents, however, as G.A. Cooke's *Topographical and Statistical Description of the Principality of Wales* says, it was a 'truly noble work,' which, when completed, would gain '4000 acres' from the sea and would save 'the lives of hundreds' as 'so dangerous are the sands of the Traeth Mawr, that a winter seldom passed without many persons having been drowned in crossing them' (1: 135).[11]

The battle between Neptune and Ceres, however, had not been settled in the fall of 1812, when the Shelleys were travelling deeper and deeper into Wales. In February 1812, seven months after its completion, the embankment was seriously damaged by a strong gale driving the high tide. The whole region rallied around, and neighbours, rich and poor alike, spontaneously offered help according to their means. When wandering into Caernarvonshire, where there were only a few small villages, the Shelleys would have felt that 'they were beyond civilization'; but they unexpectedly found at the mouth of Treath Mawr the newly built town of Tremadoc and 'an enormous building operation, involving nearly a hundred workmen, who were reinforcing a massive embankment across the mouth of the estuary to the little port of Portmadoc, and draining and clearing the land behind it' (Holmes 163). Although he admired the effect of the 'liquid mirror' as much as Peacock all his life,[12] Shelley was immediately taken by the quite different possibilities promised by this Promethean endeavour to found a new civilization: recovering land from the sea, building a town on it, and turning sand into pasture. Shelley lost no time in getting involved with Madocks's project, assisting in raising funds for the completion of the embankment. He enthusiastically writes: 'my fervid hopes, my ardent desires, my unremitting personal exertions (so far as my health will allow) are all engaged in that cause, which I will desert *but with my life*' (*Letters* 1: 330).

The Shelleys settled down in a house called Tan-yr-allt (Under the wooden cliff), which Madocks had renovated as his residential base when his plan first got off the ground at the turn of the century, but had to be let when the serious breach of the bank made him almost bankrupt. Situated on a hillside about one hundred feet above the level of the estuary, the house commanded the most splendid prospect over the environmental and social consequences of the Promethean act that started in the year of the publication of the *Lyrical Ballads*. The embankment of 1800, in which 'above 200 poor men were in constant employ' at a time of general poverty (Beazley 58), turned a 'very considerable tract of land,' which had been covered by the tide, into 'excellent pasture in three years' (Cooke 1: 135–6). A new town with a remarkably civilized urbanity was also taking shape on the reclaimed land, having 'a handsome market house,' 'a large church,' 'a manufactory for flannel,' a theatre, and a good road and transportation system (Cooke 1: 135). The great embankment was closing the whole of Traeth Mawr across its mouth in the teeth of natural hazards, and enormous practical and financial difficulties.

A view from Tan-yr-allt gives a young disciple of Godwin a broad hint as to what kind of 'weapon' is needed to win a 'bloodless victory': science and technology with humanity's reclaiming hands ('On Leaving London for Wales' 41, 44). Earlier at Oxford, Shelley was dreaming of a scientific discovery in which 'by chemical agency the philosopher ... may transmute an unfruitful region into a land of exuberant plenty,' even transforming 'the arid deserts of Africa' into 'rich meadows, and vast fields of maize and rice' (Hogg 1: 60–1). Without a new magical chemical product but with labouring human hands and will, human intelligence can improve both natural and social environments and move humankind toward a state of perfection. 'Man,' Godwin says, 'is a being of progressive nature, and capable of unlimited improvement' (*Enquiry concerning Political Justice and Its Influence on General Virtue and Happiness* 501). At Tremadoc, a new site of culture was emerging accompanied by pasture on the reclaimed land from the sea. Himself being engaged in the embankment project, Shelley's hopes for a new ideal society blossomed. He began to grind his own poetic 'weapon' at Tan-yr-allt, where most of *Queen Mab* was written. The poem, whose 'grand & comprehensive topics' are '[t]he Past, the Present, & the Future,' depicts 'a picture of manners, simplicity and delights of a perfect state of society; though still earthly' (*Letters* 1: 324, 201).

2. Fairy Mab: The Making of a Myth

The guardian spirit of 'Snowdon's ever-sacred spring,' who does not reveal her identity in 'On Leaving London for Wales' (26), turns out to be a Welsh fairy queen in *Queen Mab*. Mab's first appearance in English literature as queen of the fairies is believed to have taken place in Shakespeare's *Romeo and Juliet* (1.4.53–94). Nothing is known of her origins, except that she is a diminutive fairy on the Celtic fringe (Reeves 20–7; Briggs, *Dictionary of Fairies, Hobgoblins, Brownies, Bogies and Other Supernatural Creatures* 275). There is no mention of Cader Idris, a legendary mountain in Snowdonia, in Shelley's writings, but he may have known the bardic tradition of sleeping on the mountain in the hope that a true inspiration would be granted by a spirit. Mab, descending upon the sleeping Ianthe, strongly reminds us of this bardic myth, according to which Felicia Hemans was to write 'The Rock of Cader-Idris' (1822), but an obscure fairy and a young girl have nothing to do with the heroic bardic tradition. Nevertheless, the choice of a minor Welsh female spirit is significant for three reasons. The first is that Shelley selects a marginal local spirit to embody the universal reformer. The second is that Shelley prefers an obscure female character over a male character. The third is that Shelley's Welsh fairy has a complex relationship with a recent nationalistic movement on the Celtic fringe of Britain, in which the bardic tradition had recently been revived and many legendary heroes had risen from oblivion.

The last point is important, especially when we consider Shelley's choice of a fairy queen against the background of 'Madoc fever.' From the 1790s, the legend of Prince Madoc, who was said to have founded a Welsh-speaking community in America in the twelfth century, caught the imagination of the Welsh public, and inspired Southey to write *Madoc*.[13] Madocks's new town, Tremadoc, was also closely associated with Prince Madoc.[14] Near the mouth of the estuary of Traeth Mawr is a small rocky island from which Prince Madoc is said to have sailed to discover America; Madocks's first purchase of property in Caernarvonshire in 1798 included a farm named after this rocky island, Ynys Fadog (Beazley 53–5). According to a letter by Madocks from August 1805, his new town was called 'Pentre-Gwaelod' (Bottom Village) when it first appeared on the map (Beazley 82). Calling it 'Tre Madoc' (township or place of Madoc) was thus an afterthought, following the publication of Southey's *Madoc* in 1805. The name would have been thought worthy of a new town when the Celtic revival and

Madoc fever were still fervid. Also, the name's pun, which could be taken either as Madoc's or Madocks's town, would have pleased the founder of the town. Tan-yr-allt in the first decades of the nineteenth century was a complex site of scientific improvement, majestic nature, and Welsh myth. It is not surprising that Shelley, living there, makes use of this triad – scientific improvement, nature, and Welsh myth – at Tremadoc, but replaces a hero who promotes colonialism in the bardic tradition with a mythic figure of his own creation who mediates between nature and the human act of improvement.

In the late eighteenth century, Irish, Scottish, and Welsh nationalists emphasized the cultural origins of bardic poetry, relating it to a particular national history, while English poets created an image of the bard as an isolated, peripheral figure of imagination (Trumpener 4–6). In the dynamics of the centre and margin, the nationalistic movement in literature was considered as the revolting action by the internal 'others' against the centralized British self, while English poets, separating the internal others from the English self, tried to minimize their power by pushing them further into the margin and isolation. Southey's *Madoc* makes use of a national myth of Madoc to confirm the center-margin distinction, but unlike English poets of the previous century, Southey attempts to incorporate the internal others into the British self in order to conquer and convert the external non-Christian others, such as those in pre-Conquest Mexico. In this regard, Barrell's triad of 'this / that / the other,' which is an elaboration of Said's binary opposition, and which is geographically represented as the West, a 'manageable' Near East, and a 'terrifying' further East – 'an East *beyond* the East' – in De Quincy's Eurocentric imaginary geography (1–24), can be applied to Southey's triangle of Britain, Wales, and America with a slight modification. In Barrell's tripartite model, which draws upon Gayatri Spivak's psychoanalytical triangle of a self and two kinds of others, 'a "self-consolidating other" and an "absolute" other,'[15] the middle part is considered as a buffer against the absolute East and can be united with the West, though the 'manageable' middle part is subverting with oriental infection from within the Western self (13, 10). In Southey's cognitive map of the world, the middle part (Wales) is domesticated and cooperates with the English self in order to conquer the non-Christian Absolute Other.

By contrast, the use of a native fairy queen as a title figure is Shelley's radical strategy to disrupt the tradition and the relationship between the centre and the margin in many ways. Shelley assigns the prophetic role of the bard to an obscure female spirit, and instead of having her recall a particular national history, makes her speak of universal history. By doing so, Shelley gives a minor mythical figure a central position, transforming the traditional Mab figure into his own universal muse who advocates a new ideal society. Shelley's Mab presents a counter-myth to the nationalistic legend of Madoc. She also opposes Southey's Madoc in terms of her attitude toward the Absolute Other in America. In order to counter a national hero, Shelley chooses an obscure local fairy, and moreover, he makes use of an innocent version of Shakespeare's Mab that was well known in children's literature in the eighteenth century.[16]

When he sent the poem to the publisher in March 1813, Shelley warned him about its radical content, asking him not to print the title page before the body of the poem and to use a book form that might appeal to children of aristocratic families (*Letters* 1: 361). It has been generally agreed from this comment that Shelley chose the innocent-sounding title character in order to conceal the poem's real content and to attract an audience of aristocratic children (Behrendt 83), but the title character does much more than camouflage the poem's atheism and radicalism. The full title, 'QUEEN MAB; A PHILOSOPHICAL POEM: WITH NOTES,'[17] shows that the title character bridges the fairy tale and the serious genre of philosophical works such as Erasmus Darwin's *The Botanic Garden; A Poem ... with Philosophical Notes* (1791) and *The Temple of Nature; or the Origin of Society: A Poem. With Philosophical Notes* (1803).[18] Uniting two completely different genres, Shelley attempts to explore poetic 'contact zones,' and makes his new marginal muse cross radically different areas: the marginal region of Wales, the domestic area of women and children, and the public epic world of Madoc.

Shelley's Mab significantly departs from the contemporary images evoked by the name of the fairy queen: the frivolous and mischievous fairy queen first mentioned in Mercutio's speech in Shakespeare's *Romeo and Juliet* (1.4.53–94) and the innocent fairy queen in children's literature. Shelley's Queen Mab has her origin in the Mab of *Romeo and Juliet* as he planned to take a motto from Shakespeare (*Letters* 1: 361). Unlike his predecessors and contemporaries,[19] however, Shelley responds to Romeo's line, 'In bed asleep, while they [dreamers] do dream things true' (1.4.52), rather than Mercutio's speech. She is also worthy of her Welsh name; the Welsh 'mab' means 'a little child,' being the root of numberless words signifying 'love for children (magbar), kitten (mabgath) ... most notable of which in this connection is maginogi, the singular of Mabinogion, the romantic tales of enchantment told to the young in by-gone ages' (Sikes 14). In Shelley's version, Mab is a bringer of true dreams. She traverses the realm of fairies, which is allotted to children and young girls such as Ianthe,[20] and that of philosophical truths, conveying the vision of an ideal society in the future.

Two of the three epigraphs that follow the poem's title immediately relate the poem to the radical writings of the day. The first one, from Voltaire, vehemently accuses Christianity (*SP&P* 16n.1). The third, from Archimedes, was frequently quoted by radicals, as in the famous opening sentence of Paine's *Rights of Man, Part 2* (1792) (*SP&P* 16n.3). The second epigraph, between these two, from Lucretius, reflects Shelley's search for a new poetic space, reporting a thrilling discovery of sacred springs in a pathless region of poetry. It recalls a sacred spring on Snowdon in 'On Leaving London for Wales,' and associates Wales with not only poetry but also revolutionary actions. A 'place,' on which he can 'stand' and 'move the earth' in Archimedes's quotation (*SP&P* 16n.3), thus turns out to be Wales. It is in Wales where Shelley's youthful poetic ambition and ardent utopian hope will deliver a vision of universal truth and improvement.

3. The Female Travellers and the Vision of the World

The poem opens with a beautiful night scene described by the poet/narrator addressing Death and Sleep, who are 'so passing wonderful!' (*Queen Mab* 1.8). We are not told where the poem is set until the beginning of canto 4, in which the same nightscape is depicted in detail by Mab with a similar tone, and 'yon castled steep, / Whose banner hangeth o'er the time-worn tower' links this beautiful night scene to a view from Tan-yr-allt of the mountains across the estuary (4.12–13).[21] A Middle Eastern atmosphere, however, is created by the opening lines of cantos 1 and 4, whose tone and wording echo the opening lines of *Thalaba* (Duff 77–8), and reinforced by the images of 'fantastic oriental palaces in the heavens' built around Mab's celestial palace in canto 2 (Wallace 40). The Middle Eastern setting also creeps in through the repeated description by the poet/narrator of Ianthe's sleeping body as ruins; dismayed by the 'gloomy Power' of Death, which seems to have '[s]eized on' Ianthe, he compares Ianthe's 'lovely outline' to a 'breathing marble' that must perish and is reduced to 'loathsomeness and ruin' (*Queen Mab* 1.9, 11, 16, 17, 20). When he finds the 'breathing marble' is now 'motionless' and 'silent,' he presents her as a beautiful wreck of some huge structure (1.17, 32, 33):

> Her golden tresses shade
> The bosom's stainless pride,
> Curling like tendrils of the parasite
> Around a marble column. (1.41–4)

A beautiful body in decay appears as a ruinous Greco-Roman marble column. This is the first ruin in the poem haunted by an incredible number of ruins, and certainly it symbolizes the world in decay. At the same time, however, it suggests a special locale. Her 'peerless' neck, white as 'a marble column,' looks to be a part of the spectacular white ruins of Palmyra in Syria (1.12, 44), which struck many European travellers and archaeologists with their massive marble whiteness,[22] and which is the first site on earth Mab shows Ianthe from heaven.

We, as readers, are inclined to ask where in the world Ianthe is laid and why Mab's palace looks like an oriental palace. The superimposition of Wales and the Middle East on each other in Shelley's Romantic geography cancels the boundary between the domestic and the foreign. It offers a contrast to Barrell's geographical triad of 'this / that / the other' (10) in which the middle part is assimilated into the self, because in *Queen Mab* the middle parts, one internal within Britain and the other exotic outside Britain, are considered as a locus for those who have 'burst the chains, / The icy chains of custom, and have shone / The day-stars of their age' (1.126–8). Both places are constructed as semi-peripheries revolting against the centre. In this regard, Shelley's Romantic geography is different from Wallerstein's tripartite structure of 'core / semi-periphery / periphery.' Wallerstein introduces the concept of 'semi-periphery' for the 'political' reason that 'the upper stratum is not faced with the *unified* opposition of all the others because the *middle* stratum is both exploited and exploiter' ('The Rise and Future Demise of the World Capitalist System' 73–4). In Shelley, Wales is associated with Liberty in 'On Leaving London for Wales.' Palmyra is linked with revolutionary thoughts in Constantin Volney's *Les ruins, ou méditation sur les révolutions des empire* (1791), with which Shelley familiarized himself shortly after being expelled from Oxford in 1811 (Medwin 1: 155).

Queen Mab, being veiled in the light that beams from within, bears a marked trait of Shelley's later transcendent female epipsyches, such as the veiled maid in 'Alastor' and 'the shape all light' in 'The Triumph of Life.' The Welsh Fairy Queen, however, is slightly orientalized, and does not choose a young male disciple who is a thinly disguised Shelley, but descends on an innocent young girl. She prepares Ianthe for the calling that awaits those who have 'burst the chains, / The icy chains of custom, and have shone / The day-stars of their age' (1.126–8). Mab's phrasing evokes the image of Prometheus, but what we have to bear in mind here is that at this time Shelley bitterly criticized the myth of Prometheus. In a long prose note to *Queen Mab* (note 17) and *A Vindication of Natural Diet* (1812–13), Shelley accuses 'Prometheus (who represents the human race)' of introducing 'fire to culinary purposes' and carnivorism, which ruined 'healthful innocence' and cleared the way for all kinds of physical and social diseases: 'Tyranny, superstition, commerce, and inequality were then first known' (*SPW* 826–7). Shelley's condemnation of Prometheus has two main sources of inspiration. One is his association with the so-called Bracknell circle of radical thinkers in 1813–14 and practice of vegetarianism, which, influenced by John Frank Newton and Joseph Ristons, has medical, moral, and political implications.[23] The second important source for his accusation is Rousseau. In the opening paragraph of the second part of the *First Discourse*, Rousseau unfavourably introduces Prometheus as 'the inventor of sciences,' explaining the subject of the frontispiece that represents Prometheus, the human, and the satyr and attributing the birth of 'Sciences and Arts' to our 'vices' (2: 12).[24] Virtually every one of Shelley's criticisms against Prometheus as a founder of civilization, 'Tyranny, superstition, commerce, and inequality,' is found in Rousseau's *Second Discourse*.[25] Echoing Rousseau, Shelley questions the whole Western myth of Prometheus as a destroyer of 'healthful innocence,' and feminizes prophecy and tasks for renewal through Mab's education of Ianthe, which is to create a female, earthly version of Prometheus to fight against natural and social ills. At the same time, by placing Ianthe's body in Wales as well as in Palmyra, Shelley opens in the poem a subversive space in which Wales and Palmyra cannot be treated as manageable middle places in Barrell's triad, but can claim to be the sites of revolutionary sweetness that counter the centre from within and without.

   Mab's lessons are given in the grandest of grand tours, a space tour followed by a world tour. Shelley provides a long prose note to the 'innumerable systems [which] rolled' in the universe in order to guide the interpretation of the multiplicity and immensity of the universe that is stressed in the space trip (1.253): 'The plurality of worlds, – the indefinite immensity of the universe, is a most awful subject of contemplation. He who rightly feels its mystery and grandeur is in no danger of seduction from the falsehoods of religious systems, or of deifying the principle of the universe' (*SPW* 801). Cian Duffy considers this passage as evidence of Shelley's ongoing attempt to bring the discourse on the sublime in line with radical politics, and defines the Shelleyan sublime as an act of imagination in cooperation with 'a rational/scientific understanding of "awful" natural phenomena' that enables us to 'rightly' feel the mystery and grandeur of nature without associating it with God (*Shelley and the Revolutionary Sublime* 1–12). His point is well taken, but at this stage, in canto 1, Ianthe is not rational or scientific enough to accept the lesson the prose note offers. Only after canto 7, when she addresses a question about the existence of God, does this interpretation have more validity. Therefore, the point of the lesson here does not lead to the rejection of creator-God immediately but to the fact that all living things equally participate in this vast and multiple universe governed by the 'Spirit of Nature' (1.275): 'not the lightest leaf' is 'less instinct [=animated] with thee [=the Spirit of Nature]' and 'not the meanest worm' in the grave '[l]ess shares thy eternal breath' (1.269–74). If one of the purposes of the Grand Tour is to acquire a new sense of national identity in the experience of foreign countries, the main purpose of Mab's space tour is to invite one's imagination to 'contemplate itself, not as the centre and model of the Universe, but as one of the infinitely various multitude of beings of which it is actually composed' ('A Refutation of Deism,' *Prose* 120).

The earthly part of the educational tour begins with the ruins of Palmyra, a caravan city defeated by the Roman Empire. Mab tells Ianthe how 'Palmyra's ruined palaces' give an 'awful warning' (2.110, 118). In the late eighteenth and early nineteenth centuries, ruins were 'awful subject[s] of contemplation' that invited the viewer to muse on the transience of earthly things and the vanity of human achievement (*SPW* 801). Shelley presents the ruined city as a locus of tyranny and oppression, where '[o]blivion will steal silently / The remnant of its fame' and '[m]onarchs and conquerors' will be forgotten with the ruins (2.119–20, 121). Like 'Ozymandias' (1818), the ruins in Palmyra speak of the inevitable fall of the tyrannical empire, but unlike the sonnet, which ends with the awful nothingness evoked by the 'lone and level sands' that 'stretch far away' (14), in this poem a place ruined by human folly and tyranny needs to be recreated into a place that inspires revolutionary hope. In this regard, in creating the poem's Romantic geography, Shelley first draws on the inner geopolitical space of Volney's *Ruins*, one of the most famous works of the Revolutionary period in France and in England, which radically politicizes eighteenth-century moralistic ruin-sentiment on transience, and reformulates the ruins as a site of revolutionary thought.[26]

Shelley's indebtedness to Volney's work is obvious in his choice of Palmyra and of a protagonist's mental journey guided by a celestial spirit, which moves from contemplation of past civilizations to a vision of universal renewal. Looking from the heights at 'the whole group of ruins and the immensity of the desert,' Volney muses on '[t]he aspect of a great city deserted, the memory of times past, compared with its present state' (Volney 4–5). In his reverie, he is approached by 'the Genius,' at whose command his soul rises from his body. 'Suddenly a celestial flame seemed to dissolve the bands which held us to the earth; and, like a light vapor, borne on the wings of the Genius, I felt myself wafted to the regions above. Thence, from the aerial heights, looking down upon the earth, I perceived a scene altogether new' (14). The passage has a close resemblance to the description of Mab extracting Ianthe's soul from her body and taking her soul to Mab's celestial palace.

Shelley, however, has clear points of difference from Volney, emphasizing marginal space and otherness and insisting that human civilizations are intrinsic to nature. Shelley radically replaces Volney's male savant and his male guiding spirit with an innocent girl pupil and her tutorial goddess. By passing the cosmic vision from a fairy queen to a young girl, Shelley makes room for women in a realm of social vision, the realm that had been previously occupied by men alone. Feminizing both the granter and the grantee of the prophecy is enterprising, especially because just a few months before Anna Barbauld's 'Eighteen Hundred and Eleven' (1812) received so many hostile attacks provoked by the poem's claim to a 'prophecy' (Keach, 'A Regency Prophecy and the End of Anna Barbauld's Career' 569–77). John Wilson Croker, in an anonymous review in the *Quarterly Review*, says that they hoped that 'the empire might have been saved without the intervention of a lady-author' (309).

Another significant departure from the preceding text is the course of the mental trip to ancient ruins. Volney's route is based upon the dichotomy of centre and margin. His wanderings revolve around his mother country, starting in ancient Asia, going westward and from past to present to the Tigris, Jerusalem, Babylon, Baalbek, and to 'the most recent Europe' (Volney 7–8). He is horrified by the idea that the splendour which has departed from Asia may leave Europe as well and that the day will come when a traveller sits on the silent ruins in great European cities and 'weep[s] in solitude over the ashes of their inhabitants, and the memory of their former greatness' just as he does now in Palmyra (8). Volney's review of world history reflects the old concept of the *translatio imperii*, which was revived as the idea of progress in the eighteenth century. The progress of civilization has been westward only when seen from a Eurocentric standpoint. Volney clings to the provenance of his place-based experience, which is to him the sole centre of the world. The decay of the world is redeemed only by an apocalyptic vision that shows what is going on at that very moment in his mother country, a vision clearly referring to the States General (63–6). A universal revolution starts in France, and Volney hopes that it will spread all over the world.

In contrast, Mab and Ianthe keep going further and further in time and space without fixing any centre. In canto 1, the last thing Ianthe sees on earth during her space trip is the 'rival of the Andes, whose dark brow / Lowered o'er the silver sea' (*Queen Mab* 1.220–1). In terms of height, the 'rival of the Andes' can be either the highest in Europe, the Swiss Alps, or the highest in Asia, the Indian Caucasus (Hindu Kush), which was considered to be one of the probable sites for the birth of humankind in Shelley's day (Curran, *Shelley's Annus Mirabilis* 63–4). The Andes, however, not only boast their height but also represent the latest revolution, the independence movements among the Spanish colonies in South America in 1811 and 1812. In Anna Barbauld's 'Eighteen Hundred and Eleven' the Spirit of Progress stands on 'Andes' heights,' looking at the successful independence of Spanish colonies (324). In 'To the Republicans of North America' (1812), Shelley calls 'Cotopaxi,' a volcano in Ecuador in the chain of the Andes, to resound voices of liberty with its 'sister mountains' (21, 22).[27] In terms of the association of revolution with 'sister' mountains, the 'rival' can be either the revolutionary Andes' male opponent symbolized by the highest European mountain or its competing partner in Europe, feminized 'Mount Liberty' in Wales ('On Leaving London for Wales' 23). The two rival peaks, one of which is only indirectly referred to, create an imaginary space that enables us to go around the globe in a moment. In *Queen Mab*, marginal regions, both European and non-

European, play an important role in the history of humankind, and become the source of a possible future 'bloodless victory' ('On Leaving London for Wales' 44).

In canto 2, Mab proceeds from Palmyra to several famous ruins in the Orient: Egyptian Thebes on the Nile, Jerusalem, which has been reduced to a 'sterile spot,' and Athens, Rome, and Sparta, which have become 'a moral desert now' (2.134, 163). Shelley states clearly that the decay is not only physical but 'moral.' The palaces are 'more wretched' than the 'mean and miserable huts,' 'crumbling to oblivion' (2.165, 164, 167). Amid these vast ruins, damaged both morally and physically, there is one thing that may kindle revolutionary hopes for renewal: the 'long and lonely colonnades, / Through which the ghost of Freedom stalks' (2.168–9). The long white colonnades again remind us of Ianthe's motionless white neck. Her body 'amid ruin' (1.138), which remains on earth while her soul is at Mab's celestial palace, serves as a tiny wreck of hope that can be placed on any of those ruinous spots Mab shows her soul from above.

Corresponding to Ianthe's body as a hopeful ruin in the Old World, one unknown spot appears at the far end of the globe in the final part of the trip to the ruins. After tracing the well-known sites frequently visited by Western travellers in Europe and the Middle East, Mab and Ianthe do not then go back to European home ground, nor do they celebrate the contemporary revolutionary movements among the Spanish colonies in Central and South America. Instead, Mab directs Ianthe's attention to an obscure waste in the 'western continent':

> Spirit! ten thousand years
> Have scarcely past away,
> Since, in the waste where now the savage drinks
> His enemy's blood, and aping Europe's sons,
> Wakes the unholy song of war,
> Arose a stately city,
> Metropolis of the western continent:
> There, now, the mossy column-stone,
> Indented by time's unrelaxing grasp,
> Which once appeared to brave
> All, save its country's ruin;
> There the wide forest scene,
> Rude in the uncultivated loveliness
> Of gardens long run wild,

> Seems, to the unwilling sojourner, whose steps
>   Chance in that desert has delayed,
> Thus to have stood since earth was what it is.   (2.182–98)

In its obscurity and remoteness from contemporary Europe, the final spot significantly differs from the preceding famous cities of the past, which played a significant role in European history. Scholars usually take Shelley's 'ten thousand years' as an exaggeration, trying to identify the unnamed city with a real historical city in the American continent. Reiman and Fraistat think that the passage probably refers to the ruins of Mayan cities in Central America (*SP&P* 28n.1). Matthews and Everest consider that the city might be suggested by Tenochtitlán (the capital of the Aztecs, and the site of modern Mexico City), which was built on islands in a lake and contained Montezuma's extensive gardens, adding that Shelley had read a description of the city and its gardens in Southey's composite 'Aztlan' in *Madoc*, and dismissing Shelley's 'ten thousand years' as 'fanciful' (*PS* 1: 286–7).

As sacred chronology, which calculated the earth to be some six thousand years old, was still influential in the 1810s, Matthews' and Everest's view of Shelley's 'ten thousand years' as extravagant is reasonable if we try to identify the city in history, but it is not necessary that this ancient city be a historical one. Reiman and Fraistat in a commentary to this passage offer an interpretation of the noun phrase 'ten thousand years' as indicating 'any great number' (*CPPBS* 2: 538). I agree with them, and I would further argue that this is a visionary place that precedes any historical metropoles. Another important point in the passage is that a possible reference to Aztec civilization, which is notorious for its human sacrifice, seems to appear in a description of the present deplorable state of the spot. For 'the savage[s],' who are belligerent, are 'aping Europe's sons' (*Queen Mab* 2.184, 185). European imperialism destroyed the 'western continent,' reducing the land to a physical and moral 'waste,' where local people mimic Europeans, attacking each other. This state has been introduced long after the ancient city, which looked as old as the earth itself, flourished on the cultivated plain.

All the ruins Mab and Ianthe see – exotic ruins in Palmyra and Egyptian Thebes, biblical ruins in Jerusalem, classical ruins in Europe, and nameless ruins in the western continent – are 'desart[s],' on which one could trace what has been wiped out by time (2.163). The last one, however, is quite different from the preceding famous historical ruins familiar to contemporary Europeans. While the earlier ones are 'sterile' and 'moral desart[s],' disclosing correspondence among physical, social, and moral degeneration, the final one is a green 'desart' with columns covered with moss, and surrounded by gardens, and forests (2.134, 163, 197). Nature revealed in the 'gardens long run wild' shows 'uncultivated loveliness,' anticipating the ruins of a pleasure house entwined with parasitic flowers in 'Epipsychidion' (1821), and waiting to be cultivated again (2.195, 194, 'Epipsychidion' 498–507). Unlike the other ruins, the mossy column stone and the ruined gardens do not strike a desolate tone, nor shall they be cast into oblivion. Mab not only visualizes the ancient prosperous city on the cultivated land built by a virtuous people but also suggests its retrievability by the restoration of virtues in humans.

> Yet once it was the busiest haunt,
> Whither, as to a common centre, flocked
>   Strangers, and ships, and merchandize:
>   Once peace and freedom blest
>   The cultivated plain:
>   But wealth, that curse of man,
> Blighted the bud of its prosperity:
> Virtue and wisdom, truth and liberty,
> Fled, to return not, until man shall know
>   That they alone can give the bliss
>   Worthy a soul that claims
>   Its kindred with eternity.   (2.199–210)

This ancient 'Metropolis of the western continent' offers a prototype of a metropolis that is in harmony with nature as well as humans and welcomes '[s]trangers' from other parts of the world, though destroyed by 'wealth, that curse of man' before its possibilities are fully blossomed (2.188, 201, 204). Rousseau inveighs against luxury and commerce throughout his political writings,[28] but whereas Rousseau is not fond of cities and, in the preface to the *Second Discourse*, denounces 'all the progress of the human Species' as moving humanity 'farther away from its primitive state' (3: 12), Shelley creates his own ideal metropolis, making it predate any historical cities and allowing it to prosper in archaic times. It is a reworking of the visionary populous city at the origin of the earth that Shelley envisaged in Keswick in November 1811 (*Letters* 1: 189). Shelley does not say whether 'wealth, that curse of man,' is intrinsic to human nature or comes from outside, but he clearly states that the ancient city was first blessed with '[v]irtue and wisdom, truth and liberty' (*Queen Mab* 2.204, 206). In this respect, the Metropolis in the western continent presents itself as an antithesis to the modern metropolis of London, which is a place beneath whose 'poison-breathing shade / No solitary virtue dares to spring' (5.44–5).

The unnamed remote metropolis 'decentres' Europe by its great geographical and cultural distance from Europe's central cities. Shelley introduces the remotest other as a nameless city on the cultivated plain; it thrived in the distant past and was inhabited by a virtuous people. The 'western continent,' which is usually referred to as the New World, is as old as the Old World, and had a peaceful metropolis at its beginning (2.188). In the geopolitical imaginings of the Romantic poets, two mythical Welsh figures, Prince Madoc and Mab, go all the way from Wales to the American continent, but the contact zones they traverse present completely different geographies of the mind. In Southey's 'epic of foundation' (Bernhardt-Kabisch 111), the 'imperial city' of Astlan is retrieved with armed force and prospers under Madoc as a Christian 'White King,' while the Aztecs leave and their next stately capital is to be conquered by the 'heroic Spaniard's unrelenting sword' (*PWRS* 5: 48, 341, 395).[29] As Southey believes that 'there are but two methods of extending civilisation, – conquest and conversion' (*Correspondence* 3: 281), Madoc recreates the geography of South America by treating the distant others as objects of either of these two tools, thus inserting South America into the vicious cycle of rise and fall of empire, with one 'imperial' city superseded by another forever (*PWRS* 5: 48). On the other hand, Mab suggests the retrieval of an ideal past through human virtue.

In Shelley's Romantic geography, the notion of an ideal place is described as the 'cultivated plain' and the restoration of a happy metropolis, which is possible by those who know the cause of its loss and the means to retrieve the virtuous mind, can be achieved anywhere on earth (*Queen Mab* 2.203). Shelley's use of the word 'cultivated' goes back to an early usage of culture as cultivation, namely, the tending of nature by humans, from which is derived an extended application of the word, the cultivation of the inner nature, the human mind. For Shelley, cultivating external nature is at the same time cultivating the human mind, because in his unique view of nature, nature is replete with human presence and human and natural elements are intricately connected together: '[t]here's not one atom of yon earth /

But once was living man,' nor 'the minutest drop of rain, / That hangeth in its thinnest cloud, / But flowed in human veins' (2.211–15). Though this may look very anthropocentric, Shelley's version of the Great Chain of Being does not have a hierarchy based upon anthropocentrism. The cycle of natural processes accommodate historical cycles, and within nature's ecosystem, humans as social beings are accepted with their cities as 'cultivated plain[s]' (2.203). Thus wherever Shelley looks in the world, he envisions cities:

> And from the burning plains
> Where Libyan monsters yell,
> From the most gloomy glens
> Of Greenland's sunless clime,
> To where the golden fields
> Of fertile England spread
> Their harvest to the day,
> Thou canst not find one spot
> Whereon no city stood. (2.216–24)

Shelley's idea of multiple cultivated plains thus helps us to understand the nature of the 'Spirit of Nature' Mab passionately invokes at the end of each part of the instructive tour. The 'Spirit of Nature' is conceived as an entity that is natural and social at the same time (1.264, 3.226, 6.197). Mab, to whom is given the 'wonders of the human world' and the 'secrets of the immeasurable past' (1.168, 169), calls forth nature both in the form of scientific knowledge about the universe in the space trip, and in the form of environmental knowledge about the earth in the world trip, in order to educate the human imagination. In this regard, Mab acts as a scientific philosopher and a city muse, as Shelley links social concerns with environmental themes, and social reforms with scientific improvements. In order to 'make this Earth, our home, more beautiful,' he hopes that 'Science, and her sister Poesy, / Shall clothe in light the fields and cities of the free' (*The Revolt of Islam* [1817] 5.2254, 2255–6). In *Queen Mab*, however, the earth is not yet even 'habitable' (*Queen Mab* 8.58).

4. Wailing Ruins

Mab, as a bringer of true dreams, prepares Ianthe for 'the sick day in which we wake to weep' as we see 'healthful innocence' ruined by '[t]yranny, superstition, commerce and inequality' ('The Triumph of

Life' 430, *SPW* 827). A prosperous city in the present, which is contrasted with an ancient metropolis, is the source of all social evils that destroy nature as well as humans. It does not stand on the 'cultivated plain,' and thrives on 'gold' and 'numerous viands culled / From every clime' (*Queen Mab* 2.203, 3.46, 47–8). The word 'viands' connects commerce with carnivorism, the bloody Promethean vice Shelley wants to vanquish with his 'weapon' for a 'bloodless victory' (*SPW* 827, 'On Leaving London for Wales' 41, 44).[30] The modern metropolis is presented as '[y]on populous city,' with a 'gorgeous palace' that 'seems itself a city' as its centre (*Queen Mab* 3.23, 22, 24). Although this 'populous city' can be any city where corrupt leaders are oppressing the public, it is strongly associated with London. Shelley's vehement criticism of the English monarchs and officials of his day can be clearly heard both in the text and in the notes from canto 3 onward, echoing 'The Devil's Walk' (1812) and anticipating 'England in 1819' (1819), 'The Mask of Anarchy' (1819), and 'Oedipus Tyrannus or Swellfoot the Tyrant' (1820), whose title captures the moral as well as physical corruption of a king whose feet are morbidly enlarged by gout, a disease caused by excessive drinking and eating. The image of the king whose wanton revelry wrings the famished nation's groan, which repeatedly appears in the present poem, is one of the themes Shelley pursues in his political poems attacking contemporary Britain (Foot 50–3). It sums up how 'all-polluting luxury and wealth' make 'ruin of their hearts,' producing wars, religion, tyranny, and trade, and making humans spoilers of both nature and themselves (*Queen Mab* 8.180, 5.95).

'Yon populous city' is not reconcilable with 'yonder earth,' which presents an image of the land as blessed by nature (3.23, 192). Humans are excluded from the blessed earth: All creations 'fulfil the works of love and joy, – / All but the outcast man' (3.198–9). Shelley's hope is in Wales, as there appears a beautiful night scene viewed from Tan-yr-allt that realizes an intimate and harmonious relationship between human creation and nature represented by '[y]on gentle hills' and '[y]on castled steep,' and described in the mode of Coleridge's 'Frost at Midnight,' which confirms correspondence between internal and external nature (4.8, 12). The beautiful night, however, is not followed by the light of the day, which would locally see the embankment and other improvements turning land into green pasture. When '[t]o-morrow comes,' the whole globe is seen in violent agitation; on the 'western main' in 'southern climes,' a violent tempest is raging, and 'the vessel,' whose course may be the middle passage, 'finds a grave' beneath the abyss of the sea (4.25, 24, 20, 32); in the northern hemisphere, the fires of war are flashing, the description of which, according to Matthews and Everest, is based on Napoleon's burning of Moscow and the subsequent retreat of the French troops (*PS* 1: 299–300). The 'speaking quietude' of Wales is broken by 'the shriek, the groan, the shout' of humans all over the world (*Queen Mab* 4.3, 43).

Looking from Mab's celestial palace at these catastrophes inflicted by humans terrifies Ianthe's soul (and the readers); there are vast deserts, ruins of cities, and modern cities devastating both nature and people. Shelley, however, does not think that these disasters are 'uncaused, and irretrievable' (4.75). That is why the bird's-eye view of the whole globe is offered as a diagnosis of the 'devastated earth,' which Ianthe's soul has to learn in order to stand up 'amid ruin' and amend 'the discord-wasted land' when she goes back to earth (4.112, 1.138, 4.79). Shelley's observations of the destructive impact of humans on nature on a global scale and of the link between environmental and social degradation have their external counterparts in the observations by the naturalists and physicians on the front line of expanding geographical horizons, who, as Richard H. Grove demonstrates, initiated global environmentalism in the Romantic period (*Green Imperialism* 314–48). While medical surgeons were hired as 'naturalists' by the East India Company to develop systematic links between scientific and medical knowledge that contributed to the management of British overseas colonies (Grove, *Ecology, Climate and Empire* 66–7), naturalists and surgeons, through Hippocratic analysis of environmental changes caused by human action,[31] made an implicit critique of colonial activity. In 1771, visiting St Helena, an important replenishing point for the East India Company's ships, Sir Joseph Banks was shocked at the Company's devastation of the island, which used to be 'highly favoured by nature' (*The Endeavour Journal of Joseph Banks 1768–1771* 2: 266). He compared St Helena disapprovingly with the Cape of Good Hope, which, 'tho by nature a mere desart,' was made a 'paradise' by the Dutch, and concluded that if 'the Cape [were] now in the Hands of the English it would be a desart, as St Helena in the hands of the Dutch would as infallibly become a paradise' (2: 266).

As Alan Bewell's *Romanticism and Colonial Disease* details, with a new phase of European expansion, scientists, widening their scope to cover the whole globe, started to write a medical geography of the world, which was divided into three environmental zones – the polar, the tropical, and the temperate, the first two of which were seen as pathogenic spaces. In *Queen Mab*, humans shrink with the plants and are 'chilled' to be '[i]nsensible to courage, truth, or love' in the polar region, while they suffer in the tropical region that teems with 'earthquake, tempest and disease,' surrounded by 'blue mists through the unmoving atmosphere' that scatter 'the seeds of pestilence' (8.150, 151, 171, 168, 169). What is remarkable about Shelley's diagnosis of the health of the earth, however, is that he considers human-made disease as more malignant than natural disease and ascribes the most virulent to the most favourable clime, the middle zone where Europe is located. The 'venomed exhalations' of the 'poison-tree' produced by 'kings, and priests, and statesmen' spread '[r]uin, and death, and woe' (4.84, 83, 80, 85). The 'pestilence that stalks / In gloomy triumph through some eastern land / Is less destroying' than they are (4.188–90). They contaminate the 'bloodless veins / Of desolate society' and blight 'human flower[s]' as well as natural flowers (4.106–7, 104).

The metaphor of the 'poison-tree' points to London, which is figured as a place beneath whose 'poison-breathing shade / No solitary virtue dares to spring' (5.44–5). Shelley's use of poison tree is telling as the metaphor itself is a monstrous creation of world commerce, colonialism, and poetic imagination. The image of the upas tree, a plant native to Java, was first introduced into English literature by Erasmus Darwin in *The Loves of the Plants* (1789), and was widely used by Romantic poets.[32] The tropical poisonous tree, being transferred to British soil by world trade as well as by poetry, and tended by the baleful British social system, grows to be the poison tree of English contagion, and to blight not only British society but also the entire globe.

When the European imagination translates the anxieties of empire into images of virulent diseases, corresponding to the external shared facts, they arise in non-European places and are carried by non-European peoples into Europe. As Barrell's case study of De Quincey's mental landscape shows, Oriental diseases yield to Western medicine, and the non-European pathogenic spaces are conquered by European science and power. We, however, need to remember that non-European disease had its counterpart in Occidental disease and that these two were already intricately enmeshed in the Romantic period; while venereal disease was imported to Europe by Columbus, Europeans exported it to Tahiti, for example, and it quickly spread through the South Seas, destroying the innocence of that southern paradise. Just like the actual European disease, London as the unchallenged commercial and imperial centre spreads contagious political and economic force to eat away the health of the earth. Before the British intruded into the southern hemisphere with economic and colonial implements of 'all-polluting luxury and wealth,' people there were 'nobler' despite 'earthquake, tempest and disease,' but 'Christians,' craving for gold, turned them from fellow humans into 'bloodstained dust' or 'article[s] of trade' (8.180, 172, 171, 177, 173, 176).

Although Shelley is convinced that 'wisdom is not compatible with disease,' the hopeless situation of the present earth afflicted with 'all the varieties of disease and crimes' makes him admit that 'in the present state of the climates of the earth, health, in the true and comprehensive sense of the word, is out of the reach of civilized man' (*SPW* 808, 804). Unlike De Quincey, who depends upon the metaphor of inoculation and disinfection against Oriental disease that presupposes the myth of Europe's intellectual and military conquest of the East, Shelley relies as a last resort on the earth's 'cure' through equinoctial precession, the readjustment of the obliquity of the poles, which will restore prelapsarian happiness in a distant utopian future. Bucked up by recent astronomical discoveries and precedents recorded in 'the history of mythology, and geological researches,' Shelley presumes that 'the progress of the perpendicularity of the poles may be as rapid as the progress of intellect' (*SPW* 808).

In the poetical world of *Queen Mab*, however, what Shelley says in the prose notes is not really realized. Shelley's utopian project to regenerate the devastated geography of the earth through human intellectual amelioration comes to a halt when benevolent nature, as if a *deus ex machina*, spreads 'pure health-drops' like 'a dew of balm upon the world' (6.52, 53). Health floats as 'balmy breathings of the wind [which] inhale / Her [the earth's] virtues, and diffuse them all abroad' (8.112–13). Nature's 'balmy breathings,' which are Wordsworthian in tone, do not seem to cooperate with humans' moralistic and environmental responsibilities to progress and improve. Not humanity's but nature's 'recreating hand' will 'soon' work to recreate the earth and 'blot in mercy' human follies from 'the book of the earth' (6.56, 57). In 'On Leaving London for Wales,' Shelley refuses to indulge in this forgetful aspect of nature's healing effect. In the early cantos of *Queen Mab*, Shelley tries to diagnose the complicated entanglement of social and natural ills, and show that social reforms play an important part in healing both internal and external natures. Acting in contradiction to these political and environmental principles, however, Mab, as an executioner of a benevolent nature, simply declares: 'Let the axe / Strike at the root, the poison-tree will fall' (4.82–3). She does not explain how humans 'with changeless Nature coalescing, / Will undertake regeneration's work' (6.42–3). The lack of human participation creates great discrepancies between the present and the nebulous future, between nature's will to erase human history from the earth and Shelley's wish to transform 'all-polluting luxury and wealth' into a real form of wealth, 'the labour of man' (8.180, *SPW* 804). He has not yet found a 'bloodless' weapon that should replace the bloody axe in order to eliminate the source of contamination and recreate cities of destruction into new cultivated plains ('On Leaving London for Wales' 44).

Correspondingly, most of the last two cantos, which are intended to celebrate the arrival of the bright future, is in fact devoted to depicting retrospectively how overwhelmingly flawed and desolate the world once was. Although deserts and snowstorms disappear and scenes of the 'habitable' earth, which have Hippocratic and utopian elements, appear in the cold and tropical zones, there is no mention of temperate European countries, especially Britain, where flowers, trees, and cities should be seen to thrive where the poison tree and ruins used to be (*Queen Mab* 8.58). The gap between the present situation in Britain as well as in the world and the purely hypothetical and desired future is so striking that the latter remains unrealized even poetically despite the poem's proud announcement that '[a]ll things are recreated' (8.107).

Throughout the final two cantos, the ruins keep crumbling with dying echoes. The pyramids, which have braved the heavens in canto 2, are now driven into pieces across 'the desert where their stones survived / The name of him whose pride had heaped them there' (9.29–30). The passage, which anticipates 'Ozymandias,' presents a landscape of sand where the huge monuments have been reduced to nothingness through the workings of time. Whereas the sonnet justifies the immortality of art, in which the sculptor outlasts the defeated tyrant and his ruined monuments, all human attempts at eternity are mocked in *Queen Mab*. The marvellous art of 'breathing marble [that] glows above' the 'corpse' cannot stop the process of decomposition (9.110, 108). Here the 'breathing marble' – the phrase which is employed to refer to Ianthe's neck in canto 1 – only conceals the corpse. The final two acts of *Prometheus Unbound* do not bother to depict the evils that have disappeared after Jupiter's fall, absorbed in the sheer joy of singing the arrival of the utopian world that realizes 'the fields of Heaven-reflecting sea' and 'many-peopled continents' in harmony with nature (3.2. 18, 22). Though there is a long passage describing 'the melancholy ruins / Of cancelled cycles,' they are buried peacefully in 'the Earth's deep heart,' the scene only momentarily and sympathetically shown by the light from the Spirit of the Earth, which penetrates into the abyss of the globe (4.270–318). On the other hand, the ruins in *Queen Mab* are left ravaged by time and continue to whistle desolate and lonely tunes.

At the end of the vision of the ruins, Mab asserts that 'human things were perfected' as these ruins, 'wide scattered o'er the globe, / To happier shapes were moulded,' and that the earth 'grew / Fairer and nobler with each passing year' (*Queen Mab* 9.134, 131–2, 136–7). This is Shelley's hope: that human creations, once fragmented to atoms, will participate in the natural circulation. Unfortunately, we are never shown how the ruins are recreated and what the 'happier shapes' are like. Unlike 'Ode to the West Wind' (1819), there is no suggestion that the scattered fragments conceal ashes and sparks, the image of immortal art, nor are there the winds of imagination that blow and burn. Indeed, at the beginning of canto 5 there is a brief reference to the 'imperishable change' in the generations of humans, who are likened to fallen leaves, which, covering the ground for 'many seasons,' 'fertilize the land they long deformed' till a 'breathing lawn' and then a 'forest' appear (5.3, 7, 12, 13). This gradual development toward perfection is, however, never detailed in the utopian future. After all, the sudden arrival of the perfect future occurs only in a vision, and as Mab herself has to say at the end when her 'spells are past' and 'the present now recurs': 'a pathless wilderness remains / Yet unsubdued by man's reclaiming hand' (9.143, 144–5). There remains in reality an uncultivated wilderness that requires tremendous work by humanity's reclaiming hand.

5. The Fadeless Ruin and Humanity's Reclaiming Hand

In the Romantic geography of *Queen Mab*, there is a sharp contrast between the centre as the source of pollution and the margin as a regenerating place. London is where the poison tree spreads its dangerous exhalations of colonialism and trade, which are likened to diseases that afflict both nature and human beings all over the world. Even though 'the poison-tree will fall' (4.83), London does not show its own recreating power. By contrast, the marginal space is seen as having the power to recover health for both natural and human environments, and for both the centre and periphery. That is why Shelleyan reformers go to the contact zone, meet others in unfamiliar forms, and change themselves from within.

The ideal civilization at the beginning of the earth is located far from European centres, in an obscure waste in the western continent. The report about the ancient prosperous city in the margin that Ianthe will bring back to a central city cursed by wealth and imperial desire is an admonition from the past and the most distant other and about a way to cure a sick centre. This offers a striking contrast to what Southey's *Madoc* brings back to Wales: a story of conquest and the foundation of an empire. Southey's epic is made up of the legacy of his old utopian dream of setting up an ideal community in Pennsylvania, a Welsh myth of white Indians in the New World, which can be seen as a version of a quest for Prester John, and a missionary zeal to convert multiple others into the same – English and Christian.[33] In Southey's *Madoc*, the European eyes, seeing the 'imperial city' of a foreign people 'piled with human skulls' and filled with '[l]ong files of human heads,' justify Madoc's use of armed force to create a Christian kingdom on their religious centre (*PWRS* 5: 48, 50). The imperial eyes of Europe do not perceive the image of the savage other as mirroring their own cruelty in a different form. Shelley, however, does, referring to the present state of the 'the savage' in 'the western continent,' who, 'aping Europe's sons, / Wakes the unholy song of war' (*Queen Mab* 2.184, 188, 185–6).

It was only in the first decades of the nineteenth century that firsthand, detailed observation of ancient non-European high culture in Central and South America was available to Europeans. Alexander von Humboldt was publishing in Paris an enormous amount of research on ancient and modern Spanish America he had conducted with the assistance of Aimé Bonpland during his Spanish-American scientific expedition of 1799 to 1804.[34] Shelley's placement of the nameless ideal city of the past in 'the western continent,' rather than in India, may be related to this latest information on non-European others, in addition to the recent independence movements in Spanish colonies (2.188). A question then arises as to whether Shelley's vision of the utopian future is different from, or similar to, what Humboldt wants to see in the future when the Spanish colonies attain independence. In the preface to the *Personal Narrative of Travels to the Equinoctial*

Regions of the New Continent, during the Years 1799–1804 (1814–29),[35] Humboldt writes: 'the inhabitant of the banks of Oroonoko will behold with extasy, populous cities enriched by commerce, and fertile fields cultivated by the hands of freemen, adorn those very spots, where, at the time of my travel, I found only impenetrable forests, and inundated land' (1: li). Pratt takes this passage as a typical 'Euroexpansionist' view, asking who this future seer will be and whether the future cultivators will behold them with ecstasy (131). The same question can be raised by Shelley's future vision of the 'countless rills and shady woods, / Corn-fields and pastures and white cottages' that appear in the 'desarts of immeasurable sand,' and the 'bright garden-isles' with 'fertile vallies' that emerge from the 'trackless deeps' (*Queen Mab* 8.75–6, 70, 101, 103, 88).

Before comparing Shelley and Humboldt, however, it should be noted that imperial travellers to distant lands, including naturalists, physicians, and officers, were not on their own, but hired by or sanctioned by the authorities, such as a government, or a company granted a royal charter. They were thus deeply involved with colonialism, but in private travel accounts by colonial explorers, colonial teleology and anti-colonial ethos are inextricably enmeshed. Imperialistic as he was, Humboldt's liberal and anti-colonial view was well known through his writings. While Helen Maria Williams, the translator of Humboldt's book, remarked in her preface that she found in his narrative the progress of imperialism as 'he imprints the first step' that 'leads to civilization and all it's [sic] boundless blessings' (viii), the East India Company was so alarmed by severe criticism of colonialism in South America in Humboldt's narrative that permission for the research trip to the Himalayas and Southern Asia was never given to him despite repeated applications (Bowen 240).

It is true that there is a troubling ambivalence about the vocabulary Shelley uses in words such as 'commerce' as well as the images Shelley introduces to the future utopian vision: '[c]orn-fields and pastures and white cottages,' which are strongly reminiscent of 'the golden fields / Of fertile England' (*Queen Mab* 5.38, 8.76, 2.220–1). As Shelley shares part of his vocabulary and imagery with imperial overseas explorers, it is hard to decide how successful his attempt is in revising colonial geographies in the Romantic geography of *Queen Mab*, and to what extent he is unconsciously versus consciously a so-called liberal imperialist. One important point that differentiates Shelley from imperialists, however, is that in *Queen Mab* both the model for amelioration and the virtues to be sought after always originate in marginal places, not in the centre. An ideal city is located far back in time and far away from Europe as a model that replaces London. While the influential power from the centre 'darts / Like subtle poison through the bloodless veins' of the political and commercial networks of the British Empire (4.105–6), in Wales, an obscure marginal fairy, Mab, is recast into a chronicler of the world, and Ianthe is chosen to spread the antidote for the imperial poison, 'health-drops,' to the world (6.52). Shelley, who is disguised as Henry waiting for Ianthe to wake in the poem, wishes the wind would 'diffuse them all abroad' (8.113), as he would later wish the wind would '[s]catter, as from an unextinguished hearth / Ashes and sparks, my words among mankind!' ('Ode to the West Wind' 66–7).

The importance of marginal space is also stressed by the changes the poem makes to the gender division of the Christian epic, in which the protagonist meets a great Other, God, and is granted a vision. In the final two books of *Paradise Lost*, before the departure of Adam and Eve, God sends to them Angel Michael, who leads Adam to a high hill and shows him the vision of the future, while Eve is put to sleep. By contrast, Mab 'poured the magic of her gaze / Upon the maiden's sleep'; it is sleeping Ianthe, not wakeful Henry, who is shown the grand vision of the past, present, and future to prepare for a 'pathless wilderness' (*Queen Mab* 1.77–8, 9.144). Although Shelley's choice of an innocent young heroine as a recipient of a universal vision may be influenced by Southey's anti-war epic *Joan of Arc* (1796),[36] the attitudes of the two toward religion and God are quite different. While Southey's epic, striking a clear religious note, sees almighty God descend upon the young heroine, in Shelley's poem a pagan Welsh fairy, who denies the Christian God along with all political and religious establishments, comes to a young girl. The feminized epic grandeur of *Queen Mab* creates new cultural imaginaries about Welsh myth, against the idea of progress, London as a global centre, and the Madoc myth.

Pratt defines the contact zone as the 'space of colonial encounters' beyond Europe where 'peoples geographically and historically separated come into contact with each other and establish ongoing relations, usually involving conditions of coercion, radical inequality, and intractable conflict' (6). In the visionary contact zones of *Queen Mab*, Ianthe, guided by the fairy queen, sees many others in the form of ruins scattered all over the world. If Bakhtinian dialogism between the self and others can be considered as an important element to open a 'utopian moment' in the Saidian monolithic construct of Romantic texts (Leask, *British Romantic Writers and the East* 2), *Queen Mab* unfortunately does not make good use of many opportunities for this kind of dialogism. Those opportunities are given not only within the poem but also between the poem and the prose notes, whose social critique and scientific knowledge from the male sphere of reason are offered to assist the poem's female sphere of dreams, where female characters are given important roles.[37] Mab and Prometheus (who is criticized in a prose note), bridging these two spheres to educate Ianthe, can perform an important function of a Bakhtinian double-voiced linguistic hybridity, 'an encounter, within the arena of an utterance, between two different linguistic consciousnesses, separated from one another by an epoch, by social differentiation or by some other factor' (Bakhtin 358). Mab is able to show Ianthe the most distant other in the form of an ancient prosperous city as a counterforce against London, but she fails to redeem Prometheus, who traverses two spheres and comes into the poem as Ahasuerus, who is conjured up by Mab to answer Ianthe's question about God.

In canto 7, which marks the end of the educational journey of the past and present and is the only canto that presents Ianthe's speech, she meets a human figure who is presented as a 'monument of fadeless ruin,' Ahasuerus, who firmly refuses to surrender to God and whose 'wisdom of old age was mingled there [in his cheek] / With youth's primæval dauntlessness' (*Queen Mab* 7.261, 78–9). The figure of Ahasuerus '[m]ocking' his 'powerless tyrant's horrible curse / With stubborn and unalterable will' (7.257-8) looks back to Satan in Milton's *Paradise Lost* and forward to the Prometheus before he relinquishes the Curse in the first act of Shelley's *Prometheus Unbound*. Shelley's Ahasuerus resembles Prometheus more than the Wandering Jew, but no explicit relationship is suggested between him and the 'Prometheus (who represents the human race)' who is condemned for ushering all kinds of physical and social diseases including 'Tyranny, superstition, commerce, and inequality' (*SPW* 826–7). Moreover, Mab gives no time for Ianthe to reply to Ahasuerus, throwing him back into the abyss of dark human history, 'the dreams / Of human error's dense and purblind faith,' with a farewell wave of her wand (*Queen Mab* 7.64–5). Neither Prometheus nor Ahasuerus is reclaimed. Nor can Ianthe actively participate in meaningful dialogue with many others in the poem – Mab, Ahasuerus, and her significant other, Henry – that could lead them to a moment of awareness, unlike later earthly questers, such as Asia in *Prometheus Unbound*, and the poet/narrator in 'The Triumph of Life.' The result is that the poem, after a huge hybridizing attempt to include all – epic, romance, science, history, politics, dreams, women, and so on – only ends in a highly hypothetic abstract 'reality of Heaven,' instead of initiating a true utopian vision that alters the reality of the earth (9.1). The imaginary geopolitical space in the poem still remains 'a pathless wilderness' (9.144).

Madocks's great embankment ended in failure, and Shelley was disappointed at those various parties who thought about nothing but their own interests in embankment affairs (*Letters* 1: 334, 336; Holmes 178–82). Shelley must have realized that this Promethean project of improving the physical shape of the land for humanity's purpose pursued only economic 'improvement,' not moral 'improvement' of the place, and that the motivation for the economic improvement ran parallel to that of colonial explorers and officers who wanted to improve the 'savage' geography for their own interest, destroying its flora and fauna, its local peoples and their cultures. *Queen Mab*'s passionate singing of universal regeneration is not only a prayer for the utopian future but also a prayer for poetry that can change the bitter reality of Tremadoc, where Madoc's/Madocks's Welsh nationalistic projects left 'Nature's wound' unhealed ('On Leaving London for Wales' 54). Seeking a 'bloodless victory' (44), Shelley aims to reformulate Europeans' Promethean relationship with multifarious others, and to take humans out of the economy of Eurocentric colonialism into the 'œconomy' of nature, in which natural 'improvement' occurs. Through the Tremadoc experience, Shelley is keenly aware of the difficulty of finding an ideal place and the need for visionary improvement of a place. He has to send a quester on a real quest, exploring the untrodden realms in the globe and the mind.

2 'Alastor': A Solitary Quester and a New Eastern Geography

1. A Male Traveller in Undiscovered Lands

The last thing Ianthe saw on earth when Mab's celestial chariot 'flew far above a rock, / The utmost verge of earth' was the 'rival of the Andes, whose dark brow / Lowered o'er the silver sea' (*Queen Mab* 1.218–19, 220–1). The phrase suggests a panorama of high mountains, such as those pictured in the engraving 'A Comparative View of the Heights of the Principal Mountains and Other Elevations in the World' in John Thomson's *A New General Atlas* (1817). Thomson's plate sets the mountains in the Eastern Hemisphere against those in the Western Hemisphere (fig. 1). Although Thomson usually does not acknowledge the sources of his maps, it is clearly influenced by Goethe's 'Comparative Panorama of Mountain Tops of the Old and New World' (1813), which was inspired by Humboldt's 'Ideas for a Geography of Plants' (1807). On the left of Thomson's plate, toward the highest summit in the Western Hemisphere, appears a small dot (fig. 1, circle A), which a gloss in the border identifies as Humboldt; in 1802 he attained the highest peak in South America, Chimborazo, whose height is '19,400 [feet].' Above him is another small dot representing a bird in flight (fig. 1, circle B), which, according to another gloss, marks 'the highest flight of the Condor – 21,000 [feet].' Near the centre of the plate, toward the end of the second mountain range, is the balloon of Gay-Lussac (fig. 1, circle C; the balloon also appears on the book cover), who made the world-record ascent in 1804. A note in the border indicates that the balloon is at 'the height of 22,900 feet.' The highest summits of the Indian mountains, however, remained at that time beyond human reach.[1] Although the mapping of the globe was

John Thomson, 'A Comparative View of the Heights of the Principal Mountains and Other Elevations in the World.' *A New General Atlas* (1817), facing p. xiii. Courtesy of the Thomas Fisher Rare Book Library, University of Toronto.

gaining pace in the early nineteenth century, high mountains and unexplored regions invited Europeans to imagine their own expeditions and discoveries.

In the preface to Humboldt's *Personal Narrative of Travels to the Equinoctial Regions of the New Continent, during the Years 1799–1804* (1814–29), Helen Maria Williams argues that 'journeys by land in distant regions' are 'far more' interesting than 'sea-expeditions' with the exception of Cook's voyages (v–vi). She thinks that the former excites general interest 'not only by extending the limits of science, but by presenting new aspects of the variegated scenery of the Globe' (vi), which suggests that the pursuit of scientific knowledge in nature is connected with a new aesthetic sense of wonder. Giving extended praise to the overland traveller, she exclaims: 'Happy the traveller, with whom the study of Nature had not been merely the cold research of the understanding, in the exploration of her properties, or the solution of her problems!' (vi). She describes this happy traveller as adoring nature's 'sublimity,' following 'her steps with passionate enthusiasm, amidst that solemn and stupendous scenery, those melancholy and sacred solitudes, where she speaks in a voice so well understood by the mysterious sympathy of the feeling heart'; the reader will follow him with such 'eager delight,' wandering into 'another hemisphere,' 'the trackless deserts' and 'the untamed wilderness,' to 'mark unknown forms of luxuriant beauty, and unknown objects of majestic greatness – to view a new earth, and even new skies!' (vi–viii). The image of the traveller in Williams's preface tells us two things. First, the love of nature cultivated by Wordsworth and Coleridge and sought in the English landscape now led one's eyes to distant foreign lands beyond the European world. Second, the sublimity that nature discloses to the passionate traveller is now seen as natural resources, 'forms of luxuriant beauty' and 'objects of majestic greatness' to be devoured both by explorers on the geographical front lines and readers in metropolises with 'eager delight.'

Ever since Earl R. Wasserman distinguished the narrator as a Wordsworthian nature poet and the 'Poet' as a Shelleyan visionary poet (*Shelley* 11–41), critics recognize two main characters in Shelley's 'Alastor': one who narrates the whole poem and the other who is introduced in the main part of the poem as a 'Poet' (50). The narrator's 'solemn song' (19) is full of echoes from Wordsworth and is reminiscent of Shelley's own youthful experience, which Shelley recounts in the fifth stanza of 'Hymn to Intellectual Beauty' (1816). Similarly, the protagonist of the main part of the poem, whom the narrator introduces as a 'Poet,' was nurtured by 'solemn vision, and bright silver dream' ('Alastor' 50, 67). The narrator does not tell whether he wandered in his native land or travelled abroad, but the blissful moment of union with nature, which Wordsworth experiences, does not occur to the narrator; even though he has 'watched / Thy [Nature's] shadow, and the darkness of thy steps' and his heart 'ever gazes on the depth / Of thy deep mysteries,' Nature has never 'unveil'd' her 'inmost sanctuary' to him (20–1, 22–3, 38). The Poet has travelled widely in foreign lands, visiting 'the red volcano' that dominates '[i]ts fields of snow and pinnacles of ice,' the 'bitumen lakes' that beat with 'sluggish surge,' and the 'secret caves' that conceal numerous 'starry domes / Of diamond and of gold,' 'immeasurable halls' with 'crystal column,' and 'clear shrines / Of pearl, and thrones radiant with chrysolite' (83–94). Although the Poet has followed 'Nature's most secret steps' like her 'shadow,' there is no suggestion that Nature has ever disclosed her mysteries to him (81, 82).

It is clear that both the narrator and the Poet are educated by the English imagination cultivated by Wordsworth, Coleridge, and Southey,[2] and the Poet's course to India, motivated by interest in unknown lands, reflects Shelley's interest in the East. Hogg reports that 'he pursued with more than ordinary eagerness the relations of travellers in the East, and the translations of the marvellous tales of Oriental fancy' (1: 108). From the last few decades of the eighteenth century, the British public was able to have visual images of India based on firsthand observation and executed by professional British landscape artists.[3] The British readers were ravished with 'unknown forms of luxuriant beauty, and unknown objects of majestic greatness' – a phrase used by Williams for Humboldt's travel reports (viii) – in exotic Indian nature as well as in ancient Hindu texts translated by the members of the Asiatic Society of Bengal. Shelley, however, grants neither the narrator nor the Poet a vision of the 'inmost sanctuary' of nature ('Alastor' 38). 'Alastor,' which was composed in the fall and early winter of 1815, one year after Williams's translation of Humboldt's *Personal Narrative* started to appear, can be taken as a criticism of some aspects of the Romantic imagination and the type of Romantic discourse of the natural sublime,[4] which produces a Humboldtian type of scientific colonial traveller. The Poet in 'Alastor' has a close resemblance to the overland traveller in Williams's description, who follows 'her [nature's] steps with passionate enthusiasm, amidst that solemn and stupendous scenery, those melancholy and sacred solitudes, where she speaks in a voice so well understood by the mysterious sympathy of the feeling heart' (Williams, preface vi). Like Humboldt, the Poet travels far and wide, and some of the natural scenes he observes are described in terms that have economic implications: sublime natural objects that Nature urges him to 'love and wonder [at]' include the 'starry domes / Of diamond and of gold,' 'crystal column,' 'clear shrines / Of pearl, and thrones radiant with chrysolite' ('Alastor' 98, 90–1, 93, 93–4). Shelley makes these natural resources 'inaccessible / To avarice or pride' (89–90) in order to distinguish his Poet from overseas travellers with imperial eyes, but the Poet is far from '[h]appy,' unlike Williams's Romantic and scientific travellers (Williams, preface vi); his fate is 'dark,' and he dies 'in solitude' ('Alastor' 59, 60).

An important question arises here: how similar is the Poet to a passionate colonial explorer like Humboldt, who marks 'unknown forms of luxuriant beauty, and unknown objects of majestic greatness' in the 'trackless deserts' and 'the untamed wilderness' (Williams, preface vii–viii)? The Poet in 'Alastor' goes all the way to the vale of Kashmir, through Eastern regions, from the western Mediterranean to Egypt and Ethiopia, and beyond the Indian Caucasus, in search of the 'strange truths in undiscovered lands' (77). The rest of the chapter examines how the 'strange truths' are recorded in the physical and mental geographies the Poet traverses in the poem.

2. The Passage to the Indian Caucasus

'Alastor' has been considered a typical example of a Romantic internalized quest, removed from reality to a lonely psychological realm (Bloom, *The Visionary Company* 239). There are, however, some elements in the quest that put the poem back into historical and political contexts. The vast Eastern area the Poet covers 'closely approximates that of Alexander the Great during the triumphant years' (Raben, 'Shelley the Dionysian' 27). His abandonment of an Arab maiden and craving for a dream maid can be analysed in the context of Orientalism. The Poet's course from England to Kashmir reminds us of Kathema's reverse course from Kashmir in 'Zeinab and Kathema,' an early anti-military poem probably written in 1811.[5] The narrative structure of the earlier poem, in which the protagonist wanders in search of his (lost) ideal amid 'the strange things of a strange land' ('Zeinab and Kathema' 89), is strikingly similar to that of 'Alastor,' though the earlier poem is more concerned with the political turbulence of the day and its later counterpart concentrates more on the workings of the mind in its mental geography.

Shelley's early interest in the East and India, which lasted till the end of his life,[6] was nourished by the works of Sir William Jones and other Orientalists, various travel writings, and Southey's Oriental poems.[7] When he went to Oxford in 1810, the year of the publication of Southey's *The Curse of Kehama*, Shelley was attending University College, where Sir William Jones had studied and taught, and nearly across the road from the College was St Mary's Church, where his wife placed a monument to his memory, executed by Flaxman with an Indian figure on it.[8] In December 1812, Shelley ordered Edward Moor's *The Hindu Pantheon* (1810), William Robertson's *An Historical Disquisition concerning the Knowledge Which the Ancients Had of India* (1791), and *The Works of Sir William Jones* (1799) (*Letters* 1: 342, 344).

The India portrayed in glowing terms in the books Shelley was devouring in the early 1810s, however, would soon be threatened by British political and cultural intrusion into India. In the 1790s, writers in Britain, following Jones's portrayal of Hinduism, continued 'the survey of the virtues, learning, fortitude, and industry of this innocent and secluded race of men' with 'admiration' (Maurice 1: lxiii). Both Warren Hastings and Edmund Burke, Hastings's chief antagonist in his impeachment trials, had an imaginative respect for Indian social and cultural structures. Though there was a certain practical motivation for Hastings's patronage of Oriental studies, he wrote in a letter to Nathaniel Smith, Chairman of the East India Company: 'Such studies, independently of their utility, tend, especially when the pursuit of them is general, to diffuse a generosity of sentiment, and a disdain of the meaner occupations' (Hastings 189). On the other hand, Evangelicals, 'for whom there could be no common ground with non-Christian beliefs,' were directing hostility at Hinduism (Marshall, introduction 41–2). For them, acceptance of the existing structures supported by non-Christian beliefs was a vice. The old policy not to disturb Indian social structures and institutions was thus to be replaced by a type of Christian imperialism, supported by the middle class, which paved the way for British India. The contemporary political situation was reflected in literature. Southey condemns Hinduism as 'the most monstrous in its fables and the most fatal in its effects' in the preface to *The Curse of Kehama* (*PWRS* 8: xxiii); he refers to British Orientalists as '[o]ur *barbarian* scholars,' and massive footnotes to *Thalaba*, which use the latest research on the Eastern materials by British Orientalists, are loaded with contemptuous comments on the East: 'The little of their literature that has reached us is equally worthless' (*PWRS* 4: 29, 28).

This psychological change from admiration and wonder to hostility is later criticized as 'too self-seeking in India' by Reymond Schwab, who initiated the study of the psychological relationship between Europe and non-Europe in *La Renaissance orientale* (1950) and considered the Orient as the significant 'alter ego to the Occident' (43, 4).[9] Schwab's critical path, followed by Henri Baudet, who discussed a fundamental ambivalence in the European mind, 'a paradoxical combination of opposing motives,' which produced various images of non-Europeans (5), was significantly redirected from the quest for one's alter ego in the Oriental Renaissance to the West's desire for conquest and self-aggrandizement in Said's theory of Orientalism. What Schwab phrases as 'too self-seeking in India' Said politically and radically reconsiders as complicity of knowledge with power. In the early nineteenth century the tendency of collusion of Oriental scholarship with authority became clear. For example, when the Company opened the East India Company College at Haileybury to train young civil servants in 1805, Sanskrit was introduced into the curriculum, though it was not until 1832 that a professional chair in Sanskrit was founded in Oxford. Only about thirty years after the founding of the Asiatic Society of Bengal by Jones in 1784, Parliament was to include in the Charter Act of 1813 the 'Pious Clause,' which permitted missions to be sent to India.[10] James Mill's *History of British India* was to be published in 1817.

Contemporary literature describing the Orient was, however, more complex than Said's binary system can assume. In 1811, one year after Southey's negative portraiture of Hinduism in *The Curse of Kehama*, there appeared Sydney Owenson's *The Missionary: An Indian Tale*, which, backed up by the latest Oriental scholarship, presented a beautiful Brahman priestess as an ideal woman. Immediately after its publication, Shelley read Owenson's novel (*Letters* 1: 101, 107, 112, 130). Matthews and Everest think that *The Missionary* might have influenced Shelley's image of Kashmir as an uncorrupted earthly paradise and condemnation of imperialism in 'Zeinab and Kathema' (*PS* 1: 171). While *The Curse of Kehama* remained his favourite poem after his visit to Southey in the Lake District and his disappointment with the older poet in December (*Letters* 1: 211–12), in the letter of 20 June 1811 to Elizabeth Hitchener, Shelley admired Owenson's beautiful heroine, Luxima, as 'the Deity of virtue' (*Letters* 1: 101). As many critics have pointed out, the beautiful Brahman priestess, whose name is derived from the Indian goddess Lakshmi, strongly influenced the image of the veiled maid in 'Alastor' (Drew 255–8).[11]

The fact that *The Missionary* is set in the seventeenth century and that its protagonist is a solitary, idealistic Portuguese does not entirely remove it from British contemporary politics in India. Despite its earlier historical setting, the novel is clearly a product of the age of British expansion into India in its use of the framework of the religious/romantic quest and its identification of the Christian Hilarion as West and the Brahman Luxima as East. Similarly, the image of the narrator in the frame narrative as 'an inspired and desperate alchymist / Staking his very life on some dark hope' and as a 'dark magician' raking 'the cinders of a crucible / For life and power' intentionally sets 'Alastor' in a remote past (31–2, 682, 683–4), but the Poet's eastward course reveals the darker side of Shelley's Romantic geography, affected as it is by the history of the West's invasion of the East. Also, unlike a typical Oriental story that confirms the conquest of the East by the West, the imperialistic vein contradicts the poem's ending; it is the Poet, not the veiled maid, who is defeated and dies.

By 1815, when 'Alastor' was composed, Great Britain was becoming more and more imperialistic, annexing the greater part of the French colonies through its naval strength and standing against Russia on land in the subcontinent (Bayly, *Imperial Meridian* 3–4). Writing a poem that traces a wandering poet's overland route to Kashmir, which was not part of the territorial acquisition of the East India Company in 1815, thus raises crucial questions about the nature of the Poet's expedition and Shelley's evaluation of it. The Poet, who seeks after the imaginative female Orient as his idealized other, can be seen as an example of Saidian modern Orientalism, from which Sir William Jones was not wholly exempt, though Said distinguishes between the 'modern Orientalism' initiated by Napoleon's Egyptian expedition and the Orientalism promoted by Jones and his contemporaries in the pattern of Schwab's 'Oriental Renaissance' (*Orientalism* 122). Jones found in the East some 'true centre of population or of knowledge' by going back to 'some common source' of the East and the West that no longer exists (Jones 1: 22, 26).[12] Mab and Ianthe have found an ancient metropolis that no longer exists in an obscure waste in America in *Queen Mab*. Is Shelley, influenced by Jones, looking for some 'true centre of population or of knowledge' ? Are the 'strange truths' Shelley is seeking by tracing his protagonist's Eastern journey different from Jones's idealized ancient centre ('Alastor' 77)?

Nigel Leask, in his Saidian reading of the poem, stresses the Poet's physical desire for the East as an ideal woman. He argues that the protagonist's quest for his female 'prototype' unmasks Britain's desire for its Indian other, considering him as prefiguring 'the Victorian empire-builder, moving ever further and outwards' (*British Romantic Writers and the East* 123–4). Shelley, however, had already severely criticized the British invasion of India in 'Zeinab and Kathema,' in which the 'Christian murderers' with their 'holy book' ravage Kashmir and carry away Zeinab to England (33, 37). For Shelley, Britain's colonization of India was as deplorable as its oppression of Ireland. He writes in 'An Address, to the Irish People' (1812) that the glory England gained by '[t]he conquests in India' is 'a glory which is not more honourable than that of Buonaparte' (*Prose* 30).

Many protagonists in Shelley's poems, such as Asia, the Witch of Atlas, and the quester in 'The Triumph of Life,' are sent on a long quest journey as Shelley's imagination seeks a new habitable place in untrodden lands, whether this landscape is sought internally in the mind or externally in the remotest parts of the world. What distinguishes the Poet in 'Alastor' from other questers in Shelley's poems is his insatiable desire for 'undiscovered lands,' the desire for *terrae incognitae* that guides him to Kashmir, the Eastern sanctuary Europeans had not touched yet, and the geographical details of his eastward course. Saree Makdisi argues that the Poet's passion for foreign lands, which produces the female other that causes his restless wanderings, makes the map of 'Alastor' 'a cleaned-out slate ready for European colonization and inscription' (152). Makdisi focuses on the Poet's visit to the ruins in the Middle East, but here I will examine the Poet's entire course and demonstrate how his geographical track simultaneously mimics and criticizes the desire of nineteenth-century Great Britain to explore the globe and to fill the vast blank space with cartographic discourse.

The Poet traverses '[m]any a wide waste and tangled wilderness,' but he cannot be satisfied to 'love and wonder [at]' the secret nature revealed to him in the scenes of 'ampler majesty / Than gems of gold' in the wild unlike travelling scientists and mineralogists ('Alastor' 78, 98, 95–6). He also visits the 'awful ruins of the days of old,' which Ianthe has seen in Mab's lesson of human history (108; *Queen Mab* 2. 126–81). In these archaeological sites, a Volneyan Orientalist would expect to stimulate the sense of history. Volney laments over the transience of earthly prosperity and asks in vain why so many cities are 'destroyed' and why 'this ancient population [has not] been reproduced and perpetuated' (7) – a lament shared by Mab when looking at Palmyra. The Poet, however, is free from gloomy contemplation on *translatio imperii*, incessantly moving eastward. The Poet's eastward course is not purely imaginary; Shelley depends heavily on the journeys made by the officers of British and French trades and governments, such as James Rennell (the first surveyor-general of the East India Company), James Bruce, George Forster, C.F. Volney, and Vivant Denon. The British reading public was fascinated with the English translation of Denon's *Travels in Upper and Lower Egypt, in Company with Several Divisions of the French Army, during the Campaigns of General Bonaparte in That Country*, published in 1802 and 1803. The 'Zodiac's brazen mystery,' which the Poet saw in the ruined temples, is inspired by Denon's account and plate of the planisphere at the temple of Isis in Dendera (119; Denon 2: 313–22, plate 58).

The collusive relationship between power and knowledge is shared by both these officers and the reading public back home, driven by the fantasy that detailed cultural and historical information on the peoples and accurate cartographic information on their lands would prove European superiority and lead to better control over them. The complicity with power and maps, in this respect, emphasizes the universal feature and structuring principle of the world map, the 'omphalos syndrome,' according to which a people believes itself to be located at the centre of the world (Edgerton 26). The Poet does not seem to be bound by this 'omphalos syndrome,' which significantly distinguishes him from contemporary explorers who are on missions, working for a trading company or government, and expecting to return home with what they have discovered. The Poet wanders incessantly, leaving his 'alienated home,' never to return, and going further and further eastward, with no reference to his birthplace as a place to return to or a place of destination of his wanderings ('Alastor' 76). This very lack of a centre characterizes Shelley's unique *geo*-graphy, that is, earth-description and map-making. The geography that has neither a centre nor a home ground could not have been drawn by a proto-Victorian empire builder, because, as J.B. Harley persuasively observes, from the ancient Christian map, which centred on Jerusalem, down to the modern political map, the 'omphalos syndrome' demonstrates that the centre and the margin are always determined from an ethnocentric viewpoint (277–312). A literary version can be seen in Coleridge's 'The Rime of the Ancient Mariner,' in which the Mariner starts from the church of his native place and returns to the same church. Bernard Blackstone observes: '[in Byron's poems] we travel far afield, but always on a return ticket. *The Ancient Mariner*, not *Alastor*, is the paradigm of *Childe Harold, Lara, Mazeppa, Beppo, Don Juan*' (5).

In 'Alastor,' no place can claim to be the centre of the world in what Shelley is mapping. All those famous sites of ruins, including Jerusalem, the centre of the ancient Christian map, are passed through, until the Poet comes to 'Dark Æthiopia' in the 'desert hills' ('Alastor' 115). Contemporary scholars, based upon Diodorus, regarded Ethiopia as the most ancient civilization (Volney 15–17; Diodorus 2: 88–103). It was not until Bruce's travels in 1768 and 1772 that the land beyond the Sudan desert was investigated, and Bruce's travel account appeared more than twenty years later as *The Travels to Discover the Source of the Nile* in 1790. Just as Bruce did, the Poet retraces the well-known ruins of ancient Western civilizations, moving roughly in a reverse chronological order from Greece, the most recent pre-Christian civilization, to Ethiopia. Among magnificent columns and images in the ruins in Ethiopia, the Poet goes back in time: he kept 'poring on memorials / Of the world's youth' till 'meaning on his vacant mind / Flashed like strong inspiration, and he saw / The thrilling secrets of the birth of time' ('Alastor' 121–2, 126–8).

Going back in imagination to 'the birth of time' is what Shelley himself experienced in Keswick in 1811 and which he represented as a vast populous city in Mab's vision ('Alastor' 128; *Letters* 1:189; *Queen Mab* 2.182–210). The Poet's 'gaze' makes the meaning of the scene flash 'like strong inspiration,' but the 'thrilling secrets of the birth of time' do not manifest themselves as a concrete vision of the past. What they are is never told, which suggests that not only nature but also history does not reveal its inmost sanctuary to him yet. If they are really shown to the Poet, the poem's reticence about the details suggests that his gaze is different from that of a happy Romantic explorer like Humboldt who, upon finding 'unknown objects of majestic greatness,' would have been rapturous to report them in detail or that of the land-travellers sent from a European 'centre of calculation' who would have been as meticulously scientific and taxonomic as a 'mobile recording machine' (Williams, preface viii; Leask, *Curiosity and the Aesthetics of Travel Writing 1770–1840* 70–7). Instead, by moving abruptly from 'the birth of time' to the present desert scene in which a devoted 'Arab maiden' is ignored by the Poet, the poem reveals a certain aloofness or disengagement characteristic of the Poet's gaze ('Alastor' 128, 129). As he travels by himself, not as a representative of the British government, the African Association, or the East India Company, he would have to acquire passports from local authorities and would have to make himself as acceptable to local cultures where he is travelling as a James Bruce or a Humboldt. While wandering in nature, he 'has bought / With his sweet voice and eyes, from savage men, / His rest and food' (79–81). His eyes and song are used in exchange for food and rest, but in Ethiopia, surprisingly, he does not even look at the Arab maiden, who, devoted to him in vain, 'watched his nightly sleep, / Sleepless herself' (134–5).

The reason why the Poet's imagination does not recover the original glory of the earth Shelley envisioned in 1811 and 1813 is obvious. Although Shelley's visionary imagination aspires toward the social even in the solitary wanderings in majestic nature, the Poet, absorbed in the activity of gazing, obliterates from his field of vision local peoples. The Poet's highly focused gaze is not so much the scientific and imperialistic gaze of European explorers as an expression of his extreme solipsism. His inwardness makes him 'unknown' to people and people '[s]trangers' to him (62, 61). His utter indifference to people around him distinguishes him from those representatives of Western imperialism in Oriental tales, such as Owenson's Hilarion and Byron's Giaour, who appear as seducers and infidels to the local inhabitants.[13] The Poet's 'self-centred seclusion,' which shows traces of Wordsworth's Solitary in *The Excursion* (1814), illustrates one of the hazards of a Romantic imagination that arises from solipsism (preface to 'Alastor,' *SP&P* 73). In addition an element in the Romantic solitary imagination, if placed in a foreign setting, may weave a dream of the other in a way similar to European one-sided textual Orientalism.

It is significant that a local person who 'tend[s] his steps' is introduced as 'an Arab maiden' rather than an Abyssinian maid ('Alastor' 132, 129). Abyssinia (Ethiopia) has a long association with Christianity and the legend of Prester John.[14] It was familiar to literary readers through Samuel Johnson's English translation of the account of travels by a Portuguese missionary, Father Jerome Lobo, and through Johnson's philosophical romance *Rasselas: The Prince of Abyssinia* (1759). If we apply Barrell's theory to Abyssinia, the land is a 'manageable' East in its association with Christianity. Coleridge's 'Abyssinian maid' in 'Kubla Khan' (1816) is an interesting example of the 'manageable' Middle East to be united with the Western self against the Far East (39).[15] Coleridge includes 'within' him the symphony and song of 'an Abyssinian maid,' who, as the feminized manageable East, helps him to empower the Romantic imagination to the level of the despotic imagination of the terrifying East (42, 39). It is 'the ruined temples,' the image of which is derived from the famous temple of Isis at Dendera in Egypt, and 'an Arab maiden' living in 'her father's tent,' which Shelley's 'Dark Æthiopia in her desert hills / Conceals' ('Alastor' 116, 129, 130, 115–16). Although feminized, Shelley's Ethiopia moves toward an unknown heathen East. What is important here is that the human representation of Ethiopia as an unknown East is not described as terrifying or seducing but as the best of the 'choicest gifts' of the 'spirit of sweet human love' (205, 203). Moreover, a Saidian reading of the Poet's abandonment of the real Arab maiden for the dream maid does not work here, because the Arab maiden succumbs not to his desire for conquest but to his neglect. Surprisingly, the Poet does not seem to notice her even when he is awake and she brings 'his food, / Her daily portion, from her father's tent' and 'spread[s] her matting for his couch,' stealing '[f]rom duties and repose to tend his steps' (129–32). It is no wonder that the Poet, who fails to recognize the Arab maiden and thus misses her gift of human love, fails to visualize the 'thrilling secrets of the birth of time' Ethiopia conceals.

Leaving Ethiopia, the Poet does not take the usual route to go eastward to India. Contemporary Englishmen went via ship after the overland crossing through Egypt, Suez and Baghdad to Basra (Marshall and Williams 68–9). Instead, the Poet wanders through lands virtually untrodden by Europeans, traversing 'Arabie / And Persia, and the wild Carmanian waste' to the 'aërial mountains,' which are the Hindu Kush mountains (the Indian Caucasus) ('Alastor' 140–1, 142). The vast area from the Middle East through Persia to the Hindu Kush is conceived differently in the map of the mind between the contemporary Orientalists and the surveyors of the East India Company. In his inaugural address as president of the Asiatic Society in 1784, Sir William Jones gives the audience an imaginary map of the world that places '*Hindustan* as the centre' (Jones 1:3). He asks the audience to turn their eyes 'in idea to the North' to see on their right 'many important kingdoms in the Eastern peninsula': '[B]efore you lies that prodigious chain of mountains ... and beyond them ... the vast regions of *Tartary* ... [O]n your left are the beautiful and celebrated province of *Iran* or *Persia*, the unmeasured, and perhaps unmeasurable deserts of *Arabia* ... and farther westward, the *Asiatic* dominions of the *Turkish* sultans' (1: 3–4). Jones uses the tripartite geographical structure of Europe, Middle East, and East, similar to that of Barrell, but with a countervailing effect: 'since the language and literature of the *Abyssinians* bear a manifest affinity to those of *Asia*, since the *Arabian* arms prevailed along the *African* coast of the *Mediterranean*, and even erected a powerful dynasty on the continent of *Europe*, you may not be displeased occasionally to follow the streams of *Asiatick* learning a little beyond its natural boundary' (1: 4). Jones draws upon the religious affinity between Abyssinia and Europe and the geographical affinity between African and European civilizations. The role of the middle part is not to block and overcome the fearful further East, but to make Europe recognize another centre in India and bridge these two centres.

What Jones proposes is a Copernican revolution in the European cognitive map of the world; as the official religion of the Mughals was Islam, Hinduism was seen as 'the infernal circumference of an Islam that was itself the infernal circumference of Christianity' (B. Rajan 85). Jones and his fellow Orientalists showed that an ancient Indian culture based upon Hinduism built a centre of civilization equal to those of Europeans, with Sanskrit as a parent language of human civilization. The giaour who comes from India to tempt Vathek in Beckford's *Vathek* (1786) 'might well be the bearer of an ancient enlightenment' after Jones's discoveries (B. Rajan 85). Jones's cognitive map of the world, in which knowledge and power flow from India, epitomizes the world view of the Oriental Renaissance,[16] and offers counter-evidence against Said's ahistorical discussion of premodern Orientalism in which he mentions that Jones's view of Indic studies was 'to domesticate the Orient and thereby turn it into a province of European learning' (*Orientalism* 78).

At around the same time, the surveyors of the East India Company were trying to create a new space called '(British) India' out of the regions that were made up of various political and cultural components of Hindustan (Edney 15).[17] In 1779, after his extensive survey journeys of twelve years, James Rennell produced the *Bengal Atlas*, which was the first scientific map in India. In its use of six colours it also showed the region's political geography, in which the Company's dominion stood out in clear relief after the dismemberment of the Mughal Empire. In 1782, after returning to London and sorting through the mass of manuscript maps and descriptions that had been accumulated in the office of the East India Company, Rennell published the map of India, which became the main source for subsequent maps of India. It was entitled '*Hindoostan*,' but the centre of the map was not the subcontinent, but an extraordinarily large and elaborate cartouche celebrating the British conquest of India.[18] Rennell explains the meaning of the emblem in the cartouche in detail in the first edition of *Memoir of a Map of Hindoostan; or the Mogul's Empire* (1782):[19] 'BRITTANNIA receiving into her Protection, the sacred Books of the HINDOOS, presented by the PUNDITS, or LEARNED BRAMINS: in Allusion to the humane Interposition of the British Legislature in Favor of the Natives of Bengal, in the Year 1781. BRITTANNIA is supported by a Pedestal, on which are engraven the Victories, by Means of which the British Nation obtained, and has hitherto upheld, its Influence in India' (xii). Key elements in the design, which is wreathed with the opium poppy, the primary crop for the China trade, are Britannia, represented as a female warrior with a spear resting on a bolt of cotton cloth, then the main Indian export to Europe, and three bowing Brahmans holding documents labelled as 'Shastras,' which Rennell glosses as 'the sacred Books of the HINDOOS' (xii). Because of the ambiguity created by the posture of Britannia and the central Brahman, the emblem has been differently interpreted.[20] Rennell's intention to show the power of Britannia backed up by science and commerce is, however, clear in the verbal explanation of the cartouche. In the cartouche, although the knowledge Britannia needs is still in the hands of the Brahmans, the temple tower behind her presents her as a goddess receiving sacred Hindu manuscripts as tribute (xii). The point is that the map of *'Hindoostan'* presents the emerging modern image of (British) India, turning the subcontinent into a site of glory, conquest, and world trade. It invites the viewer to link the place with a name derived from the Hellenistic 'Indies' that signifies the traditional eastward limit of the Hellenistic world and therefore is easily associated with the Eastern expedition of Alexander the Great.

Although the subcontinent was thoroughly mapped and Indian trade routes by sea had been so well detailed that 'the soundings on the coast of Bengal' were 'better known than those in the British Channel' (Rennell, *Memoir of a Map of Hindoostan* [2nd ed.] v), the overland route to India still remained unexplored and insecure. As the vast area from the Middle East through Persia to the Hindu Kush was known to the Hellenistic Greeks, for British colonial officers and geographers, the overland routes to India meant a recovery of the legacy left by Alexander's world conquest. Rennell discusses in detail the route taken by Alexander the Great throughout the second edition of his *Memoir of a Map of Hindoostan* (1788). Eager to make ancient names correspond to modern ones, Rennell draws on sources ranging from Ptolemy to D'Anville and George Forster, whose overland journey from Kashmir to the Caspian Sea in the early 1780s partly overlaps Alexander's marches and the Poet's imaginary course from Kashmir in 'Alastor.'[21]

Alexander the Great's Eastern expedition was also a paradigm for European expansion into India for contemporary writers and travellers. In his epic *Alexander's Expedition down the Hydaspes and the Indus to the Indian Ocean* (1792), Thomas Beddoes uses Alexander's conquests as 'a pretext for impassioned anti-imperialist tirades' (R. Porter, *Doctor of Society* 166).[22] William Hodges begins his *Travels in India, during the Years 1780, 1781, 1782, and 1783* (1793) with his first glimpse of Madras from the sea; the English-founded town appeared similar to what 'a Grecian city in the age of Alexander' would have been (2). Similarly, in Owenson's *The Missionary*, entering India is linked with Alexander's invasion: 'every object, to the imagination of the Missionary, became consecrated to the memory of the enterprise of Alexander,' and Hilarion's 'historic knowledge enabled him to trace with accuracy ... those particular spots, where Alexander fought, where Alexander conquered!' (1: 37). The references to Alexander the Great stress Hilarion as a religious invader whose weapon is conversion. He wants to 'penetrate into those regions, which the spirit of invasion, or the enterprise of commerce, had never yet reached,' and to 'attack, in the birth-place of Brahma, the vital soul of a religion' that 'had so long survived the vicissitudes of time, the shock of conquest, and the persecution of intolerance' (1: 48, 49). The novel, armed with contemporary Oriental scholarship ranging from François Bernier, the first European to travel to Kashmir, to Anquetil de Perron and Sir William Jones, is illustrative of Said's notion of Orientalism. Its ending, however, runs counter to Said's monolithic argument, showing Owenson's complex and ironic treatment of the issues of European ventures into the Orient and the surge of missionary movement in Britain.

I would like to emphasize that Shelley does not trace any of the famous sites that mark Alexander's advance into India on the Poet's route to Kashmir, nor does he describe the Poet as experiencing the same excitement that Hilarion felt when entering India. Shelley does not share with Rennell a passion to make ancient names correspond to modern ones; he does not consistently follow either ancient geography or modern geography in terms of place names. The latest maps and geography books employ modern terms, such as 'Hindo Kush,' which replaces the ancient 'Caucasus,' while Shelley uses modern terms such as 'Balk' (the ancient Bactria) together with 'Caucasus' ('Alastor' 242, 353). The geographical track of the Poet from Ethiopia to Kashmir, which remains obscure in the poem, is a new overland route to India unrelated to recent British gains and discoveries or Alexander's glory. The 'aërial mountains which pour down / Indus and Oxus from their icy caves' are not identified, as if the Poet was the first to cross the mountains through that route and enter Kashmir, which was beyond the territorial acquisition of the East India Company (142–3). It is true that the vast area that the Poet covers overlaps the routes taken by Alexander or Dionysus (Raben, 'Shelley the Dionysian' 27),[23] but, whether in regard to Alexander's Eastern territory or Dionysus's invasion of India, Greek associations are intentionally omitted on the Poet's course to Kashmir. No mention is made of the cave of Prometheus, nor of the city of Nysa, which was believed to have been founded by Dionysus.[24] Nor is there any reference to the physical difficulties experienced by Alexander's armies and Western explorers in crossing the Caucasus. Both Bernier and Forster complain of the steepness of the mountain route and the barrenness and cold of the summit (Bernier 409; Forster 1: 303). On the contrary, the Poet crosses 'the aërial mountains which pour down / Indus and Oxus from their icy caves' without difficulty and in 'joy and exultation' enters Kashmir ('Alastor' 142–3, 144).

3. A Natural Bower in the Vale of Kashmir

The Poet's eastward course suggests Shelley's idea of the East as a location of paradise in the long tradition set by Sir Walter Raleigh's *History of the World* (1614), in which Ararat is identified with the Indian Caucasus for the first time (128).[25] Following Raleigh, Thomas Maurice in *Indian Antiquities* (1793–1800) identifies Ararat with the Indian Caucasus, not the mountains in Armenia (5: 490). In 'Zeinab and Kathema,' Shelley employed an idyllic picture of Kashmir as an Edenic garden of the kind first introduced by Bernier, who had praised it as a 'Terrestrial Paradise' surrounded by 'innocuous' mountains (396), used by Forster (2: 1), and popularized by Owenson's *The Missionary* and Thomas Moore's *Lalla Rookh* (1817). As Matthews and Everest point out, the description of Kashmir in 'Zeinab and Kathema,' where 'Heaven and Earth are ever bright and kind,' 'flowers and fruits are ever fair and ripe,' and 'forms [are] unpinched by frost or hunger's gripe' (93, 97, 99), is identical to that in *The Missionary* (*PS* 1: 174). Shelley's twist is to contrast Kashmir as an earthly paradise with England as hell. In England, 'blights and storms and damp forever float'; people's hearts are 'more ungenial than the zone,' which means that their hearts are colder out of proportion to the 'temperate' zone in which England is located; and '[f]amine, disease and crime even wealth's proud gates pollute' ('Zeinab and Kathema' 94, 95, 102). The contrast is taken up in *Queen Mab* as that of a regenerated earth, where '[h]ealth floats amid the gentle atmosphere, / Glows in the fruits, and mantles on the stream' and '[n]o storms deform the beaming brow of heaven' (8.114–15, 116), and London, where social and moral diseases destroy the health of the land.

'Alastor,' however, does not deck Kashmir with popular, exotic images. Nor does it use the contrast between a healthy Eastern paradise and a disease-ridden Western centre of imperialism. Instead, we are shown a natural description of a secluded Romantic place 'far within / Its loneliest dell,' where there are 'odorous plants' and 'a sparkling rivulet' ('Alastor' 145–6, 148). This simple description of the vale is markedly different from the detailed account of the Poet's travels in the wilderness and among the ancient ruins in the Middle East, which are depicted in visual terms commonly employed by contemporary travellers and explorers (81–98, 106–28). It is important to note that the vale of Kashmir, where the Poet comes all the way from the West, is not treated as a new paradise or a new centre of the world in the Romantic geography of 'Alastor.' After choosing not to trace the cities that were captured by Alexander, and not to stamp Western values and images on them in the Poet's route to the vale of Kashmir, the poem decides not to create, as Sir William Jones did, another centre in the East to compete with European glory. The lonely landscape in 'Alastor' cancels the simple dichotomy between East and West, and constitutes an imaginary contact zone in which 'strange truths' should be found (77).

In the wild, lonely inmost sanctuary in the vale of Kashmir, the Poet is visited by a 'vision on his sleep': 'He dreamed a veiled maid / Sate near him' (149, 151–2). The veiled maid, the 'prototype of his conception' (preface to 'Alastor,' *SP&P* 73), owes much to Luxima in Owenson's *The Missionary*, who appears as a 'brilliant vision [that] float[s] on his imagination' (1: 153). When first seen by Hilarion near a river in the vale of Kashmir, Luxima is described as follows: 'Before the altar ... appeared a human form, if human it might be called, which stood so bright and so ethereal in its look, that it seemed but a transient incorporation of the brilliant mists of morning'; he saw her 'resplendent locks' 'enwreathed with beams, and sparkled with the waters of the holy stream, whence it appeared recently to have emerged.' (1: 146–7). In 1811, Shelley considered her as 'divine' (*Letters* 1: 112), and her figure was to inspire Shelley to form his own resplendent female spirits, from the veiled maid to the 'shape all light' who emerges from a river in 'The Triumph of Life.' At the same time, however, Shelley recognized the danger of poetic imagination in personifying and 'embodying' a 'God': '[Y]ou have formed in your mind the Deity of virtue; this personification, beautiful in Poetry, inadmissible in reasoning in the true style of Hindoostanish devotion, you have adopted' (*Letters* 1: 101). This passage anticipates the danger of creating a 'vision in which he [the Poet] embodies his own imaginations' and which 'unites all of wonderful, or wise, or beautiful, which the poet, the philosopher or the lover could depicture,' as Shelley states in his preface to 'Alastor' (*SP&P* 73).

It is not only Luxima's ethereality but also her role associated with geography that influences Shelley's figure of the veiled maid. *The Missionary* shows how the European passion for the other conceives a transcendent female Orient in its imagination as a dream: it appears as a 'brilliant vision' that 'float[s] on his imagination,' and 'a reverie, so new and singular in its object, had stolen him from himself' (1: 153). Hilarion and Luxima stand 'finely opposed,' being put in clear binary opposition in terms of the division of roles associated with gender and geography: Hilarion is 'like the West, lofty and commanding,' while Luxima is 'like the East, lovely and luxuriant' (1: 149). The human relationship between Hilarion and Luxima is geographically presented with adjectives strongly reminiscent of Burke's aesthetic categories of the sublime and the beautiful. In *A Philosophical Enquiry into the Origin of Our Ideas of the Sublime and the Beautiful* (1757), Burke writes that 'we submit to what we admire, but we love what submits to us' (1: 273), which implies, as Suleri points out, that to be beautiful is 'potentially to be enslaved,' because a figure of the exotic other is translated into 'a mere power to defer a yielding that it foresees as inevitable and from which it draws its peculiar attention' (41). Luxima, who first looks 'like a creature formed to feel and to submit,' seems to be easily conquered by Hilarion, who looks 'like a being created to resist and to command' (Owenson 1: 149). In the second volume, however, Hilarion is forced to sustain his (European) self-image as 'immutable truth' against Luxima's image, which embodies 'the religion she professed' and is 'captivating to the senses, fatal to the reason, and powerful and tyrannic to both' (2: 59). At this point, Luxima's 'resplendent locks,' which had been suggestive of an angelic European woman at her first appearance, turn dark: 'her long dark hair floated on the wind' (1: 147, 2: 59). Her dark hair connects her with the sublimity of Indian nature, and it makes her as 'powerful' as the West represented by Hilarion. His 'pious plans' thus do not lead to a glorious conquest but to the destruction of both himself and Luxima (1: 115).

Unlike Luxima, who is finely opposed to Hilarion, in 'Alastor,' the Poet's dream maid is first shown as an idealized and feminized version of himself: the veiled maid is 'a poet' whose voice is 'like the voice of his own soul / Heard in the calm of thought,' and her theme is '[k]nowledge and truth and virtue' and 'lofty hopes of divine liberty, / Thoughts the most dear to him, and poesy' (161, 153–4, 158, 159–60). This kind of ideal mirror of oneself is to be defined later according to the concept of the epipsyche in the prose fragment 'On Love' (1818).[26] Shelley details the process and the nature of the inner creation: 'We dimly see within our intellectual nature a miniature as it were of our entire self, yet deprived of all that we condemn or despise, the ideal prototype of every thing excellent or lovely that we are capable of conceiving as belonging to the nature of man ... [It is] a mirror whose surface reflects only the forms of purity and brightness: a soul within our soul that describes a circle around its proper Paradise which pain and sorrow and evil dare not overleap' (*SP&P* 504). Leask argues that the mirroring process in 'Alastor' is a recasting of Luxima into a European epipsyche by eliding her Hindu origin and presenting instead an Enlightenment revolutionary poetess who has 'lofty hopes of divine liberty,' and considers the process as an ideological equivalent of Keats's transformation of the black-haired Indian maid into the blonde goddess Cynthia, in the poet-protagonist's 'further East' civilizing/Hellenizing mission (*British Romantic Writers and the East* 158, 124–8). His argument is insightful, but the 'further East' here is not totally recreated into an ideal mirror of the Western self. The image of the Enlightenment revolutionary poetess cannot sustain itself, but gradually metamorphoses itself while the Poet is listening to her song without seeing her, and when the Poet turns back to see her, is visualized as a seductive non-European beauty with '[h]er dark locks floating in the breath of night,' who eventually sends him to 'an untimely grave' ('Alastor' 178; preface to 'Alastor,' *SP&P* 73).

The Poet listens to the Western content of her songs, but 'strange truths in undiscovered lands' may be found in 'an ineffable tale,' which is told in the '[s]trange symphony' of her themes and 'some strange harp' she is playing ('Alastor' 77, 168, 167, 166). In the inmost sanctuary of Hinduism 'far within' Kashimir's 'loneliest dell,' the Poet may be given an opportunity to exchange the similar poetic themes between him and the veiled maid, but not having cast even a glance at the 'Arab maiden,' the 'prototype of his conception' is embodied through the sounds and images of his own creation driven by a desire for unknown truths mistaken for self-completion and sexual fulfilment (145, 146, 129; preface to 'Alastor,' *SP&P* 73). The position of the veiled maid standing and the Poet looking up and reaching toward her is the reverse position of conquering Britannia holding out her hands to receive the gifts and the Hindu literatus offering sacred knowledge in the cartouche of Rennell's map of India. In the encounter scene of the Poet and the veiled maid, what is between them, that is, what is about to be offered and to be received, changes from knowledge and truth into sexual love. He 'spread his arms to meet / Her panting bosom,' and with 'frantic gesture and short breathless cry,' she '[f]olded his frame in her dissolving arms' (183–4, 186, 187).

At this point, the relationship between the Poet and the veiled maid departs from that between Hilarion and Luxima, who hold a series of conversations that enable them to realize their cultural and religious differences, while keeping their relationship as 'father' and 'daughter' (Owenson 1: 149, 190, 189). Trembling between 'an habitual prejudice and a natural feeling,' Luxima extends to Hilarion her hands, which he takes in silence, 'excited by the conquest of a fatal prejudice,' but he drops them, recollecting that 'this was the first time the hands of a woman were ever folded in his own' (1: 224, 225). Luxima clasps them on her bosom, saying: 'Father, thou who art thyself pure, and holy as a Brahmin's thought, pray for me to thy gods; I will pray for thee to mine!' (1: 225). The Poet in 'Alastor,' as the narrator comments in alarm, 'overleaps the bounds,' in a different way driven by sexual desire (208). His power relationship with the veiled maid is probably closer to that of a bright young Muslim with a beautiful sorceress of Baal in 'The History of Maugraby the Magician' in the *Arabian Tales; or, a Continuation of the Arabian Nights Entertainments* (1794), which was often referred to as Cazotte's *Continuation* or the *New Arabian Nights*.[27] Hal-il-Maugraby sees 'in a dream a female of surprising beauty':

> This enchanting object leaned forwards to embrace him, and produced so lively and quick an effect upon the senses of the sleeper, that he raised himself to meet the caresses of his lovely visitor. He waked, thinking that he held her in his arms, but he pressed only the air ... From this moment Hal-il-Maugraby was in love; nor could he by any means remove his thoughts from the enchanting image which had seized his heart. 'Divine object,' cried he, 'Thou surely does exist, thou are not merely an illusion. You extended your lovely arms towards me ... and you have excited in me a passion which will cost me my life, if you deign not to appear again to bless my eyes!' [He] had lost even the idea of food, his eyes were turned incessantly towards the spot in which he saw the light, and his tongue ceased not to speak of the delightful phantom, except in those intervals which he gave to sighs and tears. (3: 221–2)[28]

A relationship between Cazotte's *Continuation* and Shelley's 'Alastor' may look remote, but Mary's reading list for 1815 includes *Continuation* (*Journals* 88, 641), and the story of the most powerful magician in Domdaniel was an inspiration to Southey's *Thalaba* (PWRS 4: xv). Although the scene is set in African and Islamic contexts, it is easy to see Cazotte's imagination working behind an Arabian legend,[29] and superimposing a European encounter with the dark enchantment of the female Orient on the heathen sorceress's seduction of a Muslim youth, who is made to look like a white European; he is an orphan who does not have 'that dark colour which is most usual among Africans' (*Continuation* 3: 221), and the female Orient charms and dazzles his imagination by her beauty.

The veiled maid is a complex mixture of an idealized and feminized version of himself – embodied as a Western poetess of knowledge, truth, and liberty – and the other as a female Orient that has a conspicuous source in Luxima in *The Missionary* and the sorceress of Baal in Cazotte's *Continuation*. Both the Hindu priestess and the Baalish sorceress, to borrow Balachandra Rajan's phrase, belong to 'the infernal circumference of an Islam that was itself the infernal circumference of Christianity' (85). The dream maid's body is more 'eloquent' than her intellectual themes of poetry ('Alastor' 168), and while those three images override each other, the Poet wants to choose the visual image of the dark other, which, deleting the religious difference and the Poet's own idealized intellectual concerns, carries only a hint of sexuality in its racial oppositeness.

Although the Poet does not see anything but a sensual body of a dark other, Shelley seems to be trying to reveal 'strange truths,' which are waiting to be interpreted in the foreign contact zone. The veiled maid's 'dark locks floating in the breath of night' not only associate her with dark voluptuousness but also firmly root her in Kashmir as a marked geographical trait (178). Her 'branching veins' perform to Indian music a '[s]trange symphony' and tell 'an ineffable tale' (167, 168). Tilar J. Mazzeo argues that Indian music, performed by 'a seductive woman' who evokes 'irrational sympathies,' enthralls the listener and that Shelley is interested in 'the power of Indian culture and its subalterns to seduce the imperialist' (186). I would rather emphasize the ways in which the 'strange harp' she is playing is naturalized and enlarged to be a vast Aeolian harp, such as the one in 'Ode to the West Wind' ('Alastor' 166). Behind the sensuous female body is seen a sublime Indian nature that is clad with 'the sinuous veil / Of woven wind' and produces a '[s]trange symphony' in cooperation with the 'odorous plants' of the vale and the sweeping wind (176–7, 167, 146).

The momentarily envisioned image of the dream maid as the vale of Kashmir suggests a complex, indivisible mixture of the sublime and the beautiful, the natural and the human, which stirs the Western Poet's intellectual and physical desire. Is he able to recognize strange truths in their unfamiliar forms?

Shelley offers a bower of bliss in the quiet vale for a possible true exchange of 'strange truths' and a subsequent union between the Poet and his dream maid; the vale where 'odorous plants entwine / Beneath the hollow rocks a natural bower' foreshadows the 'lovely Vale in the Indian Caucasus' full of 'fair flowers and herbs' where Asia waits for Prometheus ('Alastor' 77, 146–7; *SP& P* 235; *Prometheus Unbound* 1.829). Kashmir's natural bower in this poem, however, does not nurture a true union of the self and its other; as the Poet neglected the Arab maid, '[t]he spirit of sweet human love has sent / A vision to the sleep of him who spurned / Her choicest gifts' (203–5), and, as Frosch argues, the Poet 'sexualizes' Wordsworth's 'visionary gleam' into the 'hues of heaven that canopied his bower' (Frosch 51; Wordsworth, 'Intimations of Immortality from Recollections of Early Childhood' [1807] 56; 'Alastor' 197). Kashmir is changed into 'the vacant woods' when he wakes up ('Alastor' 195). The Poet's lament points toward '[t]he mystery and the majesty of Earth,' which suggests a Romantic traveller's failure to explore the untrodden Eastern geography (199). If Nature ever reveals her inmost sanctuary to her follower in this poem, Nature does so in the vale of Kashmir in order to take it away immediately, because its mystery and majesty are conceived and visualized by the male viewer as a sensual body of the female other.

In 'Alastor,' an attempt to project one's self-image onto the other is criticized in this way. Shelley judges the Poet's physical desire by reversing the power relationship between the Poet and the object of his desire. The female Orient is not sought after to be conquered as in *The Missionary*, nor is she defeated like Kathema's innocent Zeinab, who, stolen from 'natural' Indian society, dies in the foreign land of corruption ('Zeinab and Kathema' 100). Instead, the Poet's passion, which is similar to that stimulated by those British 'Christian murderers,' who fetch Zeinab to England as one of the spoils, is condemned ('Zeinab and Kathema' 33); the sublime Eastern geography represented by her naked body appeals to the Western sexual desire, but the desire for conquest is not fulfilled. The Poet dies unfulfilled after a prolonged search for the veiled maid.

4. From Kashimir to the Georgian Caucasus

In the vale of Kashmir, Shelley severely criticizes the Poet's burning desire for the veiled maid by turning the world into a 'cold' and 'vacant' place, in which the Poet has to wander and whose desolate landscape symbolizes dark Western history ('Alastor' 193, 195). The Poet's westward course from the vale of Kashmir is similar to that taken by Prometheus and Asia in *Prometheus Unbound* (3.3.153–5), but it is here, after the Poet flees from the beautiful vale of Kashmir, that associations with Alexander and images of the European invasion of the East come into the poem. Thus Shelley reacts to Western expansion in a completely opposite way from Rennell, who drew a separate map, 'The Countries, Situated between the Source of the Ganges and the Caspian Sea,' to add to his map of India Alexander's marches and Forster's route from India to the Caspian Sea.[30] In the Romantic geography of 'Alastor,' far from celebrating the glory of the empire, the Poet's geographical track from Kashmir reveals the darker side of the enterprise of invasion. The Poet restlessly moves in search of the veiled maid:

> He wandered on
> Till vast Aornos seen from Petra's steep
> Hung o'er the low horizon like a cloud;
> Through Balk, and where the desolated tombs
> Of Parthian kings scatter to every wind
> Their wasting dust. ('Alastor' 239–44)

Here we have Shelley's imaginary map of the East drawn to show the ravages of Western invasion recorded in the Eastern geography. The area where the Poet is wandering is observed by Shelley from the top of a nameless high mountain called simply 'Petra,' which means the rock (240), with Aornos eastward on his left, the Parthian royal tombs westward on his right, and Balk in the middle. Matthews and Everest identify 'Petra' as 'the Rock of Soghdiana,' a fortress conquered by Alexander the Great, considering Shelley's source as Quintius Curtius, not Arrian, whom he might not have read until 1817 (*PS* 1:473, 461). Aornos was also a mountain fortress that yielded to Alexander's violent attack. Balk (modern Balkh in Afghanistan) is the area between the Hindu Kush and the Oxus (modern Amu Darya), where the powerful Greco-Bactrian kingdom was created out of legacies of Alexander's eastern territories with Bactra (the Greek name for Balk) as its capital city. The ancient place name Balk reminds us that it was part of the Achaemenid Persian Empire, the first of the Persian empires, whose last king, Darius III, was defeated by Alexander, and shows us what the Poet is seeing there: the ruins of old Persian empires that fought the West, crumbling down.

The Poet's route overlaps that of Forster, who, on his way from Kashmir to the Caspian Sea, typically associated the scene with the ravages of time and prompted an eighteenth-century moralized ruin-sentiment. Forster, in his Eurocentric imagination, saw in the ruins of the Persian Empire not only 'the former grandeur and magnificence of the Persian empire' but also the past glory of the Roman Empire as well: 'where are now the Roman eagles, that were wont to stun the world with the cry of victory?' (Forster 2: 186). Reiman and Fraistat locate the place of 'the desolated tombs / Of Parthian kings' in Nysa in Bactria proper (*SP&P* 80n.8), but as Al Beljame points out, Shelley's voice, which knows Balk, brings us in imagination to Arbela (modern Erbil) and reminds us of the glory of the Parthian Empire and of the violation of the royal sepulchres by Caracalla, who fancied himself a second Alexander.[31] The devastated landscape in which the Poet is made to wander reveals the truth of Western invasions. The ruins in this passage emphasize the slaughter and desolation caused by Western invasion.

Saree Makdisi argues that the Poet 'depopulates' the Orient in order to annihilate the present Orient and invent '"Western" heritage,' displacing the Orientals, together with their own space and time, 'beyond the poem's rigorously self-imposed limits,' and making them 'remain ghosts hovering on the edges of the poem, haunting it' (142, 147). As we have seen, however, in the Romantic geography of the poem, the devastated landscape that unfolds in association with the Western intrusion into India does not affirm the Poet's search for the veiled maid or the Western invasion of the East. It is true that while seeking after his dream, the Poet continues to cut himself off from human relationships in the greater Iranian area, but it is not the case that the Poet's and the local people's spaces never cross, as if they were in 'separate spatial compartments' (Makdisi 143). Their spaces do cross, although the Poet chooses to isolate himself. The local people, like the Arab maiden, keep holding out a kind hand to the Poet. There are 'cottagers, / Who ministered with human charity / His human wants' ('Alastor' 254–6). There are opportunities in which he would receive more than what satisfies his basic human wants; like the Arab maiden, 'youthful maidens, taught / By nature, would interpret half the woe / That wasted him' (266–8). Nevertheless, their love was spent in vain, and they 'would call him with false names / Brother, and friend' and 'press his pallid hand' at his departure from 'their father's door' after being given food and a roof (268–9, 271). The Poet again neglects human kindness, sympathy, and love, fixing his eyes only on the veiled maid of his own creation and suffering more and more from isolation. He fails to take advantage of opportunities to form new and warm relations with the area in which he is wandering, and correspondingly, nature shows him only 'vacant' Eastern landscape in which are seen merely traces of a dark history of invasion.

The Poet leaves both Alexander's return route and Forster's course at 'the lone Chorasmian shore' (272).[32] It is here that the poem's Romantic geography makes the Poet realize keenly that external nature is not a space onto which one projects one's self-image. Seeing a swan flying to his 'sweet mate,' he finds himself 'wasting' his 'surpassing powers' in 'the deaf air,' and 'the blind earth, and heaven,' either of which 'echoes not' his thought (282, 288–90). Earlier when he was still in England, '[e]very sight / And sound from the vast earth and ambient air, / Sent to his heart its choicest impulses,' but he prefers 'high thoughts' to nature and seeks 'strange truths in undiscovered lands' (68–70, 107, 77). In the Middle East, '[o]bedient to high thoughts,' he 'spurned' the 'choicest gifts' that '[t]he spirit of sweet human love' has sent to him (107, 204, 205, 203). He ignores the gifts from nature and humans and instead sticks to 'a single image' of 'the Being whom he loves,' and which he himself creates (preface to 'Alastor,' *SP&P* 73).

The Poet, departing from the routes taken by Alexander and Forster, sets sail for the 'Caucasus' ('Alastor' 353). Considering the geographical details with which Shelley describes the Poet's course from Kashmir, the Post's voyage is westward to the Georgian Caucasus. The place name 'Caucasus' is, however, ambiguous.[33] Shelley makes full use of the ambiguity of the place name 'Caucasus' – it can be taken as the Georgian Caucasus in Russia, the Indian Caucasus (Hindu Kush), or the 'Caucasus' of ancient geography, a supposed continuous range from West to East[34] – and creates an imaginary space out of it to trace the workings of the Poet's mind, which produces the vision of the veiled maid. Correspondingly, all place names disappear except 'Caucasus.' When the boat moves through the cavern and goes against the current to the source of the river, it metaphorically takes him into the depths of his mind rather than returning him to human society.

The Poet's first physical overland journey, in which he discards the

Arab maiden and meets the dream maid of his own making in the vale of Kashmir, is questioned in the second boat trip to the (Georgian) Caucasus. Absent in his lonely wandering is any of the hopeful, Hellenistic tone that is evident in *Prometheus Unbound*, when Prometheus and Asia follow a similar course from the Indian Caucasus to the Georgian Caucasus after the fall of Jupiter (3.3.153–75). The Poet's upriver journey in a 'little shallop' is characterized by images of distorted self-reflections: a 'pool of treacherous and tremendous calm' is '[r]eflecting, yet distorting every cloud'; the narcissi's 'drooping eyes, / Reflected in the crystal calm' – the 'pensive task' of the 'yellow flowers' – are 'marred' by the 'wave / Of the boat's motion' ('Alastor' 299, 386, 385, 406–9). Wasserman observes that 'the crystal calm' functions as a mirror in which nature can reveal its self-fulfilment (*Shelley* 30), but the scene of the yellow flowers does not reveal the joy of self-fulfilment but warns of the danger of self-reflexiveness.

The danger of self-reflection culminates when the Poet comes to a deep well in the Caucasus Mountains, to which Shelley gives a symbolic place of origin:

> a well,
> Dark, gleaming, and of most translucent wave,
> Images all the woven boughs above,
> And each depending leaf, and every speck
> Of azure sky, darting between their chasms;
> Nor aught else in the liquid mirror laves
> Its portraiture, but some inconstant star
> Between one foliaged lattice twinkling fair,
> Or, painted bird, sleeping beneath the moon,
> Or gorgeous insect floating motionless,
> Unconscious of the day, ere yet his wings
> Have spread their glories to the gaze of noon. ('Alastor' 457–68)

Reflecting everything including the 'azure sky,' this dark 'liquid mirror' can be considered as a type of the Romantic natural mirror, in which a reflecting lake, analogous to the human mind, realizes the union between the natural and the supernatural, as in Wordsworth's 'There was a Boy' (1800). Whereas Wordsworth's 'steady' lake 'received' the 'visible scene' with 'all its solemn imagery, its rocks, / Its woods, and that uncertain heaven' into its 'bosom' ('There was a Boy' 21–5), the reflecting mirror here denies the felicity of self-reflexiveness. In Wordsworth's poem, all the reflected images in the vast frame of nature 'enter unawares into his mind' (22), but in Shelley's poem, nature would not reveal her inmost sanctuary but sends back to him his 'own treacherous likeness,' namely, his own eyes, from her 'dark depth' ('Alastor' 474, 471). When he sees his own deformed reflection, the Poet realizes that the veiled maid is only his own 'treacherous likeness.' In the reflected image the focus is on his own eyes in '[t]heir own wan light' (470). The eyes, which are a window to the external world, produce their distorted fantasies, when turned inward.

Shelley has already questioned the union of lovers who try to be each other's mirror in 'Zeinab and Kathema.' The passion for one's own likeness leads both the Indian youth Kathema and the Western Poet to a world of desolation. Both of them are too self-seeking, in search of their alter ego. In this respect, Kathema can be considered an earlier Eastern version of the Poet in 'Alastor,' making a journey from Kashmir to England, and wandering amid 'the strange things of a strange land' in search of his lost love ('Zeinab and Kathema' 89). Kathema, however, pays no attention to 'the strange things in a strange land' but looks exclusively for his lover as his double, and toward the end of the poem calmly declares his intention to 'be like to thee' when he sees 'a dead and naked female form / That from a gibbet high swung to the sullen storm' (89, 154, 131–2). By 1815 Shelley was fully aware of the danger of a self-loving mirroring process; he sends the Poet to discover the 'strange truths in undiscovered lands,' and makes him face his own 'treacherous' likeness after his object of search shifts from 'strange truths' to the lost veiled maid his imagination created ('Alastor' 77, 474).

A 'Spirit,' which is a counterpart of the veiled maid, who has appeared beside a sparkling rivulet in Kashmir, stands 'beside him' by a small river flowing from the dark fountain (479, 480). The European version of the Poet's embodiment of imagination is not veiled by nature's 'grace, or majesty, or mystery' (483). All he sees is its two 'starry eyes,' which corresponds to the veiled maid's 'beamy bending eyes,' and their 'azure smiles' suggest that the eyes are blue (490, 179, 491). Both the Spirit and the veiled maid are 'the light / That shone within his soul' which asks him to follow, but the Spirit is different from the veiled maid in its loss of sexuality (492–3). It is made an abstracted, purified Self, having no elements of otherness and being reduced to a European core – two starry 'azure' eyes. Like the narcissi on the bank, the description of the Spirit concentrates on its eyes, with which one may look for one's own likeness, but not for one's true 'antitype' in this poem. The psychological part of his journey is concluded with his discovery of the image of his life reflected in the wandering stream from the fountain (502–14), which connects him to the Solitary in Wordsworth's *The Excursion*; he ends the story of his disappointed journey to America to find the noble savage, the Rousseauian image that the European attributed to others, by saying that the goal of the river is the 'unfathomable gulf, where all is still' (3.991). What the Poet finds in his wanderings of untrodden lands is his treacherous likeness, not his true epipsyches embodied as antitypes of foreign lands.

The landscape in which the Poet dies unfulfilled is gloomy; he expires in a silent nook on the cliff, while the water falls into the 'immeasurable void' in the Caucasus ('Alastor' 569). Shelley slightly amends the dreary landscape of disappointment and death in the mental geography of the Caucasus by providing a 'pine' on the cliff that maintains itself against 'the vacancy,' singing its 'solemn song' and competing with the howl of the falling water (561–9). It is Shelley who seeks an answer to the Poet's question, 'Whither do thy mysterious waters tend?' (504), and who continues to search for an 'antitype' and recreate devastated geographies of 'undiscovered lands' in his subsequent poems.

5. Strange Truths in Undiscovered Lands

The Poet's wanderings cover the vast Eastern territory. Shelley does not terminate the Poet's wanderings at the ruins where Mab has taught Ianthe her lessons of dark human history. He seeks a new possibility beyond the birth of Western history, going further eastward, but the Poet neglects the 'choicest gifts' of human love (205), and visualizes the dream maid as a self-projection of himself, instead of meeting his true antitype, who could regenerate the world when united with a quester from the West. Consequently, the veiled maid shows him the world of devastation. As the Poet's geographical track unveils, the area is found to have been stained with the dark history of Western invasion.

The figure of the Poet who leads a solitary life of high idealism may look far from the Western intrusion into the East, but we recall that Hilarion in *The Missionary* also leads the same type of isolated life and dies in isolation and disappointment. In Landor's *Gebir* (1798), which was one of Shelley's favourite poems at Oxford (Hogg 1: 201–2), though 'generous, just, humane,' Gebir 'inhaled / Rank venom from these mansions' of his native country, 'caves abhorr'd, / Dungeons and portals that exclude the day,' and therefore must be destroyed before the wedding with the queen of Egypt (*Gebir* 6. 219, 219–20, 217–18). Similarly, even though he is 'innocuous' and 'bloodless,' and his spirit is noble ('Alastor' 101), the Poet's act of seeing cannot go beyond the very disciplinary gaze that Western explorers and intruders cast on the unfamiliar world. Wild nature in untrodden lands and the ruins of ancient civilizations can excite him, but he fails to see the Arab maiden and local people who are kind to him. This failure is noted in the poem. The crucial reason for his failure lies in the fact that the attempt to meet the real 'antitype' is confused with and impeded by the Western passion for the Orient that images the sensuous female Orient as an object of its desire and conquest.

If 'Alastor' is a poem about the 'psychopathology of empire,' it is a poem about the defeat of empire. Far from inventing a space for Western dreams of empire by cleaning out the Oriental space where the others 'turn out to be merely inferior versions of "ourselves"' (Makdisi 153), the poem creates a space in which the Poet, at the mercy of the veiled maid, is made to wander in the ravaged Eastern geography haunted by memories of Western invasion, and then in the distorted and isolated landscape of his own mental geography. Both *Gebir* and *The Missionary* do not follow the pattern of Saidian Orientalism at the end. Although both works delineate the power politics concealed in Burkean aesthetics of the sublime and the beautiful, and the female Orient loves and yields to the West (Burke 1: 273), the West does not thrive and dies unfulfilled. 'Alastor' departs from Saidian Orientalism in a different way. In place of the female Orient, who confirms the Western observer's power over the observed East, Shelley shows the Poet the erotic body of the veiled maid, which, although produced by the Poet's own imagination, is uncontrollable and indifferent to the Poet. The veiled maid 'mimics' the Poet's attitude toward the Arab maiden; she never returns the Poet's love, just as he never returns the Arab maiden's love. In spite of his desperate search for his dream, she never appears to him again. In this respect, the veiled maid as an Oriental other reverses the power relationship between East and West as well as women and men. Also, Shelley is aware that despite the original intention to seek 'strange truths in undiscovered lands,' the Poet's eyes see only what he chooses to see and fail to recognize 'truths' in unfamiliar forms ('Alastor' 77). Thus his quest changes into something that runs parallel to contemporary British expansion when, caught by her seductive aspects, he starts a desperate search for the dream maid.

In 'Alastor,' the Eastern other answers back to the Western self by not answering the Poet and by not giving him what he wants. Shelley shows the Poet as being defeated in his quest, denying the reunion with his female double. In so doing, Shelley tells us how he regards the Poet's quest, and in this aspect the poem constitutes a criticism of British expansion into India. Eastern geography, in which the Poet unsuccessfully searches for the veiled maid, is revealed as desolate, barren, and stained with the dark history of Western invasion. The Poet can never find 'strange truths' and recreate the bleak waste of the Eastern geography he has traversed. The contact zone for renewal remains 'undiscovered' in 'undiscovered lands.' The Caucasus serves as a vast sepulchre to the Poet.

Is Shelley's Romantic geography in 'Alastor' a failure? Though the Poet dies unfulfilled, in his imaginative Grand Tour to the East in search of 'strange truths,' Shelley maps the world without giving any place a central position, not taking sides with either the colonialist Rennell or the pro-Indian Orientalist Jones. What he is seeking by tracing the Poet's geographical exploration is undiscovered lands whose cultures are quite different from the British one and whose multiple truths produce a new type of epipsyche, which does not complete itself in sameness but includes its otherness. Shelley tries to combine in the figure of the veiled maid the best part of the European imagination and the otherness that belongs to Indian soil. The figure of the veiled maid is remarkable in two respects. First, her association with the local place by her 'dark locks' distinguishes Shelley's ideal embodiment of poetic imagination from other Romantic epipsyches, such as Endymion's Cynthia and Manfred's Astarte, who either purify non-European aspects or are deeply rooted in Europe. Shelley's dark-haired maid cancels the binary opposition of dark/fair commonly seen in Oriental tales, and shines as brightly as she does, because the dark local colour is neither connected with Eastern misguiding heresy nor regarded as what should be excluded from the Western self. Second, her body represents the birth of hybrid geography where not only complex relationships of East and West but also those of humans and nature are recorded. This nameless veiled maid, born out of the European Poet's imagination, initiates a new type of epipsyche in a foreign land, a female other who is associated with the land in which she is created as a genius loci and yet accepts both Eastern and Western elements. It is she who becomes the 'prototype' for Shelley's later transcendent females whose names and identities are strongly associated with places, such as Asia in *Prometheus Unbound* and the eponymous heroine of 'The Witch of Atlas.'

3 'Mont Blanc': The Questioning Traveller and a Visionary Geography of Chamonix

1. From the Accursed Mountain to the Mountain Glory

Shelley's choice of the Indian Caucasus in 'Alastor' responded to contemporary scholars and mythographers, who located Mount Caucasus in the Hindu Kush as a cradle of human civilization (Curran, *Shelley's Annus Mirabilis* 61–7). Contemporary scientists, on the other hand, promoted Mont Blanc, the highest mountain in Europe, as a rival mountain to the Indian Caucasus; they thought that the mountain concealed the secrets of the history of the earth. Whereas the Alps had long been celebrated for their sublimity, Mont Blanc was a more recent discovery despite its central position in the range. It will be useful here to trace briefly the history of Mont Blanc, to which the Romantics responded.[1]

Since 1671, when Thomas Burnet, travelling through the Alps, found himself enthralled by the sublime in nature and torn between theological condemnation of mountains and emotional praise of them, British travellers had often recorded the same exalted awe-inspiring experience of the Alps.[2] The ice-covered Mont Blanc, on the other hand, did not even have a name when Henri Justel, a Huguenot who was a librarian of Louis XIV before taking refuge in England, reported to the Royal Society in 1673 a certain Capuchin monk's discovery of a mountain *'toute de glace et cristaux'* near Geneva (Engel, *A History of Mountaineering* 21). Chamonix was to become a fashionable sightseeing place for British travellers soon after William Windham's *An Account of the Glacieres or Ice Alps in Savoy* (1744), which reports his trip to Chamonix and its 'glaciers' in 1741,[3] two years after Gray and Walpole were thrilled by the Alpine scene on their way to Italy. What is surprising, however, is that Windham, though impressed by the 'Glacieres,' did not pay any attention to the lofty mountain there and made no mention of it (4). The whole range had been vaguely referred to as 'La Mont Maudite' (The Accursed Mountain) until Peter Martel, a young Genevan engineer, taking Windham's route with his friends in the following year, measured the height of this mountain 'entirely covered with Ice, quite from the Top to the Bottom,' estimated it to be 'the Highest in all the *Glacieres*, and perhaps of all the Alps,' and for the first time called it 'Mont Blanc' (Windham 22–3).[4] The new name of the mountain was closely associated with the scientific discovery of its height.

After Martel's report, the ascent of Mont Blanc was stimulated by scientific zeal. In 1760, Horace Benedict de Saussure, a young Genevan geologist who was to become a professor of Natural Philosophy at the Geneva Academy, began visiting Chamonix regularly, and devoted himself to scientific investigations of the region. The precise measurement of high mountains with a barometer had become a major scientific endeavour, and observations by Saussure and George Shuckborough proved Mont Blanc, rather than Etna, to be the highest in Europe. In 1786, a Chamonix doctor, Michel-Gabriel Paccard, accompanied by a guide, Jacques Balmat, made his way to the summit and took barometric pressure readings. On 2 August 1787, Saussure himself, having left the valley with Marc-Théodore Bourrit and eighteen guides the day before, conquered Mont Blanc, exciting great interest in the mountain because of his celebrity. His achievement in reaching the summit, conducting experiments, and bringing back specimens from rocks on the summit was taken as an epoch-making event equal to the ascent of Everest in modern times, as Engel puts it (*Mont Blanc* 16), and thrilled the world with the anticipation that the original formation of the earth was about to be revealed.[5] Many accounts of his ascent, including his own *Brief Relation of the Voyage to the Summit of Mont-Blanc in August 1787*, publicized the mountain all over Europe.

Saussure's scientific triumph changed the image of the mountain dramatically, from a nameless, cursed mountain to an unparelleled natural wonder of Europe. The highest peak in Europe was now regarded as being able to compete with the snow-clad Indian Caucasus, the highest range in Asia. William Coxe, in his *Travels in Switzerland and in the Country of the Grisons* (1789),[6] using measurements by both ancient and modern geographers and travellers, tries to prove that Mont Blanc is 'the highest point in the old world' (2: 5–9). After comparing it with 'the Schreckhorn, the Peak of Teneriff, the mountains of the Moon in Africa, the Taurus and the Caucasus,' he proudly writes that 'some philosophers ... have drawn a presumative argument, that the Asiatic mountains are much more lofty than those of Europe. But conjectures are now banished from natural philosophy' (2: 10). William Jones and other Orientalists had been intent on considering the Indian Caucasus as a crucial site on which centred Indian, Persian, and European mythologies. But now, Europe had possibly the highest mountain on earth, and geology was about to disclose the secret origin of the globe through the examination of its rock strata.[7]

The newly discovered scientific importance of Mont Blanc is reflected in literature, too. Toward the end of George Keate's *The Alps: A Poem* (1763), Mont Blanc appears as the 'tallest Mountain' under which a tragedy happens, and the poem closes with a gloomy vision of a universal deluge in which even the Alps shall be submerged (21–5, 27).[8] The nameless Mountain Gloom in Keate's poem became the sublimest Mountain Glory in Thomas Sedgwick Whalley's *Mont Blanc: An Irregular Lyric Poem* (1788), published one year after Saussure's assent, with which 'a rich new setting was introduced into the English tradition' (J.R. de J. Jackson 195). Whalley's praise of the 'sublimest 'midst sublime' that is comparable to the biblical Mount Sinai depends upon the scientific fact; he states in a note at the outset that 'MONT BLANC, according to the most accurate measurements and calculations, is the highest mountain,' and he acknowledges at the end Saussure's ascent (5, 57).[9] Thus, in the 1790s, literature, hand in hand with science, promoted Mont Blanc as a new place for communication with the divine, making it one of the most important sites for 'Romantic mountaintop poems' (Randel, 'The Mountaintops of English Romanticism' 295).

Another important dimension Saussure's scientific triumph added to the English literary tradition is a geological reading of the rugged landscape that allows the poet to review the history of the earth. Saussure writes about the rock specimens: 'I study them, I interrogate them; and methinks that if they could answer my questions, they would unveil to me all the mysteries of the formation and revolutions of our globe' (708).[10] As Bewell discusses in detail, scientific discoveries of natural 'revolutions' in the depth of geological time had a significant impact on the Romantics' reading of natural/social 'revolutions' (*Wordsworth and the Enlightenment* 245–61). As poetry and geology between 1770 and 1820 are 'mutually constitutive through the common idiom of landscape aesthetics' (Heringman 1), both face a significant question that geological discoveries pose by opening a tremendous fissure between the sacred history and the scientific history of the earth: Is the highest mountain evidence of Providence or of the abyss of geological time? It asks not only about the existence of a creator-God but also about the place of humans in the universe. Shelley's backward-looking imagination, which tries to visualize an ideal populous city in the origin of the earth, meets a great challenge from the highest mountain in Europe. In this regard, Mont Blanc appears to Shelley as an absolute Other who confronts him with 'strange truths' lying beyond the accepted tradition of knowledge, and shakes his confidence in the centrality of humanity in nature ('Alastor' 77).

2. Travellers and the Glacial Kingdom of Chamonix

Chamonix had been among the places British travellers visited on the Grand Tour, but it was not accessible during the twenty years' war with France.[11] Shelley, Mary, and Claire Clairmont were among the first British visitors to this famous place after the Peace of Waterloo in 1815 when they travelled to Chamonix on 22 July 1816. Shelley was struck with Mont Blanc, when he saw the mountain from a distance on the way to Chamonix: 'Mont Blanc was before us ... Mont Blanc was before us but was covered with cloud, & its base furrowed with dreadful gaps was seen alone. Pinnacles of snow, intolerably bright, part of the chain connected with Mont Blanc shone thro the clouds at intervals on high. I never knew I never imagined what mountains were before' (*Letters* 1: 496–7). On the following day, they visited the source of the Arveiron and Shelley alone visited the Glacier of Boisson in the evening; on the 25th, they visited the Mer de Glace on Montenvert; on the 26th, they travelled through the Vale of Servoz and St Martin on the way back to Geneva.

Shelley as a traveller recorded his encounter with Mont Blanc in a long journal letter to Peacock composed between 22 July and 2 August 1816. Shelley as a poet composed 'Mont Blanc.' Both the revised version of the letter and 'Mont Blanc' appeared as part of Shelley and Mary's joint work, *History of a Six Weeks' Tour through a Part of France, Switzerland, Germany, and Holland: with Letters Descriptive of a Sail round the Lake of Geneva, and of the Glaciers of Chamouni* (1817), which was one of the first itineraries published after the war ended.[12] Reiman and Fraistat note that the actual scene of the poem is on a bridge over the

Arve, where the poet sees only the Arve Valley and not the summit of Mont Blanc, which is hidden by the clouds (*SP&P* 96). Their comment is supported by the poem's first title, 'At Pont Pellisier' (*Geneva Notebook of Percy Bysshe Shelley* 7), and Mary Shelley's later recollection that the poem was inspired when 'he lingered on the Bridge of Arve on his way through the Valley of Chamouni' ('Note on Poems of 1816, by Mrs. Shelley,' *SPW* 536).[13] As a careful comparison of the poem with the journal-letter and the manuscript reveals, however, the poem reflects not only this initial profound moment but also the whole experience of Chamonix, in particular Shelley's visit to the glaciers.[14]

Shelley explains in his preface that 'Mont Blanc' was composed 'under the immediate impression of the deep and powerful feelings excited by the objects which it attempts to describe' and that the poem was 'an attempt to imitate the untameable wildness and inaccessible solemnity from which those feelings sprang' (*HSWT* vi). Colbert, in his thoroughly researched *Shelley's Eye*, grounds the Shelleys' *History of a Six Weeks' Tour* and the poet's 'Mont Blanc' in the contexts of contemporary travel writing, and argues that the contemporary readers 'may have been more inclined to view "Mont Blanc" as an appendix to the sublimities of the Geneva letters' (83). While Colbert examines Shelley's attempt to discover 'an authentic language of travel' against various contemporary travel writers, landscape theorists, and reviewers on the Shelleys' *History of a Six Weeks' Tour* with a key phrase, the 'raptures of travellers' (81–115), in this chapter I focus on the difference between Shelley as a traveller and Shelley as a poet in order to examine his Romantic geography expressed in the poem, in which the poet approaches the mountain as 'inaccessible' Other by gazing, addressing, and questioning. The impact of the highest mountain in Europe forced Shelley to reconsider the idea of a mountain and the relationship between nature and humans. A striking silence about Mont Blanc both in the journal-letter and in the poem suggests Shelley's struggle with the eternal frozen world of nature that has existed from the beginning of the earth. Shelley as a poet, however, considerably differs from the astonished traveller in the journal-letter, transforming a nature that is totally alien and hostile to humans in his visionary attempt to recreate a place.

In the journal-letter, Mont Blanc does not make its appearance in the Valley of Arve nor in the glacial world of Montanvert. With the summit of Mont Blanc concealed by clouds, the rapturous blending of human and nature in a Wordsworthian manner is possible in the Valley of

Arve. The visible scene in the Valley, with the 'aerial summits' of high mountains, glaciers, majestic forests, and the roaring 'untameable' Arve, gives Shelley a sense of sublimity and wonder 'not unallied to madness' (*Letters* 1: 497). He feels that '[a]ll was as much our own as if we had been the creators of such impressions in the minds of others, as now occupied our own' (1: 497). United with the vast forms of nature and elevated to the level of creator, he is able to make nature come down to the level of a human poet, though still 'divinest': 'Nature was the poet whose harmony held our spirit more breathless than that of the divinest' (1: 497).

On the other hand, the poet and nature are intolerably opposed in the glaciers, which metonymically represent their ultimate, invisible source, the summit of Mont Blanc. Shelley is terrified to witness the 'fertile plain' being relentlessly invaded by the glaciers; they 'flow perpetually into the valley ravaging in their slow but irresistible progress the pastures & the forests which surround them, & performing a work of desolation in ages which a river of lava might accomplish in an hour, but far more irretrievably' (1:497, 500). To his horror, 'the snows on the summit of Mt. Blanc & the neighbouring mountains perpetually augment' (1: 499). With his knowledge of Saussure's work and contemporary scientific discussions of the glaciers (1: 499; De Beer, *Early Travellers in the Alps* 171–2), which are further supported by what he sees and hears from local people, Shelley is convinced of the threat posed by the perpetual increase of the glaciers. A dismal vision of the valley filled with the expanding glaciers is evoked, reminding Shelley of Buffon's 'sublime but gloomy theory' that the earth will be 'changed into a mass of frost' (*Letters* 1: 499). Buffon's *Époques de la nature* (1778), seeing the history of the earth as a cooling process, offers not only an extremely long time scale but also a shockingly dark vision of the end of the world that has nothing to do with the biblical Second Coming; the earth, which was created as a fireball some seventy-five thousand years earlier, has been losing heat and will end in an Ice Age in which all life has become extinct.

In Switzerland in 1816, seeing the mountain of ice and snow and its glaciers expanding relentlessly into human habitations, Shelley felt a much more real fear of Buffon's theory, even though in England, James Hutton presented a different theory of the earth more suitable to 'the dignity of Nature, and the wisdom of its AUTHOR' than Buffon's devastatingly atheistic vision by arguing that the earth would sustain itself endlessly through its internal heat (Playfair 486).[15] The summit of

Mont Blanc, which was the nearest to the secrets of the history of the earth as well as to God, loomed ominously as the source of destructive glaciers. Then, surprisingly, the highest, sublimest place in Europe evokes something remotest from Europe in Shelley's mind. In the white summit of the European sublime Shelley senses a fearful foreign deity, the Zoroastrian god of darkness, indifferent to human welfare and slowly destroying the world since the creation. He asks Peacock: 'Do you who assert the supremacy of Ahriman imagine him throned among these desolating snows, among these palaces of death & frost, sculptured in this their terrible magnificence by the unsparing hand of necessity, & that he casts around him as the first essays of his final usurpation avalanches, torrents, rocks & thunders – and above all, these deadly glaciers at once the proofs & the symbols of his reign' (*Letters* 1: 499). Shelley's fear of the slow but fatal descent of the glaciers into the habitable world embodies nature's tremendous and destructive power as an evil foreign deity on the summit of Mont Blanc. In *Confessions of an English Opium Eater* (1821), De Quincey was horrified to meet a Malay at Dove Cottage in the Lake District, in the symbolic heart of England (91).[16] Here in a similar but much more terrifying way, Shelley finds a tropical Eastern deity in the sublime exhibition of European nature. The boundaries between East and West are cancelled by the image of a monstrous hybrid divine form physically represented by the destructive glaciers of Chamonix and personified by the Eastern Ahriman.

Shelley's view of Mont Blanc and its glaciers in the letter stands in stark contrast to that of the admirers of the Alps in the previous century. British travellers had been fascinated by the beauty of the glaciers as a miracle of God's creation since Windham, who publicized the Mer de Glace by the trope of frozen torrents as a 'Lake put in Agitation by a strong Wind, and frozen all at once' (8). Travellers in the last decades of the eighteenth century, as typically seen in Lady Stanley of Alderley's letter in 1791, enjoyed the 'beautiful scene' of the glaciers (Engel, *Mont Blanc* 40). Helen Maria Williams, in 'A Hymn Written among the Alps,' praises 'THEE, THEE, my GOD' even where 'level with the ice-ribb'd bound, / The yellow harvests glow; / Or vales with purple vines are crown'd / Beneath impending snow' (20, 27).[17] Ramond de Carbonnières, whose philosophical interpretation of the Alpine scenes in his commentaries to Coxe's book influenced Wordsworth's *Descriptive Sketches* (1793), uses a similar image of a ruling monarch in the deadly glaciers, but reaches a completely different conclusion from that of Shelley: 'Who, but the observer of nature, would suspect that this vast tomb contains its secret laboratory, and that like the careful monarch who, in the tranquil retirement of his palace, dwells with anxiety on the happiness of his people, the mother of the world prepares in this abode, defended by such terrible avenues, the flowers with which she is to deck our plains' ('Observations on the Glacieres, and the Glaciers, by M. Ramond' 335–6).[18] For the French geologist, even those 'laboratories of ice,' which perpetually produce glaciers that invade the fertile plains below like 'lavas,' can be part of the ultimate benign plan of Mother Nature (290, 302).

For Shelley, however, the ceaseless expansion of the destructive glaciers is nothing but a menace. Though impressed by the glaciers, which appear 'as if frost had suddenly bound up the waves & whir[l]pools of a mighty torrent,' a phrase reminiscent of Windham's description of the Mer de Glace, he is overwhelmed by the inconceivable coldness, vastness, and dynamic deforming force of nature (*Letters* 1: 500): 'In these regions every thing changes & is in motion. This vast mass of ice has one general progress which ceases neither day nor night. It breaks & rises forever; its undulations sink whilst others rise. From the precipices which surround it the echo of rocks which fall from their aerial summits, or of the ice & snow scarcely ceases for one moment' (1: 500). Shelley's perception of underlying dynamism conjures up an image of something living but other than human: 'One would think that Mont Blanc was a living being & that the frozen blood forever circulated slowly thro' his stony veins' (1: 500). Mont Blanc's 'frozen blood' and 'frozen vein' anticipate the image of the Earth's 'old and icy frame' surrounded by her 'stony veins' and encircled by 'the frozen air' before her regeneration in *Prometheus Unbound* (3.3.88, 1.153, 155).

Mont Blanc is seen as being alive, in constant motion, and pulsing out cold glaciers. The image of Ahriman mentioned two days earlier on 24 July (*Letters* 1: 499) is now transformed into a torpid and terrible vast being with cold veins. Unlike the Earth in *Prometheus Unbound*, who responds to Prometheus's question, Mont Blanc appears indifferent, and Shelley cannot connect its vast forces to any direct relationship with humans, whether positive or negative. Moreover, the cold glaciers, in which Mont Blanc's frozen blood is slowly circulating, may be more destructive than the 'bloodless veins' of the tyrannical institutions that blight both society and nature in *Queen Mab* (4.106) Shelley's bewilderment at nature's glacial world is more emphatic in the printed version of the journal-letter: 'One would think that Mont Blanc, like the god of the Stoics, was a vast animal, and that the frozen blood for ever circulated through his stony veins' (*HSWT* 167). Ahriman is replaced by 'the god of the Stoics,' putting Mont Blanc back into Western philosophy, but the metaphor of 'a vast animal' reduces the loftiness of 'a living being' in the earlier statement. A confusing mixture of 'the god of the Stoics' and a gigantic animal shows that some strange truths are being revealed, but they are not able to be grasped within the accepted tradition of Western philosophy. The Stoics saw God in nature, but they thought that God's design was always good and benevolent, hence Shelley's association is misleading. Instead of assimilating the alien Eastern god into the European source of knowledge, Shelley creates through the metaphor of 'a vast animal' a monstrous hybrid of the divine and the bestial as well as the organic and the inorganic.

The journal-letter shows that Mont Blanc's glacial world did not give Shelley the same epiphanic moment of union with nature that the first generation of Romantics would have undoubtedly enjoyed. In a naturalized version of the biblical mountaintop theophanies experienced by Wordsworth, being transported to and united with the infinite power of nature through the imagination meant a blessed reunion with the (benevolent) Christian God (Monk 228; Abrams, *Natural Supernaturalism* 105–7). Wordsworth concluded his *Descriptive Sketches* with an apocalyptic scene he envisioned in Chamonix when looking upward into the 'mountain nam'd of white' and praying to 'great God' (690, 792).[19] Coleridge had a similar experience on Scafell, where he 'involuntarily poured forth a Hymn in the manner of the *Psalms*,' and he later adapted those rapturous feelings to the 'grander external objects' of the vale of Chamonix when he wrote the 'Hymn Before Sun-Rise in the Vale of Chamouny' (1802) (*CLSTC* 2: 864–5).[20]

The Mont Blanc experience of Shelley and Byron, however, was exactly opposite, evoking an evil Eastern divinity in the centre of the European sublime. Although he did experience briefly a Wordsworthian exalted correspondence with nature in the Alps and recorded it in canto 3 of *Childe Harold's Pilgrimage* (1816) (680–8), Byron did not like the 'cold sublimity' of high Alpine mountains (594). He did not go to Chamonix until shortly after the Shelleys left Geneva for England on 29 August 1816, and he scarcely mentioned Mont Blanc. Byron's Mont Blanc experience, however, contributes to the image of the Jungfrau in *Manfred* (1816), in which Byron embodies his hostility toward the destructive power of nature in the evil figure of Arimanes. As Jerome McGann rightly points out in his commentary on *Manfred*, Byron's Arimanes recalls Ebris in *Vathek* (*LBCPW* 4: 473). At the same time, however, the name, derived from the Persian god of darkness, and the throne in the Alps do remind us of Shelley's image of Ahriman sitting on the throne in Mont Blanc in the journal-letter to Peacock (*Letters* 1: 499). As the two poets were in constant touch in Geneva in the summer of 1816, it seems possible that Shelley told Byron of his vision of Ahriman's throne on the summit and referred to Peacock's unfinished *Ahrimanes* (1813–15). Cameron sees some parallels between Peacock's Ahrimanes and Byron's Arimanes, and thinks that Shelley either showed Byron a manuscript of Peacock's two-canto version of *Ahrimanes* or recited some stanzas from it by heart (*SC* 3: 239–40). I would rather think that the influence was more from Shelley; Byron might have been so impressed by Shelley's transplantation of an evil foreign god from his torrid Eastern palace to the cold Alps that he used it in his own poem to express his fear of fierce Alpine nature. For Shelley and Byron, the overwhelming power of the mountain, which leads to infinity and eternity and seems to defeat the capacity of the human imagination, evokes instead a malevolent divinity with Zoroastrian overtones.

What is important, however, is that unlike Byron, who calls up Arimanes in his poem, Shelley deletes the existence of Ahriman in 'Mont Blanc.' This is the most significant difference between the journal-letter and the poem. Shelley's resistance to the infinite power of the indifferent mountain can be considered as his answer to Coleridge's question in the explanatory note to the 'Hymn before Sun-Rise in the Vale of Chamouny': 'Who *would* be, who *could* be an Atheist in this valley of wonders!' (*STCPW* 2: 925).[21] It can also be understood, however, as his resistance to the association of 'strange truths' with terrible non-European forms. The travelling English at that time expected to find in Chamonix 'a natural temple of the Lord and a proof of the Deity by design' (Holmes 342). As a traveller Shelley resisted yielding to the overwhelming sublimity Coleridge associated with God by evoking Ahriman or by describing himself as 'an atheist' in Greek in the visitor's album (De Beer, *Speaking of Switzerland*, 162–78). Shelley as a poet, however, chooses to reinterpret what he sees around him by trying to converse with the mountain. In 'Mont Blanc,' Shelley, recording his complex psychological movement in the irregular verse scheme, attempts to decompose the anthropomorphic myth created by religion, whether positive or negative, or whether Eastern or European, to see the mountain in its purely physical existence, and to create a new humanized geography through the imagination.

3. The Everlasting Universe of Things and Nature's City

In seeking to establish a meaningful relationship with Mont Blanc, Shelley employs the new descriptive-meditative mode developed in Coleridge's conversation poems and Wordsworth's 'Tintern Abbey' (1798), a genre that Abrams has called 'the greater Romantic lyric' ('Structure and Style in the Greater Romantic Lyric' 202). The opening section traces the overflowing of the outer world through the human mind, hoping to establish a Wordsworthian interaction between the poet and the One in nature: 'The everlasting universe of things / Flows through the mind' ('Mont Blanc' 1–2). An attempt to achieve an undifferentiated unity of the inner and outer worlds is continued when Shelley tries to hear among sounds in the Valley of Arve 'a sound but half its own' (6). The phrase, ringing a faint echo of Wordsworth's 'what they half create, / And what perceive' ('Tintern Abbey' 106–7), would confirm his 'unremitting interchange' with nature ('Mont Blanc' 39), and also metaphorically interfuse thing and thought in the way discussed by eighteenth-century British empiricists such as Berkeley and Hume (Wasserman, *Shelley* 221–38).[22]

While Shelley, in a vivid description of the Valley of Arve in the journal-letter, records in detail how natural objects readily carry him to a Wordsworthian rapturous union with the infinite power of nature (*Letters* 1: 497), the abstract and speculative opening lines depart from the Wordsworthian type of descriptive-meditative poem that starts with a concrete, visible scene. Furthermore, Shelley's scepticism does not allow him to forget the position of humans in nature, awakening thoughts on the smallness of the 'feeble brook' of the human mind in front of the vast 'universe of things' ('Mont Blanc' 7, 1). It is true that terms taken from empirical philosophy and a syntax that fuses the subject and the object cancel the difference between thing and thought (Wasserman, *Shelley* 222–3), but it is also true that Shelley is astonished at the sight of the 'everlasting universe of things,' where waterfalls leap 'for ever' and a vast river 'ceaselessly' bursts ('Mont Blanc' 1, 9, 11). What is before him stands outside human time, antedating and outlasting human history. The scene he views existed before it was named the Ravine of Arve, and will exist after the extinction of humankind. Nature here can only be described without proper nouns, stripped of the marks that humans attach to things. That is why the Swiss scene appears only after section 2, when Shelley tries to make this 'awful scene' a site of encounter that can incorporate nature into human contexts (15).

The Alpine ravine has a mysterious atmosphere of the early days of the earth. Giant pines are '[c]hildren of elder time,' singing 'an old and solemn harmony' (21, 24). An 'unsculptured image' in the rocks, robed by the veil of the 'etherial waterfall,' has not been sculptured by a human hand; it is the image sculptured by geological revolutions and has existed there from time immemorial (27, 26). In the printed version of the journal-letter, the image of the rock veiled by the waterfall is described as a 'visionary image' that resembles 'some colossal Egyptian statue of a female deity' robed in 'a veil of the most exquisite woof' (*HSWT* 145).[23] The Eastern female deity makes her appearance at the foot of Mont Blanc in the travel account, paganizing the Swiss scene together with 'the god of the Stoics' (167). In the poem, however, a trace of the Egyptian goddess is obliterated, being antedated by the much more ancient 'unsculptured image.' In the same way, the scene does not allow the poet to personify the divine. Like 'a sound but half its own,' a 'Power' appears 'in likeness of the Arve,' not fully embodied or perceived ('Mont Blanc' 6, 16). Its existence, however, is sensed as the Arve 'comes down / From the ice gulphs that gird his secret throne,' and bursts like 'the flame / Of lightning through the tempest' in the valley (16–17, 18–19). It evokes a terrible masculine deity, quite unlike the 'Power' in the 'Hymn to Intellectual Beauty' (1816), who is represented as a benevolent pagan muse.

Although the Ravine has received the 'Power' from the beginning of the earth, neither the 'Power' nor its earthly reflection, the Arve, whom the poet addresses as 'thou,' descends on a mere human being (12). The Ravine produces all kinds of sounds – the Arve's commotion, singing pines and winds, the echoing caverns, and the waterfall – but Shelley fails to understand what it says. The young Shelley clasped his hands 'in extacy' when the 'shadow' of Intellectual Beauty 'fell on' him ('Hymn to Intellectual Beauty' 59–60). In Chamonix, 'the voices of the desert fail,' which suggests complete separation from nature ('Mont Blanc' 28). Shelley 'in a trance sublime and strange' addresses the Ravine of Arve as 'Dizzy Ravine!' and muses on his own 'separate phantasy' (35, 34, 36), which recalls the moment when the Poet's 'dizzy eyes' lost sight of the vision as sleep '[r]olled back its impulse on his vacant brain' in 'Alastor' (188, 191). At this moment of failure, however, Shelley's own 'human mind' becomes 'the still cave of the witch Poesy,' which serves as an internal correspondent of the natural 'caverns' at the foot of the Ravine 'echoing to the Arve's commotion,' and in which among 'the shadows that pass by / Ghosts of all things that are, some shade of thee, / Some phantom, some faint image' are sought after ('Mont Blanc' 37, 44, 30, 45–7). Unlike the Witch of the Alps in Byron's *Manfred*, Shelley's 'witch Poesy' is not a genius loci who belongs to the Ravine of Arve and can actively mediate between the temporal and the eternal; she, like Shelley, is separated from nature. According to the empirical philosophy on which Shelley heavily depends, the 'faint image' is doubly removed from the outer world. That is, there is a distinction between vivid impressions and indirect ideas; the latter are only the 'faint images' of the former.[24] Shelley's witch Poesy is an inner other of the male poet's imagination and tries to communicate with the external world, though passively and feebly, as Shelley does.

The image of epipsyche, a soul within the soul, is half naturalized and half Platonized to be an image of a cave within a cave, in which lives a female witch. The feminization of his mind as 'witch Poesy' suggests the hybrid nature of Shelley's imagination. But unlike 'Alastor,' in which the female embodiment of one's inner other is created and sought after by the passion for one's own likeness, here Shelley's imagination tries to understand and converse with 'some unknown omnipotence,' an absolute other who is external to him and whom he senses on the unseen summit (53). While Shelley's eye and ear look outward for the unseen absolute other, his poetic mind, the 'witch Poesy,' translates 'some faint image[s]' into thoughts (44, 47), but this does not mean that Shelley utilizes the small inner other of the opposite sex, because in an attempt to understand the voice of the Mountain, all personifications are to be eliminated.

When Shelley 'look[s] on high' above the ravine (52), his imagination is staggered by the immensity of the mountain: 'the very spirit fails, / Driven like a homeless cloud from steep to steep / That vanishes among the viewless gales!' (57–9). The immensity of the mountain is the immensity of geological time. The same vertigo would have been experienced by contemporary geologists when confronted with deep geological time. Visiting the famous 'unconformity' at Siccar Point in 1788, John Playfair felt that 'the mind seemed to grow giddy by looking so far into the abyss of time.'[25] Charles Lyell, a leading geologist in the 1820s, did not find solace in the vastness of geological time. In his *Principles of Geology* (1830–3), which was free from biblical chronology and established modern geology, Lyell writes: 'The imagination was first fatigued and overpowered by endeavouring to conceive the immensity of time ... Such views of the immensity of past time ... were too vast to awaken ideas of sublimity unmixed with a painful sense of our incapacity to conceive a plan of such infinite extent' (1: 63). In 'Mont Blanc,' however, at this very moment of failure, the mountain makes its first appearance, high above human reach: 'Far, far above, piercing the infinite sky, / Mont Blanc appears, – still, snowy, and serene – ' (60–1). The absence of any description of the summit of the mountain and the lack of any verb that indicates the act of seeing – Shelley uses the verb 'gaze' when he looks steadily at the Ravine of Arve and Mont Blanc's 'subject mountains' (34, 62) – may suggest that the place is too sublime to be seen.

The image of 'still, snowy, and serene' Mont Blanc, which may raise a momentary hope, immediately disappears, and in turn there appears what Shelley is really seeing: Mont Blanc's 'subject mountains' (61, 62). Their forms are 'unearthly,' though their unearthliness is far from Mont Blanc's serene whiteness (62). They are first introduced in the poem as 'the ice gulphs that gird his [the Power's] secret throne,' and their appearance – 'rude, bare, and high, / Ghastly, and scarred, and riven' – is now described in detail in geological terms (17, 70–1). Shelley fixes his eyes on the high 'primæval' mountains in the chain of Mont Blanc (99). The word 'primæval' indicates that Shelley was familiar with contemporary geological discussions, in which adjectives such as 'primitive' and 'primordial' were applied to the mountains and rocks that were 'the basis of all the great chains of mountains' and 'parts of the original *nucleus* of the globe' (Playfair 160–2).

The description of Mont Blanc's 'subject mountains' is based on Shelley's observation of the vale of Montanvert and the Mer de Glace. The 'horrible deserts' of 'ice & snow broken & heaped up & exhibiting terrific chasms' are surrounded by the precipitous mountains whose summits 'pierce the clouds like things not belonging to this earth' (*Letters* 1: 500). The scene in the poem is more terrible and desolate than the description in the letter. The frozen steeps, which have been 'hideously' and '[g]hastly' accumulated, are peopled only with a storm, raptorial birds and beasts, and the bones of the hunters ('Mont Blanc' 69, 71). Moreover, the hideous scene of ice and snow does not record any human civilizations, but carries the memories of pristine destruction, when the height of the primary mountains reveals the depth of geological time. The poet asks whether this is the scene where 'the old Earthquake-daemon taught her young / Ruin' (72–3). The question dramatizes the history of the earth's strata in which struggles of titanic forces were recorded. It also expresses Shelley's desire to see some form of life, whether supernatural or not. Though still mythologized and personified, the primordial earth is described in non-biblical terms. The deity who dominates the primal scene is a female daemon who is a personification of a natural disaster, not a terrible masculine 'Power' in section 2 or an evil Eastern deity in the journal letter.

Since the Lisbon Earthquake in 1755, a series of natural disasters, such as volcanic eruptions of Etna (1760, 1792) and of Vesuvius (1760, 1779, 1794), kept shaking eighteenth-century belief in Providence, and created doubts as to the inscrutability or evilness of the Supreme Power.[26] Shelley is trying to exorcise any kind of personified divinity, Christian or Zoroastrian, and moving to a scientific explanation. The first question is quickly reformulated: 'did a sea / Of fire, envelope once this silent snow?' (73–4). Shelley asks if the primal destruction was caused by 'a sea / Of fire,' namely, a volcanic eruption. The idea of a volcanic eruption in the Alps would have been attractive to Volcanists like Hutton in the Neptunist-Volcanist controversy of the early nineteenth century.[27] Hutton shows great interest in Saussure's discovery of the vertically placed strata in the second volume of *Voyage dans les Alpes* (36–50) as it proved the violent displacement they had suffered. Shelley records in the letter information about an earthquake near the valley of Servoz, which was first taken as a volcanic eruption fifty years earlier (*Letters* 1: 501). This may have contributed to the formation of the image of a sea of fire in 'Mont Blanc' together with the image of the earth as a fireball at its creation in Buffon's theory. Coleridge in the 'Hymn Before Sun-Rise, in the Vale of Chamouny' asks the 'Ice-falls' who created the world, and commands them to answer 'GOD!' and make the 'ice-plains echo, GOD!' (49, 59). By contrast, Shelley shares the same non-religious concerns with geologists like Saussure, who, after attaining the summit of Mont Blanc and taking the specimens from the highest rocks there, asked the questions Shelley is asking here: 'I interrogate them; and methinks that if they could answer my questions, they would unveil to me all the mysteries of the formation and revolutions of our globe' (Saussure 708). Shelley says that '[n]one can reply' to these questions ('Mont Blanc' 75), but he tries to communicate by giving the absolute Other a 'voice' that the 'adverting mind' can interpret (80, 100).

Contemporary geologists scientifically read ancient strata to understand the sublime silence of material nature, and what Shelley does in this poem is to read the geological surface of the 'primæval mountains' in the chain of Mont Blanc, more precisely, to read geological/political revolutions of the 'naked countenance of earth' (99, 98). What is characteristic of Shelley here is that he tries to make the geological reading a dialogism between the poet and inorganic other in nature. Like Saussure, Shelley asks questions, giving a 'tongue' to the wilderness and a 'voice' to the mountain so that he can relate the surrounding nature to the human world and interpret it socially (76, 80). The 'mysterious tongue' of the wilderness 'teaches' two possibilities, 'awful doubt,' or 'faith so mild, / So solemn, so serene, that man may be / But for such faith, with nature reconciled' (76, 77–9). The former is related to the possible existence of a destructive divinity, and the latter, by the phrase 'so mild, / So solemn, so serene,' adumbrates the unseen 'still, snowy, and serene' summit of Mont Blanc (77–8, 61). The image of Mont Blanc, which has remained serene after geological upheavals gives hope that 'man may be / But for such faith with nature reconciled' (78–9).[28] As Shelley wants to choose faith in nature, section 3 ends with his assertion that the silent Mountain has a voice that is ethically committed to the human world below:

> Thou hast a voice, great Mountain, to repeal
> Large codes of fraud and woe; not understood
> By all, but which the wise, and great, and good
> Interpret, or make felt, or deeply feel.   (80–3)

The Mountain, which has survived a number of catastrophes from the beginning of the earth and seen the vicissitudes of human civilizations, can foretell the inevitable termination of any political and religious tyrannies in the human world.

While Shelley envisions 'a sea / Of fire' in the 'silent snow' of Mont Blanc's 'subject mountains,' the 'naked countenance of earth,' through which a social voice of the 'great Mountain' is heard, reveals another kind of history in primeval time (73–4, 62, 98, 80). Stripped of later products of creation as well as the snow, it shows Shelley a huge 'city' in the primordial wilderness: 'dome, pyramid, and pinnacle, / A city of death, distinct with many a tower / And wall impregnable of beaming ice' (104–6). The association of mountains or precipices with domes and pyramids is not new. Bruce describes the mountains of Abyssinia by using words such as 'steeples,' 'obelisks,' and 'pyramids' (3: 128). The image of a vast city at the beginning of the earth is not new, either. As we have seen in chapter 1, the mountains and rocks in Keswick, though created after the Flood, strained Shelley's imagination to visualize a vast populous city at the beginning of history, and *Queen Mab* presents an ideal populous city of ten thousand years ago.

The significance of the image of an icy white city on the top of Mont Blanc is twofold. First, Shelley presents a city instead of evoking a personified deity. Second, this 'city' is the 'far fountains' from which '[t]he glaciers creep / Like snakes that watch their prey' ('Mont Blanc' 100–1). In the centre of the European sublime is the very source of evil, whose 'flood' like 'snakes' will destroy the whole world '[n]ever to be reclaimed' (107, 101, 114). The metaphor of a mighty city as the fountain that overflows the whole world bears a marked similarity to Wordsworth's 'vast metropolis,' which is the 'fountain' of the destiny of Great Britain as well as of 'the destiny of earth itself' (*Prelude* 8.746–8). In the Romantic geography of Mont Blanc, Shelley is confronted with a prototype of the European metropolis in the form of Mont Blanc, whose 'frozen blood' spreads like the 'perpetual stream' of globalization, destroying everything; the soil is 'mangled'; the 'dwelling-place / Of insects, beasts, and birds' is destroyed; people's 'work and dwelling' vanish (*Letters* 1: 500; 'Mont Blanc' 109, 110, 114–15, 118). This is exactly what London as the centre of destructive commerce does in *Queen Mab*. London, which is likened to the poisonous upas tree, shares the metaphor of snakes with the city of death on Mont Blanc; London's 'venomed exhalations spread / Ruin, and death, and woe, where millions lay / Quenching the serpent's famine' (*Queen Mab* 4.84–6). The 'city of death' issues a 'flood of ruin' that rains destruction on the world below ('Mont Blanc' 105, 107).

The voice coming down with the glaciers is a voice of ruin. Wordsworth heard the same voice of ruin at the foot of Mont Blanc:

> Six thousand years amid his [Mont Blanc's] lonely bounds
> The voice of Ruin, day and night, resounds.
> Where Horror-led his sea of ice assails,
> Havoc and Chaos blast a thousand vales,

In waves, like two enormous serpents, wind
And drag their length of deluge train behind.
(*Descriptive Sketches* 692–7)[29]

Wordsworth sees a clear contrast between Mont Blanc, which towers 'serene,' and the darkened valley below, where 'the slave of slaves' in Savoy is suffering (699, 706). Claire Eliane Engel says that it was never clear 'whether the mountain was in Switzerland or in the Savoy' (*Mont Blanc* 16), but Chamonix was never Swiss territory (Heringman 77). Chamonix was in the Savoy province of the Kingdom of Sardinia, and the Savoyards were tormented by Catholicism and despotism. Wordsworth in 1793 could still believe that God's benevolent plans would be ultimately realized in the French Revolution and that the revolutionary Second Flood would replace the 'voice of Ruin,' washing away human and natural evils, and the 'vales where Death with Famine scowr's, / And dark Oppression builds her thick-ribb'd towers' (*Descriptive Sketches* 693, 794–5). He asks 'great God' for 'Freedom's waves' that vanquish 'Conquest, Avarice, and Pride' and 'brood the nations o'er with Nile-like wings' (792, 793, 805).[30]

During the Napoleonic Wars Savoy was annexed to France, but at the Vienna settlements restored to Sardinia, while Geneva was admitted to the Swiss Confederation in 1814 (Birns, 'Secrets of the Birth of Time' 361). In 1816, Mont Blanc was on the border between Switzerland and the Savoy province of the Kingdom of Sardinia. Shelley was to observe with his own eyes what he had written in *Queen Mab*: the fact that the baleful effect of man-made diseases – commerce, religion, and tyranny – was severer than natural diseases. He writes that the contrast between 'the subjects of the King of Sardinia and the citizens of the independent republics of Switzerland' shows 'a powerful illustration of the blighting mischiefs of despotism, within the space of a few miles' (*Letters* 1: 482). He finds the appearance of 'the inhabitants of Evian' is 'more wretched, diseased and poor' than he have ever seen before, and notices 'the degradation of the human species' in the Chamonix regions (*Letters* 1: 482, 499).

Children are no exception. During an eight-day cruise around Lake Geneva with Byron, at Nernier, he and Byron saw children playing in the evening. 'The children here appeared in an extraordinary way deformed and diseased. Most of them were crooked, and with enlarged throats' (*Letters* 1: 480–1). In the manuscript letter to Peacock on 12 July 1816 about an eight-day cruise around Lake Geneva with

Byron, which was discovered in 1975 and which contains passages greatly revised by Shelley for publication,[31] Shelley stresses the location where he observed the deformity of children and the contrast to Switzerland: *'most of the children (this is Savoy, the King of Sardinia's domain) were exceedingly deformed and ugly very unlike those of Switzerland'* (*SC* 571 7: 29). Shelley, however, found one little boy who had 'such exquisite grace in his mien and motions,' and whose 'countenance was beautiful for the expression with which it overflowed' (*Letters* 1: 481). In the manuscript letter, Shelley adds that *'Lord Byron, a new convert to Wordsworth, reminded me of the Highland girl'* (*SC* 571 7: 29). Shelley notices in his face a seed of urbanity and corruption, 'a mixture of pride and gentleness'; it is the 'indications of sensibility,' which 'his education will probably pervert to misery or seduce to crime' (*Letters* 1: 481). Moreover, Byron, whose class-based *'vilest & most vulgar prejudices'* are noted in the manuscript letter (*SC* 571 7: 28),[32] seduced the little boy into corruption: 'My companion gave him a piece of money, which he took without speaking, with a sweet smile of easy thankfulness, and then with an unembarrassed air turned to his play' (*Letters* 1: 481).

Though he is dismayed by the local people, 'on whose stupidity, avarice & imposture engenders a mixture of vices truly horrible & disgusting,' Shelley also criticizes severely 'these vulgar great [English travellers],' who 'corrupt the manners of the people, & make this place another Keswick' (1: 500–1). Colbert points out that the phrase 'vulgar great' appeared in *Queen Mab* where Shelley condemns the 'venal interchange' of commerce (Colbert 89; *Queen Mab* 5.56, 38), and tellingly compares Shelley's accusation of British travellers with the self-congratulatory comment on the same topic by John Sheppard in *Letters Descriptive of a Tour through Some Parts of France, Italy, Switzerland, and Germany, in 1816* (1817); since Windham's visit to Chamonix in 1741, the region had become a source 'of high gratification to subsequent travellers,' who had 'carried civilization and prosperity into these solitudes.'[33] Shelley certainly wanted to correct the 'vulgar great.' He writes in the manuscript letter to Peacock: *'I had some hope that an intercourse with me would operate to weaken those superstitions of rank & wealth & revenge & servility to opinion with which he [Byron], in common with other men, is so poisonously imbued'* (*SC* 571 7: 28). Shelley, however, as an Englishman and traveller, must have found himself contributing to the 'melancholy exhibitions of tourism' in this region (*Letters* 1: 500). Shelley observes that the 'proprietor' of 'a Cabinet d'Histoire Naturelle at Chamouni' is 'the very vilest specimen' of the tourist industry that 'subsist[s] on the weakness & credulity of travellers,' but sometimes acts just like one of those 'vulgar great': 'We have bought some specimens of minerals & plants & two or three crystal seals at Mont Blanc, to preserve the remembrance of having approached it' (1:501). In 1816, the serene, white mountain symbolized a triumph of science, but it was still a 'cursed mountain' dominating the world below as a symbol of despotism and that of 'the venal interchange' of commerce and tourism exercised by British travellers (*Queen Mab* 5.38).

Unlike the young Wordsworth in 1793, Shelley in 1816, having no faith in Christianity, knowing the dire consequences of the French Revolution, and witnessing 'the degradation of the human species' caused by social and natural ills, could not resort to the Second Flood that was created by mixing religious awe and revolutionary hopes. Toward the end of 'Alastor,' when the earth is 'voiceless' and the air is 'vacant' in the mountains of the Caucasus, the narrator cannot help addressing the 'colossal Skeleton,' who is, in its 'devastating omnipotence,' the 'king of this frail world' (662, 611, 613, 614). If Mont Blanc has 'a voice' to 'repeal / Large codes of fraud and woe' as Shelley believes ('Mont Blanc' 80–1), Shelley has to channel nature's destructive flood in a way that revivifies the physically and morally ruined world.

4. The River of Life and the Unseen Summit

Shelley's glance moves from primary mountains down to the world of the Ravine of Arve. On the highest mountains, the elements, 'in scorn of mortal power,' have built a 'city of death,' and from there a 'flood of ruin' perpetually rolls down, shattering huge pines and creating a vast waste land '[n]ever to be reclaimed,' while '[t]he race of man, flies far in dread' (102–18). This scene corresponds to the part of the journal-letter in which is evoked a malign divinity. Shelley thinks that the scene is 'the most vivid image of desolation that it is possible to conceive,' and proceeds to describe the landscape in detail: 'The enormous pinnacles of ice perpetually fall, & are perpetually reproduced. – The pines of the forest which bounds it at one extremity are overthrown & shattered; – there is something inexpressibly dreadful in the aspect of the few branchless trunks which nearest to the ice rifts still stand in the uprooted soil. The meadows perish overwhelmed with sand & stones' (*Letters* 1: 499). Here the poem marks the most significant departure from the journal-letter, in which the terrible course of expanding glaciers conjures up Ahriman among his 'palaces of death & frost' in the mountain chain of Mont Blanc (1: 499). In the poem, amid the overwhelming natural ruins, Shelley successfully expels a negative deity from the scene. Instead of calling upon any kind of deity on the summit, Shelley adds, as the last component of the visionary geography of Mont Blanc, 'vast caves,' which are the source of a broad river and recreate the whole scene that is destroyed and frozen by the glaciers:

>   Below, vast caves
>   Shine in the rushing torrents' restless gleam,
>   Which from those secret chasms in tumult welling
>   Meet in the vale, and one majestic River,
>   The breath and blood of distant lands, for ever
>   Rolls its loud waters to the ocean waves,
>   Breathes its swift vapours to the circling air.   ('Mont Blanc' 120–6)

Whereas the second deluge comes down from the top of Mont Blanc in Wordsworth's eschatological vision that draws on God's promise, in Shelley's poem the 'flood of ruin' from the Mountain is transformed into a life-giving river in the 'secret chasms' located externally in the 'vast caves' of ice at the foot of Mont Blanc and internally in the abode of imagination in his human mind (107, 122, 120). The 'still cave of the witch Poesy' in the earlier section is now naturalized and enlarged to be the 'vast caves' that '[s]hine in the rushing torrents' restless gleam,' nourishing a river of life that will become the 'breath and blood of distant lands' (44, 120, 121, 124).

Shelley's own visit to the source of the Arveiron and the sacred river in Coleridge's 'Kubla Khan' contribute to recreate the scene.[34] In Shelley's day, the Arveiron was famous for its origin in a great cavern of the glacier. In the journal-letter Shelley writes that the Arveiron 'rolls impetuously from an arch of ice, & spreads itself in many streams over a vast space of the valley ravaged & laid bare by its inundations' and '[t]he glacier by which its waters are nourished overhangs this cavern & the plain, & the forests of pines which surround it, with terrible precipices of solid ice' (*Letters* 1: 498). In the journal-letter, the river was a fierce stream 'nourished' by the glacier, and together with the glacier, devastated a vast space of the valley. By contrast, in the poem, the actual Arveiron in Savoy is improved to be 'one majestic

River' by imagination, by bringing in Coleridge's sacred river Alph that issues from the 'deep romantic chasm' in the East ('Mont Blanc' 123; 'Kubla Khan' 12):[35]

> And from this chasm, with ceaseless turmoil seething
> As if this earth in fast thick pants were breathing,
> A mighty fountain momently was forced:
> Amid whose swift half-intermitted burst
> Huge fragments vaulted like rebounding hail,
> Or chaffy grain beneath the thresher's flail:
> And 'mid these dancing rocks at once and ever
> It flung up momently the sacred river.   ('Kubla Khan' 17–24)

The river, which issues at the foot of the highest peak in Europe, is described as being majestic like the sacred river in Asia. It flows to the ocean, just like the Arve, which runs from Chamonix to the Mediterranean Sea via Lake Geneva,[36] being translated into the 'breath and blood of distant lands' ('Mont Blanc' 124). Shelley does not identify the river either with the Arveiron or with the Arve, as it is created by his imagination as a hybrid of the two actual Alpine rivers and the imaginary Eastern river Alph. It is important to note that Shelley's river is a life-giving force and that it also redirects the inevitable dark course of the Alph that falls into 'a lifeless ocean' ('Kubla Khan' 28). A new great river in 'distant lands' of Europe, which Shelley creates by drawing upon the imaginary of the sacred river Alph in the East, will in turn bring fertility, 'breath and blood,' to 'distant lands' far away from Europe ('Mont Blanc' 124).

The imaginary geography of Chamonix improves that of the Caucasus in 'Alastor' as well. In 'Alastor,' on his way back to Europe, the Poet dies under the desolate and 'icy' summits, and the broad river sinks into an 'immeasurable void,' while yawning caves repeat the hollow sounds of rushing waters (353, 569). In the Valley of Chamonix, on the other hand, under the unseen summit of Mont Blanc, destruction and creation simultaneously occur when a great river of life issues forth from a glacial cavern through Shelley's imagination. In the contact zone of the Romantic geography of 'Mont Blanc,' Shelley's human imagination meets the Power's flood of ruin, melts 'the frozen blood' that circulates through 'his stony veins,' and turns it into the warm 'breath and blood of distant lands' (*Letters* 1: 500; 'Mont Blanc' 124).

The absolute Other, the 'Power,' which appears as Ahriman in the journal-letter and which is sensed as a terrible masculine deity in section 2 of the poem, is not anthropomorphized in the final vision of the mountain. The strange truths Shelley learns by interpreting nature's tongue and voice is that the Power is neither good nor evil, operating the cycle of necessity indifferently, far above the human world. 'Mont Blanc yet gleams on high: – the power is there' (127). Mont Blanc appears again, and so does the Power, but written with an initial lower-case letter. This does not mean that Shelley has domesticated the absolute Other into a little manageable other. It continues to be 'still and solemn,' but it is now recognized as the 'power of many sights, / And many sounds, and much of life and death' (128–9). In short, it still remains the other but is linked, as it is, to the physical world, '[t]he fields, the lakes, the forests, and the streams, / Ocean, and all the living things that dwell / Within the dædal earth' (84–6).

Although the mountain appears gleaming, the summit still seems hidden high above; the phrase 'on high' strongly reminds us of Shelley's flickering glimpses of icy pinnacles around Mont Blanc that shone 'on high' through the clouds on his way to Chamonix (*Letters* 1: 497).[37] Then Shelley for the first time visualizes the summit of the mountain in the imagination:

> the snows descend
> Upon that Mountain; none beholds them there,
> Nor when the flakes burn in the sinking sun,
> Or the star-beams dart through them: – Winds contend
> Silently there, and heap the snow with breath
> Rapid and strong, but silently! Its home
> The voiceless lightning in these solitudes
> Keeps innocently, and like vapour broods
> Over the snow.   ('Mont Blanc' 131–9)

Silence and coldness on the summit remind us of Saussure's account on his way to the summit of Mont Blanc. Alone on the top of Pierre-Ronde at night, Saussure, 'heightened by the imagination,' felt as if he 'had outlived the universe' and had seen 'its corpse stretched' at his feet; but he was consoled by looking at the summit of Mont Blanc, whose 'shining and phosphorical snows still gave the idea of movement and life' (682). Though Saussure found it was only the 'dwelling of silence and cold' when he reached the summit (690), Shelley tries to present the scene no one has beheld before. As in section 1, the 'everlasting universe of things' appears again ('Mont Blanc' 1). What we see there is an almost infinite length of geological time that seems to have no beginning and no end. Snow has been falling and accumulating day in and day out from the primeval past. The elements no longer build a city of death, despising the mortal, but the silent snow, ceaselessly falling, is tended by the voiceless winds on the summit. Shelley's imagination travels to the unseen summit and finds the 'home' of nature from which the 'secret strength of things' flow (136, 139).

Through his visionary improvement of the devastated and frozen landscape of Chamonix, Shelley frees Mont Blanc from anthropomorphic myth of any kind, and thaws the destructive, 'frozen blood' of Mont Blanc into life-giving 'breath and blood of distant lands' (*Letters* 1: 500; 'Mont Blanc' 124). One thing that he is not yet able to hear or visualize in the silent summit of the final section is the Mountain's voice 'to repeal / Large codes of fraud and woe' ('Mont Blanc' 80–1). The mountain, which had 'his [the Power's] secret throne' in section 2, is not only naturalized but also slightly feminized by the phrase, such as '[i]ts [the snow's] home,' and 'brood[ing] / Over' the snow (17, 136, 138–9).[38] The feminized mountain may faintly recall the image of 'Mountain Liberty,' which 'alone may heal / The pain which Custom's obduracies bring' ('On Leaving London for Wales' 23–4), but the voice of the Mountain is not yet heard '[b]y all,' nor does it correct what Shelley observes and deplores in the journal-letter: 'the melancholy exhibitions of tourism' sponsored by British travellers who corrupt the local population and destroy the places they visit ('Mont Blanc' 82; *Letters* 1: 500). If the destructive glaciers in the Chamonix region can be associated with a devastating globalizing power, they might have been first unleashed by British travellers who turned an unnamed accused mountain into a celebrated source of international tourism. Though the highest mountain in Europe was conquered by Saussure, which marks a triumph of humans over nature by the emerging new science, Mont Blanc's social and political implications still remain ambiguous.

Thus Shelley's final question at the end of the poem is left unanswered: 'what were thou, and earth, and stars, and sea, / If to the human mind's imaginings / Silence and solitude were vacancy?' ('Mont Blanc' 142–4). The answer is not given in the poem, but we may hear a faint hope, though hushed in the poem, in a passage in the journal-letter to Peacock: 'All this might scarcely be; but the imagination surely could not forbear to breathe into the most inanimate forms, some likeness of its own visions' (*Letters* 1: 481). The passage refers to Byron's and Shelley's encounter with a beautiful boy among deformed children at Nernier. Colbert, pointing out that the passage did not exist in the original manuscript letter to Peacock, maintains that in revising the letter for publication after his own encounter with Mont Blanc, Shelley may have recalled the scene as a 'suppressed footnote to "Mont Blanc"' to confirm 'sublime encounters sublimate the "degraded"' (115).[39] Seeing Byron give the boy some money, Shelley may have recalled the 'divine beauty of Rousseau's imagination' he first knew during the lake cruise (*Letters* 1: 480). Vices of society will corrupt the beautiful innocence of the child, but the human imagination can create what 'might scarcely be' even amid a physically and morally diseased place like the Kingdom of Sardinia by being influenced by a rare combination of 'a serene and glowing evening' and 'this remote and romantic village, beside the calm lake that bore us hither,' and in turn influencing and recreating the most inanimate forms of the place with its own visions (1.481). Memories of the beautiful scene at Nernier help Shelley's imagination to hear a voice to 'repeal / Large codes of fraud and woe' in its 'attempt to imitate the untameable wildness and inaccessible solemnity,' and to breathe back 'some likeness of its own visions' into the huge scene of unseen otherness in nature ('Mont Blanc' 80–1; *HSWT* vi; *Letters* 1: 481). The encounter with the inanimate and inaccessible is not one-sided, but reciprocal, though in silence. What is phrased as 'some likeness of its own visions' is no longer one's mirror image, as it is fused with the external other in its attempt to imitate what is not one's own.

If, as Frances Ferguson says, 'Mont Blanc' shows 'the palpable improbability of looking for anything but silence from the mountain' despite seeking the mountain's voice and tongue (202), the poem's failure to hear what the mountain says in answer to its final question is partly due to its mode of the lyric, which does not allow the poet to develop dialogues with the external others represented as the mountain and creative/destructive deities, Christian and pagan alike. The Alpine experience of Shelley and Byron produces Shelley's 'Mont Blanc' and Byron's *Manfred*. Both concern the deified elements, scornful of mortal power, on the summit, but choose different modes of poetry. In order to defy and challenge the transcendental elements of nature, Byron dramatizes a human will and passion in Manfred's struggle against personified powers, the Witch of the Alps and Arimanes. On the other hand, Shelley develops a geological/political reading of Mont Blanc in the mode of the greater Romantic lyric in 'Mont Blanc' in order to dispel divine personifications. His strategy is successful in recreating a cosmic geography of the 'everlasting universe of things' ('Mont Blanc' 1), but leaves a series of unanswered questions in the poem, and makes the silent, barren mountaintop remain associated with human suffering, whether in Europe or Asia, and whether the suffering is caused by the transcendental power or human evils. Images of a city of death appear again and again in his subsequent poems. In *The Revolt of Islam*, Laon is bound on a 'mighty column' that pierces the sky on a hilltop near Constantinople (Istanbul) (3.1198–377).

All of the unanswered questions in 'Mont Blanc' require the more extensive and objective modes of narrative and drama for their full investigation. 'Mont Blanc,' Sperry notes, is 'in many ways a preliminary sketch for *Prometheus*' (68). Shelley's Mont Blanc experience is not completed in his visionary recreation of the Chamonix valley in 'Mont Blanc.' Two years after 'Mont Blanc,' in *Prometheus Unbound*, Shelley carefully investigates the questions he left unanswered in the earlier lyric. The highest peak in Europe is transferred to the Indian Caucasus, and conflict among the human imagination, evil deities, and necessity is dramatized in Prometheus, Asia, Jupiter, and Demogorgon.

4 *Prometheus Unbound*: The Eastern and Western Lovers on the Highest Mountain

1. Prometheus Bound

Although Shelley himself does not mention anything about the genesis of *Prometheus Unbound*, which was begun in September 1818 and finished late in 1819, Mary Shelley, in a letter to Leigh and Marianne Hunt from Savoy in 1823, remembers that it was when Shelley made a return visit to the Savoy scene in 1818, two years after 'Mont Blanc,' that 'the idea of his Prometheus' occurred to him (*LMWS* 1: 357).[1] Mary describes in detail the Montagne des Eschelles, the lofty mountain on the border between France and Savoy, which they visited on 26 March 1818: '*The rocks which cannot be less than 1000 feet in perpendicular height sometimes overhang the road on each side & almost shut out the sky. The scene is like that described in the Prometheus of Aeschylus – Vast rifts & caverns in the granite precipices – wintry mountains with ice & snow above – the loud sounds of unseen waters within the caverns, & walls of topling rocks only to be scaled as he describes, by the winged chariot of the Ocean Nymphs*' (*Journals* 200). The vast wintry precipices of the Montagne des Eschelles would have reminded Shelley and Mary of a Greek tragic place of 'a catastrophe' where 'reconciling the Champion with the Oppressor of mankind' occurred (preface to *Prometheus Unbound*, *SP&P* 206). With the memory of Mont Blanc's 'præmæval mountains,' whose hideous shapes were 'rude, bare, and high, / Ghastly, and scarred, and riven,' the frozen landscape in the Savoy province would have produced an image of the '[b]lack, wintry, dead' peak in the Indian Caucasus where Prometheus is chained in the opening scene of *Prometheus Unbound* ('Mont Blanc' 99, 70–1; *Prometheus Unbound* 1.21).

The image of Prometheus, the founder of human civilization, chained to the icy precipice, however, might well have haunted

Shelley even since 1816. Shelley's reading list of 1816 in Mary's *Journals* includes 'Prometheus of Eschylus [sic]-Greek' (97). While in Geneva, Shelley was reading Greek dramatists intensively, especially 'Æschylus's *Prometheus*, whom he considered the type of Milton's Satan' (Medwin 161). Mary records that Shelley was translating *Prometheus Bound* in July 1817 when he was in the middle of writing *The Revolt of Islam* (*Journals* 177–8). What we have to bear in mind, however, is that a dangerous Promethean fire-bringer, who is associated with European intellect and civilization, appears again and again in Shelley's work, from a long note to *Queen Mab* to the image of Rousseau in 'The Triumph of Life.' In a long note explaining the depravity of the physical and moral nature of man in canto 8 of *Queen Mab*, Shelley accuses Prometheus of applying fire to 'culinary purposes'; the introduction of eating meat leads to all human vices, especially '[t]yranny, superstition, commerce, and inequality' (*SPW* 827). The vices introduced by Prometheus culminate in *The Revolt of Islam*, where the revolutionary fire-bringer Laon, who envisages himself filling the world with 'cleansing fire' in Argolis, Greece, experiences a fearful mountaintop vision when he is bound to a pillar upon the hill; Laon eats his lover's flesh for his own preservation (2.784–92, 3.1316–41). In this chapter, we shall see how Shelley recreates a place of 'a catastrophe' and the myth of Prometheus who initiates all political and social ills (preface to *Prometheus Unbound*, *SP&P* 206).

Shelley's choice of the Indian mountains as a place for 'reforming the world' shows his belief in the healing power in the margin (preface to *Prometheus Unbound*, *SP&P* 208). It is also influenced by contemporary Europe's keen interest in the Prometheus myth and eager anticipation of a new revelation in ancient India when syncretism was breaking the boundaries of classical antiquity.[2] The Indian Caucasus had been given special attention in Britain since Sir Walter Raleigh in *The History of the World* (1614) identified the highest Indian peak with Mount Ararat, whereas the traditional classical sources considered it to be the mountain in Armenia (113–28). While serious efforts were made to establish the authorized Greek texts of Aeschylus's works in the first decade of the nineteenth century, comparative mythology extended into India, equating Prometheus with other mythological figures such as Noah, Japheth, or Magog, and discussing Milton's placement of Ararat and Eden in the East against the Orientalists' discoveries. The linkage between the Indian Caucasus and Prometheus was confirmed by a British Orientalist, Francis Wilford, who reported an Indian version of the story of Prometheus and the eagle and identified Mount Meru, a sacred mountain in the Indian geography, with the Indian Caucasus ('On Mount Caucasus' [1801] 511–14; 'An Essay on the Sacred Isles in the West, with Other Essays Connected with That Work' [1809] 258–9).

Shelley was a prodigious reader and kept up with these scholarly trends. The book order list he sent to Thomas 'Clio' Rickman, the London bookseller and reformer, toward the end of 1812 includes Aeschylus, both '[o]riginal and translation, if possible, united,' Confucius, *The Works of Sir William Jones* (1799), Robertson's *Historical Disquisition concerning the Knowledge Which the Ancients Had of India* (1791), Garcilaso de la Vega, Diderot, poems by Wordsworth, Coleridge, and Southey, and Godwin's works (*Letters* 1: 344–5).[3] The order list was an immediate response to Godwin's long letter of December 10 recommending the Greek and English classics (*Collected Novels and Memoirs of William Godwin* 80–2), but there are quite a few in the list that were not suggested by Godwin but show that Shelley was lifting his eyes beyond the European world.

In repositioning Prometheus's bondage from the Georgian Caucasus of Aeschylus's *Prometheus Bound* and from the Alps to the Indian Caucasus, however, Shelley marks a salient difference from syncretic mythologists and Orientalists. He transfers to the East the ruinous sterility of a site where 'a catastrophe so feeble as that of reconciling the Champion with the Oppressor of mankind' occurred, and the icy devastation of Mont Blanc caused by British globalizing power and embodied as a 'flood of ruin' (preface to *Prometheus Unbound*, *SP&P* 206; 'Mont Blanc' 107). The highest Eastern peak that appears in the first act of *Prometheus Unbound* is made cold and disastrous by two ruinous mountains carried from the West. Here the West and the East, the self and the other, are intricately meshed. In order to unbind Prometheus and regenerate the devastated Eastern/European geography, Shelley uses Eastern elements, dialogue, and hybridity.

2. Hybridity and the Contagion of Good

In Shelley's day, the Indian Caucasus was known as 'Hindoo-Kho' (the modern Hindu Kush in north India and Afghanistan). According to Abraham Rees's *Cyclopaedia* (1819–20), 'Hindoo-Kho' is the '*Indian Caucasus* of Alexander' (18), and the 'Caucasus' is 'in *Ancient Geography*, the name of highest and most extensive range of mountains in the northern part of Asia' (7).[4] Rees mentions the meaning of 'Caucasus' in Persian and in some other Eastern languages. In the former, as *'cau* or *coh* signifies a mountain,' Caucasus refers to 'the mountain of the Chasas, an ancient and formidable tribe, who inhabited this immense range from the eastern limits of India, to the confines of Persia'; in the latter Caucasus means *'white'* and 'snow' (7). The Eastern Mountain of White, where a 'formidable' Eastern tribe lived, is marked under masculine/militaristic European expeditions, including literary ones, into the East from Alexander the Great, through Milton, to Johann Friedrich Blumenbach. Since Joseph Raben's 'Shelley's *Prometheus Unbound*: Why the Indian Caucasus?' (1963), the first paper to examine the importance of the Indian Caucasus and the mountains' associations with Alexander the Great, two critics, Curran and Leask, have discussed the poem in detail in relation to the political and cultural contexts of contemporary Europe. Curran, focusing on pan-European interest in syncretic mythology, stresses Shelley's effort to 'extend the religious contexts of *Prometheus Unbound* beyond those assumed from Milton' (*Shelley's Annus Mirabilis* 60), while Leask points out a political link between Shelley's transfer of Prometheus to the Indian Caucasus and the Western anthropological discovery of the mountains as the origin of 'the "Caucasian" races, a term coined by Blumenbach in 1775 [for 1795]' (*British Romantic Writers and the East* 143).[5] Though I am indebted to both critics, I would argue that the Indian setting functions as a place of interaction between East and West, rather than just a foreign land into which the Western self makes a one-sided foray and extends itself.

Unlike Mont Blanc, although ruined by European expeditions, the highest range in Asia had not been surmounted yet, and its association with the dawn of civilization must have attracted Shelley in many ways as a place in the margin that could offer an alternative Romantic geography. Shelley's dislocation of the geography and chronology of the Western myth shatters European boundaries. Weinberg mentions that in *Prometheus Unbound* Shelley sets English literature free from 'English insularity' to graft it onto 'the mainstream of European culture' (9), but Shelley goes much further than that: Shelley aims at 'embodying the discoveries of all ages, & harmonizing the contending creeds by which mankind have been ruled' (*Letters* 2: 71). This may sound similar to Southey's interest in world religions. Southey, looking back at a time when he was 'a school-boy at Westminster,' says: 'I had formed an intention of exhibiting the most remarkable forms of Mythology which have at any time obtained among mankind, by making each the ground-work of a narrative poem' (*PWRS* 8: xiii). Moreover, in writing a series of epics with foreign settings, Southey finds non-Christian religions 'false' and 'monstrous,' and always wants 'English knowledge and the English language diffused to the east, and west, and the south' (*PWRS* 8: xxiii, *Correspondence* 2: 243).

It is important to note here how Shelley's attitude differs from Southey's, especially because Shelley discusses the 'beneficial innovation' generated by 'European feelings' and the 'contagion of good' that infects the East when he refers to the civilizing role of Christian missionaries in the subcontinent in 'A Philosophical View of Reform,' which was drafted while he was completing *Prometheus Unbound* in its four-act form (*CWPBS* 7: 17, 18). Shelley writes: 'the zeal of the missionaries of what is called the Christian faith will produce beneficial innovation there, even by the application of dogmas and forms of what is here an outworn incumbrance' (7: 17). The passage, comparable to Southey's firm belief that 'there are but two methods of extending civilisation, – conquest and conversion' (*Correspondence* 3: 281), has been taken as revealing Shelley's imperialistic bias. Shelley, however, had already expressed his doubts about conversion as early as 1811 (*Letters* 1: 201), and in this passage he is critical of the ways in which the 'zeal' is conveyed. While Southey intends to alchemize the barbarous other into the Christian self, 'transmuting lead into gold' by pouring Christian essence into an Oriental setting (*PWRS* 4: 29), Shelley's 'contagion of good' intends to eventually foster something that is different from the self.

The point of Shelley's passage is his belief that the 'zeal' for 'beneficial innovation,' which far outweighs the means of conversions, should help an Indian spirit of liberty despite the missionaries' intention to homogenize the heathen (*CWPBS* 7: 17). What is important about 'European feelings' is that while European 'beneficial innovation' exercises in India, there is a 'thing to be sought': 'they [the Indians] should, as they would if they were free, attain to a system of arts and literature of their own' (7: 18). In *A Defence of Poetry*, Shelley observes that in 'modern England,' the promoters of the 'narrower' kind of utility, who 'have their appointed office in society,' are intent on 'banishing the importunity of the wants of our animal nature' and 'dispersing the grosser delusions of superstition' (*SP&P* 529); while they have tended to 'exasperate at once the extremes of luxury and want,' 'Poet or poetic philosophers,' who are promoters of true utility, aspire to realize the multiplicity of 'highest idealisms' (529, 518). The 'contagion of good' can be seen in this context as a figure of the sympathetic imagination that realizes multiple 'idealisms,' by 'going out of our own nature' and '[identifying] ourselves with the beautiful which exists in thought, action, or person, not our own' ('A Philosophical View of Reform,' *CWPBS* 7: 18; *A Defence of Poetry*, *SP&P* 518, 517).

Shelley's use of 'European feelings' and 'beneficial innovation' to emancipate non-European countries is thus different from the civilizing activities of the British missionaries and officers in India. Moreover, the 'beneficial innovation' does not necessarily come from the West. In *Prometheus Unbound*, it is not the others, as in Reginald Heber's famous missionary hymn, 'From Greenland's Icy Mountains' (1819), who 'call us to deliver / Their land from error's chain' from 'India's coral strand' (*The English Hymnal with Tunes* 709). It is Prometheus, the founder of European civilization, who is chained on the Indian Caucasus. Images of faraway places, represented mainly by the East, in Romantic discourse often evoke not only an 'exotic' earthly paradise to replace the lost Eden but also a locus of contagion, where Europeans, coming into contact with their 'others,' face infection and death; In Mary Shelley's *The Last Man* (1826) a worldwide plague arises on 'the shores of the Nile,' spreading east and west, and all people – Africans, Asians, Americans, and Europeans – 'hug her' in their 'bosom' and perish, except Lionel Verney (127, 139); De Quincey records his fear of the 'cancerous kisses' of the Eastern others (109); A lucky survivor from a disease-stricken East would return home as a colonial invalid, impaired or tainted by the foreign climate, like Coleridge's 'lank, and brown' Ancient Mariner whose eyes, like Eastern evil eyes, are 'glittering' ('The Rime of the Ancient Mariner' 226, 228). In *Prometheus Unbound*, however, Eastern elements also contribute greatly to improve the sick, devastated landscape of the Indian Caucasus. The initiator of Prometheus's liberation is Asia, his lover and a daughter of Oceanus from whom the Asian continent receives its name (Herodotus 2: 245; Lemprière 103). She acts as an Eastern version of 'contagion of good,' and the cooperation and union of Prometheus and Asia transforms the frozen Indian Caucasus and regenerates the world.

In using the myth of Prometheus, Shelley is much more enterprising and bolder than syncretic mythologists and Orientalists in two respects. First, influenced by contemporary geological thought such as Buffon's, Shelley's timescale is much longer than biblical chronology could allow. Scholars in comparative mythology take pains to confine ancient studies within biblical history. Even Sir William Jones, who was keen to promote a much older original centre of civilization in India, expresses his firm belief in the orthodox chronology; in his famous essay 'On the Gods of Greece, Italy, and India,' he declares that his hypothesis and its proofs would 'in no degree affect the truth and sanctity of the *Mosaick* History' (Jones 1: 276). By contrast, Shelley does not hesitate to exceed six thousand years of biblical history. At the beginning of the play, '[t]hrice three hundred thousand' years have passed since the creation of the earth (*Prometheus Unbound* 1.74).

Second, Shelley includes foreign characters in his pantheon on the Indian Caucasus. Both Demogorgon and Asia are almost unknown in classical mythology and neither of them appears in Aeschylus's play. Shelley's Demogorgon is quite similar to the Demorgorgon of Antoine Banier's *The Mythology and Fables of the Ancients Explain'd from History* (1739–40), the most influential of the eighteenth-century rationalist mythographies. Banier, paraphrasing Boccaccio's account of Demogorgon, writes that the name means 'the *Genius* of the Earth,' and that this god is 'a Being before the World, even before *Chaos* itself,' who 'answers but indifferently to the Idea the first Philosophers form'd of him' (1: 119–20).[6] This description suits well an embodiment of Shelley's idea of Necessity as the unseen formless principle of the world. Asia is a very minor figure in classical mythology, though Herodotus considers her as 'the wife of Prometheus' (2: 245). A keen interest in pagan gods in the eighteenth century was not restricted to scholars. Many 'Pantheons' were available for the general public; Andrew Tooke's *Pantheon* (1698) continued to be used, and *Bell's New Pantheon* was published in 1790. In these books, Asia is only briefly introduced as 'a daughter of Oceanus by his wife Pamphyloge' (Bell 1: 98).

While the original meaning of Demogorgon's name suggests the genius loci of the whole earth, Asia's name points to a more specific locality on earth. Lemprière, whose *Classical Dictionary* was a standard reference book for Shelley's generation, contemplated on the history of the continent named after the obscure Oceanid. He explains the gradual expansion of the area called Asia: 'The name of Asia was applied by Homer, Herodotus, and Euripides, to a district of Lydia, watered by the Cayster, and in which the geographers of a later age distinguished a tribe called Asiones, and a city called Asia. It appears probable that the Greeks, in proportion as their knowledge was enlarged, extended this name by little and little, from the district to which it was applied, until it embraced the whole of Asia Minor, and ultimately the other extensive countries of the east' (103). In Shelley's play, both Asia and her sister Ione have Eastern elements in their names. Moreover, the Indian setting of the lyrical drama stresses Asia's Eastern character, connecting her, like Keats's obscure Titaness 'born of most enormous Caf' ('Hyperion: A Fragment' [1820] 2.53),[7] more with the subcontinent than with Asia Minor.[8] Shelley replaces Hesione, the Greek wife of Prometheus, who has no important role in Aeschylus's *Prometheus Bound*, with this obscure Oceanid, and makes her wait for Prometheus in the vale of Kashmir. In doing so, Shelley attaches great importance to Asia as Prometheus's epipsyche and saviour, in a way that reminds us of his transformation of a marginal Welsh spirit into a universal fairy queen of revolutionary power in *Queen Mab*. While the dialogue between the poet and the unseen Power was purely European in 'Mont Blanc,' by adding Asia and Demogorgon Shelley creates a cosmopolitan dialogue.

Shelley expresses the relationship between Prometheus and Asia through two sets of metaphors, one based on the gender opposition of 'masculine' rationality and 'female' imagination and the other on the geopolitical opposition of Europe and Asia (Leask, *British Romantic Writers and the East* 121). Their different geographical and cultural associations enable them to escape the fatal dead end of the mirror relationship, from which Shelley's previous political poems, 'Zeinab and Kathema' and *The Revolt of Islam*, could not escape.[9] On the other hand, as in Owenson's *The Missionary*, the gendered and geopolitical opposition between the European and Eastern lovers loads the binary opposition between reason and imagination with the problems of Orientalism, making the terms associated with the East – 'female' and 'imagination' – subordinate to the West.

Leask argues that Shelley rethinks these binary stereotypes through 'a radical exercise of imagination' to orientalize a Greek myth, 'a reverse acculturation which frees the Orient from its formerly negative or supplementary connotations' (*British Romantic Writers and the East* 122, 143). The subordinate geopolitical triad, 'Asia/female/imagination,' is reformulated so as to cancel the binary stereotypes by presenting Asia as an active harbinger of the new Promethean Age, and Prometheus as a negative and passive prisoner (122, 141–54). It is true that Asia's role as a quester and Prometheus's immobility overturn the stereotypical division of roles based on gender and geography, but a reversal of gender roles – the passive hero and the active heroine – is one of Shelley's strategies for giving power to the marginal. It is not necessarily geographically oriented, as seen in Ianthe and Henry of

Queen Mab and in Laon and Cythna of *The Revolt of Islam*.[10] The important point is why the correlation of gender and geography with colonizer and colonized is broken in *Prometheus Unbound*.

What makes the play a truly 'utopian moment' in Romantic discourse is, as Leask argues, the introduction of hybridity, transmission, and interaction between the self and the others (*British Romantic Writers and the East* 2). Leask emphasizes the overturning of hierarchy between East and West, and 'the admission of a principle of hybridity' in Asia's dialogue with Demogorgon, which, he conjectures, alludes to Rammohun Roy's translation of the *Kena Upanishad* in the *Monthly Magazine*, the first translation from the Vedanta that entered as a 'hybridized discourse' into 'the heart of the western literary canon' (149–51). Leask's argument is insightful, but I would seek hybridity within Shelley's poetry and see the play's 'utopian moment' not in the reversal of hierarchy but in the interactions of the two main characters, dialogues with inanimate forms, and 'contagion[s] of good' from the West as well as from the East.

Both Prometheus and Asia are liberated from the stereotypical geographical images without losing their different cultural elements, but their liberation presupposes the mingling and exchanging of their essence, that is, hybridization. Hybridization in Shelley is, however, not limited to this text; some of Shelley's earlier poems also represent the hybridization of qualities. 'Alastor' enters into the lyrical drama when Asia in the vale of Kashmir sees the dream of a glowing form; the Western Poet's search for his Oriental other is hybridized or 'orientalized' by an Eastern female quester whose journey is motivated by her love, not lust, for her Western lover. 'Mont Blanc' finds its way into the dialogue between Asia and Demogorgon in the underground cave of the Indian Caucasus, making Asia a hybrid female poet who takes over Shelley's unanswered questions, and the lyrical drama in turn presents an absolute Other in India who responds to Shelley.

Correspondingly, Shelley employs a new hybrid mode of 'Lyrical Drama,' a new poetic mode that alludes to Wordsworth and Coleridge's *Lyrical Ballads* and combines the lyric and the drama (preface to *Prometheus Unbound, SP&P* 206). In the mode, all kinds of voices – Greek, Italian, English, and Indian, and lyrical and social – and imagery 'drawn from the operations of the human mind' offer important opportunities for dialogue that can cross zones of political, social, geographical and cultural differences (*SP&P* 207). In replacing the lost drama of Aeschylus with his own version of the Promethean myth, Shelley multiplies the lyric voice characteristic of the English Romantics in the social structure of the drama, the genre in which, Shelley thinks, 'the connexion of poetry and social good is more observable ... than in whatever other form' (*A Defence of Poetry*, *SP&P* 521). Shelley thinks that the 'great specimens of the Athenian drama' are the 'most perfect in the kindred expressions of the poetical faculty,' making the fullest use of 'language, action, music, painting, the dance, and religious institution to produce a common effect in the representation of the highest idealisms of passion and of power' (*SP&P* 518). The scenic beauty of Italy where Shelley lived also contributes greatly to the lyrical drama. The poem was 'chiefly written upon the mountainous ruins of the Baths of Caracalla,' among 'the flowery glades, and thickets of odoriferous blossoming trees' that entwined with the 'immense platforms and dizzy arches suspended in the air,' and the 'bright blue sky of Rome,' and the effect and the new life of 'the vigorous awakening of spring in that divinest climate' were 'the inspiration of this drama' (preface to *Prometheus Unbound*, *SP&P* 207).

3. Two Mountaintop Experiences

It is important to note that the Indian Caucasus and the vale of Kashmir first appear in the play as 'desolate and frozen' places of banishment at the far end of the world (*Prometheus Unbound* 1.828). The 'far Indian vale' is the 'scene of her [Asia's] sad exile' (1.826, 827). This bleak landscape where Prometheus is chained shares nothing with the early-nineteenth-century European image of the Indian Caucasus as the site of the dawn of human civilization that embraces an earthly paradise in its bosom. Nor does the cold gloomy peak bear any resemblance to Mount Meru, a sacred mountain-paradise at the centre of the Hindu geography, which Francis Wilford identifies with the Indian Caucasus. Instead, the barren Indian mountain reflects the history of the Western invasion of India in which Prometheus's mountain prison was transferred to India.

Shelley is not the first to situate Prometheus's place of confinement in India; Arrian's *Anabasis Alexandri* introduced Eratosthenes's interpretation that 'the Macedonians' spread the rumour that 'a cave among the Parapamisadae' was 'Prometheus's cave, where he had been chained' and that 'the Macedonians transferred, in their account, Mount Caucasus from the Pontus ... towards India, and called Mount Parapamisus Mount Caucasus, all for the glory of Alexander' (2: 11). Prometheus was chained on the Georgian Caucasus by Jupiter and then the place of bondage as well as its name was transferred eastward to the Indian Caucasus to glorify Alexander's conquest of India. The history of invasion, however, goes further back; there is no obvious allusion to Alexander's Eastern expedition in *Prometheus Unbound*, but the play makes mention of 'Bacchic Nysa,' a city believed to have been founded by Dionysus in his expedition to India (3.3.154). Arrian says that when Alexander reached Nysa, he felt that he would 'go even farther' in 'rivalry with Dionysus' achievements' (2: 7). Arrian also refers to several writers who report Alexander's triumphant, militaristic marches 'in mimicry of the bacchic revelry of Dionysus' (2: 191). The original image of Dionysus's Eastern expedition, described in the opening scene of Euripides's *Bacchae*, is quite unmilitary, blending as it does the joys of wine with singing and dancing (1–167). Alexander's military conquest of India and his rivalry with Dionysus's vast Eastern progress, however, certainly changed the merrymaking image of the wine god's activities. For example, Nonnos's *Dionysiaca*, which Shelley ordered in December 1817 (*Letters* 1: 575, 585), depicts in detail the god's military conquest of India commanded by his father, Zeus.[11] The image of Dionysus as a military conqueror of the East is also seen in *Bell's New Pantheon* (1: 115). The barren Indian landscape in which Prometheus is held captive is where the Poet in 'Alastor' wanders, and where Dionysus came triumphant and Alexander ravaged at will. It is not difficult to see Shelley's criticism of the Western invasion of India in the gloomy image of Prometheus's mountain prison and the desolate vale of Kashmir in the opening scene.

The play begins with Prometheus's mountaintop experience. Alone on the barren precipice,[12] Prometheus addresses

> Monarch of Gods and Dæmons, and all Spirits
> But One, who throng those bright and rolling Worlds
> Which Thou and I alone of living things
> Behold with sleepless eyes! (*Prometheus Unbound* 1.1–4)

Shelley divides the transcendent presence that rules the world into two, the 'One' and the 'Monarch of Gods and Dæmons.' The former is the non-anthropomorphized 'One,' or Necessity, which Shelley has apprehended in 'Mont Blanc' and which appears as Demogorgon in the present play. The latter, which Prometheus is addressing, is the anthropomorphized 'Mighty God' or 'Almighty,' personified as Jupiter, the worst tyrant Western civilization has ever created (1.17, 18).

Prometheus's opening speech marks a significant reorientation in his response to the evil Almighty. Here Shelley makes a new use of Romantic theophanies on the mountaintop. Unlike Wordsworth and Coleridge, Shelley, speaking through Prometheus, does not want to be united with the Almighty, nor does he defy the Supreme Power as Byron did in the Alps. Prometheus tries to forego his hatred of the Power's 'ill tyranny' (1.19): 'Disdain? Ah no! I pity thee' (1. 53). At the same time, Prometheus also faces the 'Curse' he uttered when he was chained, and asks inanimate forms in nature – 'Mountains,' 'Springs,' 'Air,' and 'Whirlwinds' – what his 'Curse' was that has blighted the earth (1.58, 59, 62, 64, 66). The Indian mountain in act 1 appears as cold and intolerable as Mont Blanc, but the Asian peak answers Prometheus's enquiry in a way the European mountain would not do; instead of a terrible masculine deity, Mother Earth appears and sympathizes with Prometheus.

In order to recall and revoke the Curse that Prometheus used to destroy his enemy, the Earth advises him to meet his own image. The Indian Caucasus thus provides a place to meet the transcendent as well as one's own self. The visions of slaughter and bloodshed in human history that Prometheus sees on the mountain are at the extreme opposite to the rapturous bright theophanies that we associate with the first generation of Romantic poets. When the shadow of Jupiter is conjured up from among '[Prometheus's] own ghost, or the ghost of Jupiter, / Hades or Typhon, or what mightier Gods / From all-prolific Evil' and repeats Prometheus's Curse (1.211–13), it becomes clear that 'when Prometheus first spoke it he was, in a very real sense, Jupiter,' as he countered a wrong with another wrong, and that 'Prometheus [is] facing his own former self in Jupiter's ghost' (Wasserman, *Shelley* 259–60). The visions delivered as his torture by the Furies, Jupiter's servants, prove that it is Prometheus who founded European civilization as a 'city of death' ('Mont Blanc' 105). His fire, burning in an insatiable desire for conquest, turns arts of civilization into arts of slaughter: 'Many a million-peopled city / Vomits smoke in the bright air' (*Prometheus Unbound* 1.551–2). Even 'a disenchanted Nation,' which springs 'like day from desolation' and dedicates itself to truth, freedom, and love, is inevitably enmeshed in bloody civil wars and wars of conquest, and ends in 'the vintage-time for Death and Sin' (1.567–74).[13]

The dark visions Prometheus sees in the Indian Caucasus are the hardest part of his torment and a most terrible mountaintop experience, because it was Prometheus himself before he was chained to the Indian Caucasus who was 'the Oppressor of mankind' and brought to humanity terror, tyranny, and slaughter, and 'pain, pain ever, forever' (preface to *Prometheus Unbound*, *SP&P* 206; *Prometheus Unbound* 1.635). This is exactly the image of Prometheus that Rousseau uses to condemn 'the development of the sciences and arts' that 'has corrupted our morals' (2: 21). How could Prometheus's former self be recreated into the Prometheus of this play, who is 'the type of the highest perfection of moral and intellectual nature, impelled by the purest and the truest motives to the best and noblest ends' (preface to *Prometheus Unbound*, *SP&P* 207)? Shelley's answer is Prometheus's long-forgotten Eastern lover.

Prometheus's relinquishment of the Curse, his true liberation from his former self, and the recovery of the devastated Indian landscape are not possible without his long-forgotten Asia. The vale of Kashmir, when it first appears in the play, exhibits no trace of the earthly paradise it used to be, withered by Prometheus's Curse and left barren after he forgot Asia in the sufferings of his captivity. Panthea asks Prometheus: 'Hast thou forgotten one who watches thee / The cold dark night, and never sleeps but when / The shadow of thy spirit falls on her?' (*Prometheus Unbound* 1.821–3). The passage, which recalls the image of the Arab maiden in 'Alastor,' asks the Western self to correct its indifference to the real Eastern other. Remembering Asia is the first step in revoking the Curse and allowing the recovery of the world.

By remembering Asia, the founder of Western civilization realizes what he needs to refashion himself to be a bringer of true civilization: 'Asia! who when my being overflowed / Wert like a golden chalice to bright wine / Which else had sunk into the thirsty dust' (1.809–11). What is lacking in the Greek hero is supplied by his Eastern epipsyche. It is important to note that the epipsyche is recognized not as a mirror but as a being that is different from, but complementary to, the self. At the same time, however, the simile of Asia as a golden chalice that received Prometheus's overflowing being is, as Balachandra Rajan points out, 'uncomfortably close to the gendered imperialism of a set piece by Owenson' (154). Prometheus's memory of Asia as a chalice is said in the past tense. Now that he recognizes what enables him to relinquish the Curse is 'love,' which is a distinctly Eastern characteristic in the geographical division of roles and attributions between East and West, his relationship with Asia is to be changed from that expressed in the metaphor of pouring and receiving (*Prometheus Unbound* 1.824). Being remembered terminates Asia's 'sad exile,' which changes her from a chalice that passively receives Prometheus's spirit into an active spirit emanating 'the ether / Of her transforming presence' (1.827, 831–2). Their spirits, however, have to be 'mingled' (1.833). Otherwise, the vale of Kashmir, which is regenerated by Asia's essence, 'would fade,' and 'this ravine' where Prometheus is bound remain 'desolate and frozen' (1.832, 828). The regeneration of the earth cannot be accomplished by either Prometheus or Asia alone.

Prometheus's overflowing ether is conveyed to Asia by Panthea, to whom came two dreams, only one of which she remembered. In the dream she saw Prometheus's mental liberation: 'his pale, wound-worn limbs / Fell from Prometheus' (2.1.62–3). Then she felt his presence 'flow[ing] and mingl[ing]' through her blood till it became his life and his grew hers, and she could hear him calling Asia's name when her being was 'condensed' again (2.1.80, 86). This can be taken as sexual intercourse, and as Sharon Ruston discusses (112), invites comparison with Jupiter's account of his rape of Thetis, who cannot sustain the 'quick flames' of his 'penetrating presence' and '[l]ike him whom the Numidian seps did thaw / Into a dew with poison, is dissolved' (3.1.38, 39, 40–1). Ruston emphasizes the similarities between the two scenes and interprets Panthea's dream as 'the imposition of one principle of vitality on another' (112). I would rather stress the most important difference between the two scenes: the nature of Prometheus's presence, though quite similar to that of Jupiter, does not consume its object of desire with 'poison,' and Panthea is 'condensed' again (*Prometheus Unbound* 3.1.41, 2.1.86). Prometheus's 'life-blood,' though only half is transfused as Panthea receives only one dream, makes Panthea act as if she were a carrier of a contagious disease (2.1.105). She infuses it into her sister Ione through her 'parted lips' and their 'intertwining arms' (2.1.103, 106). The infusion of his 'life-blood' into Asia, however, is not immediate, but deferred. She first reads Prometheus's 'written soul,' which Panthea carries in her eyes as his dream (2.1.110). As Panthea is not able to accept the whole content of the dream, the dream takes the form of a sexual encounter, and Prometheus appears as if he were the resplendent dream figure in 'Alastor': in Panthea's dream what is emphasized in the 'immortal shape' is 'his soft and flowing limbs,' 'passion-parted lips,' and 'keen faint eyes,' from which love streams forth like 'vaporous fire' (2.1.72, 73, 74, 75). The figure in the dream appears differently in Asia's reading. Instead of a burning sexual fire issuing forth from his face and limbs, she sees 'a shade,' or 'a shape' which she recognizes as Prometheus: "tis He, arrayed / In the soft light of his own smiles which spread / Like radiance from the cloud-surrounded moon' (2.1.120–2). At this moment, Asia becomes Prometheus's epipsyche, and Prometheus her epipsyche. His 'written soul' in the dream becomes her soul within the soul, and she starts her journey to follow Panthea's 'other dream,' which departs from her and asks them to follow (2.1.110, 132). Although she, like the Poet in 'Alastor,' cries 'Prometheus, it is thou – depart not yet!' (2.1.123), her quest is not motivated by sexual desire but by the desire to liberate the other. It is only after Asia reads both dreams preserved in Panthea's eyes that Aisa 'link[s]' her hands with Panthea's and starts her quest (2.1.207).

Asia changes from a passive woman in her 'sad exile' in the vale of Kashmir to an active quester, going all the way with Panthea to a *'Pinnacle of Rock among Mountains'* (*SP&P* 243). Panthea describes the peak:

> Hither the sound has borne us – to the realm
> Of Demogorgon, and the mighty portal,
> Like a Volcano's meteor-breathing chasm,
> Whence the oracular vapour is hurled up
> Which lonely men drink wandering in their youth
> And call truth, virtue, love, genius or joy –
> That maddening wine of life, whose dregs they drain
> To deep intoxication, and uplift
> Like Mænads who cry loud, Evoe! Evoe!
> The voice which is contagion to the world.   (*Prometheus Unbound* 2.3.1–10)

As Panthea's account of the oracular vapour suggests, it is not the fierce force of nature that alarms her.[14] She is uneasy with the place's haunting memory of Bacchus's Indian conquest, in which the Maenads' 'Evoe! Evoe!' resounded over the mountains (2.3.9). The priestesses of Bacchus were originally 'a troop of bold, enthusiastic women, who attended Bacchus in his expedition to the Indies, and materially contributed to his conquests' (Bell 1: 115). The 'oracular vapour,' which is likened to the 'maddening wine of life' whose 'deep intoxication' is a 'contagion to the world' (*Prometheus Unbound* 2.3.4, 7, 8, 10), not only evokes the inspired dancers but also recalls Dionysus's use of wine in his Indian conquest described in Nonnos; the Indians, upon drinking the god's wine, 'went mad,' 'struck up a dance,' and after the 'wild revel' fell asleep to be 'at the mercy of Dionysos and his weak women' (Nonnos 2: 41). The 'maddening wine of life' looks back to Prometheus's simile of himself as a wine, and the Poet in 'Alastor' may be one of those 'lonely men' who drink it while 'wandering in their youth' and call it 'truth, virtue, love, genius or joy.' The effect of the vapour, however, is nullified by the scene Asia views from the mountain. Asia tells her sister to see the view the mountain offers before the vapour 'dim[s]' her brain (*Prometheus Unbound* 2.3.18).

The volcanic summit in the Indian Caucasus, which is the '[f]it throne for such a Power! Magnificent!,' is strongly contrasted to the icy precipice where Prometheus is bound, the snow-capped Alps which offers a site that leads to deities – whether Christian or pagan, benevolent or evil – and the Indian mountain described as a sacred place of Indian religion by Europeans (2.3.11). In Thomas Maurice's *Indian Antiquities or Dissertations of Hindostan* (1793–1800), the Indian Caucasus, with the vale of Kashmir as 'a proper residence for the austere sect of the Saivites,' is presented as sublime but gloomy. Maurice, describing those mountains 'covered with eternal snow' and 'ris[ing] one above the other in a style of horrid grandeur' as an Eastern counterpart of Mont Blanc, thinks that 'the mind of the Hindoo, intimidated by the grand and majestic objects with which he is encircled, should be the sport of superstitious terrors'; 'human nature may well shudder' at and 'human fortitude may be well staggered' by the mountains 'most stupendous in height and the most rugged in form' (5: 433–4). Shelley's Indian peak is neither the heathen Mountain Gloom as Maurice describes nor an Indian counterpart of the European Mountain Glory. On the high peak that looks down on the vale of Kashmir, Asia maps the world differently. The prospect from the mountain draws her breathless admiration for the sublunary earth, even if it may be only the 'shadow of some Spirit lovelier still' and 'evil [should] stain its work' (*Prometheus Unbound* 2.3.13, 14). Asia's mountaintop experience is not the appreciation of the manifestation of a deity, but the acceptance of the earth and all creations as 'weak yet beautiful' (2.3.15). Her view affirms Shelley's faith in human creative power and his wish to 'make this Earth, our home, more beautiful' with humanity's reclaiming hands (*The Revolt of Islam* 5.2254), a wish he first expressed in *Queen Mab*.

Shelley repeatedly organizes the geography of a place with a method borrowed from the prospect poem, hoping to discover an ideal place, but he never fails to find traces of bloodshed, tyranny, and false religion.[15] Here, however, we have a most beautiful and comprehensive prospect from the mountaintop, which counters nature's cold city of death on Mont Blanc, showing the beauty of the earth at dawn and anticipating the renewal of the earth. Asia says:

> Beneath is a wide plain of billowy mist,
> As a lake, paving in the morning sky,
> With azure waves which burst in silver light,
> Some Indian vale ... Behold it, rolling on
> Under the curdling winds, and islanding
> The peak whereon we stand – midway, around
> Encinctured by the dark and blooming forests,
> Dim twilight lawns and stream-illumed caves
> And wind-inchanted shapes of wandering mist;   (2.3.19–27)

The sea of mist under the high mountain reminds us of Wordsworth's Snowdon episode, the quintessential mountaintop vision experienced by the Romantics.[16] Shelley, however, gives an epiphanic moment not to a male European poet but to a female Asian spirit standing on the Indian peak, presenting a new version of the mountaintop experience. He leads Asia not to a natural supernaturalism in which the self is borne up to the transcendent, but to a full-hearted affirmation of earthly things as they exist.

The high white mountains that characterize the geography of the East counter Mont Blanc in many respects. Whereas the cold European summit flatly rejects 'feeble' human beings and freezes the world by perpetually flinging 'a flood of ruin' ('Mont Blanc' 7, 107), in the East 'the keen sky-cleaving mountains / From icy spires of sunlike radiance fling / The dawn' (*Prometheus Unbound* 2.3.28–30). A coming avalanche, associating nature's tremendous force with the infinite power of the human mind, anticipates a great change both in the natural and human worlds:

> – Hark! the rushing snow!
> The sun-awakened avalanche! whose mass,
> Thrice sifted by the storm, had gathered there
> Flake after flake, in Heaven-defying minds
> As thought by thought is piled, till some great truth
> Is loosened, and the nations echo round
> Shaken to their roots: as do the mountains now.   (2.3.36–42)

As Cian Duffy argues, this passage employs an 'explicitly sublime natural phenomenon' as 'a figure for *gradual* political change, that is, as a figure for an ideological rather than a violent revolution' (*Shelley and the Revolutionary Sublime* 174). Unlike the glaciers of Mont Blanc, which are '[s]low rolling on' to destroy the whole world ('Mont Blanc' 102), the snows that descend on the summit roll down to invite the nations to awaken.

While the famous European peak boasts of its highest position in the West, the summit where Asia stands and views the world is known only as a *'Pinnacle of Rock among Mountains'* (*SP&P* 243). Its namelessness suggests its marginal location and Shelley's strategy of recreating the world from the periphery. The peak, which commands a magnificent view of India, is certainly influenced by Mount Meru, the sacred centre of the world in Indian mythology that was identified with the Indian Caucasus by Wilford. Shelley's Indian mountain, however, does not claim to be the centre of the world. What is more, this peak is Shelley's imaginary creation, fusing Eastern and Western elements; it owes as much to Mount Vesuvius as to Mount Meru.[17] Shelley climbed Mount Vesuvius on 16 December 1818 and was impressed by its 'tremendous & irresistible strength' (*Letters* 2: 62). While Mount Meru is not a volcano, the pinnacle, out of whose 'Volcano's meteor-breathing chasm' gushes out 'the oracular vapour,' resembles the summit of Mount Vesuvius in the midst of which 'stands the conical hill from which the volumes of smoke & the fountains of liquid fire are rolled forth forever' (*Prometheus Unbound* 2.3.3, 4; *Letters* 2: 62). When he visited Pompeii two days later, Shelley saw Vesuvius dominate the Italian scene: 'the single summit of Vesuvius [was] rolling forth volumes of thick white smoke,' and its 'subterranean thunder' and 'distant deep peals' seemed to 'shake the very air & light of day which interpenetrated our frames with the sullen & tremendous sound' (*Letters* 2: 73). The actual and the imaginary, the West and the East, merge to form a great mountain on which Asia is shown the beauty and strength of earthly things.

It is not only the nameless Indian peak that is the product of hybridization between East and West. The whole scene reflects hybridity. Asia, viewing the Indian landscape from the summit as an English Romantic poet might, proceeds to converse with the invisible Power, the 'One pervading,' 'the Eternal, the Immortal' residing in the mountain (*Prometheus Unbound* 2.3.79, 95), an experience which clearly develops out of Shelley's own Mont Blanc experience. Geographical binary oppositions between East and West are broken down when this Eastern female spirit takes over Shelley's unanswered questions on Mont Blanc. The Mont Blanc scene is, however, completely reconstructed and reversed in the Eastern scene. The unseen Power on the white summit of the European mountain is transferred to the 'ebon throne' deep down beneath the volcano in India and appears as 'a mighty Darkness / Filling the seat of power' (2.4.1, 2–3). Instead of soaring to an invisible height, Asia goes to 'the Deep, to the Deep, / Down, Down,' through the volcanic crater, the 'mighty portal' of Demogorgon's cave, to the Power's underworld realm (2.3.54–5, 2). Unlike the European poet whose imagination was dazzled by the flight to the invisible Power and who was overwhelmed by the cold sublimity of the mountain, Asia is not affected by falling the length of the chasm, nor does she hesitate to ask questions of 'Demogorgon, a tremendous Gloom' (1.207).

The dialogue between the subject and the unseen Power becomes cosmopolitan with the addition of Asia and Demogorgon. There are two inquiring spirits, male and female, who represent Europe and Asia respectively, and two unseen Powers, the classical tyrant-god in heaven and the much more ancient invisible presence under the Indian Caucasus. Like Shelley, who had to read and interpret the 'mysterious tongue' of the mountain ('Mont Blanc' 76), Asia has to interpret Demogorgon's language, which does not belong to this world. When she arrives at Demogorgon's cave, Asia is still caught in the same mental state that Prometheus was in prior to his internal liberation. She too wants the name of the one who 'made terror, madness, crime, remorse' and 'Hell' so that 'curses shall drag him down' (*Prometheus Unbound* 2.4.19, 28, 30). Demogorgon's unintelligible statements on 'God,' referring to the non-anthropomorphized principle of the world rather than to a personified deity, however, lead Asia to change the way she sees the world (2.4.8).

Unlike the unseen Power on Mont Blanc, whose cold eternity has nothing to do with humanity and who does not answer Shelley's questions, Demogorgon gives Asia an opportunity to review Western history. It is here in the Indian underground cave and by Asia, Prometheus's geographical other, that the history of Western civilization founded by a mythical fire-bringer and ruled by Jupiter is reinterpreted. The evils and vices, for which Prometheus was bitterly indicted by the Furies in act 1, are now attributed to Jupiter. With Jupiter's reign, '[f]irst famine and then toil and then disease, / Strife, wounds, and ghastly death unseen before, / Fell' on humankind (2.4.50–2). Although Prometheus 'tamed' fire, which is 'like some beast of prey / Most terrible, but lovely,' for humans fire is still a double-edged weapon; when used 'beneath / The frown of man,' it 'tortured to his will / Iron and gold, the slaves and signs of power, / And gems and poisons, and all subtlest forms / Hidden beneath the mountains and the waves' (2.4.66, 66–7, 67–8, 68–71). Moreover, '[s]cience,' a symbol of European intellect, 'struck the thrones of Earth and Heaven,' though they 'fell not' (2.4.74, 75). The misuse of fire by humans is pointed out, and Prometheus is seen as giving to humans 'alleviations' of their miseries (2.4.98).

Asia, still looking for an answer that can 'repeal / Large codes of fraud and woe' ('Mont Blanc' 80–1), is not sure whether a ruler can be a slave at the same time, to which Demogorgon answers that '[a]ll spirits are enslaved which serve things evil' and that 'the deep truth is imageless' (2.4.110, 116). Here, part of 'strange truths' is revealed as a reinterpretation of Western history, while another part of them, which is Demogorgon's truth, is, like Demogorgon himself, 'imageless' and 'a voice / Is wanting' (2.4.115–16). Earlier in 1811, when reading Owenson's *Missionary*, Shelley considered the relationship between truth, imagelessness, and inaudibility: 'I was against it [personification of a divinity] for the sake of truth' (*Letters* 1: 101). He also said that 'virtue's voice is almost inaudible, yet it shakes upon the brain, upon the heart' (1: 101). In 1816 Shelley thought that Mont Blanc had 'a voice' 'not understood / By all, but which the wise, and great, and good / Interpret, or make felt, or deeply feel' ('Mont Blanc' 80, 81–3). In *Prometheus Unbound*, before partly answering Asia's questions (which are Shelley's as well), Demogorgon adds: 'If the Abysm / Could vomit forth its secrets' (2.4.114–15). These secrets cannot be visualized nor heard as 'the deep truth is imageless' and 'a voice / Is wanting' (2.4.115–16), but they can be felt upon the heart, interpreted, and deeply understood upon the brain through the dialogue between Asia and Demogorgon, which enables Asia to gain what she has lacked, the unseen, inaudible, and strange 'truths' that disentangle divinity and power from knowledge (2.4.122). When the true knowledge about history and the deep, imageless truth about the non-anthropomorphized power behind the revolving universe are added to what she knows by intuition – love – Asia liberates herself, and like Prometheus in act 1, she is able to choose 'eternal Love' over the curse (2.4.120).

4. The Geography of Love

Although both Prometheus and Asia are led through dialogue with the others to choose Love over the Curse, it is Asia's experience, not that of Prometheus, which physically initiates the golden age. If one sees the climax of the play in the fall of Jupiter, Asia's acquisition of European knowledge, which leads to the dethronement of Jupiter, can be considered as a version of Bhabha's mimicry. At the same time, however, one might be disappointed that the strategy of mimicry does not function as it should; Demogorgon as a deus ex machina drags Jupiter to Hell; Asia does not overturn the power relations between East and West but merely strengthens Western hegemony by contributing to Prometheus's 'Victory' and 'Empire' (4.578). Indeed, the ambivalence of the coming Promethean Age is seen in these words, 'Victory' and 'Empire,' as Prometheus's relinquishment of the Curse cannot be announced without using the language of despotism and imperialism. Although Prometheus does not reign but instead withdraws into a cave with Asia after his liberation, a voice is still wanting which can articulate Prometheus's renouncement of the Curse and his retirement from the world in their proper terms. Thus, as Karen Weisman says, from 'the deep truth' that is 'imageless,' 'we learn of the inherent inefficacy of our metaphors and myths, and so, like Asia, we also learn both the danger of and the inescapable need and compulsion for interpretation, in the terms of what we do claim as knowable' (95). Within this limitation, Shelley makes the geographical other find and speak strange truths, and seeks the realization of multiple idealisms after Jupiter's reign. That is why there are still two more acts after Asia's revelation.

The 'beautiful idealisms' of *Prometheus Unbound* begin to be realized with the final scene of act 2, where Asia comes back from Demogorgon's realm (preface to *Prometheus Unbound*, *SP&P* 209). The arrival of the second golden world, which results from the 'mingling' of Asia's and Prometheus's presence, from the hybridization of Western and Eastern elements, is celebrated in song by all creations in the utopian world. First, Asia's inner liberation is outwardly shown by her transfiguration on *'the Top of a snowy Mountain'* (*SP&P* 252). Panthea recalls the day Asia was born; she stood '[w]ithin a veined shell, which floated on' among 'the Ægean isles, and by the shores / Which bear thy name,' and the love that burst from her 'illumined Earth and Heaven / And the deep ocean and the sunless caves, / And all that dwells within them' (*Prometheus Unbound* 2.5.23, 25–6, 28–30). While Panthea's remark draws upon the classical birth of Venus Aphrodite, Asia's Eastern identity does remain under her name. Her voyage in a shell among 'the Ægean isles' and by the shores of Asian countries reminds us of Lemprière's account of gradual expansion of the area called Asia as well as Baudet's remark on the hybrid origin of Greek civilization, which 'was born in Asia': 'although the Greeks shaped the

European spirit by opposing Asia, they were nevertheless oriented toward Asia' (Baudet 4–5).

By recasting a minor Oceanid into a great radiant goddess of love and beauty who aligns herself with Aphrodite/Venus, Shelley distances a transfigured Asia from the stereotypical Western images of the female East. She is elevated above sensuous Eastern women such as Cleopatra, Owenson's Luxima, or Shelley's own veiled maid in 'Alastor.' She also shares nothing with Keats's exotic and gloomy Asia, who was 'born of most enormous Caf' and whose face was 'dusky' and 'not so fair'; who leaned on the tusk of an elephant, 'prophesying of her glory' and 'in her wide imagination stood / Palm-shaded temples, and high rival fanes, / By Oxus or in Ganges' sacred isles' ('Hyperion: A Fragment' 2.53–63). Neither can she be identified with the political icon of the distressed woman of the ravaged East.[18] *Bell's New Pantheon* refers to a relief on which a goddess bearing the name of the Eastern continent 'appears in deep distress for the sufferings and desolation of her people' at 'the destruction of that city [Troy]' by the early Greeks (1: 98). The sad woman exiled in the far Indian vale in act 1 becomes a female quester following the dream of her lover in order to deliver him, and his liberation transforms her into a radiant goddess on an Indian mountaintop filling the world with the light of love.

Asia as Love, who gives her 'sympathy' to 'the whole world,' acquires the image of the world's mother, a role attributed to Lakshmi but not to the Western goddesses of love and beauty (*Prometheus Unbound* 2.5.34). In Sir William Jones's 'A Hymn to Lacshmí,' the goddess appears as the 'world great mother' and '[a]ll nature glow'd, whene'er she smil'd or blush'd' (6: 359).[19] The radiant figure of selfless maternal love on the Indian Caucasus, which embraces the whole world gently and indiscriminately, is what Shelley needs to counter the unseen Power on Mont Blanc and its mechanical operation of the world. Asia and the Spirit of the Earth in the form of a winged child who calls her 'Mother' crystallize the image of universal love in the second golden world (*Prometheus Unbound* 3.4.24), an image Shelley had been working on since *Queen Mab*, whose utopian vision sees a human baby 'before his mother's door, / Sharing his morning's meal / With the green and golden basilisk' (8.84–6). In *The Revolt of Islam*, the Statue of Love on the great pyramid is presented as a 'Woman sitting on the sculptured disk / Of the broad earth, and feeding from one breast / A human babe and a young basilisk' (5.2161–3). A human baby and a basilisk in the earlier poems are united into a hybrid spirit, the Spirit of the Earth, in the form of a child in *Prometheus Unbound*; its forehead emits a 'tyrant-quelling' light like 'a green star' whose 'emerald beams' are 'twined with its fair hair' (4.272; 3.4.3, 4).

How does love work in recreating the world after Prometheus's liberation? Shelley describes love's universality and borderlessness as love's 'infection,' so to speak, in an interesting medical/ecological way. Asia infuses love into the air on the snow-capped mountain, and 'the air we breathe is Love' (2.5.95). The first thing Prometheus does after his liberation and reunion with Asia is to kiss the old and sick 'Mother Earth' into renewal (3.3.84). In act 2, scene 1, we have seen Prometheus's ether transmitted to Ione and Asia via Panthea. The infection here, however, is immediate and global. The Earth cries in exultation:

> Thy lips are on me, and their touch runs down
> Even to the adamantine central gloom
> Along these marble nerves – 'tis life, 'tis joy,
> And through my withered, old and icy frame
> The warmth of an immortal youth shoots down
> Circling.   (3.3.85–90)

In act 1, Prometheus told Mother Earth of his decision not to utter any curse again: 'Mother, let not aught / Of that which may be evil, pass again / My lips' (1.218–20). His lips, which have withered the Earth, now revitalize her. The Earth grows young again just as when Prometheus was born from her bosom as the warm life-giving force that regenerates the whole globe: '[j]oy ran, as blood within a living frame,' from her 'stony veins' to the last fibre of thin leaves of the trees trembling in 'the frozen air' (1.153–6). Phrases, such as the 'old and icy frame' and 'stony veins' (3.3.88, 1.153), remind us of Mont Blanc, whose 'frozen blood' forever circulates slowly through his 'stony veins' (*Letters* 1: 500). Here Prometheus's power can infuse joy and energy into the cold veins of the Earth.

Prometheus's healing kisses may be seen as a kind of royal touch on a global scale,[20] but they also spread a contagious, though benign, disease. We remember that the same lips have uttered the Curse, which infected the Earth, inducing her own curse, 'the contagion of a mother's hate' (*Prometheus Unbound* 1.178). The Earth's contagion afflicted the whole world with all kinds of natural catastrophes – floods, famine, and plague – making her 'wan' and 'dry' (1.176). Maddened by

Prometheus's pain, the Earth released in anguish the 'oracular' breath from a 'Cavern' – the same 'oracular vapour' gushing out from Demogorgon's 'mighty portal' – which in turn maddened people and made them 'oracular' (3.3.128, 124, 2.3.4, 2). Those who inhaled her contagious vapour 'lured / The erring nations round to mutual war / And faithless faith,' filling the human world with 'shrieks of slaughter' (3.3.128–30, 1.80). Prometheus's power is a 'contagion to the world,' whether it overflows as the 'bright wine' of love or as 'maddening wine' whose 'dregs' mislead not only ambitious tyrants but even 'lonely men' in 'their youth' into the path of evil (2.3.10, 1. 810, 2. 3.7, 5). It is Asia's presence that transforms his emanation from a curse into love.

As in the revival of the vale of Kashmir in act 1, to revitalize the sick, withered world it is necessary that Prometheus's and Asia's essences be mingled. Infection and mingling are the keys to global renewal. The sources of contagion, Prometheus and Asia, are spreading love by air and by touch. John Barrell discusses the interaction between East and West in terms of the process of inoculation against disease, demonstrating how De Quincey fears the Oriental infection and 'cancerous' kisses that intrude into his Western body (De Quincey 109). In *Prometheus Unbound*, however, we see a completely different use of 'contagion' in the relationship between East and West. It is not the East but the West (Prometheus) that acted as a virulent disease, ravaging the earth as far as the vale of Kashmir. In this respect, Prometheus's Curse represents the Western invasion of the East as Occidental infection, or, worse still, as it devastated the whole globe, it represents the 'venomed exhalations' of the globalizing power of the British Empire that dart '[l]ike subtle poison through the bloodless veins' of the societies and afflict the world with 'all-polluting luxury and wealth' (*Queen Mab* 4.84, 106, 8.180). What is important here, however, is that the Eastern infection, love, finds its way into the Western intellect to counter the Western curse. Moreover, Europe's reception of Eastern love enables Prometheus's power to become universal love, which is a kind of supergerm that carries a good influence whose process of infection nothing can resist.

Love as infection cancels boundaries of class, race, and nation, mingling self and other, just as pollution and contagious diseases cross these boundaries. In the Spirit of the Hour's report on 'the haunts and dwellings of mankind,' thrones are now 'kingless,' and people are '[e]qual, unclassed, tribeless, and nationless' (*Prometheus Unbound* 3.4.127, 131, 195). In contrast to the kisses of the Oriental other De

Quincey fears, love's infection spreads to heal and cure. It does not hesitate to touch the sick and the ugly. Prometheus kisses the sick, ugly Earth, and Earth's breath rises with 'a serener light and crimson air' (3.3.133). Asia's love, like the warm beams of the sun, penetrates and illuminates 'Earth and Heaven' and 'all that dwells within them' (2.5.28, 30). The atmosphere replete with love touches and cures ugly human beings all over the globe. They are transformed, being liberated not only from tyranny but also from their own evil. The change is shown by the falling off of the deformed self-image, which is exactly opposite to what happened to the Poet in 'Alastor,' who, terror-stricken, encountered his treacherous image reflected on the fountain. Here the sky becomes a great reflecting and reforming mirror on which human nature is reflected. The Spirit of the Earth reports that the 'ugly human shapes and visages' fell off and '[p]ast floating through the air, and fading still / Into the winds that scattered them,' and that those humans after 'some foul disguise had fallen' seemed 'mild and lovely' (3.4.65–70). In the universal celebration of the second golden world, humanity is compared to a leprous child who is cured by healing springs and returns healthy to his mother (4.388–93).

The Romantic geography of *Prometheus Unbound* is a geography of love. For the first time in Shelley's writing fire is not associated with destruction. A recreated Eastern goddess of love spreads 'love' like 'the atmosphere / Of the sun's fire filling the living world' and a Greek fire-bringer is unbound as a bringer of love and regeneration, his kisses and breath revivifying the decaying earth and turning even the rigid volcanic crater into a 'green heaven' (2.5.26–7, 3.3.40). In a prologue scene set in Argolis, Greece, in *The Revolt of Islam*, Laon envisions himself arising like 'a sulphurous hill' that 'on a sudden from its snows has shaken / The swoon of ages,' and bursts and fills the world with 'cleansing fire' amid the 'rocking earthquake' (2.785–90). The human Prometheus's 'cleansing fire' is a revival of the 'sea / Of fire' that Shelley imagined to have enveloped the primary Alpine mountains, but his fire cannot recreate the earth after burning the world to ashes (*The Revolt of Islam* 2. 788, 'Mont Blanc' 73–4).[21] Writing to Peacock about his first impression of Vesuvius, Shelley says: 'Vesuvius is, after the glaciers the most impressive expression of the energies of nature I ever saw' (*Letters* 2: 62). It was neither 'the overpowering magnificence, nor above all the radiant beauty of the glaciers,' but 'their character of tremendous & irresistible strength' that attracted Shelley's attention (2: 62). Shelley saw, many thousands of years after the 'sea / Of fire' took place ('Mont Blanc' 73–4), its most recent Italian counterpart: 'This plain was once a sea of liquid fire' (*Letters* 2: 62). A 'vast stream of hardened lava, which is an actuall image of the waves of the sea changed into hard black stone by enchantment,' is described in a similar way in which Shelley depicted the glaciers in 1816: 'The lines of the boiling fluid seem to hang retarded in the air & it is difficult to believe that the billows which seem hurrying down upon you are not actually in motion ... The lava like the glacier creeps on perpetually with a crackling sound as of suppressed fire ... & in one place it gushes precipito[us]ly over a high crag, rolling down the half melted rocks & its own burning waves; a cataract of quivering fire' (2:62–3). The tremendous energies of Vesuvius are transferred to the Indian Caucasus, but they do not destroy the world with burning waves. The volcanic force of the Indian Caucasus, being combined with love, does not wrap the world with devastating lava.[22] It is neither a sea of destructive fire nor an icy 'flood of ruin' ('Mont Blanc' 107), but a sea of love, which envelops the world when Demogorgon rises from the depth of the Indian Caucasus in the final act to celebrate the union of Prometheus and Asia:

> a mighty Power, which is as Darkness,
> Is rising out of Earth, and from the sky
> Is showered like Night, and from within the air
> Bursts, like eclipse which had been gathered up
> Into the pores of sunlight – the bright Visions
> Wherein the singing spirits rode and shone
> Gleam like pale meteors through a watery night.
> (*Prometheus Unbound* 4.510–16)

The second flood the mighty Power brings is a flood of bright visions that sing and celebrate the arrival of the utopian world.

Unlike the unseen Power in 'Mont Blanc,' which never makes its appearance nor answers Shelley's questions, Demogorgon affirms the possibility of humanity's reclaiming hand. While the 'singing spirits' are celebrating the union of Prometheus and Asia (4.515), Demogorgon describes an internalized geography of the Promethean Age, drawing a new map of the human heart where Prometheus as Wisdom and Asia as Love are united. The craggy, cold mountain at the end of the world, which represents Prometheus's inner landscape in Act 1, is now transformed into a mountain-shaped 'wise heart' from which love arises and 'folds over the world its healing wings' (4.558, 561). Love has to climb patiently all the way up the 'slippery, steep / And narrow verge of crag-like Agony' (4.559–60); this is what Prometheus has done internally and Asia externally in the play.

5. Cities and Ruins

In *Prometheus Unbound*, the arrival of the second golden age revives the pristine happiness that was enjoyed in ancient days. Accordingly, with the reunion of Prometheus and Asia, some legendary cities are restored from the past. A most significant example is '*the Island Atlantis*,' which re-emerges from under the sea immediately after Jupiter's fall (*SP&P* 257). All that is known about this island-city comes from two of Plato's dialogues, the *Timaeus* and the *Critias*. Plato says that the island was 'opposite' the strait called 'the Pillars of Hercules' and that it was 'larger than Libya [Africa] and Asia combined' (*Timaeus and Critias* 37). The 'Pillars of Hercules' are the two points of land bordering the Strait of Gibraltar, a boundary of the known world at that time. According to Plato, this great island kingdom is said to have been suddenly submerged beneath the sea by a deluge nine thousand years before Solon's time,[23] which dates the island-city as more than eleven thousand years old.

The location of Atlantis had been discussed widely since the Middle Ages. Although the myth of Atlantis was well known, the island did not appear on any of the medieval maps that also included legendary places such as the Garden of Eden and the kingdom of Prester John.[24] Three different interpretations of the myth developed. After the European discovery of America in 1492, scholars began connecting Atlantis and America by way of biblical history. Thomas Taylor, in his translation of Plato published in 1804, interprets the island as 'that which we call America,' but adds that Plato's dating of Atlantis contradicts 'the generally-received opinion respecting the antiquity of the world,' that is, biblical chronology (*Works of Plato* 2: 434, 573). On the other hand, during the Enlightenment, there arose a new nationalistic view of Atlantis, which Pierre Vidal-Naquet calls 'a national Atlantis' ('Atlantis and the Nations' 321). This is a version of the European search for their origins, in which nations claimed positions of primacy at the beginning of civilization by considering themselves as heirs to Atlantis.[25] In comparative mythology, the linkage between the Indian Caucasus and Atlantis, which Shelley might have known, was explored. Jean Sylvain Bailly writes that the Atlantide descended on the summit of the Indian Caucasus after the Deluge in his *Lettres sur l'Atlantide de Platon et sur l'ancienne histoire de l'Asie* (1779), which, translated into English as *Letters upon the Atlantis of Plato* in 1801, influenced Keats's invention of Asia's parentage in Caf (Hungerford 146). Francis Wilford combines comparative mythology with a nationalistic Atlantis theme in 'An Essay on the Sacred Isles in the West, with Other Essays Connected with That Work.' Comparing Greek and Indian texts, he interprets the sacred white isles in the West in Hindu myth as Atlantis and identifies the isles with England and Ireland, giving his native country the status of a paradise in the west in the ancient world. His identification was well known even before the essay was published. It was sufficiently prevalent, and George Stanley Faber had a section on it in *The Origin of Pagan Idolatry* (1816) (1: 392–401).[26]

The appearance of Atlantis emphasizes the importance of marginality and remoteness in Shelley's world map. It is one of those 'many-peopled continents' and '[f]ortunate isles' (*Prometheus Unbound* 3.2.22, 23), strongly recalling an ancient metropolis that prospered more than ten thousand years earlier in the far west in *Queen Mab* (2.182–203). The antediluvian city, which only leaves its remains in the waste in *Queen Mab*, is restored as the redeemed Atlantis from beyond biblical history. Shelley's island-city is not related to any of the three interpretations of the Atlantis myth. It does not resonate with contemporary revolutionary movements in North and Central America, or 'a national Atlantis.'[27] While in Wilford's view of the world his home country occupies a central position in the world both in ancient and modern times, Shelley's Atlantis appears on the margin, far from Britain or the Indian Caucasus.

What is most important, however, is that Shelley does not represent the island as a belligerent seafaring nation, as does Plato. In the *Works of Plato* translated by Thomas Taylor, it was a 'mighty warlike power' that from the Atlantic Ocean 'spread itself with hostile fury over all Europe and Asia' (2: 469). Blake reincarnates Plato's imperial warlike power in both Britain and America, seeing Atlantis as a dubious achievement in *America: A Prophecy* (1793) (plate 10: 5–11) and *A Descriptive Catalogue* (1809) (number 5: 'The Ancient Britons').[28] After the overthrow of Napoleon, seafaring Britain emerged as Europe's chief power; its image could be likened to Plato's great imperial sea power. Shelley criticizes the great warlike power of the centre as does Blake, but in a different way. In *Prometheus Unbound*, no connection is implied between Britain and the island that rises after Jupiter's fall. Moreover, the peaceful island and the calm sea with 'fair ships' embody a powerful critique not only of Plato's imperial sea power but also of contemporary Britain (*Prometheus Unbound* 3.2.25). The Ocean reports the abolition of naval battles and the slave trade: ships are '[t]racking their path no more by blood and groans / And desolation, and the mingled voice / Of slavery and command' (3.2.29–31).

Atlantis is not, however, the final destination of Prometheus and Asia. Shelley tries to restore another city in the 'far goal of Time,' which is located 'beyond the peak / Of Bacchic Nysa, Mænad-haunted mountain, / And beyond Indus, and its tribute rivers' (3.3.174, 153–5). It has two important places: the Cave and the Temple of Prometheus. The former refers to the cave of Prometheus near Bamiyan, which was considered to be the site of Eden by Wilford ('On Mount Caucasus' 495), and the latter refers to the annual celebration of Prometheus as a fire-bringer in Athens (Hungerford 196–204). Their coexistence suggests Shelley's wish to have both an Indian earthly paradise and an ideal Greek city in a place where Prometheus and Asia will build a new human civilization. What is striking is that despite its classical Greek features, the Temple of Prometheus is hybrid:

[The Temple is] Distinct with column, arch and architrave
And palm-like capital, and overwrought,
And populous most with living imagery –
Praxitelean shapes, whose marble smiles
Fill the hushed air with everlasting love. (*Prometheus Unbound* 3.3.162–6)

As Frederic S. Colwell details, the 'palm-like' capitals associate the architecture with 'Egypt or the east,' and an 'arch' aligns it with 'Rome, the east, or the Renaissance' ('Figures in a Promethean Landscape' 126).[29] The 'marble smiles' of 'Praxitelean shapes' are also a curious mixture of the stern Greek sculptures and the soft smiles of Eastern figures (*Prometheus Unbound* 3.3.165). Colwell's comment is worth citing: 'The temple is, like the union of Prometheus and Asia, a fusion of east and west; as relics of the golden age, the enigmatic smiles adorning it antedate the classical west' ('Figures in a Promethean Landscape' 127).

From the Earth's speech about the final goal 'beyond the peak / Of Bacchic Nysa, Mænad-haunted mountain, / And beyond Indus and its tribute rivers,' Prometheus's and Asia's destination can be also taken as the Georgian Caucasus, recreating the place where Aeschylus's Prometheus compromises with Zeus and where the Poet in 'Alastor' dies in despair (*Prometheus Unbound* 3.3.153–5). We, however, do not have to decide whether this 'far goal of Time' is in India, Greece, or the Georgian Caucasus (3.3.174). It could be anywhere in the world, as the description of the Temple of Prometheus, which is 'deserted now' but whose image 'ever lies' in 'the windless and chrystalline pool' (3.3.167, 160, 159), has its origin in an ancient civilization in the secret valley of Bethzatanai, Lebanon, in *The Assassins* (1814–15). In the prose fragment, the 'mountains of everlasting snow' conceal the 'fertile valley,' where the 'men of elder days' accomplished the 'profoundest miracles' of '[t]he human spirit and the human hand,' and where there was a temple 'dedicated to the God of knowledge and of truth': 'Piles of monumental marble and fragments of columns that in their integrity almost seemed the work of some intelligence more sportive and fantastic than the gross conceptions of mortality lay in heaps beside the lake and were visible beneath its transparent waves' (*Prose* 126–7). The Temple and Cave of Prometheus and the recreated Atlantis represent the emergence of a multifaceted peaceful new centre in the world.

While act 3 glimpses the revival of ancient cities, act 4, the final act, gives a detailed report of what has become in the Promethean Age of the evil civilizations of past and present, just before the love-duet of the Earth and the Moon begins. Going further back in geological time, Shelley presents his version of the history of the earth as an extraordinary vision of subterranean geography revealed under the 'tyrant-quelling' light of the Spirit of the Earth (*Prometheus Unbound* 4.272). The beams of light shooting from the Spirit pierce into the interior of the earth and first show inorganic and mineral strata:

> Infinite mine of adamant and gold,
> Valueless stones and unimagined gems,
> And caverns on chrystalline columns poised
> With vegetable silver overspread. (4.280–3)

Those precious substances are concealed deep in the earth beyond reach of humans, unlike those in Asia's account of human history in Demogorgon's cave that were 'tortured' beneath the 'frown of man' and became 'the slaves and signs of power' (2.4.68, 69). In 'Mont Blanc,' geological features of the primary mountains reveal no trace of humanity, but here beneath the most ancient geological strata are hidden 'the melancholy ruins / Of cancelled cycles' (4.288–9). The beams lay bare the relics of the vanished civilization at the core of the earth. The relics are of 'dead Destruction, ruin within ruin!' (4.295), and the wrecks, all of which are military – 'helms and spears,' 'scythed chariots' and so on – indicate the nature of the civilization (4.290, 292).

Now Shelley unfolds 'the secrets of the Earth's deep heart,' tracing back the history of the earth from the beginning to the time when all was swallowed by a great cataclysm (4.279):

> The wrecks beside of many a city vast,
> Whose population which the Earth grew over
> Was mortal but not human; see, they lie,
> Their monstrous works and uncouth skeletons,
> Their status, homes, and fanes; prodigious shapes
> Huddled in grey annihilation, split,
> Jammed in the hard black deep; and over these
> The anatomies of unknown winged things,
> And fishes which were isles of living scale,
> And serpents, bony chains, twisted around
> The iron crags, or within heaps of dust
> To which the tortuous strength of their last pangs
> Had crushed the iron crags; – and over these
> The jagged alligator and the might
> Of earth-convulsing behemoth, which once
> Were monarch beasts, and on the slimy shores
> And weed-overgrown continents of Earth
> Increased and multiplied like summer worms
> On an abandoned corpse, till the blue globe
> Wrapt Deluge round it like a cloak, and they
> Yelled, gaspt and were abolished; or some God
> Whose throne was in a Comet, past, and cried –
> 'Be not!' – and like my words they were not more.   (4.296–318)

A number of details in the passage are derived from James Parkinson's *Organic Remains of a Former World* (1804–11) and Cuvier's *Essay on the Theory of the Earth* (1813) (Grabo, *A Newton among Poets* 177–80; Hungerford 209–11),[30] but Shelley's unique cosmogony does not follow the theories of either the religious British paleontologist or the atheistic French geologist.

Shelley would not have agreed with Parkinson's view of the earth as having gone through five creative stages, each corresponding to a 'day' in the Genesis account, and under divine supervision (Parkinson 3: 449–53). The passage, which depicts the 'anatomies' of large prehistoric creatures, the gigantic marine invertebrates and the 'earth-convulsing behemoth' drowned in the deluge (*Prometheus Unbound* 4.303, 310), evokes the full horror of the catastrophe and the complete extinction of species, the horror which early-nineteenth-century readers would have felt when Cuvier's theories on comparative anatomy and cataclysmic change gave the coup de grâce to orthodox chronology; through a careful investigation of fossil creatures that had no living counterparts and whose distribution in a stratigraphic column revealed the number and order of global revolutions, Cuvier confirmed that some species had become extinct due to sudden catastrophes in previous stages, despite the Bible's assertion that two individuals of each were saved in Noah's ark (*Essay on the Theory of the Earth* 57–60, 88–103). Shelley, however, differs from Cuvier at a most important point. The French catastrophist nonchalantly infers from the absence of human fossils that long before the birth of humanity the earth had gone through a series of geological stages, each of which ended with a sudden catastrophe that caused the complete extinction of some organisms (*Essay on the Theory of the Earth* 102–27). On the other hand, Shelley reverses the history of the earth by placing 'the melancholy ruins / Of cancelled cycles,' the remains of the earliest civilization formed by some extinct intelligent race, at the very first period of the earth (*Prometheus Unbound* 4.288–9). Shelley has a civilization built and then destroyed at the very beginning.

Why is Shelley locating the relics of civilization at the very core of the earth beneath the fossils of antediluvian creatures in contradiction to the common knowledge of geology? Critics have puzzled over Shelley's chronology of the events in the passage. Carl Grabo, unable to find any source for the vanished civilization, makes the far-fetched suggestion that Shelley might have been inspired by 'the superior tribe of monkeys of Helvetius's surmise,' which is mentioned in Erasmus Darwin's *Temple of Nature* (*A Newton among Poets* 65, 180). As we have seen in chapter 1, whenever possible, Shelley's imagination seeks a resplendent populous city further and further back in time. In the passage quoted above, Shelley reaches the beginning of geological time. The phrase 'mortal but not human' strikes a faint mythological echo of Hesiod's races of giants, but the vivid details of the passage link the 'mortal but not human' races more with pre-Adamite races, who, Shelley considers, built the first city and were destroyed by a catastrophe (*Prometheus Unbound* 4.298). The shockingly heretical idea of 'pre-Adamite races,' which was first suggested by La Peyrère in 1655, became well known in late-eighteenth-century England (Fiona Stafford 57–8, 187). Beckford's *Vathek*, which both Shelley and Mary read in 1815 (*Journals* 90), has a passage toward the end that might have given a hint to Shelley's idea of the antediluvian world; Eblis shows Vathek and Nouronihar the 'treasures of pre-adamite sultans,' 'their fulminating sabres,' and the 'various animals that inhabited the earth prior to the creation of ... the father of mankind' (111). Together with Cuvier's theories, the idea of pre-Adamite races was very provocative in the early nineteenth century. In Byron's 'Cain' (1821), which owes much to Cuvier's theories and the pre-Adamite world of *Vathek*, Lucifer shows Cain phantoms of now extinct pre-Adamite races and animals in Hades (2.2.41–190). This scene forces Byron to add a note to the preface; he has to state that Cuvier's theories prove the biblical Flood to be a historical event and that Lucifer's account of a former world is 'a poetical fiction' (*LBCPW* 6: 229–30).[31]

Shelley presents the pre-Adamite civilization as splendid but warlike, making it the prototype for all the cities of destruction in human history, those historical cities which Shelley has repeatedly criticized and left crumbling into ruin and wailing to the wind from *Queen Mab* onward. In 'Mont Blanc,' Shelley does not go deeper than the 'naked countenance of earth' (98). In *The Revolt of Islam*, the 'everlasting wail' of the ruins never ceases in Greece, even though Laon wishes that it be 'no more!' when 'truth's steady beams' are cast upon 'the vast stream of ages' (2.756, 775 774, 770). Here in the final act of *Prometheus Unbound*, Shelley not only envisions a trace of civilization in the geological abyss but also finally entombs, in the deepest bosom of the earth, the ruins of cities of destruction. Unlike Beckford, who conjures up 'the fleshless forms of the pre-adamite kings' to be tortured (112), Shelley puts the antediluvian civilization peacefully to eternal sleep. Those cancelled cycles are still grotesque and the 'ruin within ruin' (*Prometheus Unbound* 4.295), but they are given, in the heart of the earth, a place of rest, which is momentarily revealed by the green basilisk-like light of the Spirit of the Earth and then returned to eternal darkness.

6. Songs, Dance, and the Children of Light

The structure of the lyrical drama, which admits many different voices, enables characters to achieve meaningful dialogue with their others. It multiplies the lyric voice characteristic of the English Romantics in the social structure of the drama. It also interweaves different voices into a polyphonic symphony of 'a perpetual Orphic song' (*Prometheus Unbound* 4.415). This is exactly what is lacking in the closed mental theatre of Prometheus, the male European intellect, and needs to be supplied by Asia. From act 2, scene 5, where Asia comes back from Demogorgon's cave, all the main characters except Prometheus join the universal celebration by singing and dancing. Asia sings 'My soul is an enchanted Boat' in response to the voice in the air singing the 'Life of Life' lyric (2.5.48–110). Love's infection is rapturously appreciated by the spirits' 'Life of Life' lyric and Mother Earth's exuberant song of joy after Prometheus's kiss. Even Demogorgon arises from the underground and concludes the global epithalamion, in which the Earth, the Moon, spirits, and earthly creations sing and dance with joy, answering Shelley's question about 'the human mind's imaginings' in 'Mont Blanc' (143). Demogorgon ascertains that humans are able to 'hope, till Hope creates / From its own wreck the thing it contemplates' when Prometheus and Asia are united, whether the world is ruined by wars, natural calamities, or the Supreme Power (*Prometheus Unbound* 4.573–4).

The universal theatre in act 4, in which all earthly creations and arts participate in celebrating the arrival of the utopian world, liberates the closed mental theatre of the Greek tragedy, and realizes the ideal Greek open theatre Shelley imagined Greeks had beheld under the Italian sky when visiting the ruins of Pompeii in December 1818. Shelley says that Greeks 'lived in harmony with nature, & the interstices of their incomparable columns, were portals as it were to admit the spirit of beauty which animates this glorious universe to visit those whom it inspired' (*Letters* 2: 73). This open theatre is a space where 'beautiful idealisms' – plural idealisms, not a single idealism – are celebrated by singing and dancing in *Prometheus Unbound*. Ronald Tetreault thinks that Shelley's interest in the Italian opera helped 'the classically-minded Shelley' to restore 'music and dance to the theatre' and to liberate Aeschylean tragedy into the 'beautiful idealisms' of the lyrical drama; he proceeds to maintain that '[t]he roots of Shelley's art are never single but always manifold and syncretic,' considering Shelley's lyrical drama to be 'two-fold tradition,' 'Greek and Italian, ancient and modern' ('Shelley at the Opera' 149). I would like to extend this important insight by including Eastern roots in Shelley's multiple traditions.

If 'European feelings,' arising from Romantic lyricism, radicalism, and Italian scenes, contribute to the 'beneficial innovation' of the cold

Indian summit in the early parts of the lyrical drama, equally 'beneficial' feelings from the East answer back to them, improving the Greek setting and presenting a universal theatre (*CWPBS* 7: 19). The Cave of Prometheus near Bamiyan appears in the Greek setting. Demogorgon comes to celebrate from the Indian cave. The Temple of Prometheus is a hybrid architecture with Eastern capitals and arches. The austerity of the Greek style is softened by Eastern influence. Also, Eastern feelings of love contribute to transform the wild Greek singing voice in the play, the Maenads' 'Evoe! Evoe!' into a 'perpetual Orphic song' (*Prometheus Unbound* 2.3.9, 4.415).

In 'Note on Sculptures' (1819), Shelley describes the sculpture of four Maenads on an altar dedicated to Bacchus: 'One – perhaps Agave with the head of Pentheus, has a human head in one hand and in the other a great knife; another has a spear with its pine cone, which was their thyrsus; another dances with mad voluptuousness; the fourth is dancing to a kind of tambourine' (*CWPBS* 6: 323). Shelley is struck by the sculptures' drunkenness and insanity, which are morally abominable but contribute to the production of a marvellous piece of art: 'The tremendous spirit of superstition aided by drunkenness and producing something beyond insanity, seems to have caught them [the Maenads] in its whirlwinds, and to bear them over the earth,' and it was 'a monstrous superstition only capable of existing in Greece because there alone capable of combining ideal beauty and poetical and abstract enthusiasm with the wild errors from which it sprung' (6: 323). Shelley's conclusion on Greek art is that the Greeks 'turned all things, superstition, prejudice, murder, madness – to Beauty' (6: 323). As Timothy Webb persuasively argues, Shelley 'seems to be softening his characteristically rigourous moral attitude,' with aesthetic excellence making morally repellent subjects acceptable (*Shelley* 213–14). Shelley's revision of Greek art by improving the lost drama of Aeschylus, however, aims at the 'beautiful idealisms of moral excellence' (preface to *Prometheus Unbound*, *SP&P* 209). To achieve this end, Shelley complements Prometheus with Asia and creates an alternative space where European and Eastern elements can mingle and interact.

The geography of the Promethean Age is thoroughly mapped in all its dimensions, on the land, on the sea, under the ground. Prometheus and Asia, however, disappear into the Cave. Demogorgon calls all creations one by one in the grand finale of the play, starting with the Earth; when it comes to humanity's turn at the very end, 'All,' not 'Man,' answers Demogorgon (*SP&P* 285, *Prometheus Unbound* 4.549).

Although the spirits emanating from the human mind sing of future civilization, they are not fully human. There is at least one thing missing in the lyrical drama, or one thing that remains in its potentiality: a new populous city of recreated humans born from the unity of Prometheus and Asia. Prometheus plans to make '[s]trange combinations out of common things / Like human babes in their brief innocence' in the Cave of Prometheus (3.3.32–3). Acts 3 and 4 are crowded with spirits in the form of hybrid children. The Spirit of the Earth is a winged child whose beams are a basilisk's. A 'winged Infant' in the chariot of the Moon looks a hybrid between European and Asian; it 'gleam[s] white' but its eyes are 'Heavens / Of liquid darkness' (4.219, 222, 225–6). Like Asia, who is called 'Child of Light' (2.5.54), these infant spirits are children of light. They appear in the celebration but are not ready to sing and dance. Similarly, the Temple of Prometheus, which was once filled with the torch-bearing 'youths' who honoured Prometheus, is now 'deserted,' waiting to be populated again (3.3.168, 167).

The Temple with marble figures preserves its eternal image and 'everlasting love' on the 'unerasing waves' of the lake (3.3.166, 160), suggesting 'beautiful potentiality' in humankind (Webb, *Shelley* 221–2). If the universal epithalamion of the Earth and the Moon symbolically celebrates the union of Prometheus and Asia, where are these possibilities and potentialities in humanity suggested in acts 3 and 4 to be realized? The next chapter will seek an answer to this question in another marginal place – the interior of Africa. In August 1820, Shelley made a solitary expedition to the top of Monte San Pellegrino, which is situated above Lucca and looks over the 'fertile' country under the 'gladsome sunny heaven' (Mary Shelley, 'Note on The Witch of Atlas, by Mrs. Shelley' *SPW* 388). On coming back from the delightful three-day excursion, he composed 'The Witch of Atlas' in three days.[32] The poem, inspired by this walking tour in the Apennines under the hot sun, was set in Mount Atlas in North Africa and presented the cheerful journey of a female hybrid cross between Europe and Africa, at a time when cross-breeding between white and black races was falling more and more into disfavour.

5 'The Witch of Atlas': The Hybrid Explorer and Shelley's Joyous Challenge

1. Hybridity and Colonial Exploration

With its plurality of 'beautiful idealisms' suggesting a plurality of cultures (preface to *Prometheus Unbound*, *SP&P* 209), *Prometheus Unbound* reaches a climax of Shelley's poetic quest. At least one thing is, however, left untouched in the play: the birth and growth of a hybrid spirit, a true mixture resulting from the union of two cultures. Asia is portrayed as a mother, and correspondingly a spirit of the Earth appears in the form of a winged child, calling her Mother; but it has no biological tie with Asia, nor does it call Prometheus Father. The progeny of the Promethean Age remains in its beautiful potentiality. The unborn child of Prometheus and Asia, however, has a counterpart in the play: '[t]hat fatal child, the terror of the Earth,' begotten by Jupiter as 'a strange wonder' (*Prometheus Unbound* 3.1.19, 18). Jupiter recounts the result of his rape of Thetis, who is, like Asia, a sea-nymph, but unlike her, 'veiled in the light / Of the desire' (3.1.34–5):

> Two mighty spirits, mingling, made a third
> Mightier than either – which, unbodied now
> Between us, floats, felt although unbeheld,
> Waiting the incarnation.   (3.1.43–6)

Jupiter's 'fatal child' before its embodiment as Demogorgon is the result of the 'mingling' of two 'mighty spirits,' and '[m]ightier than either' of its parents; it is described in terms characteristic of the hybrid, or the 'half-caste children' as were understood in Shelley's day. The word 'hybridity' in the early nineteenth century referred to the offspring of two different species that were different from either of the parents. When Blumenbach considered human cross-breeding under the theory of hybridization and hybrid degeneration in the third edition of 'On the Natural Variety of Mankind' (1795),[1] he observed the human hybrid as springing from 'the intercourse of different varieties of one and the same species,' and being 'like neither parent altogether, but participating in the form of each, and being as it were a mean between the two' (202, 201, 215–18).

It is ironic that the replacement of the physical union of Prometheus and Asia with that of the Earth and the Moon and the dethronement of Jupiter by his 'fatal child' mirrors the shift in British colonial policy toward interracial marriage. Beginning in 1791, the East India Company prohibited Anglo-Indians – the mixed-race offspring of British officers and Indian women – from holding either civil or military office, and discouraged mixed marriage. Like all early European empires, however, its initial policy had been to encourage intermarriage with local women in order to spread British influence in geographical areas where acclimatization was difficult and in order to build up the armies of Anglo-Indians for further territorial expansion.[2] Hyam has persuasively argued that this change of policy was a reaction to the uprising in the Caribbean island of Santo Domingo in 1791, which led to the independence of the Republic of Haiti in 1804 (*Empire and Sexuality* 117). Due to the reversal of the policy, no Anglo-Indians were left in the British Army by 1808.[3] In the early nineteenth century, the offspring of British-Indian marriages began to be feared as a new hybrid race; they were only half 'English' and their 'other' blood would be subversive. The 'vague apprehensions' about 'the danger' that might result from an increasing mixed race in India were probably recorded in print for the first time by George Annesley, Viscount Valentia, who was commissioned by the East India Company to visit its possessions (Stark 71; Leask, *Curiosity and the Aesthetics of Travel Writing 1770–1840* 177). In *Voyages and Travels to India, Ceylon, the Red Sea, Abyssinia, and Egypt, in the Years 1802, 1803, 1804, 1805, and 1806* (1809),[4] Valentia expresses his concern about rapidly increasing 'half-cast[e] children,' who are forming 'the first step to colonization, by creating a link of union between the English and the natives.' Imagining the future when 'this intermediate cast[e]' will become 'too powerful for control' and ultimately destroy their father's country, he proposes that 'the evil ought to be stopt' (1: 197–8).[5]

Hybrid plants and animals were considered to be sterile. The *Ency-*

clopædia Britannica defines the hybrid as 'a monstrous production of two different species of plants, analogous to a mule among animals,' and adds that its seeds 'will not propagate' (3rd ed. [1797] 8: 795; 5th ed. [1817] 10: 693). In the emerging study of human races, the problem of human hybridity, especially the mixing of the black and white races, played a central role in the monogenesis/polygenesis controversy, in which there was heated discussion over whether humanity composed a single species or several different species. Blumenbach, who believed in biblical monogenesis, rejected the idea of the different races of humanity as different species. He did not follow the biological model in which the hybrid was sterile, but he attributed degeneration in humankind largely to racial crossings. His theory of varieties of humanity caused by degeneration from the pure original race – a position he assigned to the Caucasian race – left room for the idea of a hierarchy in the human family, which eventually led to an unorthodox yet appealing idea of the human races as different species. It was well known that human beings from different lands had mixed with each other and that such unions had been fertile.[6] The theories of race were not genuinely scientific, however, being closely entwined with colonialism, in which physical fascination and fear of different races were two sides of the same coin.

Robert Young, in *Colonial Desire: Hybridity in Theory, Culture and Race*, cogently examines in detail the concept's nefarious and entangled connections with sexual and economic desire in the history of Western fantasies of race from the late eighteenth century to the present, emphasizing the original historical implications of the concept. Though the historical trajectory of the concept of hybridity started in biology and botany,[7] Young argues that it was 'the nineteenth century's word' in the context of race and ethnicity, by citing evidence in the *OED*; its significant early usage in the interracial context was found in Josiah Nott's reference in 1843, with one earlier occurrence in 1813 (*Colonial Desire* 6). To be precise, in Young's view, it was the mid-nineteenth century's word that emerged in the development of racial and cultural theories. Various reactions to the emergent notion of hybridity or its antecedents in the period of English Romanticism – especially those of Romantic poets – are largely missing in his discussion, which makes a short cut from J.S. Mill to Matthew Arnold by way of Herder's concept of culture (55–89). In the early nineteenth century, the term, still taking shape, eluded easy classification, being applied to crossings of different species, whether animals, birds, plants, or humans, and representing intermediate zones and states between animals and humans, varieties of humans, and different races in humankind.[8] Gilbert White observed the 'hybrid pheasant' in his journals (65–6). Shelley's 'The Sensitive Plant,' which was written in the spring of 1820, revolves around a variety of mimosa, a hermaphrodite plant native to Brazil, which confused contemporary naturalists as 'one of the most frequent examples of those ambiguous border-forms sharing both vegetable and animal characteristics' (Wasserman, *Shelley* 157).

Shelley was fully aware and critical of the complicity of knowledge and imperial power in the contemporary discussion on the hybrid. A few months after 'The Sensitive Plant,' in August 1820, he wrote two poems, each of which presents a human hybrid, a male and a female respectively, and their appellations reflect their biological and cultural identities. 'The Witch of Atlas' traces an African journey by a 'witch,' a hybrid female spirit, who is born from colonial miscegenation of Apollo's deflowering of a nameless African maid. 'Oedipus Tyrannus or Swellfoot the Tyrant,' which was begun a few days after the completion of 'The Witch of Atlas,' satirizes George IV and closes with a speech by the monstrous hybrid Minotaur, who represents Britain:

> I am the Ionian Minotaur, the mightiest
> Of all Europa's taurine progeny –
> I am the old traditional Man-Bull;
> And from my ancestor having been Ionian,
> I am called Ion, which, by interpretation,
> Is JOHN; in plain Theban, that is to say,
> My name's JOHN BULL. (2.2.103–9)

Wordplay produces a monstrous 'Man-Bull,' alias John Bull, on whom three different myths converge: he is a son of Greece and Britain, Zeus disguised as a white ox and Europa, and the adulterous Pasiphae and an ox. The Minotaur's biological hybridity is transferred to Britain by linguistic hybridity, which disturbs both its self-image as an heir to ancient Greece and its place as the most powerful country in Europe.

The Minotaur is in every respect a male counterpart of the hybrid protagonist of 'The Witch of Atlas,' who, like Jupiter's 'fatal child' (*Prometheus Unbound* 3.1.19), is born from the rape of a local nymph by a powerful European god. While the hybridity of the grotesque British heir to all Europe anticipates the contribution of 'All Europe' to 'the making of Kurtz' in Conrad's *Heart of Darkness* (117), a female hybrid in 'The Witch of Atlas' is a colonial hybrid. The desire of conquest, kindling both physical fascination with and fear of different races, is fulfilled both politically and sexually in colonization and miscegenation. Blumenbach reported that 'Ethiopian and Mulatto women' were 'particularly sought out by Europeans' (248), but the colonial and sexual conquest of female others was undermined by the resulting racial mixing. As we have seen, a social fear of children of mixed blood was observed in India, and in the West Indies created a social disgust at the contamination of white blood with black blood in cross-breeding between the white and black races.[9] Though British scientists generally supported the monogenetic view in accordance with the Enlightenment humanitarian belief in universality and equality, 'Christian theology,' and the anti-slavery movement, a turning point came with William Lawrence's *Lectures on Physiology, Zoology, and the Natural History of Man*, published in 1819.[10]

Ruston explores the importance of Lawrence's book in the context of emergent scientific principles of life that were 'committed to a radical political and unorthodox religious agenda,' tracing the book's immediate suppression for its unorthodox religious views, and its survival in America and in a pirate edition that was first published in 1823 and went through nine editions until 1848 (24–73).[11] My particular interest here is in Lawrence's modification of the concept of human hybrid. Lawrence, who published a translation of Blumenbach's *Short System of Comparative Anatomy* in 1807, was more concerned with 'making precise comparisons between men and animals' than his colleagues in approaching the natural history of humans (Kitson, introduction xix). Although considering different human races as 'varieties of a single species,' he establishes an analogy between the human crossing and the animal hybrid, regarding them as 'the fruit of such unnatural intercourse' (Lawrence 235, 255). Lawrence proceeds to say: 'The intellectual and moral character of the Europeans is deteriorated by the mixture of black or red blood; while, on the other hand, an infusion of white blood tends in an equal degree to improve and ennoble the qualities of the dark varieties' (260). Lawrence's theory was widely quoted, reflecting the direction in which racial attitudes in Britain were moving.[12]

The scales were turned out of favour of mixed children, changing them into monsters, 'the fruit of such unnatural intercourse' (Lawrence 255). It was at this very time that two beautiful hybrid women, Shelley's Witch of Atlas and Byron's Haidée in *Don Juan*, appeared on the British literary scene, making a poetic reflection on British colonialism in Africa and the problem of hybridity. Haidée's African background and her Greek pirate father are mentioned in canto 2, which was published in 1819, but it is not until canto 4, which was published in 1821, that detailed information of her West African origin is provided. 'The Witch of Atlas' was included in the *Posthumous Poems* in 1824, as the publisher, Charles Ollier, refused to publish it during Shelley's lifetime. Joseph Lew argues that corresponding to the contemporary political situation, even in Byron's Oriental Bowers of Bliss, children of mixed blood are 'aborted,' 'let alone reared' (197). But the poets do produce them, and they are born as colonial hybrids in Africa. Shelley's Witch and Byron's Haidée are not among those typical female others who are clad in Oriental epithets in Romantic exotic poems; issuing from a powerful Greek explorer and a nameless African maid, they are hybrids of Caucasian and non-Caucasian, their birth reflecting Western colonial activities. The Witch of Atlas is conceived by Apollo's *aura seminalis* when the 'all-beholding Sun' in his 'wide voyage o'er continents and seas' deflowers 'one of the Atlantides' ('The Witch of Atlas' 57–9). Haidée's father, Lambro, is a complicated figure recalling the Lambro of 'The Bride of Abydos' (1813) and the historical Lambros Katzones, a famous Greek revolutionist who became a pirate (*LBCPW* 3: 441); while pursuing 'o'er the high seas his watery journey' with 'the spirit of old Greece,' he is a villainous 'Greek' pirate involved in 'the slave-market' and the 'Turkish trade'; and a 'Moorish maid, from Fez' gives birth to his sole heiress (Byron, *Don Juan* 3.111, 432; 2.1009, 1006, 1007; 4.431).

2. The African Witch and a Southern Geography

The view that Shelley's 'The Witch of Atlas' reflects the history of British colonialism fundamentally differs from the traditional evaluation of the poem in the mainstream of Shelley studies which echoes Mary Shelley's grieving view of the poem as a deliberate escape from the human realm into 'the airiest flight of fancy' ('Note on The Witch of Atlas, by Mrs. Shelley,' *SPW* 389). Shelley's 'airiest flight of fancy' was, on the one hand, seen as a 'trifle' by T.S. Eliot (93) and dismissed as a 'flight' from 'reality' and 'sensibility' by the New Critics (Pottle 297), and on the other, was highly evaluated as characteristic of 'Shelleyan poetic virtues' by Bloom, who takes 'The Witch of Atlas' as the best example of Shelley's mythopoetic mode (*Shelley's Mythmaking* 184,

165). Jerrold E. Hogle, in his excellent 'Metaphor and Metamorphosis in Shelley's "The Witch of Atlas"' (1980), follows Bloom but, taking one further step to equate a mythopoeic creation with superlative poetry from a deconstructionist point of view, considers the poem to be a playful and endless series of metaphors that have no origin.

As critics have concentrated on the mythopoeic aspect of the poem, Shelley's mapping of the Southern Hemisphere in the poem has not been examined until recently and has not been fully explained. The first investigation of the poem's detailed geographical reference is Frederic S. Colwell's source study, 'Shelley's "The Witch of Atlas" and the Mythic Geography of the Nile' (1978), in which Colwell charts the Witch's Africa as a mythical land with reference to classical geographers, in particular Herodotus, and contemporary British cartographers and explorers. Colwell, however, thinks little of the Witch's African characteristics, pushing her into the realm of imagination by equating her with the Witch Poesy in 'Mont Blanc' and the Witch Memory in the 'Letter to Maria Gisborne' (1820). As the Witch of Atlas is conceived in the 'chamber of grey rock,' which can be seen as equal to the 'still cave of the witch Poesy' in the poet's mind ('The Witch of Atlas' 63; 'Mont Blanc' 44), she represents the poetic imagination; but to be more precise, born as she was in a cave on Atlas, she is an African version of the embodiment of poetry. Debbie Lee in 'Mapping the Interior: African Cartography and Shelley's *The Witch of Atlas*' (1997) stresses contemporary political associations rather than Herodotean ones. She argues that Shelley criticizes the male British explorer's imperialistic desire for the female other by giving the maiden-as-Africa the power and versatility with which to cross the continent that no European traveller had conquered. Insightful as it is, Lee's discussion focuses on the Witch's trip to the interior of Africa, which is only one part of her travels, and ignores two important aspects of the Witch – her hybridity and her complex relationship with her parent cultures – which make the poem more than a mere criticism or parody of contemporary British penetration of Africa.

The poem is worthy of serious critical scrutiny for the very reason that its title character is a hybrid. While her mother is 'one of the Atlantides' ('The Witch of Atlas' 57), who are 'a people of Africa near Mount Atlas' (Lemprière 111), her maternal origin tends to be ignored by Shelleyans, who stress her paternal, classical background. Carl Grabo observes that being the daughter of Apollo and a sea-nymph who embodies concepts in 'neo-Platonism,' the Witch of Atlas is 'a goddess of the classical mythology' and a 'healer' whom Shelley creates in 'a gay mood' (*The Meaning of 'The Witch of Atlas'* 3, 18, 23). Timothy Webb argues that the poem is Shelley's own version of the Homeric 'Hymn to Mercury,' which he translated in ottava rima in July 1820, making 'the delightful child god of the original' undergo 'a sex-change' and reappear 'in the feminine guise of the Witch of Atlas' (*Shelley* 210). If so, the question arises as to whether the word 'witch' has no derogatory meaning, though G. Wilson Knight thinks it does, both in terms of her geographical attributes and her link to the poetic imagination (226). It is not only a sex-change that she undergoes; a delightful Greek child-god is transformed into a delightful child-goddess on the margin, coming into the world as a hybrid child of a Greek god and an African nymph. She is a marginal spirit like Queen Mab, who is both a bringer of dreams and a healer, and like Asia, she reflects her geographical identity in her name. Unlike Shelley's earlier geographical others, she is born a hybrid, as a result of Apollo's rape of an African nymph. Her marginality and hybridity – her birth on Mount Atlas, her femininity, and her mixed blood as daughter of a Greek god and an Atlantid – have to be examined thoroughly by tracing her delightful and effortless boat trip across the African continent, which is set against contemporary British exploration of Africa promoted by the African Association.

There is a sharp sense of geography working in the dedicatory poem 'To Mary' even before the main narrative begins with the conception of the Witch. Shelley compares the title character with Wordsworth's Ruth and Lucy, those idealized English girls who flourish only on English soil and haunt the Lake District as genii loci after their deaths. The comparison points to a difference between Englishness and foreignness, centre and margin, as the innocent girls in the heart of England are contrasted to Shelley's African 'witch' of Atlas, who appears on the border of the known and the unknown. When Shelley says that '[his] Witch indeed is not so sweet a creature / As Ruth or Lucy' ('To Mary' 33–4), the reader might feel that Shelley's creature will escape the sad fates of those English girls, who are at the mercy of the father (biological or symbolic) or the lover. Lucy 'died' after '[t]hree years she grew in sun and shower' and Nature declared this child to be his (Wordsworth, 'Three years she grew in sun and shower' [1800] 39, 1). Ruth was half deserted by her father when a child, and when she grew to be a blooming maid, she was abandoned by a youth who came from 'Georgia's shore' (Wordsworth, 'Ruth' [1800] 19).

The Witch is neither sweet nor weak like Lucy or Ruth, but she is so powerfully beautiful that for her beauty one would prostate oneself: 'If you unveil my Witch, no Priest or Primate / Can shrive you of that sin, if sin there be / In love, when it becomes idolatry' ('To Mary' 46–8). What kind of beauty does she have if we cannot distinguish between a deadly sin and an ultimate blessing when she is unveiled? Shelley leaves it unsaid as it is the reader's task to find her beauty by reading the main poem. The image at the end of the dedicatory poem, however, would have made the contemporary reader halt between two conflicting images: an innocent child comparable to Ruth or Lucy and a dark seductive female East in the Oriental tale. Her image, for which one revels in the sin of idolatry, certainly aligns her with Luxima in Owenson's *The Missionary*, Shelley's own veiled maid in 'Alastor,' and the beautiful priestess of Isis in Thomas Moore's *The Epicurean, a Tale* (1827),[13] all of whom belong to the exotic and erotic female East who excites the desire of the European imagination.

Owing to classical allusions around the Witch and her similarities with the Asia of *Prometheus Unbound*, critics tend to associate her with the regions recognized as the 'Orient'; Carlos Baker and Joseph Raben even shift the location of Mount Atlas from Morocco to Ethiopia, identifying it with the fabulous Mountains of the Moon (C. Baker 206; Raben, 'Shelley the Dionysian' 35). Her geographical tie with Atlas in Morocco does impress on her the undeniable mark of Africa, however. Atlas, the place name she carries, was the boundary between the known and the unknown, between white and black. The 'South of mount Atlas,' Cuvier says, is the area for the 'Negro race,' which is sharply distinguished from the 'Caucasian, to which we ourselves belong' (*The Animal Kingdom* 1: 43). The Witch of Atlas carries an image of the female East into territories beyond Morocco, and can be taken as an example of the female East transferred to Africa or an Orientalization of Africa. Martha Pike Conant includes in the literary chart of the 'Orient' North Africa and Abyssinia,[14] and mentions that Africa, when annexed to the 'Oriental world,' appears as a land of mystery associated with witchcraft, and 'at every turn one may meet African magicians' (xv–xvi, 3). One of her examples is 'The History of Maugraby the Magician' in Cazotte's *Continuation*, which maintains that the 'most pernicious production of Africa' is not savage animals such as crocodiles and serpents but 'the magicians' and their sanctuary at 'the House of Daniel of Tunis [Dom-Daniel]' (3: 142). Unlike the female East, the female Africa, when attracting the Western imagination, takes the form of a powerful sorceress belonging to a dark power, as seen in the image of a beautiful witch in 'The History of Maugraby the Magician' in Cazotte's *Continuation*. As I have briefly mentioned in chapter 2, Cazotte's story influences Shelley's 'Alastor' in terms of the encounter between the European imagination and the female other, but here it has special relevance in its association of magic with Mount Atlas. The word 'maugraby' signifies inhabitants of North Africa, in particular, Moroccans (Kidwai 104), and Maugraby in the story has a splendid magic palace protected by the 'tops of Mount Atlas' (*Continuation* 3: 64).

The beautiful and mysterious witch symbolizes the land of wonder and enchantment. To unveil the Witch of Atlas in Shelley's dedicatory poem, in this sense, is to strip the mysterious veil from the hidden riches of the unexplored dark continent, where the African Association had been sending explorers and seeking commercial and colonial opportunities. Britain's colonial gaze yearns to demystify and conquer the site of otherness that fulfils dreams of masculine exploration and masculine desire simultaneously. When penetrating the interior of Africa, Mungo Park felt a 'passionate desire to examine into the productions of a country so little known' and to 'render the geography of Africa more familiar' to his countrymen so that Britain could gain 'new resources of wealth' and 'new channels of commerce' (1: 2). The new resources concealed in the unexplored interior of Africa looked more attractive after the abolition of the slave trade in 1807. In *An Account of Timbuctoo and Housa, Territories in the Interior of Africa, by El Hage Abd Salam Shabeeny* (1820), James Grey Jackson says that 'the discovery of the inmost recesses would follow the path of commerce, and that continent, which had baffled the researches of the moderns as well as the ancients, would lay open its treasures to modern Europe' (201). To European eyes, Africa appears to be an unexplored treasure house, whose inexhaustible riches, which are symbolized as the physical beauty of the female Africa, European explorers want to explore and possess.

Correspondingly, Shelley's preliminary introduction of the Witch reflects a complex and ambiguous relationship between unveiling and exploring, the explorer and the explored object, and centre and margin. What is important is that the Witch is not only the subject to be unveiled; she is herself an explorer of Africa. In the final stanza, Shelley compares the Witch with the eponymous character of Wordsworth's *Peter Bell* (1819) in terms of beauty concealed under the surface: 'If you strip Peter, you will see a fellow / Scorched by Hell's hyperequatorial climate / Into a kind of a sulphurous yellow' ('To Mary' 41–3). Stripping Peter and sneering at his hue burned black by the 'hyperequatorial climate' implicitly suggests his failure as an explorer in comparison with the Witch. Shelley seems to be laughing at Wordsworth's cowardice, which prevents him from exploring the deep heart of Africa and from 'uplift[ing]' even 'the hem of Nature's shift' ('Peter Bell the Third' 316, 315).[15] Unveiling and exploring are synonymous here, but the Witch is not only an object of unveiling and exploration but also an explorer in her own right. When Shelley asks the reader to 'unveil' the Witch, he is inviting us to explore and unveil a new beauty in the female Africa, who is quite different from other Romantic witches, such as Lamia and Geraldine, who are ugly when undressed. She is emerging from numerous conflicting images – a sweet creature, an African witch, a female East, an embodied imagination, and a female explorer.

3. Mount Atlas and the Mythic Geography of the Land of Wonders

Before discussing the main part of the poem, it will be useful to briefly trace the history of British exploration of the interior of Africa. In the early decades of the nineteenth century, European explorers and temporary residents in North Africa began to carefully collect information on the interior of the continent from North African travellers and merchants and send reports to the African Association. Geographers back home, including James Rennell, who collaborated with the African Association after returning from Bengal, were locating important geographical sites and major cities with considerable accuracy by analysing those reports, whether these places were actually visited or known only by second-hand information. Geographical knowledge of Africa was rapidly increasing; while the third edition of the *Encyclopædia Britannica* (1797) has only three and a half pages for 'Africa' (1: 225–8), the fifth edition (1817) expands to twenty-one pages, presenting the latest knowledge of Africa provided by travel reports (1: 254–75). Nevertheless, large parts of the interior remained unknown. The reviewer of Hugh Murray's *Historical Account of Discoveries and Travels in Africa* (1817) deplores 'the state of geographical science in the nineteenth century': 'so imperfect, indeed, is our knowledge of this vast continent, that in what are deemed to be best charts, full two-thirds of it appear a blank' (299). John Thomson's *A New General Atlas*

(1817) leaves a large blank space in the interior, marking it 'unknown' or 'unexplored' (3, 4, 6, 47, 49).

The interior of Africa south of the Atlas Mountains, where Shelley's poem is set, remained as obscure as it had been in the days of Herodotus. Shelley depends heavily upon Herodotus's account of Africa in Books 2 to 4 in the *History* (Colwell, 'Shelley's "The Witch of Atlas" and the Mythic Geography of the Nile' 70–90), but it was not only Shelley who relied upon the classical historian. The section on Africa in the fifth edition of the *Encyclopædia Britannica* begins with Herodotus (1: 254). Rennell considered the mapping of Africa to be a reconstruction of Herodotus's geography in *The Geographical System of Herodotus* (1800), always comparing explorers' reports with Herodotus's accounts and looking for new trade centres in the mysterious interior of Africa. The Garamantes, a fabled people in Fezzan in classical accounts, who appear at the celebration of the Witch's birth in Shelley's poem, are identified with the present Fezzaners by Rennell; they are 'the most enterprising merchants of Africa,' as they are 'the most advantageously placed of any inland country in Africa, for the purposes of commerce'; Fezzan is 'not only situated on the line of the *shortest* and *convenient*, and therefore *principal* communication between the Mediterranean sea, and the centre of Africa, but also in the line between Western Africa, Egypt, and Arabia, comparing to the ancient state of Palmyra, placed in the midst of desert and forming a *link* of connection between other sites' (*The Geographical System of Herodotus* 615–19). Herodotus is useful to Rennell for colonial purposes; unlike other classical geographers, he took great interest in and had detailed knowledge of the course of the Niger,[16] the source and mouth of which were the goals of British geographers and explorers charting the inland parts of Africa (*The Geographical System of Herodotus* 4–5).

The Atlas Mountains, in which Shelley's poem opens, were called 'the pillar of heaven,' whose shape was 'a complete circle' (Herodotus 2: 389). In the early nineteenth century, James Grey Jackson adored the 'magnificent and truly romantic mountains' whose immensely high summits were 'continually covered with snow' and almost 'inaccessible,' and under which spread forests and countries 'abounding in all the necessaries and luxuries of life' (*An Account of Timbuctoo and Housa, Territories in the Interior of Africa, by El Hage Abd Salam Shabeeny* 75, 92, 76, 106). The Atlas range bears the same mythical importance as the highest mountains Shelley treated in his earlier poems, but the lofty mountain in this poem is different from the cold barren Indian Caucasus in the opening of *Prometheus Unbound* or from the summit of Atlas where 'the Genius of the South' sits on the 'tempest-cinctured throne' in 'Henry and Louisa' (1809) (166, 167). Shelley creates a beautiful green mountain at the earth's 'prime' ('The Witch of Atlas' 52), and superimposes on it Monte San Pellegrino, which is surrounded by 'fertile' country and the 'handsome intelligent' peasantry (Mary Shelley, 'Note on "The Witch of Atlas," by Mrs. Shelley' *SPW* 388). Atlas stands high as a centre of the primordial world as well as that of unexplored Africa. It is home to myriad creatures, and its local peoples enjoy a pastoral life.

To this symbolic centre of untrodden Africa far from Europe, the 'all-beholding Sun,' who is later identified as 'Apollo,' comes in his 'wide voyage o'er continents and seas' ('The Witch of Atlas' 58, 293, 59). In an adaptation of a Homeric hymn, 'Song of Apollo,' which is one of the mythological lyrics in 1820 written in the same mythmaking mode as 'The Cloud' and 'The Witch of Atlas,' Apollo is identified with the sun and associated with the searching light of truth; in a proud voice, the Greek god introduces himself as 'the eye with which the Universe / Beholds itself, and knows it is divine' (31–2). He asserts that '[a]ll harmony of instrument and verse, / All prophecy and medicine' are his (33–4). In 'The Witch of Atlas,' the 'all-beholding Sun' is also associated with exploration. In the opening of the poem, the light of the sun not only penetrates the grey cavern in Africa; Apollo is thrilled at the discovery of '[s]o fair a creature' he has never seen, and simply acts out what European explorers dream (60): 'He kissed her with his beams, and made all golden / The chamber of grey rock in which she lay – / She, in that dream of joy, dissolved away' (62–4).

Apollo's deflowering of a nameless African beauty on Atlas is described in the beautiful language of dreams, but what he does is very close to Jupiter's rape of Thetis, whom Jupiter addresses as 'bright Image of Eternity,' who is 'veiled in the light / Of the desire which makes thee one with me' (*Prometheus Unbound* 3.1.36, 34–5). Thetis could not sustain 'the quick flames, / The penetrating presence' of Jupiter and was dissolved '[l]ike him whom the Numidian seps did thaw / Into a dew with poison' (3.1.38–9, 40–1). Unlike Thetis, the nameless African nymph is thoroughly consumed by Apollo, undergoing a series of meteorological changes, from 'a vapour' and 'a cloud' into 'a meteor,' and finally going out of the earth's circulating system, never to return ('The Witch of Atlas' 65, 66, 69). Although leading to the nymph's transformation into 'one of those mysterious stars /

Which hide themselves between the Earth and Mars' (71–2), this consummation is once and for all, and effected by Apollo's overwhelming power and colonial desire.

Does this opening represent a scene of triumph of Europe over Africa? Shelley does not say so. For, 'in that cave a dewy Splendour hidden / Took shape and motion: with the living form / Of this embodied Power, the cave grew warm' (78–80). The cave on the summit of Atlas serves as a womb for the secretly conceived hybrid. As the 'fatal child' of Jupiter resulting from the 'mingling' of the '[t]wo mighty spirits' is 'a third / Mightier than either' and regarded as 'a strange wonder,' the witch of Atlas is born as a 'wonder new' (*Prometheus Unbound* 3.1.19, 43–4, 18; 'The Witch of Atlas' 88). Unlike Haidée in *Don Juan*, who is raised in a Greek island under her father's control, the hybrid nurtured within the 'enwombed rocks' of the loftiest African mountain is completely independent of its father, and is a 'Power' from its conception ('The Witch of Atlas' 126, 80):

The 'Power,' when coming into being, appears as a 'lovely lady garmented in light / From her own beauty' like the transfigured Asia, but she has distinct local traits, looking more like a dark queen of Africa than a 'Heliad' (81–2, 584). Being associated with night, the heart of light is darkness.

>   – deep her eyes, as are
> Two openings of unfathomable night
>   Seen through a Temple's cloven roof – her hair
> Dark –   (82–5)

The image of a ruined temple open to the night sky suggests an ideal interaction between humans and nature, which Shelley imagined Greek 'upaithric' architecture would have had (*Letters* 2: 74).[17] At the same time, it offers a clear contrast to the Temple of Prometheus, which, drawing on the Greek/Roman model, opens to the 'bright and liquid sky' (*Prometheus Unbound* 3.4.118). The correspondence between microcosm and macrocosm, reflected in the Witch's eyes, which are likened to the vault of heaven, enables us to see her as a great 'Power.' The colour of her eyes, however, inevitably makes us aware that she is a dark queen of Africa, stressing the dark marginality of a newly born hybrid. She belongs to the night here and later in her travels on the Nile, and it should also be noted that the description of her appearance focuses on her eyes and hair with an emphasis on darkness, just as 'Afric' is visible through Haidée's 'large dark eye' (Byron, *Don Juan* 4.441, 447). Their dark appearance is what fascinates European travellers.

The beauty of the African female hybrid is, however, much more powerful and dangerous than the exotic physical attraction of the stereotypical female Orient. 'Afric,' which is 'all the sun's,' has infused into Haidée 'deep Passion's force' (*Don Juan* 4.441, 447). Although her image oscillates between white Greece and black Africa, '[t]he fire burst[s] forth from her Numidian veins, / Even as the Simoom sweeps the blasted plains' (4.455–6). Numidia is the Roman name of a region of Africa, north of the Sahara, which roughly corresponds to modern Algeria. What was known about Numidia in the early nineteenth century was mostly drawn from classical historians; in the age of Herodotus, the people of this country were called either Africans or Libyans and Numidians, who were famous for being excellent warriors (Gilbert 214; *Encyclopædia Britannica* [1817] 15: 90; Lemprière 537). Haidée's 'Numidian veins' thus have a strong association with warlike blood as well as with African soil tempered by the burning sun and Simoon, the hot blast which blows in the deserts of Africa. Her glance is as 'black as death,' being likened to 'the swiftest arrow' and 'the snake late coil'd, who pours his length, / And hurls at once his venom and his strength' (Byron, *Don Juan* 2.930, 934, 935–6).

In Shelley's poem, it is clear that European reason and imagination are irresistibly attracted to the dark charms of the Witch: 'the dim brain whirls dizzy with delight / Picturing her form' ('The Witch of Atlas' 85–6). Her beauty, however, not only dazzles European reason and imagination but attracts all living creatures – animals, mythical beasts, and humans. Moreover, those who have seen her cannot fix their thought '[o]n any object in the world so wide, / On any hope within the circling skies, / But on her form, and in her inmost eyes' (142–4). The danger that leads the Poet in 'Alastor' to his untimely death is occurring on a universal scale. But it is here that Shelley makes his beautiful Witch something more than an African enchantress or a sensuous female East. He sharply separates her from the latter two types of the female other and elevates her to a benevolent queen. The Witch is aware of her own dangerous beauty and tries to avoid becoming the source of 'idolatry' ('To Mary' 48). She weaves and puts on a 'subtle veil' of mist and light, which is a 'shadow for the splendour of her love' ('The Witch of Atlas' 151, 152).

Having the Witch on the throne, Mount Atlas is flooded with all sorts of creatures coming to celebrate her birth. Shelley's long catalogue of the worshippers, including legendary races, 'herdsmen and mountain maidens,' animals and monsters, and even 'lumps neither alive nor dead,' shows that Mount Atlas is mythical and that the world of Atlas represents the atlas of the world mapped in the format of the European ancient and medieval world map, which filled the utmost corners of the world with legendary animals and fabulous races (129, 135). The worshippers of the Witch are not limited to local races such as the 'Garamant[es]' and 'Pigmies' (130, 133). Classical demigods and nymphs are present, reflecting Lemprière's account of Atlas as the place where 'all the gods of antiquity received their birth' (Lemprière 111). 'Polyphemes,' one-eyed giants, come all the way from Sicily, from the world of *The Odyssey* ('The Witch of Atlas' 133). Shelley's Atlas also abounds in monstrous races, the fabled races that John Block Friedman names 'Plinian' after the Roman encyclopedist whose catalogue of unusual humans and subhuman creatures was so widely read (5). Those 'bosom-eyed' correspond to Pliny's 'Blemmyae,' who 'have no heads, their mouth and eyes being attached to their chests' ('The Witch of Atlas' 136; Pliny 253),[18] but those monstrous races were reported by contemporary explorers, too. James Grey Jackson records second-hand information on the dog-faced race, the tailed race, and the race having one eye in the breast and connects their Arabian names with corresponding classical sources (*An Account of Timbuctoo and Housa, Territories in the Interior of Africa, by El Hage Abd Salam Shabeeny* 198–9).

No living forms are to be seen on the top of the barren highest peak in 'Mont Blanc' nor in the Indian Caucasus in *Prometheus Unbound*, but here, for the first time in Shelley's poems, a high mountain grows green in the centre and is densely populated. Shelley's Atlas presents the mythical image of Africa commonly held in ancient times, but he does not show any fear or revulsion for the unknown or the unfamiliar.[19] This stands in sharp contrast to ancient and medieval mapmakers, who transformed peoples in distant lands into mysterious creatures, and to the more scientific eighteenth-century colonial cartographers, who reduced such areas to a vast blank space. The Atlas world is a social place with all kind of living things from all over the world, which invites us to compare Mount Atlas with London as Wordsworth describes it. As the city gathers 'all specimens of man,' ranging from 'the Swede, the Russian' to 'Moors, / Malays, Lascars, the Tartars and Chinese, / And Negro ladies in white muslin gowns,' Wordsworth is convinced that the vast metropolis is the 'fountain' of his 'country's destiny / And of the destiny of earth itself' (*Prelude* 7.236, 239, 241–3, 8.747–8). But the 'Power,' which is situated on the 'emerald throne' on the summit guarded by 'many a star-surrounded pyramid / Of icy crag cleaving the purple sky,' does not reign but leaves the country ('The Witch of Atlas' 80, 120, 350–1).

Like Queen Mab, to whom is given the 'wonders of the human world to keep,' the 'Power' of Mount Atlas inherits a number of 'magic treasures,' the most important of which are the 'scrolls of strange device' concerned with love and peace that were written by a 'Saturnian Archimage' and stored in the cave from time immemorial (*Queen Mab* 8.49; 'The Witch of Atlas' 154, 185, 186). This 'Archimage' of Atlas marks a salient difference from the evil African magicians of the *Continuation*, Spenser's villainous Archimago whose books contain evil charms, and Shelley's Spenser-inspired 'weird Archimage,' who plots 'dark spells' and 'devilish enginery' in the 'Letter to Maria Gisborne' (106, 107). The sacred writings of Atlas teach how to 'quench the earth-consuming rage / Of gold and blood' of humans, and 'unbind / The inmost lore of Love' ('The Witch of Atlas' 190–1, 198–9). With these 'magic treasures' the Witch of Atlas can reign her world peacefully and is even capable of redeeming the whole globe, but her qualities inherited from Apollo forbid her to 'love' the denizens of Atlas. Shelley does not let the 'Power' reign the world who cannot love the world it rules.

Her immortality sharply distinguishes her from the rest, and the magic gift Apollo gives her makes her self-contained and happy to be 'alone' and 'aloof' (209, 249). The mortal 'Ocean-Nymphs and Hamadryades, / Oreads and Naiads' cannot compete with their immortal counterparts, the Witch's own thoughts embodied by her 'mighty Sire' as the aerial servants who, clothed with 'the Ocean foam, / Or with the wind, or with the speed of fire,' 'work whatever purposes might come / Into her mind' (217–18, 214, 211–12, 213–14). When they offer to do her bidding, the Witch rejects them, showing them a vision of the end of the world. 'The fountains where the Naiades bedew / Their shining hair' will be 'drained and dried,' and '[t]he boundless Ocean like a drop of dew / Will be consumed – the stubborn centre must / Be scattered like a cloud of summer dust,' and she tells them: 'ye with them will perish one by one' (226–7, 230–2, 233). This is a very stern vision of the future, and it is worth noting that the Witch would not use her magic devices and knowledge to prevent the golden world from being dried up, though, unlike 'the surviving Sun' who '[s]hall smile on' the 'decay,' she is sympathetic to those mortals and 'must sigh' and 'weep' (234–6). There is a conflict between love and self-love in her when she rejects the local mortals and decides to leave the world she dominates. The 'wonder new' born in Atlas is taken as 'love' by the locals, but does not truly develop her qualities as love, as defined in the broader social context and exercised by 'poets or poetical philosophers,' or 'unacknowledged legislators of the World' in *A Defence of Poetry* (*SP&P* 529, 535).

In her preparation for the trip, the Witch breathes her 'living spirit' into a magic boat and creates a travel companion, 'Hermaphroditus' ('The Witch of Atlas,' 314, 388). Shelley attempts to answer a question of hybridity – whether the hybrid is a monster or a beautiful new product. The Witch kneads, with 'liquid love,' 'fire and snow,' the image of which looks back to the transcendent crimson fire of the Witch's secret fountain and the melting snow on it and suggests a mixture of the immortal and the mortal (323, 321). Two opposite things, mixed together with love, produce a 'fair Shape' that does not resemble either fire or snow (325). Hermaphroditus 'far surpass[es] / In beauty that bright shape of vital stone / Which drew the heart out of Pygmalion,' and its countenance is 'such as might select / Some artist that his skill should never die, / Imaging forth such perfect purity' (326–8, 334–6). Nevertheless, this beautiful hybrid is a 'sexless thing' (329).

Shelley does address the central problem of the hybrid, when he makes Hermaphroditus 'sexless' (329). Immediately after its sexlessness is mentioned, however, Shelley praises its youthful androgyny:

>   It seemed to have developed no defect
> Of either sex, yet all the grace of both –
>   In gentleness and strength its limbs were decked;
> The bosom swelled lightly with its full youth –   (330–3)

Reading this passage, we wonder if the word 'sexless' means sterility; it seems to reflect pre-pubescent asexuality, because later in the poem the Witch herself, who is 'chaster' than holy Dian '[b]efore she stooped to kiss Endymion,' is likened to 'a sexless bee' (587, 588, 589). Reiman and Fraistat comment that the 'sexless bee' is the 'undeveloped female (neuter) bee' who is 'the worker that collects honey and produces wax to store the honey for food in the winter' (*SP&P* 385 n.7). In the early nineteenth century it was well known that there were three kinds of bees – the queen (female), the drone (male), and the worker bee (neuter) – but opinions varied regarding the sex and fecundation of bees. *The Encyclopædia Britannica* (1817) explained that worker bees were originally of the female sex and that they were capable of becoming queen bees if nursed in a particular manner that could develop the female organs properly (3: 121–43). Thus I would think that the 'sexless bee' is a young queen bee in her virginity rather than a worker neuter that has the female organs obliterated at its last metamorphosis, and that the phrase refers to the Witch in her maidenhood, not to her sexlessness.

The real problem, however, is that she creates Hermaphroditus as her self-reflection and that at this stage she loves only herself or that which is made exactly as she is. Hermaphroditus's 'perfect purity' reminds us of Shelley's earlier theory of the epipsyche as 'a mirror whose surface reflects only the forms of purity and brightness,' according to which the 'Poet' in 'Alastor' embodies his ideals as the veiled maid ('The Witch of Atlas' 336; 'On Love,' *SP&P* 504). During the Witch's boat trip with Hermaphroditus, it thus acts as a perfect embodiment of the narcissistic concept of love. It is far from being companionable and loving, sleeping almost all the time in its own happy dreams. It has no volition, like a 'robot,' serving the Witch only when she needs it (Bloom, *Shelley's Mythmaking* 200). The Witch orders Hermaphroditus to sit at 'the prow' and takes her seat beside 'the rudder' ('The Witch of Atlas' 343, 344). With narcissistic self-love as her boat's driving power, the Witch starts her voyage as her father did, leaving Atlas never to return.

Haidée, who is a human hybrid under her Greek father's protection, cannot perform functions of hybridity such as mimicry, as she is dominated by her father and dies of grief after her father separates her from Juan. Shelley's Witch, who is produced by a mixing of the white and black races as well as the immortal and the mortal, develops qualities of the hybrid more fully when she becomes completely independent from either parent, leaving the Atlas Mountains. Bhabha, looking at early-nineteenth-century English colonialism through the lens of late-twentieth-century critical insight, shows how the English Bible, the symbol of English authority, being translated, misread, and displaced, turned into 'signs taken for wonders,' and became the colonial hybrid text, which disclosed a different voice of the other whose '"denied" knowledges' subverted and estranged the voice of authority (*The Location of Culture* 102–22). Shelley investigates possibilities of hybridity in real time by tracing a female hybrid from her birth as a 'wonder new' on Atlas to her exploration of Africa in which she is incessantly changing her identity, mimicking and undermining her European father's 'wide voyage o'er continents and seas' ('The Witch of Atlas' 88, 59). Her journey shows that Shelley's 'airiest' flight is not escapism ('Note on The Witch of Atlas, by Mrs. Shelley,' SPW 389). In her independence from her European father and the uncontrollable joyous energy with which she crosses the continent, the Witch confuses and outdoes European supremacy in the colonial situation, opening a liberating space that presents an alternative to both contemporary Western attempts to penetrate Africa and the Poet's eastward expedition in 'Alastor.'

4. A Geography of Exploration: Timbuctoo, the Austral Lake, and the British Penetration of Africa

The Witch's magic boat is closely associated with love and exploration. According to Shelley, it was either a boat created by Apollo from Venus's chariot and given to his daughter or a boat that Love piloted round 'the circumfluous Ocean' ('The Witch of Atlas' 312). The Witch's boat, into which she breathes her 'living spirit' and on which Hermaphroditus sits at the prow, is also closely related to Asia's boat in her song of 'My soul is an enchanted Boat' (314; *Prometheus Unbound* 2.5.72–110).[20] In Asia's imaginary boat trip, the boat of her 'desire,' guided by the spirit of music who 'like an Angel sit[s] / Beside the helm' and 'lifts its pinions' to catch the winds, 'sail[s] on, away, afar' and forever to the realm where 'never mortal pinnace [has been] glided' (2.5.94, 75–6, 85, 88, 93). The destination of the magic boat is 'a diviner day' in Asia's vision (2.5.103), but in 'The Witch of Atlas' it is sought on earth in the untrodden depths of Africa, where Wordsworth's magic 'little Boat' wants to go in the prologue to *Peter Bell* (1819) (4). When the magic boat invites Wordsworth to explore 'the secrets of a land / Where human foot did never stray' in 'the depth' of 'burning Africa,' the inmost place in Africa, which is as '[f]air' and 'cool' as evening skies, does not appeal to the poet and he chooses to go back to 'the town' where he was 'born' and where things are livelier than anywhere else (96–7, 99, 100, 98, 99, 66).

Wordsworth's homeward tendency, which gives his native place a central position, contrasts with the Witch's never-ending journey further and further away from home, but as Roland A. Duerksen points out (18–20), a reference to a '[f]air' and 'cool' spot in the heart of 'burning Africa' in Wordsworth's poem has some special relevance to the Witch's destination in the 'Austral waters' beyond Timbuctoo

(*Peter Bell* 98, 99, 100; 'The Witch of Atlas' 423). Wordsworth composed *Peter Bell* in the spring of 1798, a few months after Park returned from his exploration of the course of the Niger (*PWWW* 2: 527–9).[21] The Witch's southward course is one that Wordsworth declines to take and that Park and other Western explorers have not been able to complete successfully. She sails through the 'panther-peopled forests' ('The Witch of Atlas' 347), which seem to correspond to the land of the Garamantes, 'a country abounding with wild beasts' (Herodotus 2: 377), to 'the Austral waters' beyond 'the fabulous Thamondocana' ('The Witch of Atlas' 423, 424). The word 'Thamondocana' not only sounds ancient but also suggests a faithful transcription of the local pronunciation of the city's name, like Captain Jobson's 'Tombakonda' in *The Golden Trade* (1623) (102), giving us a chance to review the history of the English search for the mysterious city, driven by 'human cupidity beyond all others – *gold*' (Murray 165) from the early seventeenth century.[22] When Park's first eyewitness report on the Niger enabled Britain to see 'new resources of wealth' in a practical light, the fabled city re-emerged as a new centre from behind the fantastic legends and rumors that surrounded it (Park 1: 2).

The geographical track of the Witch's boat trip overlaps the most doomed area in the history of exploration.[23] Still, explorers had been sent one after another in vain because, as W. Young, secretary to the African Society, says in the preface to *The Journal of Frederick Horneman's Travels* (1802), Park's discoveries would open a gate for 'every commercial nation to enter and trade from the west to the eastern extremity of Africa' and 'the thorny track of a Park or a Horneman' would become 'the beaten road of the merchant' (ix–x).[24] Britain would only later realize 'the expediency of a military escort' in the attempts to penetrate Africa (Park 2: 93). Park's second and last mission in 1805, which was ordered by the government, was the first expedition that was accompanied by a considerable number of soldiers.[25] In 1815 the African Institution, which was founded in 1807 to promote humanitarian policies, honored Park by publishing his last journals and letters, proposing further expeditions protected by an armed force, and mentioning the riches that British commerce would enjoy after the opening of the heart of Africa.[26] The government sent three more expeditions between 1816 and 1821, but all of them failed. Although widely known as 'the great centre of the commerce of Fezzan, Cairo, and the countries of the north of Africa' (*Encyclopædia Britannica* [1817] 1: 265), no Europeans saw Timbuctoo till 1826.[27] It is, as Byron says, an 'impracticable place' where 'Geography finds no one to oblige her / With such a chart as may be safely stuck to' (*Don Juan* 12.555, 556–7).

Earlier at Oxford, Shelley described to Hogg one of his wildest scientific dreams, a dream that would remove the darkness of the interior of Africa: 'Why are we still so ignorant of the interior of Africa? – why do we not despatch intrepid aeronauts to cross it in every direction, and to survey the whole peninsula in a few weeks? The shadow of the first balloon, which a vertical sun would project precisely underneath it, as it glided silently over that hitherto unhappy country, would virtually emancipate every slave, and would annihilate slavery for ever' (Hogg 1: 63). We can trace the Witch's magic boat trip to the 'Austral waters' beyond Timbuctoo and her later gliding through the Nile back to this balloon ('The Witch of Atlas' 423). When the boat flies, driven by Hermaphroditus's wings, it looks like a big surveying balloon. What the Witch's playful boat trip illuminates, however, is the unhappy fate of the European explorers who toiled their way in vain to the source of the Niger and the unattainable city, which the British government was so anxious to reach at the cost of huge sums of money and loss of life.[28] In particular, the Witch's imaginary trip in a magic boat 'oared' by Hermaphroditus's 'enchanted wings' beyond 'the fabulous Thamondocana' to the 'Austral waters' offers a striking contrast to Park's final boat trip to the termination of the Niger from Sansanding near Timbuctoo, where Park rebuilt a broken canoe into a schooner and named it His Majesty's Schooner *Joliba* (407, 424, 423; Park 2: 80).[29] Even after having lost ninety per cent of the party, Park was able to maintain amazingly high spirits: '[On board] I this day hoist the British flag, and shall set sail to the east with the fixed resolution to discover the termination of the Niger or perish in the attempt' (2: 80). The reality of the expedition, however, was very dark. The editor of the journals comments: '[t]his voyage, one of the most formidable ever attempted, was to be undertaken in a crazy and ill appointed vessel, manned by a few Negroes and four Europeans!' (2: 77). Although Park was inclined to think that 'the termination of this mysterious stream' could be the sea, a local guide informed him that the Niger, after passing Kashna, ran 'directly to the right hand, or the South,' and the river was generally believed to end in 'some great lake or inland sea' (2: 78, 80). The word 'Austral,' by which Shelley means 'southern,' is vague, but the 'Austral lake,' which is located beyond Timbuctoo and reflects the 'Antarctic constellations' visible in the whole southern hemisphere, must be a large unknown inland lake beyond the equator ('The Witch of Atlas' 428, 427).

In the early nineteenth century four possibilities were discussed for the termination of the Niger, and the possibility of some inland lake, which corresponded with ancient and medieval opinions, was thought to be a rational answer (Park 2: 355–66). Colwell argues that Shelley 'prefer[s] the accounts of the classical historians and geographers to the less fanciful ones of his contemporaries,' and maintains that Shelley maps the Witch's journey according to Herodotus's account of the Nile, tracing 'the course of the Nile from its mysterious fountain source within the witch's Atlas cave' to 'the Nile delta' in Egypt ('Shelley's "The Witch of Atlas" and Mythic Geography of the Nile' 70–1). Shelley, however, has located the source of the Nile in the 'secret Aethiopian dells' ('To the Nile' [1818] 2), and in 'The Witch of Atlas,' the Nile flows from 'the steep / Of utmost Axumè' in Ethiopia to Cairo and Alexandria (499–500). There is no identification of the 'Austral waters' under the equator with the source of the Nile in the northeast mountainous area in the poem. As discussed earlier, Herodotus's account, which mistakenly located the source of the Nile in the west, served as a starting point for the contemporary accounts of the source of the Niger. The Niger was eagerly sought after by European explorers in the first two decades of the century, and topical and exciting enough to be alluded in the prologue to Wordsworth's *Peter Bell*. The Witch's magic boat takes up the voyage to the source of the Niger Wordsworth's little magic boat has given up. Thus I would suggest that the Witch's river journey from Atlas is more related to the Niger and that she covers a considerable part of Africa, going southward from Atlas to the Austral lake, crossing the continent to Ethiopia, and then moving up the Nile to Egypt.

The figure of a virgin queen travelling easily in the interior of Africa is interpreted as the triumph of Africa over British expeditions by Lee ('Mapping the Interior' 169–84), but at this point in the poem the figure of an Apollonian explorer is superimposed on that of a queen of Africa in an ambiguous fashion. It is easy to see a reversal of colonial power in a magical female African explorer looking triumphantly down on Western male explorers, but the contrast between the two as a direct criticism of the British penetration of Africa is not explicitly written. Moreover, there is something in the Witch's effortless boat trip that makes her exploration a dream version of the exploration of the interior of Africa, something that colonial and imperial Britain would have wished for. First, the Witch's hair, which was described as black at her birth, is now 'radiant,' revealing her Apollonian elements, when she orders Hermaphroditus to 'extend amain / Its storm-outspeeding wings' and the boat, propelled by Hermaphroditus's 'enchanted wings' and moving easily against the fierce torrents towards the upper springs, goes from Timbuctoo to the 'Austral waters' ('The Witch of Atlas' 413, 421–2, 407, 423).

Second, no local forms are to be seen from Atlas to the Austral lake, while the world of Atlas is filled with all kinds of peoples and animals. In *Frankenstein* (1818), when asking Victor to create his companion, the monster assures him that no human beings shall see them again as they will go to 'the vast wilds of South America' (120). Unlike South America or Australia, the area where the Witch has travelled is not uninhabited. Contemporary European travellers' difficulties did not lie in travelling alone in primeval forests, but in establishing friendly relationships with local societies. An absence of local peoples and animals suggests that the Witch's boat trip follows the scientific colonial map of the eighteenth and nineteenth centuries, which spreads a vast silent space, ignoring human presence in distant non-European regions. A geography of mythology is now replaced by that of exploration and imperialism.

Third, on arriving at the lake, the Witch calls the 'armies of her ministering Spirits,' which are her own thoughts to which Apollo's magic power gave tangible forms, and orders them to perform military duties ('The Witch of Atlas' 459):

> In mighty legions million after million
> They came, each troop emblazoning its merits
>   On meteor flags, and many a proud pavilion
> Of the intertexture of the atmosphere
> They pitched upon the plain of the calm mere.   (460–4)

What they do is frame 'the imperial tent of their great Queen' (465). If the Witch's boat trip to the lake refers to Park's voyage in the *Joliba*, here on the lake the Witch mimics British colonial activities.[30] The tone is that of conquest and empire-building. 'Canopus and his crew,' the Argonauts who symbolize Western exploration, are clearly impressed on the crystal surface of the lake (428). A dream of empire can be extended to include the entire Southern Hemisphere and the South Pole. The description of the stormy and frozen landscape with 'the solid vapours hoar' and 'the incessant hail' is very similar to that of a southern land of ice and snow reported in the second voyage of James Cook and used in Coleridge's 'The Rime of the Ancient Mariner' (435, 443). Leask argues that in 'Alastor' the Poet 'prefigures the Victorian empire-builder, moving ever further and outward' (*British Romantic Writers and the East* 124); but it is probably the Witch on the Austral lake who best exemplifies Leask's view of the Shelleyan solitary quester as an imperial explorer. A modern reader would be tempted to see in the 'great Queen' in the 'imperial' tent on the Austral lake an anticipation of the Queen of England, who was born in 1819 and in whose honour the largest African lake, which is the chief reservoir of the Nile, was to be named Victoria in 1858 ('The Witch of Atlas' 465).[31]

After seeing the sheer delight in mock-military actions of the Witch, who can be seen as a 'radiant' Apollonian queen and a triumphant African queen alike, we cannot simply say that a figure of the free and powerful female Africa is a condemnation of British attempts to penetrate into Africa. During the course of her trip, she is still shifting between the two poles of Europe and non-Europe, love and self-love, and the familiar and the foreign. In the Austral lake, the Witch is presented as an imperial queen, whether European or non-European, and Shelley deplores her complete indifference to mortal plights (441–8). In her hybridity the Witch cancels the binary opposition between the invader and the invaded, but she is merely repeating and imitating European colonial actions here, reflecting a disturbing image of European exploration in her non-European identity as queen of Africa. This can be seen as what Jan Nederveen Pieterse calls 'an assimilationist hybridity' which he locates at the one end of the spectrum of '*continuum of hybridity*,' and in which 'the centre predominates' (277). This may be one way in which the hybrid goes beyond its parent culture, but Shelley's Witch does go to the other end of Pieterse's '*continuum of hybridity*' to subvert the centre in her own way, for her destination is not the Austral lake. If the journey upriver presents a symbolic quest that will cure a diseased European civilization through an exercise of power and knowledge as in Conrad's *Heart of Darkness*, it is important to note that the Witch parts with Hermaphroditus and the magic boat she inherited from her European father here in the middle of her wanderings. Although the Witch has moved her throne to the Austral lake, she does not settle with Hermaphroditus in her 'imperial' tent ('The Witch of Atlas' 465). Earlier in Mount Atlas she had refused the nymphs because she did not want to 'weep,' but here hearing 'all that had happened new / Between the earth and moon,' she both 'wept' and 'laughed outright' (235, 476–7, 480), which shows that she is ready to go down to the populated world again. It is significant that Hermaphroditus, a symbol of self-love, silently disappears after they come to the Austral lake and does not accompany the Witch's never-ending wanderings, in which, gliding down the Nile, she visits human cities at night in the final part of the poem. It is in this part of the poem that Shelley details another kind of hybridizing activity by the Witch.

5. A Hybrid Geography

The geography of exploration and imperialism in the Austral lake gives way to another kind of geography when the Witch makes nightly visits to the cities on the Nile. In the sonnet 'To the Nile' the river is described as bringing down the waters from its 'aërial urn' in the 'secret Aethiopian dells' over 'Egypt's land of Memory' (7, 2, 9). The floods that descend from the highest mountain in Ethiopia, unlike the freezing 'flood of ruin' of Mont Blanc, symbolize fertility, which embraces both good and evil, as both 'fruits and poisons' spring wherever the mighty stream flows ('Mont Blanc' 107; 'To the Nile' 12). In 'The Witch of Atlas,' it is along the course of the Nile that the harmonious landscape of nature and city, which is called the 'cultivated plain' in *Queen Mab* (2.203), unfolds. In 'the hours of sleep,' she 'glide[s] adown old Nilus,' which 'threads / Egypt and Æhiopia, from the steep / Of utmost Axumè' and spreads '[h]is waters on the plain,' where 'crested heads / Of cities and proud temples gleam amid / And many a vapour-belted pyramid' ('The Witch of Atlas' 497, 498, 498–500, 502, 502–4). The Nile is presented as a genius loci of Africa, covering the vast part of the continent and blessing both nature and cities with his water. The Nile welcomes the hybrid daughter of Apollo and an Atlantid, letting her glide down his watery courses. The Witch is associated with night and becomes almost identical with the Nile, which makes her different from an Apollonian explorer.

Flowing from the remote source in mountainous 'Axumè' in Ethiopia, the river takes the Witch all the way down to its delta on the Mediterranean in Egypt formed by 'Mœis and the Mareotid lakes' (500, 505), which are Lake Moeris (Birket-Qarun) near Cairo and Lake Mareotis (Mariout) near Alexandria, respectively. Those two ancient names of the lakes point to the special geographical features of Egypt in ancient geography – its ambiguity – which made Herodotus distinguish Egypt from the rest of Africa as well as from Asia, which was well known in the early nineteenth century (Herodotus 2: 239; Rennell, *The Geographical System of Herodotus* 3, 410–11). Lake Moeris is located near a branch of the Nile that separates Egypt from Asia, while Lake Mareotis is near a branch of the Nile that separates Egypt from Africa (Pliny 253, 269, 267). Ever since Herodotus, Egypt has been an in-between place, between East and West, Europe and Africa, and the familiar and the foreign.

In the early nineteenth century, before the whitening of Egypt had started,[32] Europe was simultaneously fascinated and terrified by the dark, mysterious origin of the most ancient non-white civilization in Africa. It was not Europe, but it was not Europe's other, either, because it could be Europe's origin. Charles François Dupuis argued in the *Origine de tous les cultes* (1795) that all mythologies and religions including Christianity could be traced back to Egypt,[33] and it was this ancient civilization 'from which the Greeks had derived a great part of their arts and of their religion' (*Encyclopædia Britannica* [1817] 1: 256). At the same time, however, Egypt's exotic foreignness and ancientness evoked fearful images and associations that linked it more closely with the ancient civilizations of Asia. For example, in De Quincey's mental landscape, the ancient civilizations of Asia, Chinese and Indian, are jumbled together under nightmarish images of tropical regions and form a loathsome opposite to Europe. Egypt is attached to this horrible Asian climate that is governed by the 'ancient, monumental, cruel, and elaborate religions' of old Asia instead of being incorporated into the 'wild, barbarous, and capricious superstitions of Africa' (De Quincey 108).

If a human cross between black and white races was a biological hybrid who terrified and fascinated Europeans at the same time, Egypt was a cultural hybrid that showed problems of hybridity on a much larger scale and in much more complicated ways. Egypt was a point of exchange among Europe, Africa, the Middle East, and the further East, attracting travellers and merchants and offering a threshold to the East.[34] It was associated with pharaonic religion, but inhabited by different peoples with different religions including Muslims and Christians. Egypt's indeterminacy and hybridity made it difficult to place the country in the East-West binary opposition. Nor does it fit in Barrell's 'this / that / the other' triad, as it cannot be appropriated. The European approach to it was demonstrated in Napoleon's expedition to Egypt, which was accompanied by the Commission of Arts and Sciences, consisting of 120 savants, in order to 'make it [Egypt] totally accessible to *European* scrutiny' (Said, *Orientalism* 83). Shelley, however, approaches Egypt's hybridity and indeterminacy differently by making the Witch explore the 'peopled haunts of humankind' ('The Witch of Atlas' 523). The silent uninhabited geography of the Austral lake is replaced by the hybrid geography of peopled Egypt.

The Witch's travel in the Nile Valley is suggested simply by the two lakes, the only place names, whether ancient or modern, to appear. Thus the poem moves in an opposite direction from 'Alastor,' which details a solitary explorer's wanderings in the Middle East. There is no mention of the cities that were subject to ancient or modern deeds of conquest, such as Canopus (Abukir) or Alexandria; the former was visited by the heroes of the Trojan War and was a battlefield of the recent triumph of Nelson (Rennell, *The Geographical System of Herodotus* 523–5); the latter, which is the 'perpetual monument of the genius and talents of Alexander the Great' (Pinkerton, *Modern Geography* 3: 834), was a starting point of Napoleon's campaign, which followed the footsteps of Alexander the Great and unveiled the marvellous mysteries of Egypt with the aid of his corps of scholars. The Witch's nightly glide along the Nile can be contrasted with Napoleon's river campaign under the parching African sun, just as her effortless boat trip to the Austral lake parallels Park's last boat trip. But here, instead of mimicking European exploration, the Witch offers a third way, an alternative to both the military and the intellectual conquest of others – she reveals in a new hybrid space what European exploration of Africa cannot find.

The vantage point enjoyed by Shelley and the Witch from above the Nile differs from the cold scrutinizing gaze of Western exploration. The bird's-eye view of the Nile Valley first captures a lively civilization embraced by the Nile. The surface of Lake Moeris at night is observed still preserving the scene of a harmonious unity of humans and animals of the remote past, the image of 'naked boys bridling tame Water snakes / Or charioteering ghastly alligators' ('The Witch of Atlas' 507–8). The scene echoes Coleridge's 'Rime of the Ancient Mariner,' where the Mariner sees and blesses the water snakes in the lonely ocean; but Shelley's scene is not only distinctly Egyptian but also a reconciliation between nature and human civilization, because both boys and beasts 'slept' in 'the great Labyrinth' (511), which is, according to Herodotus, the pyramids of the City of Crocodiles on Lake Moeris (1: 455–9).

The Nile Valley represents an urban civilization on the margin, teeming with life, far from the centres of Europe. In particular, it makes a contrast to Italy, where Shelley had been living. The city of cities in Europe, Rome, is defined as a 'point within our day and night' of the 'pendulous Earth' and is 'at once the Paradise, / The grave, the city, and the wilderness' (*Adonais* [1821] 421, 417, 433–4). At the heart of urban civilization in Africa are lives lived among gleaming pyramids, 'tombs, and towers, and fanes' ('The Witch of Atlas' 519), while Rome embraces death at its core, centring on 'one keen pyramid with wedge sublime,' the pyramidal tomb of Caius Cestius in the Aurelian wall under which spreads a field of graves where 'a newer band / Have pitched in Heaven's smile their camp of death' (*Adonais* 444, 448–9). Rome is a centre that leads to heaven by way of death, but the Nile Valley affirms the continuity of life by reflecting all the images of the sublunary world on the water. The enormous vistas of cities on the Nile are epitomized in the reflected shadows of massive architecture and are represented in the present tense: 'within the surface of the River / The shadows of the massy temples lie / And never are erased – but tremble ever' ('The Witch of Atlas' 513–15). W.B. Yeats in 'The Philosophy of Shelley' persuasively observes that the Witch 'sees all human life shadowed upon its waters in shadows that "never are erased but tremble ever"' (85).

The reflected images on the water register human architecture that, for the first time in Shelley's poetry, is not falling into ruin. In *Queen Mab* the gleaming pyramids are destined to crumble into nothing beside the eternal Nile (2.126–33). In the 'Ode to Liberty,' written just before 'The Witch of Atlas' was composed, Shelley cannot sustain a similar image of Athens. He sees the reflection of the city on the water:

> Within the surface of Time's fleeting river
>   Its [Athens's] wrinkled image lies, as then it lay
> Immovably unquiet, and for ever
>   It trembles, but it cannot pass away! (76–9)

Despite Shelley's wish, however, the image cannot last at the end of the poem when the waters of time begin raging and swallow the poet. In the poem that is set in Africa, finally, the watery images stay in the water forever, reflecting all the lives lived above, and they keep their three-dimensional 'massy' solidity even while floating, which supports the human will to create and last midway in the Heraclitean flux of time ('The Witch of Atlas' 514). The Nile scene is made universal as an image of life on the fleeting river of time. Even if some parts of the image are to be overcast by the clouds, which 'can doom [them] to die' (516), the trembling image stays forever on the river, affirming the continuity of human civilization, generation after generation, and civilization after civilization.

Moreover, this visionary landscape contributes to the transformation of a pathogenic European space, as another example of a beautiful innovation from the East. One year after in the summer of 1821, the scene reappears in 'Evening: Ponte Al Mare, Pisa,' one of the finest of Shelley's 'Pisan poems':

> Within the surface of the fleeting river
>   The wrinkled image of the city lay,
> Immovably unquiet, and forever
>   It trembles, but it never fades away. (13–16)

This present Italian scene is recreated by revising the visionary image of Athens that fails the drowning poet in the 'Ode to Liberty' with the imaginary landscape of the Nile Valley, and resists the gathering gloom that surrounds the Italian city whose underlying reference is 'one of Dante's infernal cities' (Holmes 683).

The Witch in the Nile Valley who visits 'mortals in their sleep' is a developed form of the Spirit of the Earth in *Prometheus Unbound*, who calls Asia 'Mother' ('The Witch of Atlas' 528; *Prometheus Unbound* 3.4.24). Wandering the world, the Spirit of the Earth 'walks through fields or cities while men sleep,' '[w]ondering at all it sees' (3.4.12, 15). While the Spirit of the Earth just sees and wonders, the Witch of Atlas goes one step further, being involved with the mortals and '[s]cattering sweet visions from her presence sweet' like the transfigured Asia on the Indian Caucasus who showers love on the earth ('The Witch of Atlas' 524). It is significant that the Witch's epipsyche, Hermaphroditus, is absent from the Nile Valley. As we have seen, Hermaphroditus is the Witch's own self-image, which she, like the Poet in 'Alastor,' creates as an object of love. The minimization of Hermaphroditus's role in the boat trip and its silent disappearance from the Nile scene suggest a criticism of the narcissistic conception of love. This also indicates that the Witch is moving from self-love to true love; she is changing from a narcissistic traveller like the Poet in 'Alastor' to a bringer of love and dreams, thus assuming a characteristic associated with Asia in *Prometheus Unbound*.

Parting from the fair 'Image' of herself, the Witch goes into labyrinths of cities, seeing all sorts of human beings, from the emperor down to nameless commoners, both rich and poor, and young and old (326). The Witch, who passes through 'the peopled haunts of humankind' with her 'light feet' and scatters 'sweet visions,' is likened to 'the spirit of that wind / Whose soft step deepens slumber' in a way that associates her with the 'evanescent visitations' of poetry whose 'footsteps are like those of a wind over a sea' in *A Defence of Poetry* (521–4; *A Defence of Poetry*, *SP&P* 532). The 'Power,' who has led a solitary life in the Atlas Mountains and created Hermaphroditus as her travel companion, meets others clothed in mortality in the Nile Valley. Earlier she has refused semi-immortal nymphs, but she now penetrates the souls and dreams of sleeping people, and finds in those mortal forms 'living spirits' ('The Witch of Atlas' 570):

> to her eyes
> The naked beauty of the soul lay bare,
>   And often through a rude and worn disguise
>   She saw the inner form most bright and fair –   (570–3)

Here the Witch clearly acts like poetry as described in *A Defence of Poetry*: '[Poetry] strips the veil of familiarity from the world, and lays bare the naked and sleeping beauty which is the spirit of its forms' (*SP&P* 533). Another side of Apollo, the god of poetry, reveals itself in the Witch in the way in which the power of poetic imagination functions best, piercing crude outward appearances to reach the beauty of the human soul.

In *A Defence of Poetry*, Shelley elucidates many roles of poetry, but here I am concerned with its 'visitations' and its influences experienced as 'the interpenetration of a diviner nature through our own,' which is the meeting and hybridization of a divine spirit and a mortal being (*SP&P* 532). The Witch recognizes the beauty of the mortal human soul and the existence of a living spirit in it, and interpenetration occurs: 'And then, she had a charm of strange device, / Which murmured on mute lips with tender tone, / Could make that Spirit mingle with her own' ('The Witch of Atlas' 574–6). It is for these imperfect mortal forms that she uses a magic treasure from her hoard in the Atlas cave, performing the miracle of love. What takes place is not only the union of transcendental and mortal spirits; the self and the other, the European psyche and the African psyche are mixed with each other in love and poetic imagination. The Witch transmutes her father's act of lust into love, and uses her '[m]ightier' qualities differently from the violent way in which Jupiter's '[d]etested prodigy,' the 'fatal child' incarnated as Demogorgon, dethrones Jupiter (*Prometheus Unbound* 3.1.44, 61, 19). The European explorer and god of poetry enters into and consumes a beautiful local nymph. The Witch crosses between black and white and mortal and immortal, but this crossing is spiritual and leads to almost all the effects that are attributed to poetry in *A Defence of Poetry*, especially love that functions as a moral means, which is 'a going out of our own nature, and an identification of ourselves with the beautiful which exists in thought, action, or person, not our own' (*SP&P* 517). She cancels boundaries between the self and the others, dream and reality, life and death, by revising the dreams of the sleepers.

The Witch's affectionate gaze into labyrinths of cities and the souls of people is different from the scrutinizing gaze Napoleon's expedition cast on Egypt, which, aiming at a military and intellectual conquest of Egypt, organized the viewed world from a vantage point that safely separated the Western self from the observed other. Her willingness to 'mingle' with local sleepers also offers a strong contrast to the contemporary Europeans' dislike of mixing with local people. Thomas Walsh, a British military officer, thought that one of the big advantages of sailing on the Nile lay in the avoidance of local inns, 'miserable cravanseraïs, disgusting to an European, where you must sleep upon dirty carpets ... lying promiscuously with Turks, Arabs, &c.' (252). Similarly, in an opium dream, De Quincey is in fear of being 'kissed, with cancerous kisses, by crocodiles' and being 'laid, confounded with all unutterable slimy things, amongst reeds and Nilotic mud' (109).

The Witch's Nile trip shows the third way of being involved with those who are different from oneself; not by way of conquest or observation, but by way of the 'great secret of morals,' love, which is a sympathetic recognition of the beauty in the other and an imaginary identification of the self with what is different (*A Defence of Poetry*, *SP&P* 517). In the Nile Valley the Witch manifests a hybridity that combines love and poetic imagination, in which European and non-European qualities are mingled without the one being assimilated into the other. Shelley hybridizes the Witch's non-European and European qualities into a new hybrid female explorer, a dark queen of Africa and Apollonian goddess of poetry. Accordingly, the Nile Valley becomes a hybrid space that symbolizes a possible alternative Africa, where the female hybrid exploring goddess, in her own playful way, 'unite[s]' people with 'visions clear / Of deep affection and of truth sincere' ('The Witch of Atlas' 663–4), engaged with all people, kings, priests, peasants, mariners, young lovers, and old men, and thus overturns the deeds of European male explorers, represented by her father, Apollo, who desire, conquer, and consume the continent.

6. Shelley's Joyous Challenge

The Witch's hybridity differentiates her from the female other as well as from the European self. As a female hybrid explorer she maps Africa differently from those engaged in contemporary British attempts to penetrate Africa. By tracing her journey from Atlas to the Nile Valley, Shelley presents three different kinds of African geography: a mythical or medieval geography of the Atlas Mountains, a colonial geography of the Austral lake beyond Timbuctoo, and a hybrid geography of the Nile Valley. The Witch moves not only in space but also in time, which shows another dimension of hybridity that concerns the experience of *'mixed times (tiempos mixtos),'* which is 'the coexistence and interspersion of premodernity, modernity and postmodernity' (Pieterse 272). In terms of narrative sequence, the mapping style of each geography is progressive. The final part of her trip is set in a hybrid geography, Egypt, which offers an alternative mode of mapping the other to the contemporary mode of exploring the other, such as Napoleon's Egyptian expedition.

As Shelley emphasizes the poem's irony by saying in the last stanza that all that the Witch does is 'pranks' fit for a daydream in 'garish summer days' ('The Witch of Atlas' 665, 671), 'The Witch of Atlas' can be seen as an imposition of the poet's dream on the vast interior of Africa, ignoring what Africa was experiencing externally with the slave trade and internally with wars among tribes, and reconstructing an imaginary geography based purely upon Western texts from Herodotus to Rennell. Even so, Shelley's poem shows how language and imagination can affect a text that can be taken as a typical piece of Orientalism, breaking a one-sided relationship between two different cultures from within the genre. Both Shelley's 'The Witch of Atlas' and Keats's *Lamia* (1820) show that Africa was the last possibility for a poetic imaginary reconstruction of a place. Written almost simultaneously and dealing with the same themes, the two poems strikingly differ in the treatment of the central figure, the hybrid African witch.

Keats's Lamia, a hybrid between a snake and a human whose 'gordian shape of dazzling hue' is '[s]triped like a zebra, freckled like a pard, / Eyed like a peacock,' is composed of all African animals and birds (1.47, 49–50). But when she is undressed, '[n]othing but pain and ugliness' remains, and she is demystified by the cold Western gaze (164). On the contrary, Shelley's Witch is triumphant, and when unveiling her, the reader will find a surpassing beauty, just as the Witch finds the inmost beauty of the mortal soul in the poem. The significant difference between Keats's Lamia and Shelley's Witch demonstrates that literature can accommodate different images of the other even within the same age and that a given culture is subject to change through contact with another.

The 'visionary rhyme' of 'The Witch of Altas' is 'light,' and its ottava rima, like that of *Don Juan* and Shelley's own translation of the 'Hymn to Mercury,' is 'infinitely comical,' tracing the Witch's endless delightful journey ('To Mary' 8; 'The Witch of Atlas' 522; *Letters* 2: 218). But this very lightness shakes the rigid imposition of one culture upon the other that Orientalism presupposes. The poem's playfulness and its marginal female protagonist outlast and laugh at the seriousness and epic glory that always accompany male exploration of the vast untrodden land. Shelley's imagination, taking the form of a female hybrid in the poem, introduces crossings between the self and the other, liberates the space penetrated and disclosed by Western explorers, and presents a most fruitful Romantic geography of hybridity and love. What is unveiled in the heart of Africa in the poem is the beauty of the hybrid Witch and the inmost beauty of the soul of the other, which can be found in all peoples: a beauty that cannot be found by Western colonial desire but that, discovered by the liberating imagination, can alter African geography.

Because hybridity was not at all a positive concept of the day, the poem is layered with irony at many levels. The serio-comic ottava rima makes the Witch's journey a never-ending holiday excursion at the surface, but it is laden with deep human sorrow, responding to the contemporary British exploration of Africa. Marilyn Butler argues that in the poem 'a sad consciousness of human suffering' is treated according to the classical theme that 'from the gods' eye view life is an occasion for laughter rather than tears' (*Peacock Displayed* 305). As Judith Chernaik points out, however, Shelley's poems in 1820 humanize traditional Greek gods (130–8), and in 'The Witch of Atlas,' Shelley makes one step further, adding to the immortal hybrid a sympathy for earthly creations. In this poem, the separation between the two worlds, between the mortal and the immortal as well as the self and the others, is always undermined by hybridity, crossings between gods and mortals as well as between Europeans and Africans. Many of the passing classical references in the poem revolve around miscegenation between gods and mortals: Apollo and an Atlantid, Aurora and Tithonus, Venus and Adonis, and Diana and Endymion. Shelley thinks that the Witch's 'charm of strange device,' with which she mingles her spirit with a human spirit, is the key that could transform those relationships ('The Witch of Atlas' 574). It is clear that the Witch is more and more involved with human affairs as the poem progresses. The Witch has not been very sympathetic toward the nymphs, but she is changing during the journey to such an extent that she recognizes the inner beauty breathing under the imperfect mortal form in the Nile Valley, engaging both human beings and spirits in her 'sweet ditties' (667). Like Asia's enchanted boat, the Witch sails and sings forever, and goes freely between the sublunary and transcendental worlds, '[h]armonizing this Earth with what we feel above' and transforming the places she passes through into the '[r]ealms where the air we breathe is Love' (*Prometheus Unbound* 2.5.97, 95).

Shelley changes the image of a female Africa completely from a seductive enchantress to an invincible hybrid queen-explorer who crosses the African continent easily and freely. Shelley's likening of the Witch to a 'sexless' bee puts her back into the contemporary racial debate to her disadvantage ('The Witch of Atlas' 589), but this sexlessness is not so much the third sex or infertility as pre-pubertal asexuality. In the dedicatory poem 'To Mary,' the 'visionary rhyme' is likened to 'a young kitten' and 'the silken-winged fly,' which is the 'youngest of inconstant April's minions' (8, 5, 9, 10). This feminine youthfulness effectively counters the image of imperial youth, by which Burke expresses for the first time the apprehension of 'the adolescence of the colonizing mind' in his speech on Fox's Indian Bill delivered in December 1783 (Suleri 32). Burke condemns the British officers in India, '[y]oung men (boys almost)' who 'govern there, without society, and without sympathy with the natives,' but only with 'all the impetuosity of youth'; Burke is terrified and indignant at 'the desperate boldness of a few obscure young men,' who having obtained 'a power of which they saw neither the purposes nor the limits, tossed about, subverted, and tore to pieces, as if it were in the gambols of a boyish unluckiness and malice, the most established rights, and the most ancient and most revered institutions, of ages and nations' (Burke 5: 402, 427). As Suleri argues (111–31), Burke's image of young colonizers found its way into the figure of adolescent hybrid like Kim in Kipling's *Kim* (1901), but the 'desperate boldness of a few obscure young men' was also seen in British explorers in Africa in the early nineteenth century, and was to resurface in imperial narrative at the turn of the twentieth century to meet the most voluptuous female Africa like Ayesha in H. Rider Haggard's *She* (1886). In this respect, it is important to stress that the feminine adolescence of Shelley's Witch keeps her at a discreet distance from both Ayesha and Kim.

The irony that accompanies the Witch's double identity thus does not lead to a dark aporia of history; instead, it is pregnant with a new world view, simultaneously voicing the superiority and the disadvantage of hybridity. The poem in its joy at singing 'no story, false or true' and delight in the playful excursion of the hybrid young muse on the margin succeeds in replacing the continent torn by wars and penetrated by European explorers with an alternative geography in the advent of British colonization of Africa ('To Mary' 4). The Romantic geography of 'The Witch of Atlas' shows that the margin is capable of producing a new power through a meeting of two different cultures, in the form of the hybrid. A new 'Power' in the margin is neither the self nor the other but a complex mixture of the two. A brief comparison between Shelley's Witch and Conrad's Kurtz is worth making here. Despite his actual experience in the Congo and his intended criticism on imperialism, Conrad's imaginary Africa centres upon the figure of Kurtz, who represents the hybrid of 'All Europe' (117). Whereas Conrad's Marlow should seek a white man in the dark heart of Africa, the hybrid female protagonist in Shelley's poem finally finds true beauty in the naked spirit concealed under the dark skin. The female hybrid Power sings and heals in her endless wanderings. She lifts the dark veil of Africa to show that what the heart of darkness conceals is neither gold nor riches, but the naked beauty of the human soul, and in so doing, redirects the course of exploration from colonial desire to love, which transforms both the explorer herself and the geography she explores.

Conclusion

The central theme of this book has been Shelley's Romantic geography, and throughout the chapters a range of connected themes and concepts have been discussed, often in a positive light. In particular, the concept of hybridity has been examined and shown to have a number of constructive values for Shelley. Many scholars, however, would think that it is overtly optimistic; Shelley's oeuvre would look different if his quest for visionary improvement of sick places was to go round Africa and return to Europe, to the last unfinished work, 'The Triumph of Life,' in which culminate the moments of pessimism that are more and more prominent in Shelley's later works. It is to this work that we should turn now before summing up the book as a whole.

Toward the end of his short life, Shelley found himself torn between colonial desire, shame for it, and resignation. In the autumn of 1821, Shelley was dreaming of going to India. After asking Peacock about a possible employment opportunity in India, Shelley ordered James Mill's *History of British India* on 11 October (*Letters* 2: 357). In the same month Peacock wrote a reply; he does not like Shelley's 'Indian project,' which he thinks does not suit Shelley's mind and body at all, and also adds its practical impossibility. 'The whole of the Civil Service of India is sealed against all but the Company's covenanted servants' who are trained from an early period of life (*Letters* 2: 361n.5). In a letter to Hogg on 22 October, Shelley writes: 'I have some thoughts, if I could get a respectable appointment, of going to India, or any where where I might be compelled to active exertion, & at the same time enter into an entirely new sphere of action. – But this I dare say is a mere dream, & I shall probably have no opportunity of making it a reality' (*Letters* 2: 361–2). He is more and more aware of his own complicity in colonialism, and correspondingly, in 'The Triumph of Life,' the destructive Power in 'Mont Blanc' comes back more powerfully. The icy colonial Power, which creates a white desert where '[n]one can reply,' revives as the Life's white light that 'deform[s]' everything from Europe as far as to 'some Indian isle' under the 'tropic sun' ('Mont Blanc' 75; 'The Triumph of Life' 468, 486, 485).

The poem opens with a narrating poet/quester, who is a thinly disguised Shelley, standing on 'the steep / Of a green Apennine' (25–6). He turns his back to the scene of prayer at dawn, the scene strongly reminiscent of Coleridge's universal morning prayer in the 'Hymn Before Sun-Rise in the Vale of Chamouni.' Once again, Shelley is confronted with the origin of Europe, but this time not with the sublime in nature, but with the Promethean figure that prepared for the French Revolution and the age of Romanticism. During the summer of 1816, Byron, Shelley, and Mary made two discoveries: the cold sublimity of the Alps and 'a fellow Promethean' in Rousseau (Edward Duffy 53).[1] They read Rousseau's work extensively, and visited places associated with him. Shelley 'first knew the divine beauty of Rousseau's imagination, as it exhibits itself in Julie' when he and Byron were touring around Lake Geneva by boat in late June (*Letters* 1: 480). In canto 3 of *Childe Harold's Pilgrimage*, Byron shifts from a brief Wordsworthian praise of high mountains to his true theme, the 'One, whose dust was once all fire,' which 'set the world in flame, / Nor ceased to burn till kingdoms were no more' (719, 763–4). In *A Defence of Poetry*, Shelley lists Rousseau among great poets and thinkers, and emphasizes in a note that 'Rousseau was essentially a poet' (*SP&P* 530n.2). For Shelley, Rousseau is one of those 'Poets or poetical philosophers' who produce 'true utility,' and thus are 'the unacknowledged legislators of the World' (*SP&P* 529, 535). It took, however, more than five years before Rousseau became a central theme in his poetry. Whereas in 1816 he was caught by a 'trance sublime and strange' in which he tried to interpret the mountain's voice for himself ('Mont Blanc' 35), the Shelleyan quester of his last poem is visited by a 'strange trance' and in the dream vision meets Rousseau, who is chosen as his Virgilian guide ('The Triumph of Life' 29).

Rousseau, however, does not appear as a bright fire-bringer. He is instead presented as a withered plant distorted by the sick 'clime' of Europe (467); the narrating poet with horror realizes that what he thought was 'an old root which grew / To a strange distortion out of the hill side' is 'one of that deluded crew,' and that 'the grass' which he thought 'hung so wide / And white' is 'his thin discoloured hair' and 'the holes it vainly sought to hide / Were or had been eyes' (182–7). Rousseau identifies the shape in the flying chariot as 'Life,' whose 'icy cold' light deforms everything in its way (180, 78). Rousseau's terrible distortion and the metaphor of humans as plants growing on the soil suggest that European colonial 'Power' destroys all who were born there; even Geneva-born Rousseau, who was regarded as advocating revolutionary thought, was no exception. In 1816, both Shelley and Mary made a sharp distinction between 'the subjects of the King of Sardinia and the citizens of the independent republics of Switzerland' as 'a powerful illustration of the blighting mischiefs of despotism, within the space of a few miles' (*Letters* 1: 482; *HSWT* 117). Now Shelley faces the question of contamination of European colonial Power and the fate of Landor's Gebir, who, though 'generous, just, humane,' 'inhaled / Rank venom' of his native country (*Gebir* 6.219, 219–20). The disfigured Rousseau in the poem says:

> if the spark with which Heaven lit my spirit
> Earth had with purer nutriment supplied
>
> 'Corruption would not now thus much inherit
> Of what was once Rousseau.   ('The Triumph of Life' 201–4)

In the hallucinatory superimposition of images of the protagonist's dream vision on those of Rousseau's, Shelley presents two kinds of 'Power': a 'shape all light' and a 'cold bright car' of Life (352, 434). Shelley's increasing pessimism makes the 'shape all light,' Rousseau's epipsyche, an ambiguous entity. Her birth, which is witnessed by Rousseau, takes place in the 'azure clime' of Europe's 'young year' (310, 311). She, however, has many traces from Shelley's earlier non-European epipsyches. She emerges from 'the Sun's image radiantly intense' that burned on the waves of the issuing fountain that 'glowed / Like gold' (345, 346–7); the scene reminds us of the birth of the Witch of Atlas in the 'chamber of grey rock' that Apollo had 'made all golden,' and 'the Deity of virtue,' which Shelley found in the image of Luxima in Sydney Owenson's novel, whose 'resplendent locks' were 'enwreathed with beams, and sparked with the waters of the holy stream, whence it appeared recently to have emerged' ('The Witch of Altas' 63, 62; *Letters* 1: 101; Owenson 1: 146–7). Unlike the Witch, though, her tender beauty is inseparable from the violence with which 'her feet, no less than the sweet tune' trample the 'fires' of the gazer's mind into 'the dust of death' ('The Triumph of Life' 382, 388). The intricate mixture of violence and poetry points to a more immediate reality than the world of the Witch of Atlas, looking back to a nameless 'Shape,' which rises as a 'mist, a light, an image' from nowhere in 'The Mask of Anarchy' (1819) (110, 103): the 'Shape arrayed in mail / Brighter than the Viper's scale' moves with a 'step as soft as wind' over the prostrate multitude and slays Anarchy, whose 'Pageant swift and free' goes all over England, '[t]rampling to a mire of blood / The adoring multitude' (110–11, 118, 51, 40–1). Anarchy's triumphal procession, which has an obvious source in the Hindu chariot of the Juggernaut (*SP&P* 317n.8), is a local manifestation of colonial Power inspired by the Peterloo Massacre. Its image is elaborated and extended into that of the Car of Life in 'The Triumph of Life,' which rages from Europe to 'some Indian isle,' and to which is chained 'a captive multitude' from 'Imperial Rome' down to the Enlightenment (486, 119, 113).

If the relationship between the 'Shape' and Anarchy runs parallel to that between the 'shape all light' and the cold light of Life, can the 'shape all light' be considered as a counter-hegemonic force powerful enough to subvert the Power from the centre? It is difficult to answer this question. For, while her 'light' is 'half extinguished' by the coming new light of Life's car, her cup of Nepenthe forcefully awakes Rousseau in 'this valley of perpetual dream' to 'the sick day' in which he 'wake[s] to weep' (429, 397, 430). That is, although her light is 'forever sought, forever lost' in the sick day of the European colonial Power, she at least forces Rousseau to be aware of his complicity in colonialism (431).

What is important is her impact on Rousseau's mind. Her cup of 'bright Nepenthe' reminds us of the Witch's 'christal vials' of 'liquors clear and sweet' ('The Triumph of Life' 359; 'The Witch of Atlas' 182, 177), but the effect is quite different. Whereas the Witch's liquors 'medicine the sick soul to happy sleep' and 'change eternal death into a night / Of glorious dreams,' the 'bright Nepenthe' in this poem causes a violent change in Rousseau's consciousness ('The Witch of Atlas' 178–80; 'The Triumph of Life' 359). As soon as his lips touch the cup, his brain becomes 'as sand' (405):

'Where the first wave had more than half erased
  The track of deer on desert Labrador,
    Whilst the fierce wolf from which they fled amazed

'Leaves his stamp visibly upon the shore
   Until the second bursts – so on my sight
Burst a new Vision never seen before.   (406–11)

The image of the deer chased by a wolf looks back to the white desert of Mont Blanc where 'the eagle brings some hunter's bone, / And the wolf tracks her there' ('Mont Blanc' 68–9), on which Stuart Peterfreund comments: 'Power residing in Mont Blanc is responsible for territoriality, predation and conflict' (123). As Mont Blanc's white wilderness is devoured by snake-like glaciers, waves wash and erase traces on the Labrador shore.

Many critics have examined this desert scene, but no one, to my knowledge, has discussed the special relevance of this northern locality. Though Donald Reiman and Paul de Man rightly consider that it is a 'sandy beach' (*Triumph* 67; de Man 99–100), they do not give any thought on where this 'sandy beach' is and why. Edward Duffy returns the disfigured Rousseau to the historical context of the French Revolution, but he ignores the fact that it is a beach, and fails to consider why it has to be Labrador; he maintains that 'Rousseau's mind as a wolf-haunted, Labradorean desert' is an 'obviously unattractive image' and that the metaphor of 'the brain as a cold desert' is 'a deliberately sinister parody of the epistemological image at the base of eighteenth century radicalism' (129, 130). I would locate Labrador in the context of the history of British colonialism. In the early nineteenth century Labrador and Newfoundland 'barely existed in the European consciousness' (Baehre 11). Shelley brings this almost forgotten northern area to British consciousness in the Romantic geography of the poem in order to recall Britain's empire-building scheme in 'Labrador, or New Britain,' which was known as a colony 'most inhabitable' but 'inhabited by the Esquimaux' in the late eighteenth century (Tytler 309, 276). Newfoundland was regarded as 'England's oldest colony' (Hough 26),[2] and the Treaty of Paris in 1763 settled a dispute over rival claims to Labrador, confirming that Britain possessed Newfoundland and Canada including Labrador (Gosling 95).

The landscape of the 'desert Labrador' thus takes Rousseau back to the 1760s, a decade crucial both for British colonialism and Rousseau's own life. Far from Europe, Labrador became a complex contact zone; the British, French, and Americans all claimed fishing rights in its waters; European fishermen, traders, and the Unitus Fratrum, more commonly known as Moravian missionaries, were commercially and culturally involved with Inuit, Beothuk, and other native peoples; its coasts James Cook mapped between 1763 and 1767; its flora and fauna Joseph Banks researched on his first overseas expedition in 1766.[3] Back in Europe, the historical Rousseau was writing his major works and wandering about Europe, including a visit to England in 1765; in 1762 he published *Julie ou la nouvelle Héloïse*, *Du Contract social, ou principes du droit politique*, which was banned in Geneva, and *Émile ou de l'éducation*, which was banned in France and Geneva, and deprived him of citizenship of Geneva. The latter half of the 1760s fairly closely corresponds to the period of his composition of *The Confessions* (Kelly, Masters, and Stillman xxxiii).

According to Baehre, Labrador and Newfoundland were seen as remote and obscure 'extension[s] of Europe' (11), though Labrador served as the base for the richest fishery, to which European fishermen came every summer. In the 1760s, when Britain was fervently trying to monopolize trade and the fishery and to maintain its naval strength, however, the area became a theatre of conflicting powers and interests. On being appointed governor and commander-in-chief of Newfoundland in 1764, Sir Hugh Palliser took a series of quick-fire actions; while restricting the French and American fishing claims, he ordered a survey of the coasts, issued passports to the Moravians, and prohibited English fishermen from plundering and killing indigenous people. Among others, Palliser wanted to establish a friendly relationship with the Indians. He issued the 'Order for Establishing Communication and Trade with the Esquimaux Savages on the Coast of Labrador, 1765,' in which he declared that he endeavoured 'to establish a friendly communication between His Majesty's subject[s] and the said natives on the coast of Labrador, and to remove these prejudices that have hitherto proved obstacles to it.'[4] Until Palliser's proclamation, Europeans and indigenous people had been killing each other. Joseph Banks records a second-hand report on the tense relationships between Europeans and locals in his diary. 'Our people' are 'in a continual state of warfare with them firing at them whenever they meet with them & if they chance to find their houses or wigwams as they call them Plundering them immediately,' while they 'in return Look upon us in exactly the same Light as we Do them Killing our people whenever they get the advantage of them & Stealing or Destroying their nets whenever they find them' (*Joseph Banks in Newfoundland and Labrador, 1766* 132). George Cartwright, who was a trader and entrepreneur and lived in Labrador between 1770 and 1786, writes in his journals that 'our fishermen' are 'much greater savages than the Indians themselves, for they seldom fail to shoot the poor creatures, whenever they can,' adding that '[w]ith horror, I have heard several declare, they would rather kill an Indian than a deer!' (*A Journal of Transactions and Events* 1: 86).

The home government utilized the Moravian missionary enterprise to establish friendly relations, and monopolize trade, with indigenous people. Palliser met in London with Jens Haven, a Moravian missionary who desired to establish a mission on the coast of Labrador, and allowed him and three other Moravians to go to Chateau Bay on board the HMS *Niger*. In return for the navy's support, Haven gave Palliser his journals, which detailed their exploration in Labrador. In 1769, the British government granted the Moravians a place for a permanent settlement, and accorded them permission for missionary activities and trade with native people. There were traders and entrepreneurs who tried to be on good terms with locals. Cartwright writes on the first page of his journals that his purpose is dual: 'carrying on various branches of business upon the coast of Labrador' and 'endeavouring to cultivate a friendly intercourse with the Esquimaux Indians, who have always been accounted the most savage race of people upon the whole continent of America' (*A Journal of Transactions and Events* 1: 1). Even though they meant well, however, both the Moravians and British traders like Cartwright were, on the whole, unarmed imperialists who acquiesced to the purposes of British imperial policy in this area.

The landscape of Labrador in early writings is characterized by dreariness and a sequence of predation. In 'Journals of the Two Brethren Jens Haven & C.A. Schloezer to Explore the Coast of Labrador, in the "Hope" Schooner from the 23d July to the 3d September 1765,' Haven reports that two days after they landed on the 'Rocky and Barren' coast and 'saw plainly in the sandy Beach footsteps of both Indians & Europeans, also of Bears & Foxes,' they 'shot two large Deer, of the Moore kind' while rowing along the shore (*Joseph Banks in Newfoundland and Labrador, 1766*, Pt. 3. 215, 214, 217).[5] In his poem *Labrador: A Poetical Epistle*, Cartwright describes a chain of slaughter among deer, wolves, and humans near 'the Ocean's shore,' or on a 'dreary Desart all, of Ice and Snow,' where wolves 'in plenty' appear and, driven by hunger, 'seek for Deer' (5, 23, 24).[6] After recounting how a 'Hind' seeks her safety from 'the Wolf's dire wiles,' he asks his friend whether he would like to shoot 'a stout Rein-deer' or would prefer to hunt a 'voracious Wolf' along the 'sandy beeches' (5, 12, 14); then he depicts a deadly chase of a wolf, who, 'rushing forward, singles out his Deer' (24):

> Greedy of Blood, and with keen Hunger press'd,
>   This he pursues, regardless of the rest.
> With well strung Sinews, both maintain the Strife;
> The one for Food – the other runs for Life.   (25)

It is not certain whether Shelley knew Labrador through books or hearsay; there are no extant records of his sources. He might have heard of this remote colony from Byron, whose grandfather, John Byron, had succeeded Palliser in the governorship of Newfoundland, and, following Palliser's policies, issued a proclamation on 7 May 1771 that forbade 'every one to molest the Brethren in their settlement, or to male-treat the poor Esquimaux in any wise' (United Brethren in Christ 6). Although there was little writing on Labrador in the early nineteenth century, the passages cited in the previous paragraph sum up the image of Labrador that would have found its way into the minds of contemporary British readers and formed the imagined geography of a faraway cold land of predation. Wolves hunt deer with 'dire wiles' and 'artful skill' (Cartwright, *Labrador* 5, 24); when humans, whether European or Indian, find their footsteps, they hunt them with guns and traps; and Europeans and Indians kill each other. After the flagship of the governor of Newfoundland, the HMS *Antelope*, went to Newfoundland in 1762, the northern shore continued to be soaked in blood. English settlements were attacked by French warships when Britain was at war with France in 1793, and ravaged by American privateers especially after the War of 1812 broke out. Shelley may have wanted to create new traces on the sand again and again until the old traces of bloodshed were erased.

The appearance of lights in the sky – the 'shape all light' for whom 'Iris her many coloured scarf had drawn' and the 'coming light' of Life for whom '[a] moving arch of victory, the vermilion / And green and azure plumes of Iris had / Built high over her wind-winged pavilion' ('The Triumph of Life' 352, 357, 412, 439–41) – bears some similarity to a common phenomenon of 'mock sun' (parhelion) reported by early travellers in Labrador. The phenomenon refers to a bright spot (or sometimes spots) that appears in the sky caused by the refraction of sunlight through ice crystals in the atmosphere, being 'very luminous, and beautifully tinged with all the various colours of the rainbow'

(Trusler 99). How do these lights in the Labrador scene relate to the historical Rousseau's life? Critics have sought biographical parallels for the 'oblivious' valley and the subsequent disfigurement of Rousseau, who 'plunged' the 'thickest billows of the living storm' of Life's light ('The Triumph of Life' 331, 467, 466).[7] I would like to link Rousseau's experience in the 'oblivious valley' (539) to the historical Rousseau's tendency to 'forgetfulness' he mentions in *The Confessions*; 'as soon as I have written a thing one time I no longer remember it at all' (5: 294). And I would argue that the glimmering lights in the Labrador scene are internally transferred back to Europe to evoke the so-called 'illumination of Vincennes' in the historical Rousseau's mind, in which 'first crystallized' his important notions of 'the natural goodness of man' and the social origin of wickedness (Melzer 29).[8] The vision took place in 1749, but was first mentioned in the second letter to Malesherbes in 1762, and later in *The Confessions*.[9]

In 1762, Rousseau, in an early attempt to write an autobiography, told Malesherbes that he was struck by 'a sudden inspiration' when walking from Paris to Vincennes to visit the prison where his friend Diderot was confined; he felt his mind 'dazzled by a thousand lights,' while 'crowds of lively ideas presented themselves' with such 'a strength and a confusion' that, in 'an inexpressible perturbation,' he fell 'under one of the trees of the avenue' for half an hour (5: 575). He addresses Malesherbes: 'Oh Sir, if I had ever been able to write a quarter of what I saw and felt under that tree, how clearly I would have made all the contradictions of the social system seen, with what strength I would have exposed all the abuses of our institutions, with what simplicity I would have demonstrated that man is naturally good and that it is from these institutions alone that men become wicked' (5: 575). Of these 'crowds of great truths' that 'illuminated' him under that tree, it was only 'the prosopopeia of Fabricius' that Rousseau managed to write 'on the spot,' and the ideas were 'weakly scattered' in his three principal writings, 'that first discourse, the one on inequality, and the treatise on education' (5: 575). The 'prosopopeia of Fabricius' refers to the *Discours sur les sciences et les arts* (*First Discourse*),[10] in which Rousseau invokes the dead Fabricius: 'O Fabricius! What would your noble soul have thought if, resorted to life to your own misfortune, you had seen the pompous appearance of that Rome saved by your valor and better glorified by your worthy name than by all its conquests?' (2: 11). The apostrophe to the dead Fabricius runs parallel to Shelley's conjuring of the disfigured Rousseau in the poem. If prosopopeia is defined as 'the fiction of an apostrophe to an absent, deceased, or voiceless entity' in order to 'confer upon it the power to speech,' and then 'confer a mask or a face (*prosopon*)' as in de Man's 'Autobiography as De-Facement' (75–6), what takes place on the hillside when Rousseau is first introduced into Shelley's poem is not 'a reverse prosopopoeia' (Wang 637), for a face is given to a 'voice' that answers Shelley's question ('The Triumph of Life' 180). The narrating Shelley gives 'a voice' of the dead a disfigured face, because he knows what happened to Rousseau after the publication of the award-winning treatise. Rousseau himself, recollecting this most important vision in his life twenty years later, in book 8 of *The Confessions*, writes: '[in the vision] I saw another universe and I became another man' (5: 294). At the same time, however, he bewails the fate of a man who discovered and tried to preserve the principle of the natural goodness of man in a corrupt society that afflicted humans: '[F]rom that instant I was lost. All the rest of my life and misfortunes was the inevitable effect of that instant of aberration' (5: 295). The vision was, in retrospect, illusory.

Arthur Melzer suggests that the vision of Vincennes offers Rousseau both the foundation for his thought on the structure of society and the 'ways to cure men's deformity' (81). Like Godwin and Rousseau, Shelley believes in the natural goodness of man and thinks that the evils that originate in society are curable. Instead of merely criticizing corrupt society and grieving for those who are deformed, in this final poem, Shelley, as a European, is prepared to perceive and accept that the deformity is deeply rooted in European society. Shelley makes Rousseau plunge into the light of Life, which, accumulating all the evils of the past, has been and will be blighting both Europe and the world at large. What is more, Shelley chooses as his Virgilian guide the disfigured Rousseau, who asks Shelley to 'from spectator turn / Actor or victim in this wretchedness' ('The Triumph of Life' 305–6). Shelley's resolution to face his complicity in the evils of European society here is a telling rejoinder to Mary's modern Prometheus, Victor Frankenstein, who refuses to take any responsibility for his hideous progeny. Victor waves aside a 'sight tremendous and abhorred'; the 'shape,' which appears on the summit of Montanvert as if to respond to Victor's apostrophe to '[w]andering spirits,' turns out to be 'the wretch' he himself 'had created' (Mary Shelley, *Frankenstein* 76).

The moment when Rousseau, one of the most important philosophers of the Enlightenment, bears his bosom to 'the clime / Of that cold light' and commits himself to Eurocentric colonial power, critiques of colonialism emerge from within the sick European centre, not from beyond the colonial divide ('The Triumph of Life' 467–8). In 'the sick day in which we wake to weep,' the 'shape all light' appears as a new unclassifiable phenomenon (430, 352). Unlike the transfigured Asia, however, who establishes herself as Love, which opposes the cold colonial Power emanating from Europe, she looks similar to the colonial Power. The disfigured Rousseau, no matter how hard it may be, tries to distinguish between these two kinds of Power, asking Shelley to '[b]ehold a wonder worthy of the rhyme / Of him [Dante]' (471–2). What Rousseau wants Shelley to see is the 'shape all light' who is almost unseen but keeps her 'obscure tenour' in the coming light of Life (352, 432). The word 'wonder' reinforces her association with the Witch of Atlas, who was born as a 'wonder new,' but it also connects her with 'a strange wonder,' Jupiter's unborn hybrid, who, '[m]ightier than either [of the parents]' and 'unbodied now,' 'floats, felt although unbeheld, / Waiting the incarnation' ('The Witch of Atlas' 88; *Prometheus Unbound* 3.1.18, 44, 45–6). All those hybrid progenies are born from the very source of European colonialism and imperialism, and mightier than the parents. The problem is how to exercise their counter-colonial powers. After Dante, it has become extremely difficult to talk about the nature of transfiguring power of Love. Two different kinds of transfiguring Powers, one deforming and one curing, have been almost indistinguishable, because the 'wondrous story' is told in 'words of hate and awe,' namely, the language of colonialism, and '[t]he world can hear not the sweet notes' of singing spirits of light ('The Triumph of Life' 475, 478). Rousseau's 'words' were thus 'seeds of misery – / Even as the deeds of others' (280–1). Nevertheless, a Shelleyan quester would dare to paint '[f]igures ever new / Rise on the bubble' against erasing waves of the all-encompassing Power, and continue to ask: 'what is Life?' (248–9, 544). This is the question Shelley has asked from the beginning to the end of his life in 'the sick day in which we wake to weep' (430). As we have seen in the previous chapters, the question can be variously rephrased: 'What is the Power?' 'What is colonialism?' 'What has made the earth pathogenic?'

In *Queen Mab* Shelley likens the 'Power' that '[p]ollutes whate'er it touches' to a 'desolating pestilence' (3.176–7). Comparing Shelley's concept of disease with James Annesley's medical view of miasmas that 'float in the atmosphere,'[11] Alan Bewell casts an eye-opening light on the Shelleyan 'Power': 'power *is* disease; it is the force that creates pathogenic spaces in the world' (*Romanticism and Colonial Disease* 209). The Shelleyan Power *is* disease, but there are two kinds disease: a globalizing, all-polluting power and a counter-hegemonic contagious power that cancels the geopolitical dichotomy between centre and periphery to create new cultural imaginaries. Tracing six different constellations of the locality and particularity of 'Romantic geography' in Shelley's poems, the present book has demonstrated that it is neither through dispensing medicine nor militaristic conquest that Shelley endeavoured to cure pathogenic spaces and inhospitable landscapes. The key to cure the colonial landscape is in the minds of people, which can emit an opposing contagious power of love, assisted by the imagination that can separate itself from power. The visionary improvement of the internal contact zone requires merging endogenous/exogenous understandings and acceptance of others, and that is why hybridity, which ushers mutualities, negotiations, and changes in the inner contact zones, and forces the self to grow, is so important in the Shelleyan Romantic geography.

The concept of Romantic geography has been broadened since we started off in the introduction. Each chapter has added an extra dimension of the concept in relation to hybridity. In *Queen Mab*, the place from where to counter the all-polluting imperial power is found in the 'cultivated plain' in the margin (2.203). The Romantic geography of 'Alastor' reveals the dark history of Western invasion of the East, but it also produces a new type of Shelleyan epipsyche that is nameless and hybrid with marked geographical traits in its body. Hybridity works as an allopathic disease from the margin in 'Mont Blanc' and *Prometheus Unbound*, whose Romantic geography realizes a plurality of 'beautiful idealisms' (preface to *Prometheus Unbound*, *SP&P* 209). The Romantic geography of 'The Witch of Atlas' presents the most fruitful effects of hybridity internally in the Witch's penetration into mortal others and externally in a city at night on the Nile as a possible future model of the recreated 'cultivated plain.' In 'The Triumph of Life,' the Labrador shore as Rousseau's brain shows a birth of European consciousness that, keenly aware of its complicity with colonialism, revisits the colonial past/present, and is determined to live the tensions between imperialism and idealism.

Shelley's Romantic geography sees, through contact with others, new poetic modes and themes realizing new possibilities of marginality and hybridity. Shelley, however, knows that hybridization is a very painful and long process. Even in an idealized revision of the

Promethean myth, the bound Prometheus has been 'eyeless in hate' for '[t]hree thousand years' and love as a 'patient power' undergoes 'dread endurance' before creating a geography of love on the Eastern mountaintop in the distant future (*Prometheus Unbound* 1.9, 12, 4.557, 559). Because hybridity was a negative concept in culture as well as in science in the nineteenth century, we should not celebrate it without reservation as if it were the cultural hybridity of the twentieth century, turning a problem into a virtue.[12] In the Romantic period, the concept was oscillating between a negative trope and new possibilities. Behind the plural idealisms of *Prometheus Unbound* lies the unbodied, hybrid 'fatal child' of Jupiter (3.1.19). In 'The Witch of Altas,' the female hybrid by colonial miscegenation is given only a hint of growth, being kept at the stage of the pre-pubescent asexuality.

The 'shape all light' of 'The Triumph of Life,' the final Shelleyan epipsyche, is a very complex and ambiguous entity developed from his previous epipsyches of hybrid construction of self and others. She becomes almost indistinguishable from the colonial Power from the centre of Europe, because Shelley chooses to continue his effort to cure 'the sick day in which we wake to weep' rather than staying in the 'oblivious valley' ('The Triumph of Life' 430, 539). Had his life not been terminated abruptly off the Gulf of Spezia at the age of twenty-nine, we would have seen a series of visionary making and unmaking in the Labrador sand to rewrite the European colonial mind. As a Shelleyan quester in the poem takes over the disfigured Rousseau's experience, we in the twenty-first century have to complete Shelley's unfinished quest. The Romantic geography of Shelley's final poem is both colonial and postcolonial, where we, with Rousseau, have to write and rewrite numberless times '[f]igures ever new' arising from our internal contact zone against rushing waves of colonialism and globalization, however painful it may be (248).

From our present vantage point, which has seen globalization as a new kind of political and social phenomenon that impacts on all aspects of the postcolonial age, Shelley's effort to account for the nature of pathogenic spaces and to improve them by the imagination can be viewed as an endeavour to tackle with an early form of the same predicament that confronts us now. From his early career, Shelley has been alert to an unnameable force, metaphorically presented by disease, radiating in immediate ways that engage technological, economic, political, and cultural realities from a discrete geographical and cultural centre. This all-deforming colonial force can be considered as globalization that takes a form of homogenization, or Westernization that compresses multiple worlds into one. Shelley has been seeking counter-hegemonic energies in 'the human mind's imaginings' in order to cure pathogenic spaces ('Mont Blanc' 143). In his later poems, while the colonial past/present is revisited, remembered, and crucially interrogated by two Romantic heroes, Prometheus and Rousseau, unnamed hybrid progenies, impregnated by imperial power but mightier than it, are changing the devastated colonial geographies, producing alternative Romantic geographies.

Karen O'Brien in 'Poetry against Empire: Milton to Shelley' emphasizes a counter-tradition of anti-imperialism poetry from Milton to Shelley. Though she ends the tradition with Shelley, his disfigured Promethean characters and nameless hybrid progenies set a new path that urges us, living in the twenty-first century, to interrogate the colonial past/present and improve morally and physically the disease-stricken earth all before us.[13] Both Shelley and his contemporaries whom I have treated in this book are acutely aware of and alarmed by colonial expansion, and try to see possibilities of hybridity, but they have not yet found a term to articulate what they see and feel in these new types of interaction or mutuality between the self and others that are about to be developed. The protagonist of 'The Witch of Atlas' and the 'shape all light' in 'The Triumph of Life' are nameless, as the concept they embody has not been fully grasped in their age.

In the third act of *Prometheus Unbound*, when Demogorgon, the 'fatal child, the terror of the earth,' drags down Jupiter as '[t]he conqueror and the conquered,' a tremendous catastrophe 'on Caucasus' '[b]urns far along the tempest-wrinkled Deep' (3.1.19, 78, 3.2.12, 9). Shelley does not end the play here. Nor does he end his quest for Romantic geography with the utopian world of *Prometheus Unbound*. He continues difficult attempts to revisit, question, and cure 'the sick day in which we wake to weep' ('The Triumph of Life' 430). In our century, conqueror and conquered, colonizer and colonized, and good and evil are intrinsically and inextricably mixed, as is the figuration and disfiguration of the 'shape all light' in Shelley's unfinished final poem. The visionary baton passed on from Shelley to us is then to squarely face the colonial past/present, and keep drawing, as disfigured Rousseau does, 'a new Vision never seen before,' turning an unbearable colonial light into a new Romantic geography (411).

Notes

Introduction

1 References to Wordsworth's *Prelude* are to the 1805 version unless otherwise stated.
2 I am grateful to James Alvey for pointing out this passage. References to Rousseau's work are to *The Collected Writings of Rousseau*, under the general editorship of Roger D. Masters and Christopher Kelly.
3 References to Burke's work are to *The Writings and Speeches of Edmund Burke*, under the general editorship of Paul Langford.
4 References to Wordsworth's poems except *The Prelude* are to *The Poetical Works of William Wordsworth*, edited by Ernest de Selincourt and Helen Darbishire.
5 References to Peacock's work are to *The Works of Thomas Love Peacock*, edited by H.F.B. Brett-Smith and C.E. Jones.
6 Bentham thinks that the values of arts and sciences are exactly in proportion to the pleasure they yield. He writes in *The Rationale of Reward* (1825): 'Prejudice apart, the game of push-pin is of equal value with the arts and sciences of music and poetry' (206). The book is based upon two sets of manuscripts that were published under the title of *Théorie des peines et des recompenses* in Paris in 1811, translated by M. Dumont, who added his own renditions. It was John Stuart Mill who made this remark much more famous than Bentham's original.
7 Quotations from Byron's poems are taken from *Lord Byron: The Complete Poetical Works*, edited by Jerome J. McGann
8 Grosrichard's book, unlike Said's, failed to appeal to a wider audience, attracting only specialists in French literature and psychoanalysis. As its English translation did not appear till 1998, it has been largely unknown

in English-speaking countries. Only Lowe briefly touches on him (55, 63, 65).

9 Lowe's concept of 'heterotopicality' is an elaboration of Foucault's notion of other space as 'heterotopioa.' Foucault's 'Des espaces autres,' which was based upon his lecture in 1967, was not part of his official corpus as it was not prepared for publication by the author himself, though it was posthumously published.

10 Wallerstein's theory has developed since the early 1970s. I will discuss later in chapter 1 Wallerstein's elaboration of the concept into the tripartite structure of 'core, semi-periphery, and periphery' ('The Rise and Future Demise of the World Capitalist System' 57–85). In the 1930s and 1940s, long before Wallenstein, Argentinian economist Raúl Prebisch was examining why Latin America did not share in the profits of economic and technological progress enjoyed by the countries in the centre and developed his own centre-periphery concept, which has been an inspiration for generations of Latin American and other scholars (Di Marco 3–13).

11 Gallagher and Robinson published their joint work, 'The Imperialism of Free Trade,' in the *Economic History Review* in 1953, which became a foundation for their subsequent writings. The article was reprinted many times, and I quote from Gallagher's collection of essays. In the mid-1990s, a complex reassessment of the Gallagher-Robinson thesis was made in the gentlemanly capitalism thesis of P.J. Cain and A.G. Hopkins.

12 The dating of the emergence of globalization has been contested. See, for example, Flynn and Giraldez, Osterhammel and Petersson, and Robertson and White 1–44.

13 Most of Bhabha's important essays are collected in *The Location of Culture* (1994). In his later essays, however, his emphasis shifts from the operations of the colonial other that affect the colonizer's identity formation to the issues raised by postcolonial situations.

14 The original meaning will be discussed in detail in chapter 5.

15 Another example is Christopher L. Miller's *Blank Darkness: Africanist Discourse in French* that applies Said's method to French writings on Africa.

16 For the dating of the manuscript, see *SC* 6: 951–5.

1. Queen Mab

1 While Buffon's 'la sombre abîme du temps' and Cuvier's comparative anatomy extended the history of the earth much further than the six thousand years of sacred history, the Greco-Roman antiquity was sud-

denly found to be 'partnered and preceded by the other great civilizations of Asian, and in the case of Egypt, African antiquity' (Julian Robinson 108). Cook's three scientific voyages to the Pacific in the 1770s brought knowledge of *Terra Australis incognita* to Europe. The African Association (the Association for Promoting the Discovery of the Inland Parts of Africa) was established in 1788 with Sir Joseph Banks as one of its leading members.

2. The 1701 new edition of the Authorized Version of the Bible inserted in the margin James Ussher's famous dating of the creation of the earth in the year 4004 BC, and Ussher's chronology of six thousand years was accepted as 'The Received Chronology' (Cohn 95). In 1813, when Shelley completed *Queen Mab*, William Buckland at his inaugural lecture as Reader of Geology at Oxford attempted to demonstrate the consistency of geological records with the Mosaic writings.

3. Timothy Morton examines the conterminousness of nature and culture from a different angel in 'Nature and Culture' (185–207).

4. This thought is at the basis of Rousseau's *First Discourse*. See, for example, Rousseau 2: 15–18. Shelley ordered the *First Discourse* from Lackington, the largest bookshop in England, in September 1815 (*Letters* 1: 433), but he should have been familiar with Rousseau's thought much earlier through writings by English radicals, such as Godwin's *Political Justice*.

5. In July 1811, Shelley went for a month to the estate of his cousin at Cwm Elan, near Rhayader, in Wales. On returning from Wales, he eloped with Harriet Westbrook to Edinburgh and married in August. For the next two years, Shelley lived with Harriet in Keswick, Lynmouth, and Tremadoc, paying two visits to Ireland.

6. For the system of exploitation of the domestic colonies of Wales, Scotland, and Ireland by the metropolis, see Hechter.

7. Cameron takes the 'rocks to ruin hurled' as those 'rolled down the mountains in order to build the embankment (*EN* 192). It may be so, but I would agree with Matthews and Everest, who think that the scene more probably refers to 'geological signs of the working of Necessity,' such as accumulated rocks on Mont Blanc (*PS* 1: 260; 'Mont Blanc' 69–73).

8. For Madocks and his embankment project, see Beazley. Madocks's embankment was part of his regional plan, which was the most advanced and most idealistic regional plan of this period. In the first decades of the nineteenth century, Madocks's embankment project and his new town received much attention and was referred to as a 'wonder of Wales' (Beazley 118).

9 For the significant influence of Madocks's embankment and Tremadoc on Shelley, see Foot 207–8 and Holmes 163–77. For the importance of Wales as 'a potential staging-post for wider social reform' (182), see Cian Duffy, '"One Draught from Snowdon's Ever-Sacred Spring": Shelley's Welsh Sublime.'
10 Shelley's first meeting with Peacock took place in London in November 1812, and Peacock's novel was written in 1815, when Shelley took a house in Bishopsgate, near Peacock's residence at Marlowe, forming a warm friendship with him. The novel has Foster and Escot – the characters strongly reminiscent of Shelley and Peacock – quote or paraphrase freely notes from *Queen Mab*.
11 The embankment, which was intended to reclaim land and to brave the storms of the Irish Sea on one face and the floods of the Glaslyn on the other, was also designed to be a carriage road. It was, however, never completed for lack of funds.
12 See, for example, *Letters* 2: 60–1 and 'To Jane. The Recollection' (1821).
13 Welsh scholars' and patriots' mythologizing of the past sometimes went so far as to invent a past that had never existed. For 'Madoc feaver,' see Gwyn A. Williams. The subject of Madoc was suggested to Southey by his close friend, Charles Watkin Williams Wynn, who claimed descendence from Prince Madoc's brother Rhodri, and to whom Southey's poem was dedicated (Bernhardt-Kabisch 109).
14 I am grateful to Alan Bewell for pointing out to me the connection between Tremadoc and Madoc.
15 Spivak is influenced by Foucault's notion of the relations of power and knowledge and Lacan's distinction between two kinds of 'Other,' 'the little other' and 'the big Other,' that cannot be assimilated into the ego. She argues that in the broader contexts of imperialism and colonialism, 'the absolute Other' cannot be transformed into 'a domesticated Other' that consolidates the imperialist self ('Three Women's Texts and a Critique of Imperialism' 253).
16 The successful promoter, John Newbery, publicized the innocent image of Queen Mab holding court in a bean blossom in the 1750s (Pickering 223). In 1752, a collection of nine French fairy tales by Countess d'Aulnoy was published under the general title of *Queen Mab*, and went through a fifth edition in 1799. The book adds at the end 'Queen Mab's Song,' in which the tiny fairy queen invites her elves for their nightly dance and pranks, the details of which are reminiscent of the Mercutio speech (366–7). Reiman first noted the book as a possible source of Shelley's poem (*SC* 5: 284). In the early nineteenth century, however, fairies, especially those of

native origin, were considered dangerous, and fairy tales, except those from the French literary tradition, were generally disapproved of in children's literature under the influence of Locke's *Some Thoughts Concerning Education*. In the preface to *Poetry for Children* (1803), Lucy Aikin proudly says that 'dragons and fairies, giants and witches, have vanished from our nurseries before the wand of reason' (iii). Queen Mab seems to have been an exception.

17 I cite the title page of the 1813 edition from the facsimile edition, *Queen Mab 1813*, edited by Jonathan Wordsworth.
18 Shelley was reading Darwin at Cwn Elan in the summer of 1811 (*Letters* 1: 129). For the important influence of Darwin's poems on *Queen Mab*, see King-Hele, *Erasmus Darwin and the Romantic Poets* 193–200.
19 Henry Fuseli portrayed Mab as a nocturnal spirit of nightmares in the 1780s and 1790s. Charlotte Dacre's 'Queen Mab and Her Fays' in *Hours of Solitude* (1805) presented the 'little wily queen' as a bringer of erotic nightmares to the young (37). Francis Douce's annotation on Shakespeare in 1807 considers Mab as a spiteful local spirit (2: 180–1). It is only after 1814 and only in two paintings, 'Queen Mab, Shakespeare, *Romeo and Juliet*, I, 4' (1814) and 'Queen Mab Visits Two Sleeping Women' (1810–20), that Fuseli depicted her as a benevolent little messenger of good dreams.
20 Shelley modelled Ianthe on Harriet Shelley and the character's name was to be given to their first child, who was born on 23 June 1813.
21 The castle in the quoted lines is identified by Matthews and Everest as Harlech Castle, which can be seen on a hill six miles across the estuary from Tan-yr-allt (*PS* 1: 299).
22 Robert Wood in *The Ruins of Palmyra: Otherwise Tedmor in the Desert* (1753) writes: '[T]he hills opening discovered to us, all at once, the greatest quantity of ruins we had ever seen, all of white marble, and beyond them to the Euphrates a flat waste, as far as the eye could reach, without any object which shewed either life or motion. It is scarce possible to imagine any thing more striking than this view: So great a number of Corinthian pillars, mixed with so little wall or solid building, afforded a most romantic variety of prospect' (35). For the ruins of Palmyra, see Marshall and Williams 11, 68; Rose Macaulay 68–77.
23 For Shelley's association with the 'Bracknell circle' including William Lawrence, William Lambe, and John Frank Newton and the political implications of Shelley's vegetarianism, see Morton's *Shelley and the Revolution in Taste*. The word 'vegetarianism' had not been used in the Romantic age. The word appeared to have been in currency after the formation of the Vegetarian Society at Ramsgate in 1847. Timothy Morton

mentions that the preferred term for 'vegetarian' in Shelley's day was 'Pythagorean' ('Nature and Culture' 196).
24 The frontispiece is reproduced in Rousseau 2:2 .
25 See, for example, 3: 22–4, 43–67, 71, 82–3.
26 An anonymous English translation of Volney's work was immediately published by Joseph Johnson in 1792, followed by two subsequent editions in 1794 and 1796, and many editions from various publishers throughout the next century (Rigby 24).
27 For Shelley's keen interest in the independence movements in South America, see *Letters* 1: 253–4, 272.
28 See, for example, Rousseau 2: 14–16, 3: 78.
29 As the edition does not provide the line number, in my citations from Southey's poems, the page number is used instead of the line number.
30 Shelley considers a flesh diet, which was introduced by Prometheus who symbolizes Western civilization, to be one of the reasons for the fall of humans (*SPW* 826–7).
31 In the eighteenth century Hippocratic philosophy concerning the relationships between the external environment and human health was essential to the training of all Western physicians (Grove, *Ecology, Climate and Empire* 42). Hippocrates's medical and ethnographical treatise, 'Airs Waters Places,' was also well read by humanistic thinkers. Montesquieu's widely read *The Spirit of the Laws* (1748) repeated Hippocrates's formula and popularized the close relations of ethnic and cultural differences with climactic and environmental ones. See Hippocrates 65–137; Montesquieu 231–45, 278–84; Glacken 567–78; Sargent 168–222.
32 In canto 3 of *The Loves of the Plants*, Darwin mentions in a footnote an account of the Javanese poison tree by N.P. Foersch, and cites, in the 'Additional Notes' section at the end of the work, Foresch's article, which, translated from Dutch into English, appeared in the *London Magazine* in 1783 (*The Loves of the Plants* 106–7, 167–71). While the image was widely used, Thomas Stamford Raffles in *The History of Java* (1817) criticizes Darwin as popularizing the image of the plant as a 'malignant spirit' based upon 'an extravagant forgery' that 'the romance of Foersch' has created, and replaces it with a description of the upas tree by an American physician and naturalist Thomas Horsfiled (1: 44–5).
33 The overseas mission was a phenomenon that started in the 1790s. Most of the chief British missionary societies were founded between the end of the eighteenth century and the early nineteenth century (Hyam, *Britain's Imperial Century 1815–1914* 50–1).
34 They were the first non-Spaniards who were allowed to go beyond the

coasts and port cities in Spanish America. Humboldt's extensive account of his equinoctial travels, published mostly in Paris between 1807 and 1834, covered botany, zoology, astronomy, geography, archaeology, and political economy, and amounted to thirty-two volumes.

35 This is an English version of the *Voyage aux regions équinoxiales du nouveau continent*, translated by Helen Maria Williams.

36 It was not until Jules Quicherat's book on Jeanne d'Arc, *Procès de condamnation et de réabilitation de Jeanne d'Arc dite la Pucelle d'Orléans* (1841–9), that Joan became a world-wide heroine. Before Quicherat's monumental work, she was not so well known, and Southey's originality consisted in expanding the legend and 'making, not a saint or martyr out of her, but a heroine' (Haller 101–3). Book 9 of Southey's *Joan of Arc* reports a vision received by the heroine while she is sleeping.

37 The poem and the prose notes have not been put together in later editions until *The Poems of Shelley*, edited by Geoffrey Matthews and Kelvin Everest.

2. 'Alastor'

1 Impressed by Humboldt's work, Goethe produced the plate as a sepia print in Weimar in 1813, and then an improved version as a copper engraving appeared in Paris in the same year. In Goethe's version, the mountains of Europe are placed on the right and set against those of South America; and Humboldt, Saussure, and Gay-Lussac's balloon are shown (Hein, 'Humboldt and Goethe' 53).

2 See, for example, William Keach's 'Obstinate Questionings: The Immortality Ode and *Alastor*,' and Marilyn Butler's 'Shelley and the Question of Joint Authorship.'

3 See, for example, William Hodges's two-volume *Select Views of India* (1785–8), the *Oriental Scenery* (1795–1808) by Thomas Daniell and his nephew William, and Henry Salt's *Twenty-Four Views Taken in St Helena, the Cape, India, Ceylon, Abyssinia and Egypt* (1809).

4 For the concept of the 'natural sublime' in the Romantic period, see Cian Duffy, Heringman, Monk, and Nicolson.

5 For the date of the poem, see *SP&P* 6n.1.

6 See *Letters* 2: 361.

7 Shelley's first encounter with Sir William Jones's poetical works might have taken place in Dr Lind's library while he was being taken care of by Dr Lind during his last two years at Eton (Peck 1: 25).

8 I owe this information to Jay Macpherson.

9 The English version appeared in 1984 with the foreword written by Said.
10 The official attitude of the East India Company in not disturbing Indian social and cultural structures, strongly supported by Parliament in the 1770s and 1780s, met a great challenge from the Evangelical Charles Grant, a director of the East India Company, who, after his return to Britain, played a significant role in the Indian Home Administration both as a member of Parliament and as a leader of the Clapham Sect. Though most of the directors of the East India Company and most of the members of Parliament were against Grant's proposal, the Evangelical campaign eventually forced Parliament to insert the 'Pious Clause' in the Company's charter in 1813 (Embree 141–57).
11 Edward Moor's *The Hindu Pantheon*, which Shelley ordered in 1812 (*Letters* 1: 342), gives a detailed explanation of the goddess (203–4).
12 References to Jones's work are to *The Works of Sir William Jones*.
13 Hilarion is the 'daring Infidel' who denied their gods and 'seduced ... the most celebrated of their religious women' (Owenson 3: 222). The Turkish term 'Giaour' means a non-Muslim.
14 For the legend of Prester John in the Middle Ages and the subsequent history of the relationship between Abyssinia and Europe, see Hallett.
15 Quotations from Coleridge's poems are taken from *Poetical Works*, edited by J.C.C. Mays, unless otherwise stated. As for the poems that have more than one version, it is very difficult and sometime almost impossible to decide which version(s) Shelley read, as is typically shown in the case of 'The Rime of the Ancient Mariner,' which was continuously and considerably revised immediately after the publication of the original 'The Rime of the Ancyent Marinere' in 1798 (Stillinger 171, 16–21; Percy Bysshe Shelley, *Letters* 1: 345, 548; Mary Shelley, *Journals* 642). For 'Kubla Khan,' I quote from the facsimile edition by Jonathan Wordsworth, *Christabel 1816*.
16 A similar view is expressed in the review of the initial achievements of the Asiatic Society in the *Monthly Review* (1797) by Alexander Hamilton, a member of the Asiatic Society and a professor of Sanskrit and Hindu at the East India Company College at Haileybury: 'the channels of Indian knowledge and Indian wealth shall have again become impervious to the western world' (408).
17 The East India Company conducted surveys at its own expense and owned maps as its property.
18 The map is held at the British Library, Oriental and India Office Collections. It can be seen on the Eighteenth Century Collections on Line.

19 A few months after the publication of the whole map of India in December 1782, the *Memoir of a Map of Hindoostan; or the Mogul Empire* appeared. The much fuller second edition was published in 1788 and reprinted in 1792 and afterwards. I quote from the text of the first edition published in 1783. For the complex publication history of Rennell's Map and *Memoir* due to the constant updates to the map, see Edney 99–100.

20 The question is whether Britannia is receiving the sacred manuscripts from the central Brahman or giving them to him. See, for example, Edney 13–15, Raj 223–4, Ludden 254.

21 In the preface, Rennell mentions his indebtedness to Lord Mulgrave for a copy of Forster's route from Kashmir to the Caspian Sea (vi). Forster's journey was made in 1782, but it was in 1790 in Calcutta that the first volume of his journey appeared. Forster died at Nagpore in 1792, and it was not until 1798 that an unknown editor collected his papers and published in London a two-volume book of his journey, entitled *A Journey from Bengal to England*. There is no record that Shelley referred to Forster when he composed the poem.

22 Opinions differ as to Beddoes's use of Alexander's conquest of India. While Porter sees in the poem a view of Indian history '[f]rom Alexander to Warren Hastings' as 'a chronicle of "crime"' by European soldiers (*Doctor of Society* 166–7), Leask finds a hint of 'radical imperialism' (*British Romantic Writers and the East* 92–3).

23 Dionysus was thought to be a great conqueror of the East as early as Euripides's day and was assimilated into a human conqueror, Alexander, as seen in Nonnos's *Dionysiaca* (H. Rose 1: xiv). The European invasion into India will be also discussed in detail in chapter 4.

24 These two place names will be discussed more in detail in chapter 4.

25 I am grateful to Robin Jackson for pointing out Raleigh's book.

26 For the date of the essay, see SC 6: 638–41, The 'Julian and Maddalo' Draft Notebook 171, and Barker-Benfield 97.

27 This is Robert Heron's translation of *La suite des mille et une nuits* (1788–9), which was a joint work of Dom Denis Chavis and Jacques Cazotte. It was first published in four volumes in London, Dublin, and Edinburgh in 1792, and then appeared as a three-volume set in London in 1794.

28 I quote the *Continuation* from the 1794 edition.

29 *La suite des mille et une nuits* is a collection of Oriental tales adapted from an Arabian manuscript, and it can be regarded as a product of European fantasy about the East. It is a joint work of Dom Denis Chavis, who translated the Arabian manuscript, and Jacques Cazotte, who recast not only the style but also the content of Chavis's manuscript by adding episodes

of his own freely to the original story (Shaw 79–80). Although many of the tales are based on genuine Arabian sources, Cazotte handled the material with so much freedom and invention that the first impression of Alexander Russell, a contemporary Orientalist, was that the work was 'spurious' (1: 386), and Martha Pike Conant considers it as 'pseudo-translation' (41–2). 'The History of Maugraby' is one of those tales that have no source in Chavis's manuscript, though the story of Maugraby itself was well known in Arabian folklore (Shaw 80).

30 The map is inserted between pages 200 and 201 in the second edition of the *Memoir of a Map of Hindoostan*.
31 Al Beljame first connects these lines to Caracalla's outrage (113). For Caracalla's advance into Parthia, see Dio 356. For Caracalla's identification with Alexander, see Herodianus 1: 413–14. Identification with Alexander was a claim to be a champion of the East, and it was thus frequently made by Roman emperors.
32 Forster sailed from the southern side of the Caspian Sea to Astrakhan, from where he walked to St Petersburg by way of Moscow.
33 Due to Shelley's ambiguous use of 'Caucasus' and 'Chorasmia,' which is the region between the Caspian and the Aral seas, critics differ in the actual location of 'Caucasus.' Reiman takes the Poet's voyage as eastward from the Aral Sea to the headwaters in the Indian Caucasus through the Oxus (*Percy Bysshe Shelley* 22, 142n.8), but as Cameron argues, his voyage is westward from the Caspian Sea to the Georgian Caucasus, because the Poet sees from the sea the 'etherial cliffs / Of Caucasus' (352–3), which is not visible from the Aral Sea (*Shelley* 610–11n.10).
34 John Pinkerton, in his *Modern Geography* (1807), gives the range the modern name 'Hindu Kush' and denies the connection with the Georgian Caucasus assumed by the ancients (2: 346–9, 438).

3. 'Mont Blanc'

1 For the history of Mont Blanc, I am indebted to Claire Eliane Engel's *A History of Mountaineering in the Alps* and *Mont Blanc*, Gavin de Beer's *Early Travellers in the Alps*, and David Hill's *Turner in the Alps*.
2 For the change in English attitude toward mountains between the late seventeenth century and the early nineteenth century, see Nicolson and Monk.
3 Windham took with him seven friends, including a professional explorer, Richard Pococke, and organized his expedition in a military manner, as the Geneva border was not peaceful (Engel, *Mont Blanc* 15). Windham,

following the local usage, distinguishes between 'glacieres' and glaciers. The former are 'Mountains of Ice, which not only never melt, but always increase by the falling of fresh snow' and are mostly 'of immense height' and sometimes 'split from Top to Bottom' (Windham 9).

4 Martel's report, taking the form of a letter to Windham, is incorporated in Windham's pamphlet. Martel compares his measurement of Mont Blanc with that by Fatio de Duillier, who referred to the mountain as 'the *Maudite*' (Windham 28).

5 Contemporary geologists, believing the age of rocks might be ascertained by their composition, established a threefold grouping of rocks into the Primary, the Secondary, and the Tertiary. They thought that the highest 'primary' peaks in the central zone of the Alps preceded the Flood, which created the 'secondary' mountains that surround the central core.

6 Coxe published the letters he had written during his tour in Switzerland in 1775 as *Sketches of the Natural, Civil and Political State of Switzerland* (1779), which was translated into French by Ramond de Carbonnières, one of the founders of French geology, in 1781. After three further tours in 1779, 1785, and 1787, the expanded version, *Travels in Switzerland and in the Country of the Grisons*, appeared in 1789.

7 James Hutton's *The Theory of the Earth* (1795) heavily depended upon Saussure's research on the Alps. Alexander von Humboldt found the strata of the Jura Mountains to be a separate unit in 1795.

8 As the edition does not have the line number, I indicate the page number.

9 As the edition does not have the line number, I indicate the page number.

10 Part of Saussure's *Voyage dans les Alpes* (1779–96) is printed as 'An Account of the Attempts That Have Been Made to Attain the Summit of Mont Blanc. Written in the Year 1786' in the fourth volume of Pinkerton's *A General Collection of the Best and Most Interesting Voyages and Travels* (1809). All quotations from Saussure are taken from Pinkerton's collection.

11 The French invasion of Savoy in September 1792 denied British travellers access to Chamonix, and after Britain's involvement with the conflict in early 1793, the Continent was closed to the British till 1815, except for the short period of the Peace of Amiens in 1802.

12 By the 1790s there had been several travel reports about Switzerland, such as Coxe's book and its French translation with notes and commentaries by Ramond de Carbonnières (1781), and Helen Maria Williams's *A Tour in Switzerland* (1798). There had been no proper English guidebook of Switzerland, however, till 1818, when Daniel Wall translated and expanded Johann Gottfried Ebel's *Manuel du voyage en Suisse* (1804–5) as *The Traveller's Guide through Switzerland* (Hill 161).

13 Shelley does not mention the bridge until they are on the way back to Geneva (*Letters* 1: 501). On the other hand, Mary writes of the bridge on their way to Chamonix (*Journals* 114–15).
14 For a close comparison of the poem with the journal-letter and the draft, see Chernaik 49–52, and Erkelenz's comment in the introduction to *The Geneva Notebook of Percy Bysshe Shelley* (xxv–vii).
15 The wider reading public was acquainted with Hutton's *Theory of the Earth* through *Illustrations of the Huttonian Theory of the Earth* by John Playfair, who was Hutton's friend and student.
16 I quote from Hayter's edition based upon the original version of the *Confessions of an English Opium Eater* that appeared in the *London Magazine* in 1821.
17 The poem appears in the second volume of *A Tour in Switzerland* (16–19). The book does not have the line number, and I provide the stanza number.
18 'Observations on the Glacieres, and the Glaciers, by M. Ramond' appears in the appendix attached to Helen Maria Williams's *A Tour in Switzerland* (2: 279–352).
19 The lines that describe Mont Blanc and the subsequent apocalyptic vision (690–755, 782–809) are omitted in the final 1849 version. I will discuss these lines in detail later in this chapter.
20 Coleridge himself never went to Chamonix. The poem is based on his Scafell experience and Friderika Brun's 'Ode to Chaumony' (1791), which celebrates the sunrise in the valley of Chamonix.
21 Coleridge's 'Hymn' was first printed in the *Morning Post* on 11 September 1802 and then reprinted in *The Friend* (no. 11., 26 Oct. 1809). Charles Robinson details Shelley's access to Coleridge's *The Friend* either in the original 1809 version or in the reprinted 1812 version ('The Shelley Circle and Coleridge's *The Friend*' 269–74).
22 In 'A Refutation of Deism,' Shelley writes that '[m]ind cannot create, it can only perceive' (*Prose* 122), and again in the essay 'On Life' (1819) he states: 'I confess that I am one of those who am unable to refuse my assent to the conclusions of those philosophers, who assert that nothing exists but as it is perceived' (*SP&P* 506). Shelley was influenced by Berkeley's theory of immaterialism based on the principle *esse est percipi* (being depends on being perceived), but he was more sceptical than Berkeley, who was against any philosophical theories that could nurture atheism or scepticism. As Wasserman mentions (*Shelley* 136), Shelley's excited report of the Arve in the letter – 'All was as much our own as if we had been the creators of such impressions in the minds of others, as now

occupied our own' (*Letters* 1: 497) – may suggest Berkeley's God, but this impression never finds its way into the poem.

23 The account is not in Shelley's original letter to Peacock. It is based on Mary's description of the rock in her journals, but she does not use the Egyptian association. She writes: '*It struck the head of the visionary Image & gracefully dividing then fell in folds of foam, more like cloud than water, imitating a viel* [for veil] *of the most exquisite woof; – It united then, concealing the lower part of the statue* (*Journals* 113–14).

24 In *A Treatise of Human Nature* (1739–40), Hume distinguishes between impressions and ideas. The perceptions that enter into the mind with most force and liveliness are '*impressions*,' under which name, sensations, passions, and emotions 'make their first appearance.' On the other hand, '*ideas*' are 'the faint images of these [the impressions] in thinking and reasoning' (1: 11).

25 *Transactions of the Royal Society of Edinburgh* 4 (1803): 39, quoted in Hallam 33.

26 The violent earthquake that attacked Lisbon in November 1755 and the sufferings of its victims shocked all Europe. In his 'Poème sur le Désastre de Lisbonne' (1755), Voltaire records his confrontation with the evilness of Providence and his denial of all hope except that for a serene afterlife given to those who still believe in Providence. Shelley faces the same terrifying question, but he answers it differently in 'Mont Blanc' and *Prometheus Unbound*.

27 Wasserman interprets the passage as '[Shelley's] own variants of the two current theories of the origin of mountains, the Neptunian and the Catastrophic' (*The Subtler Language* 227), but I take it that the passage refers to the Catastrophist theory. The term Volcanist was interchangeably used with Catastrophist and Plutonist in the Romantic period. For an excellent discussion of the Neptunist-Volcanist controversy of the early nineteenth century, see Hallam 1–29.

28 For the interpretation of '[b]ut' (79), I follow Chernaik (43–4, 59n.10) and Wasserman (*Shelley* 235), taking it as an adverb meaning 'only' rather than as a preposition meaning 'except.' Their reading is based on the cancelled variants, '[w]ith such a faith' and '[i]n such a faith' (*Geneva Notebook of Percy Bysshe Shelley* 19).

29 Wordsworth followed the biblical chronology of six thousand years in 1793, but in the 1849 version the phrase was replaced by '[f]rom age to age' (579).

30 When writing *The Prelude* twelve years later, however, Wordsworth did not hide his disappointment at 'soulless' Mont Blanc and its 'dumb

cataracts and stream of ice' in which he could find neither revolutionary hopes nor the voice of a Father-God (6.454, 458). He had to be consoled by the 'five rivers broad and vast' in the vale of Chamonix, which made 'rich amends [for glaciers], / And reconciled us to realities' (6.460–1).

31 The manuscript shows that what has been published as two separate letters, as in Jones's *Letters* (1: 480–8, 488–91), turned out to be one single letter that contains important passages which have not been included in any published text. I quote *SC571*, which reproduces the original letter.

32 Shelley's criticism of Byron is mentioned in the second letter to Peacock on 17 July 1816 in Jones's *Letters* (1: 491), but entirely omitted in the published version of the journal-letter.

33 John Sheppard, *Letters Descriptive of a Tour through Some Parts of France, Italy, Switzerland, and Germany, in 1816* (Edinburgh: Oliphant, 1817) 196–7, quoted in Colbert 90.

34 Charles Robinson discusses Shelley's probable access to Coleridge's 'Kubla Khan' prior to his composition of 'Mont Blanc' (*Shelley and Byron* 36–7). According to Robinson, although Shelley did not receive Coleridge's *Christabel* volume until 26 August 1816, he may have known the poem already either in a manuscript transcription of the poem or through Byron, who, when they exchanged ghost stories on 18 June may have recited part of the poem, either from memory, from a manuscript transcription, or from the May edition of *Christabel: Kubla Khan, a Vision; The Pains of Sleep* which he received before August.

35 Valerie Grosvenor Myer observes that Saussure's account of the Arveiron in the *Voyages dans les Alpes* (2: 16) is reflected in the description of the Alph in 'Kubla Khan' (176–7). If so, Coleridge repositions the Arveiron in Xanadu, and Shelley brings it back to Europe without losing all the mythical and exotic images of the Alph.

36 The Arve, which issues at the foot of Mont Blanc in the Valley of Chamonix, flows into Lake Geneva, out of which the Rhone flows through France to the Mediterranean Sea.

37 The summit was again concealed when Shelley, Mary, and Claire Clairmont were travelling back to Geneva on the 26th: '[t]he scenery had lost something of its immensity, thick clouds hanging over the highest mountains' (*Letters* 1: 501).

38 Mary Shelley feminizes Mont Blanc as well: '[we saw] at a distance, surrounding all, the beautiful Mont Blanc, and the assemblage of snowy mountains that in vain endeavour to emulate her' (*Frankenstein* 163).

39 Colbert's conjecture is stimulating, and I would take it as evidence of

Shelley's continued effort to improve the degraded environment. It remains uncertain, however, whether Shelley wrote it after he saw Mont Blanc.

4. *Prometheus Unbound*

1 Mary omitted this fact in her 'Note on *Prometheus Unbound*' (*SPW* 271).
2 The first English translation of Aeschylus's *Prometheus Bound* by Thomas Morell, with the Greek and Latin texts, appeared in 1773. Between 1796 and 1825 there were seven collected editions and fourteen editions of individual dramas of Aeschylus published in England (Curran, 'The Political Prometheus' 434).
3 The Bodleian Library possesses what is said to be Shelley's copy (Shelley adds. g.1), which is C.G. Schütz's edition (*Shelley's Pisan Winter Notebook [1820–1822]* 493). Schütz's five-volume *Tragoediae*, which begins with *Prometheus Vinctus*, appeared in 1809.
4 I am grateful to Robin Jackson for pointing out Rees's *Cyclopaedia*. As *The Cyclopaedia* does not provide the page number, I indicate the volume number.
5 Blumenbach's 'On the Natural Variety of Mankind,' the first academic work on human race classification, was published in 1775, but he used the new term 'Caucasian' for the first time in the third edition, published in 1795. References to Blumenbach are to *The Anthropological Treatises of Johann Friedrich Blumenbach*, translated by Thomas Bendyshe.
6 Zillman in his variorum edition of *Prometheus Unbound* says that Peacock's reference to Demogorgon based on Boccaccio in a note to his *Rhododaphne* (1818) is a possible source for Shelley's Demogorgon, as Shelley saw Peacock daily at Marlow in 1817 when Peacock was writing the poem (313).
7 Caf is not mentioned in Greek mythology but frequently appears in Oriental romances as 'horrible Kaf' (Beckford 50, 137n.1). It is identified with the Indian Caucasus.
8 References to Keats's poems are to *John Keats: Complete Poems*, edited by Jack Stillinger.
9 When the epipsyche is not a true antitype of the self but merely a mirror reflecting the self, the mirroring process always ends in death. The mirror relationship between Zeinab and Kathema is intensified in the incestuous relationship between Laon and Cythna, who are brother and sister in the original version of the poem, *Laon and Cythna*. In the revised *Revolt of Islam*, Cythna is brought up with Laon as his sibling and later adopts the

name of Laone, which suggests that she is nothing more than his 'second self' (2.875).

10 Henry passively watches the sleeping Ianthe, while she is on an educational journey with Mab. Laon is driven out of his senses after the cruel punishment on the top of a pillar upon the mountain and confined in a lonely tower for seven years, while Cythna is leading a revolutionary movement.

11 I am grateful to Jay Macpherson for pointing out the relevance of Nonnos's *Dionysiaca* in this context.

12 Although Panthea and Ione are seated at his feet, they are placed there as reporters for the audience, never participating in the dialogue between Prometheus and supernatural spirits. They do not even speak to Prometheus except at the very end of act 1.

13 This refers to France in 1798–1815.

14 It is possible that despite the comma following 'chasm,' the simile is meant to include everything from '[l]ike' in line 3 to the end of Panthea's speech in line 10. The vapour, however, is actually gushing out of the mountain when Asia asks her sister to turn away from the maddening vapour and look at the prospect from the summit before it 'dim[s]' her 'brain' (2. 3. 18).

15 See, for example, *Queen Mab* (2.135–210), 'Alastor' (240–4), *The Revolt of Islam* (5.1720–8), 'Lines Written among the Euganean Hills,' and 'The Triumph of Life.'

16 Of course Shelley was not able to read *The Prelude*, which was published in 1850, but we should note that in Wordsworth's works the image of the sea of mist under the summit made its first appearance in the Alpine landscape at dawn in the 1793 version of the *Descriptive Sketches* (492–505), from which most of the details of the moonlit Snowdon landscape were taken.

17 For the parallels between Shelley's description of the Indian peak and Italian volcanoes, see Matthews, 'A Volcano's Voice in Shelley' 211–12.

18 Marilyn Butler mentions that Robert Lowth, in his Oxford lectures on the Old Testament (1754), influentially discussed the recurring figure of a mourning woman who symbolized 'a defeated city or people, Jerusalem or Israel as a whole,' and adds that his allegorical reading of the dispossessed women was popularized and used in different contexts by Macpherson, Owenson, and other writers. Zeinab in Shelley's 'Zeinab and Kathema,' who is hanged in Britain, can be considered in this context, as '[h]er name in Latin is Zenobia, after the patriot queen of

ancient Palmyra' who was defeated by the Roman empire ('Orientalism' 419–20, 424).
19 See also Moor 132, 447.
20 I am referring to the healing touch ritualized and practised by French and English kings from the Middle Ages to the end of the eighteenth century. It was believed that scrofula, 'King's Evil,' was healed by being touched by a king. For a history of royal touch, see Bloch.
21 Laon's name is derived from the Greek word for the people (J.R. de J. Jackson 252). For the Promethean milieu in *The Revolt of Islam*, see Curran, *Shelley's Annus Mirabilis* 36.
22 The destructive aspect of Demogorgon's volcanic power is briefly mentioned, in comparison with 'the lurid smoke / Of earthquake-ruined cities o'er the sea,' prior to the reunion of Prometheus and Asia (2.4.151–2), but the description is minimized.
23 The Athenian lawgiver Solon was born in 638 BC (?) and died in 559 BC.
24 For the history of Atlantis after Plato, see Pierre Vidal-Naquet's 'Atlantis and the Nations.' It is only in late-twentieth-century seismological research that the possible location of Atlantis in Crete has been suggested (Vitaliano 12).
25 It started with Olof Rudbeck's *Atlantica* (1679–1702), in which the famous Swedish scientist painstakingly tried to show that Atlantis was nothing but Sweden.
26 Before the publication of his research, however, Wilford had discovered that most evidence was forged by his pundits. He rejected the forgeries, publishing what was left as 'An Essay on the Sacred Isles in the West, with Other Essays Connected with That Work,' and sent a letter to *The British Critic* to explain the whole affair (Rev. of *Asiatic Researches. Vol 6* 401). Nevertheless, Wilford's theory on the white isles was very popular, especially in Ireland throughout the nineteenth century (Vidal-Naquet, 'Atlantis and the Nations' 323).
27 In *Hellas* (1821), however, the 'far Atlantis' refers to the United States of America (70).
28 References to Blake's illuminated books are to *The Illuminated Blake*, edited by David V. Erdman. References to Blake's other works are to *The Complete Poetry and Prose of William Blake*, edited by David V. Erdman. Blake is well aware of the end of Plato's story: both the imperial Atlantis and the antediluvian Athens, after being heavily involved in war, were suddenly sunk under the sea in a night and a day by a deluge.
29 Colwell, examining carefully Shelley's interest in architecture, which went back at least to 1811, and his thorough knowledge of the classical

orders and canons, mentions that '[i]t is unlikely that Shelley would have botched his details' ('Figures in a Promethean Landscape' 127).

30 Shelley obtained a copy of Parkinson's work early in 1812 (*Letters* 1: 214, 255). He mentioned Cuvier's *Leçons d'anatomie comparée* in a note to *Queen Mab* and *A Vindication of Natural Diet*, but his references were made via William Lambe's *Reports on the Effect of a Peculiar Regimen on Scirrhous Tumours and Cancerous Ulcers* (1809) (*PS* 1:407). Cuvier's new theory on the earth, which first appeared as a preface to his major publication, *Recherches sur les ossemens fossiles* (1812), went through several editions as *Discours sur les revolutions de la surface du globe*, and its English translation by Robert Kerr, *Essays on the Theory of the Earth*, went through three editions between 1813 and 1817.

31 See also McGann's commentary on the poem (*LBCPW* 6: 645–55, 659–61).

32 Shelley, Mary, and Claire went to Lucca on Friday, 11 August. Shelley alone made a walking tour to the mountain, departing at dawn on Saturday and returning late on Sunday night exhausted. He began composing the poem on Monday morning and completed it two days later, on 16 August (*Journals* 329).

5. 'The Witch of Atlas'

1 In the first edition of this famous treatise published in 1775, Blumenbach considers the human hybrid as a cross between a human being and an animal, adding that 'the Supreme Being' ensures that such 'disgusting kind of unions' will be 'futile' (80). The concept of the human hybrid as a cross between two different human races first appears in the third edition.

2 For the interracial marriage policies of the early European countries, see Henriques. For the situation in India, see Stark.

3 The Company prohibited intermarriage in 1835.

4 Quotations from Valentia are taken from the extended four-volume version published in 1811.

5 Valentia's observation needs to be juxtaposed with the Indian context in which those mixed children were seen; born and educated as Christians, they had no relationship with their Indian relatives, who had cast out their mothers. Even after the Company dismissed them, they showed remarkable loyalty to their fathers' country, and performed valuable services in the Indian Mutiny of 1857.

6 The definition of 'man' in the *Encyclopædia Britannica* (1817) asserts the

superiority of the white race but considers different races as 'varieties' of a single species and human hybrids as 'prolific' (12: 543–5).

7 Animal hybrids had been known from ancient times, but scientific interest in hybridity arose in the area of horticulture after the sexual function of plants became known at the end of the seventeenth century. In the eighteenth century Linnaeus made many experiments on the cross-fertilization of plants, producing various hybrids.

8 It was only after the Victorian period that the idea of human hybridity was applied to the dominant culture, as is the case of Matthew Arnold, who, as Young demonstrates, claimed that hybridity was a distinct feature of English culture (*Colonial Desire* 55–89).

9 Edward Long, in his widely circulated *The History of Jamaica* (1774), claimed to find decreasing fertility in mulattos and considered it as evidence of degeneracy, despite the large hybrid population in the West Indies.

10 For Shelley's association with Lawrence, see Ruston. It is possible that Shelley first met Lawrence in 1811, when he was thinking of becoming a surgeon after his expulsion from Oxford. Shelley briefly attended anatomical lectures given by John Abernethy at St Bartholomew's Hospital, and Lawrence was an assistant to Abernethy's anatomical course. In 1813 and 1814, Shelley was part of the 'Bracknell circle,' to which Lawrence also belonged. In 1815, Lawrence became a Professor of Anatomy and Surgery to the Royal College of Surgeons, and in 1817, Shelley consulted Lawrence about his health (*Letters* 1: 429; *LMWS* 1: 41).

11 After the publication of the book, the governors of Bridewell and Bethlem hospitals suspended Lawrence from his position as surgeon, forcing him to retract its materialistic and atheistic statements and suppress the circulation of his book. Lawrence was subsequently restored to the Royal College of Surgeons. In 1829, he succeeded Abernethy's position, deserting his radical friends. In 1837, he was appointed Surgeon Extraordinaire to the new Queen Victoria.

12 By the 1840s, polygenist arguments were in the ascendancy.

13 Alciphron is struck by 'a new feeling' when he glimpses a beautiful Egyptian priestess, Alethe, from a distance: '[H]ad this bright vision but lingered another moment before my eyes, I should, in my transport, have wholly forgotten who I was and where, and thrown myself, in prostrate adoration, at her feet' (Moore 34).

14 See also Butler, 'Orientalism' 395–6.

15 Using both internal and external evidence, Cameron argues persuasively

that Shelley had read Wordsworth's poem, which was published in April 1819, before he wrote 'Peter Bell the Third' in October 1819, and thus it is certain that Shelley read Wordsworth's poem before the composition of 'The Witch of Atlas' in August 1820 (*Shelley* 351–2, 626–7n.21).

16 Herodotus himself mistook this river for the Egyptian Nile.
17 Shelley thinks that the 'upaithric' Greek temples exemplified their 'perpetual commerce with external nature' (*Letters* 2: 74). Frederick Jones comments on 'upaithric,' which means 'open to the air, having no roof' (2: 74n.10).
18 Shelley's description of 'such shapes as haunt / Wet clefts' may correspond to the 'Trogodytae [Cave-dwellers]' in Atlas ('The Witch of Atlas' 134–5; Pliny 250). The '[d]og-headed' probably refers to the 'Cynocephali' ('dog-head'), who were believed to live in the mountains of India ('The Witch of Atlas' 136; Friedman 15).
19 Pliny writes: 'The Atlas tribe have fallen below the level of human civilization' and '[t]he Satyrs have nothing of ordinary humanity about them except human shape' (251, 253).
20 I am grateful to Alan Bewell for suggesting this connection.
21 It is possible that Wordsworth had Park's exploration of the course of the Niger in mind when writing of the cool, beautiful spot in deep Africa in *Peter Bell*. Although Park failed to reach the source of the Niger and Timbuctoo, his return and his report on the interior of Africa excited the public.
22 Hakluyt's *Voyages, Navigations, Traffiques, and Discoveries of the English Nation* (1598–1600) records the rich cities called Tombuto and Gago, and Leo Africanus's account of the visit to the flowering empire on the Niger in 1526 (Hakluyt 3: 6–7; Leo 5). The English expedition to advance to the country of gold in the heart of Africa was arranged in 1618, and Richard Jobson managed to collect information on the city where the houses were covered with gold (Jobson 102). The Royal African Company dispatched a few expeditions to the area in the early eighteenth century. A five-volume new edition of Hakluyt's work was published between 1810 and 1812. Purchas's *Pilgrimage* includes Leo Africanus's account and an extract from Jobson's report (5: 309, 6: 243).
23 For the details of European attempts to reach Timbuctoo, see Murray, Curtin's *The Image of Africa*, and Gardner.
24 Horneman, a young German academic, was the first modern European to cross the Sahara, but died on the bank of the Niger.
25 Park led a party consisting of forty-four soldiers, four carpenters, and a draftsman, all of whom perished.

26 The Earl Camden, secretary of state for war and the colonies, entrusted Park's original documents to the African Institution. The anonymous editor of the documents prefixes a long 'Account of the Life of Mungo Park' that includes Park's letters, an 'Addenda' to Park's journals, and the account of his death reported by Isaaco and Amadou Fatouma (Park 2: 3–116).
27 In 1826, Alexander Laing reached the city, but was killed shortly after leaving it. It was not until 1828 that the first European, René Caillié, returned from the city alive.
28 For the extremely high casualty rate among British explorers and officers in West Africa between 1790 and 1830, see Curtin, *The Image of Africa* 483–6.
29 Both Shelley and Mary read Park's *Travels in Africa* (1799) in 1814, and *Journals of a Mission to the Interior of Africa in 1805* (1815) in 1816 (*Letters* 2: 481).
30 Between 1818 and 1819, James Grey Jackson repeatedly insisted on a radical change in the colonial policy in Africa, proposing 'a grand plan' that would replace the current system of solitary explorers and 'secure the command of the commerce of Africa to Great Britain' (*An Account of Timbuctoo and Housa, Territories in the Interior of Africa, by El Hage Abd Salam Shabeeny* 201, 252–75, 495; 'Hints concerning the Colonization of Africa' 652–4).
31 The existence of a large lake that is the chief reservoir of the Nile had been known to the ancient geographers and the Arabs, and Purchas mentions a large lake under the equator as a source of the Nile (7: 405). No one in Shelley's day, however, confirmed the existence of Victoria Nyanza, which was to be discovered by J.H. Speke on the present borders of Kenya, Uganda, and Tanzania when he was seeking the source of the Nile in 1858.
32 The racial identity of this melting pot was still ambiguous in the early nineteenth century (Brace et al. 129–64). For the attempts to de-Africanize Egypt in mid-century academia, see Bernal's *Black Athena* and Robert Young's *Colonial Desire* (118–41). Bernal's historiographical naivety and the historical validity of the existence of African Greeks are criticized by *Black Athena Revisited* (1996), edited by Lefkowitz and Rogers, but it was a serious attempt from within the West to discredit a Greece that was considered as the origin of European civilization.
33 Dupuis's view was very influential in Napoleon's Egyptian expedition (Bernal 182–4).
34 From the mid-eighteenth century British travellers used the Red Sea and

the overland crossing through Egypt as quicker ways of going to India (Marshall and Williams 68–9).

Conclusion

1 Early suggestions of Rousseau and his negative view of Prometheus are discussed in chapter 1.
2 Newfoundland was first claimed for King Henry VII in 1497 by John Cabot, and Labrador was first legally possessed by the Hudson's Bay Company under the royal charter of King Charles II in 1670. By the Treaty of Utrecht (1713) the proposed dividing line was drawn from Cape Grimmington on the Labrador coast to Lake Mistassini, which gave almost the whole east coast of Labrador to the French. For the history of Labrador, see Gosling.
3 Banks was probably acquainted with the Moravians through his mother, and the Moravian missionaries in Labrador collected plants for him in 1765 (Mason 57).
4 I quote Palliser's account from Gosling 172.
5 Lysaght, the editor of the materials relating Joseph Banks's Canadian expedition in 1766, transcribes and includes the diaries of the Moravians in Newfoundland and Labrador between 1764 and 1765 in the third part of his edition. I quote from this edition.
6 Cartwright's *Labrador: A Poetical Epistle* was first published in 1785. I quote from the 1792 edition. As the edition does not provide the line number, in my citations from Cartwright's poem, the page number is used instead of the line number.
7 For example, Matthews links Shelley's narrative to the real Rousseau's situation at Les Charmettes in 1737–8, described in books 5–6 of *The Confessions*, immediately after which he plunged into the living storm of social and political life ('On Shelley's *The Triumph of Life*' 108). Cian Duffy associates the scene with Rousseau's brief stay on the Isle St Pierre in 1765, mentioned in book 12 of *The Confessions* (*Shelley and the Revolutionary Sublime* 199).
8 The connection between the mental landscape of Labrador and the 'illumination of Vincennes' was suggested to me by James Alvey.
9 The letters to Malesherbes were included in the *Œuvres completes de J.J. Rousseau, citoyen de Genève* (1782). The English translation of Rousseau's letters, *Original Letters of J.J. Rousseau, to M. de Malesherbes, M. D'Alanbert, Madame la M. de Luxembourg, & c.*, was published in 1799.
10 When he was visited by the vision, Rousseau was reading the announce-

ment for the prize competition proposed by the Academy of Dijon. In 1750 the Academy of Dijon awarded Rousseau the prize for his *Discours sur les sciences et les arts*, which was published early in 1751. Shelley ordered the book from Lackington, the largest bookshop in England, in September 1815 and again in December 1817 (*Letters* 1: 433, 585). It is, however, not certain whether he got it or not, because the title does not appear on the itemized list of books sent that accompanied Lackington's January 1818 financial statement, nor is it in the Shelleys' reading list in Mary's journal (*SC* 9: 230–1; *Journals* 670).

11 James Annesley, *Researches into the Causes, Nature and Treatment of the More Prevalent Diseases in India* (1828) 45, quoted in Bewell, *Romanticism and Colonial Disease* 211.

12 The (re)evaluation of the concept of hybridity in society and in culture is in line with that in science. It is only in the early twentieth century, more than forty years after Gregor Mendel presented 'Versuche über Pflanzenhybriden' ('Experiments in Plant Hybridization') in 1865, that Mendelian inheritance was 'rediscovered,' and contributed to the genesis of a new discipline of genetics, in which cross-breeding and polygenic inheritance are positively seen as enriching gene pools.

13 In this regard, we may find a modern version of the disfigured Rousseau in David Lurie of Coetzee's *Disgrace* (1999), who lives a purgatorial life of being 'no longer European but not yet African' (Coetzee, *White Writing* 11). This dilemma is as deep as the colonized's *'almost white but not quite'* (Bhabha, *The Location of Culture* 89).

Bibliography

Abrams, M.H., ed. *English Romantic Poets: Modern Essays in Criticism.* New York: Oxford UP, 1960.
- *The Mirror and the Lamp: Romantic Theory and the Critical Tradition.* Oxford: Oxford UP, 1953.
- *Natural Supernaturalism: Tradition and Revolution in Romantic Literature.* New York: Norton, 1971.
- 'Structure and Style in the Greater Romantic Lyric.' *Romanticism and Consciousness: Essays in Criticism.* Ed. Harold Bloom. New York: Norton, 1970. 201–29.
Aeschylus. *Aeschyli Prometheus Vinctus: ad Fidem Manuscriptorum Emendavit Notas et Glossarium Adjecit Carolus Jacobus Blomfield.* Ed. Charles James Blomfield. Cambridge: Cambridge UP, 1810.
- *Prometheus Bound (Aischylou Promētheus Desmōtēs).* Trans. Thomas Morell. London: Longman, 1773.
- 'Prometheus Bound.' *Aeschylus.* Trans. Herbert Weir Smyth. Loeb Classical Library. London: Heinemann, 1963. Vol. 1. 211–315.
Aikin, Lucy. *Poetry for Children: Consisting of Short Pieces to Be Committed to Memory Selected by Lucy Aikin.* 2nd ed. London: Tabart, 1803.
Allott, Miriam. 'Keats's *Endymion* and Shelley's "Alastor."' *Literature of the Romantic Period, 1750–1850.* Ed. R.T. Davies and B.G. Beatty. Liverpool: Liverpool UP, 1976. 151–70.
Alvey, Miyamoto Nahoko. 'Love as Infection: Hybridity and Multiple Idealisms in *Prometheus Unbound.*' *Poetica* 54 (2001): 71–92.
- '"Strange Truths in Undiscovered Lands": *Alastor* and a New Eastern Geography.' *Corresponding Powers: Studies in Honour of Professor Hisaaki Yamanouchi.* Ed. George Hughes. Cambridge: Brewer, 1997. 63–77.
Ambashthya, Brahmadeva Prasad. Preface. *James Rennell's Memoir of a Map of*

Hindustan or the Mughal Empire. By James Rennell. Ed. Brahmadeva Prasad Ambashthya. Delhi: N.V., 1975. v–vii.
Anderson, Benedict. *Imagined Communities: Reflections on the Origin and Spread of Nationalism.* Rev. ed. London: Verso, 1991.
Arabian Tales; or, a Continuation of the Arabian Nights Entertainments. Consisting of Stories, Related by the Sultana of the Indies, to Divert Her Husband from the Performance of a Rash Vow. Exhibiting a Most Interesting Picture of the Religion, Laws, Manners, Costumes, Arts, and Literature of the Nations of the East. In Three Volumes. Newly Translated from the Original Arabic into French, by Dom Chaves, a Native Arab, and M. Cazotte, Member of the Academy of Dijon. 3 vols. Trans. Robert Heron. London: Faulder, 1794.
Archer, Midred, and Ronald Lightbown. *India Observed: India as Viewed by British Artists 1760–1860.* London: Victoria and Albert Museum, 1982.
Arnold, David. *The Problem of Nature: Environment, Culture and European Expansion.* Oxford: Blackwell, 1996.
Arrian, Lucius Flavius. *Anabasis Alexandri.* Trans. E. Iliff Robson. 2 vols. Loeb Classical Library. London: Heinemann, 1929–33.
Rev. of *Asiatic Researches.* Vol. 6. *The British Critic* 25 (1805): 401–8, 521–33.
Aulnoy, Countess d'. *Queen Mab: Containing a Select Collection of Only the Best, Most Instructive, and Entertaining Tales of the Fairies; ... Written by the Countess d' Aulnoi ... To Which Are Added a Fairy Tale, in the Ancient English Style, by Dr. Parnell: and Queen Mab's Song.* 5th ed. London: Vernor, 1799. *The Eighteenth Century* (1992): fiche reel 5619, no. 16.
Bachelard, Gaston. *The Poetics of Space.* Trans. Maria Jolas. Boston: Beacon, 1964.
Baehre, Rainer K. Introduction. *Outrageous Seas: Shipwreck and Survival in the Waters off Newfoundland, 1583–1893.* Montreal: McGill-Queen's UP, 1999. 1–62.
Bailly, Jean Sylvain. *Lettres sur l'Atlantide de Platon et sur l'ancienne histoire de l'Asie: pour server de suite aux letters sur l'origine des sciences adressées á M. de Voltaire.* London: Elmsly, 1779.
Baker, Carlos. *Shelley's Major Poetry: The Fabric of a Vision.* 1948. New York: Russell, 1961.
Baker, E.H. 'Critical and Explanatory Notes on the Prometheus Desmotes of Æschylus, with Stricture on the Notes and the Glossary to Mr. Blomfield's Edition. No. 2.' *Classical Journal* 4 (1811): 209–22.
Baker, John Jay. 'Myth, Subjectivity, and the Problem of Historical Time in Shelley's "Lines Written among the Euganean Hills."' *ELH* 56 (1989): 149–72.

Bakhtin, M.M. *The Dialogic Imagination*. Ed. M. Holquist. Trans. C. Emerson and M. Holquist. Austin: U of Texas P, 1981.

Banier, Antoine. *The Mythology and Fables of the Ancients Explain'd from History*. 4 vols. 1739–40. New York: Garland, 1976.

Banks, Joseph. *The Endeavour Journal of Joseph Banks 1768–1771*. Ed. J.C. Beaglehole. 2nd ed. 2 vols. Sydney: Angus, 1963.

– *Joseph Banks in Newfoundland and Labrador, 1766: His Diary, Manuscripts and Collections*. Ed. A.M. Lysaght. Berkeley: U of California P, 1971.

Barbauld, Anna Letitia. *The Poems of Anna Letitia Barbauld*. Ed. William McCarthy and Elizabeth Kraft. Athens: U of Georgia P, 1994.

Barcus, James E., ed. *Shelley: The Critical Heritage*. London: Routledge, 1975.

Barker, Francis, et al., eds. *Europe and Its Others: Proceedings of the Essex Conference of the Sociology of Literature July 1984*. 2 vols. Colchester: U of Essex P, 1985.

Barker, Francis, et al., eds. *Politics of Theory: Proceedings of the Essex Conference of the Sociology of Literature July 1982*. Colchester: U of Essex P, 1983.

Barker-Benfield, B.C., ed. *Shelley's Guitar: An Exhibition of Manuscripts, First Editions and Relics, to Mark the Bicentenary of the Birth of Percy Bysshe Shelley, 1792/1992*. Oxford: Bodleian Library, 1992.

Barrell, John. *The Infection of Thomas De Quincey: A Psychopathology of Imperialism*. New Haven, CT: Yale UP, 1991.

Barrow, Ian J. *Making History, Drawing Territory: British Mapping in India, c. 1756–1905*. Cambridge: Cambridge UP, 2003.

Baudet, Henri. *Paradise on Earth: Some Thoughts on European Images of Non-European Man*. Trans. Elizabeth Wentholt. New Haven, CT: Yale UP, 1965.

Bayly, C.A. *Imperial Meridian: The British Empire and the World 1780–1830*. London: Longman, 1989.

– *Indian Society and the Making of the British Empire*. Cambridge: Cambridge UP, 1988.

Beazley, Elisabeth. *Madocks and the Wonder of Wales*. 2nd ed. Aberystwyth, UK: P & Q, 1985.

Beckford, William. *Vathek*. Ed. Roger Lonsdale. Oxford: Oxford UP, 1983.

Beddoes, Thomas. *Alexander's Expedition down the Hydaspes and the Indus to the Indian Ocean*. London: Murray, 1792. *The Eighteenth Century* (1990): fiche reel 3938, no. 3.

Behrendt, Stephen C. *Shelley and His Audiences*. Lincoln: U of Nebraska P, 1989.

Beljame, Al, trans. *Alastor ou le génie de la solitude: Poème traduit en prose française avec le texte anglais en regard et des notes par Al Beljame*. Paris: Hachette, 1895.

Bell, John. *Bell's New Pantheon; or Historical Dictionary of the Gods, Demi-Gods, Heroes, and Fabulous Personages of Antiquity*. 2 vols. London: British Library, 1790.

Bentham, Jeremy. *The Rationale of Reward*. London: Hunt, 1825.

Bernal, Martin. *Black Athena: The Afroasiatic Roots of Classical Civilization*. Vol. 1. New Brunswick, NJ: Rutgers UP, 1987. 3 vols.

Bernhardt-Kabisch, Ernest. *Robert Southey*. New York: Twayne, 1977.

Bernier, François. *Travels in the Mogul Empire AD 1656–1668*. Trans. Archibald Constable. Delhi: Chand, 1891.

Bewell, Alan. *Romanticism and Colonial Disease*. Baltimore: Johns Hopkins UP, 1999.

– 'Romanticism and Colonial Natural History.' *Studies in Romanticism* 43 (2004): 5–34.

– *Wordsworth and the Enlightenment: Nature, Man, and Society in the Experimental Poetry*. New Haven, CT: Yale UP, 1989.

Bhabha, Homi K. *The Location of Culture*. London: Routledge, 1994.

–, ed. *Nation and Narration*. London: Routledge, 1990.

Birns, Nicholas. 'Secrets of the Birth of Time: The Rhetoric of Cultural Origins in *Alastor* and "Mont Blanc."' *Studies in Romanticism* 32 (1993): 339–65.

– '"Thy World, Columbus!": Barbauld and Global Space, 1803, "1811," 1812, 2003.' *European Romantic Review* 16 (2005): 545–62.

Blackstone, Bernard. '"The Loops of Time": Spatio-Temporal Patterns in "Childe Harold."' *Ariel* 2, no. 4 (1971): 5–17.

Blake, William. *The Complete Poetry and Prose of William Blake*. Rev. ed. Ed. David V. Erdman. New York: Anchor, 1988.

– *The Illuminated Blake: William Blake's Complete Illuminated Works with a Plate-by-Plate Commentary*. Ed. David V. Erdman. New York: Dover, 1974.

Blank, G. Kim. *Wordsworth's Influence on Shelley: A Study in Poetic Authority*. London: Macmillan, 1988.

Bloch, Marc. *The Royal Touch: Sacred Monarchy and Scrofula in England and France*. Trans. J.E. Anderson. London: Routledge, 1973.

Bloom, Harold. *Anxiety of Influence: A Theory of Poetry*. London: Oxford UP, 1973.

Bloom, Harold, et al. *Deconstruction and Criticism*. New York: Seabury, 1979.

– *The Ringers in the Tower: Studies in Romantic Tradition*. Chicago: U of Chicago P, 1971.

- *Shelley's Mythmaking*. New Haven, CT: Yale UP, 1959.
- *The Visionary Company: A Reading of English Romantic Poetry*. London: Faber, 1962.
-, ed. *Romanticism and Consciousness: Essays in Criticism*. New York: Norton, 1970.
Blumenbach, Johann Friedrich. *The Anthropological Treatises of Johann Friedrich Blumenbach*. Trans. Thomas Bendyshe. 1865. Boston: Milford, 1973.
Bostetter, Edward E. *The Romantic Ventriloquists: Wordsworth, Coleridge, Keats, Shelley and Byron*. Seattle: Washington UP, 1963.
Bosworth, A.B. *Conquest and Empire: The Reign of Alexander the Great*. Cambridge: Cambridge UP, 1988.
Bourget, Marie-Noële, Christian Licoppe, and H. Otto Sibum, eds. *Instruments, Travel and Science: Itineraries of Precision from the Seventeenth Century to the Twentieth Century*. London: Routledge, 2002.
Bowen, Margarita. *Empiricism and Geographical Thought: From Francis Bacon to Alexander von Humboldt*. Cambridge: Cambridge UP, 1981.
Brace, C. Loring, et al. 'A Test in Ancient Egypt and the Case of a Death on the Nile.' *Black Athena Revisited*. Ed. Mary R. Lefkowitz and Guy MacLean Rogers. Chapel Hill: U of North Carolina P, 1996. 129–64.
Brand, C.P. *Italy and the English Romantics: The Italianate Fashion in Early Nineteenth-Century England*. Cambridge: Cambridge UP, 1957.
Brantlinger, Patrick. *Rule of Darkness: British Literature and Imperialism, 1830–1914*. Ithaca, NY: Cornell UP, 1988.
Breckeridge, Carol A., and Peter van der Veer, eds. *Orientalism and the Postcolonial Predicament: Perspectives on South Asia*. Philadelphia: U of Pennsylvania P, 1993.
Briggs, Katharine. *A Dictionary of Fairies, Hobgoblins, Brownies, Bogies and Other Supernatural Creatures*. London: Lane, 1976.
- *The Fairies in English Tradition and Literature*. Chicago: U of Chicago P, 1967.
Bruce, James. *Travels to Discover the Source of the Nile: in the Years 1768, 1769, 1770, 1771, 1772, and 1773*. 5 vols. Edinburgh: Ruthven, 1790.
Bryant, Hallman B. 'The African Genesis of Tennyson's "Timbuctoo."' *Tennyson Research Bulletin* 3 (1981): 196–202.
Bryson, Norman. *Vision and Painting: The Logic of the Gaze*. London: Macmillan, 1983.
Burke, Edmund. *The Writings and Speeches of Edmund Burke*. Ed. Paul Langford. 9 vols. to date. Oxford: Clarendon, 1981–.
Butler, Marilyn. 'Hidden Metropolis: London in Sentimental and Romantic

Writing.' *London – World City 1800–1840*. Ed. Celina Fox. New Haven, CT: Yale UP, 1992. 187–98.
- 'Orientalism.' *The Romantic Period*. Ed. David B. Pirie. London: Penguin, 1994. Vol. 5 of *The Penguin History of Literature*. 10 vols. 1987–94. 395–447.
- 'The Orientalism of Byron's *Giaour.*' *Byron and the Limits of Fiction*. Ed. Bernard Beatty and Vincent Newey. Liverpool: Liverpool UP, 1988. 78–96.
- *Peacock Displayed: A Satirist in His Context*. London: Routledge, 1979.
- *Romantics, Rebels and Reactionaries: English Literature and Its Background*. New York: Oxford UP, 1985.
- 'Shelley and the Question of Joint Authorship.' *Evaluating Shelley*. Ed. Timothy Clark and Jerrold E. Hogle. Edinburgh: Edinburgh UP, 1996. 42–7.

Butter, Peter. *Shelley's Idols of the Cave*. Edinburgh: Edinburgh UP, 1954.

Byron, George Gordon, Lord. *Byron's Letters and Journals*. Ed. L.A. Marchand. 13 vols. London: Murray, 1973–94.
- *Lord Byron: The Complete Poetical Works*. Ed. Jerome J. McGann. 7 vols. Oxford: Clarendon, 1980–93.

Cain, P.J., and A.G. Hopkins. *British Imperialism: Innovation and Expansion, 1688–1914*. London: Longman, 1993.

Cameron, Kenneth Neill. 'The Political Symbolism of *Prometheus Unbound.*' *PMLA* 58 (1943): 728–53.
- *Shelley: The Golden Years*. Cambridge, MA: Harvard UP, 1974.
- *The Young Shelley: Genesis of a Radical*. New York: Macmillan, 1950.

Cannon, Garland. *Oriental Jones: A Biography of Sir William Jones (1746–1794)*. London: Asia, 1964.

Caracciolo, Peter L. 'Introduction: "Such a Store House of Ingenious Fiction and of Splendid Imagery."' *The Arabian Nights in English Literature: Studies in the Reception of the Thousand and One Nights into British Culture*. Ed. Peter L. Caracciolo. London: Macmillan, 1988. 1–80.

Carl H. Pforzheimer Library. *Shelley and His Circle 1773–1822*. 10 vols. to date. Cambridge, MA: Harvard UP, 1961– .

Carnall, Geoffrey. *Robert Southey and His Age: The Development of a Conservative Mind*. Oxford: Clarendon, 1960.

Cartwright, George. *A Journal of Transactions and Events, During a Residence of Nearly Sixteen Years on the Coast of Labrador; Containing Many Interesting Particulars, Both of the Country and its Inhabitants, Not Hitherto Known*. 3 vols. Newark, Upper Canada [Niagara-on-the-Lake, ON]: Allin and Ridge; London: Robinson and Stockdale, 1792.
- *Labrador: A Poetical Epistle; with Explanatory Notes: Addressed to a Friend*. Newark, Upper Canada [Niagara-on-the-Lake, ON]: Allin and Ridge; London: Robinson and Stockdale, 1792.

Chandler, James. *England in 1819: The Politics of Literary Culture and the Case of Romantic Historicism*. Chicago: U of Chicago P, 1998.
Chernaik, Judith. *The Lyrics of Shelley*. Cleveland: Case Western Reserve UP, 1972.
Clark, Timothy. *Embodying Revolution: The Figure of the Poet in Shelley*. Oxford: Clarendon, 1989.
Clifford, James. *The Predicament of Culture: Twentieth-Century Ethnography, Literature, and Art*. Cambridge, MA: Harvard UP, 1988.
Coats, Sandra. 'Shelley and the Promethean Myth.' *Conference of College Teachers of English Studies* 48 (1983): 40–7.
Coetzee, J.M. *Disgrace*. London: Secker, 1999.
– *White Writing: On the Culture of Letters in South Africa*. New Haven, CT: Yale UP, 1988.
Cohn, Norman. *Noah's Ark: The Genesis Story in Western Thought*. New Haven, CT: Yale UP, 1996.
Colbert, Benjamin. *Shelley's Eye: Travel Writing and Aesthetic Vision*. Aldershot: Ashgate, 2005.
Coleridge, Samuel Taylor. *Biographia Literaria: or Biographical Sketches of My Life and Work*. Ed. James Engell and W. Jackson Bate. The Collected Works of Samuel Taylor Coleridge 7. Princeton, NJ: Princeton UP, 1983.
– *Christabel 1816*. 1816. Ed. Jonathan Wordsworth. Oxford: Woodstock, 1991.
– *The Collected Letters of Samuel Taylor Coleridge*. Ed. Earl Leslie Griggs. 6 vols. Oxford: Clarendon, 1956–71.
– *The Complete Poetical Works of Samuel Taylor Coleridge*. Ed. Ernest Hartley Coleridge. 2 vols. Oxford: Clarendon, 1912.
– *The Friend*. Ed. Barbara E. Rooke. 2 vols. The Collected Works of Samuel Taylor Coleridge 4. Princeton, NJ: Princeton UP, 1969.
– *Marginalia*. Ed. George Whalley and H.J. Jackson. 6 vols. The Collected Works of Samuel Taylor Coleridge 12. Princeton, NJ: Princeton UP, 1980–.
– *The Notebooks of Samuel Taylor Coleridge*. Ed. Kathleen Coburn, Merton Christensen, and Anthony John Harding. 5 vols in 10. Bollingen Series 50. Princeton, NJ: Princeton UP, 1957–2002.
– *Poetical Works*. Ed. J.C.C. Mays. 3 vols in 6. The Collected Works of Samuel Taylor Coleridge 16. Princeton, NJ: Princeton UP, 2001.
– *Shorter Works and Fragments*. Ed. H.J. Jackson and J.R. de J. Jackson. 2 vols. The Collected Works of Samuel Taylor Coleridge 11. Princeton, NJ: Princeton UP, 1995.
– *Sibylline Leaves 1817*. 1817. Ed. Jonathan Wordsworth. Oxford: Woodstock, 1990.

Colley, Linda. *Britons: Forging the Nation, 1707–1837.* New Haven, CT: Yale UP, 1992.
- *Captives: Britain, Empire, and the World, 1600–1850.* London: Cape, 2002.
Colwell, Frederic S. 'Figures in a Promethean Landscape.' *Keats-Shelley Journal* 45 (1996): 118–31.
- *Rivermen: A Romantic Iconography of the River and the Source.* Kingston: McGill-Queen's UP, 1989.
- 'Shelley on Sculpture: The Uffizi Notes.' *Keats-Shelley Journal* 28 (1979): 59–77.
- 'Shelley's "The Witch of Atlas" and the Mythic Geography of the Nile.' *ELH* 45 (1978): 69–92.
Conant, Martha Pike. *The Oriental Tale in England in the Eighteenth Century.* New York: Columbia UP, 1908.
Connell, Philip. *Romanticism, Economics and the Question of 'Culture.'* Oxford: Oxford UP, 2001.
Conrad, Joseph. *The Collected Works of Joseph Conrad.* Ed. Ford Madox Ford. Vol. 6. New York: Doubleday, 1926. 26 vols.
Cook, James. *A Voyage towards the South Pole and round the World: Performed in His Majesty's Ships the Resolution and Adventure, in the Years 1772, 1773, 1774 and 1775.* 2 vols. London: Cadell, 1777.
Cooke, G.A. *Topographical and Statistical Description of the Principality of Wales.* 2 vols. London: Sherwood, n.d.
Coxe, William. *Travels in Switzerland and in the Country of the Grisons: In a Series of Letters to William Melmoth, Esq., from William Coxe.* 2nd ed. 3 vols. London: Cadell, 1791.
Croker, John Wilson. Rev. of *Eighteen Hundred and Eleven*, by Anna Barbauld. *Quarterly Review* 7 (1812): 309–13.
Cronin, Richard. *Shelley's Poetic Thoughts.* New York: St Martin's, 1981.
Cross, Ashley J. '"What a World We Make the Oppression and the Oppressed": George Cruikshank, Percy Shelley, and the Gendering of Revolution.' *ELH* 71 (2004): 167–207.
Curran, Stuart. *Poetic Form and British Romanticism.* Oxford: Oxford UP, 1986.
- 'Political Prometheus.' *Studies in Romanticism* 25 (1986): 429–55.
- *Shelley's Annus Mirabilis: The Maturing of an Epic Vision.* San Marino, CA: Huntington, 1975.
Curtin, Philip, D. *The Image of Africa: British Ideas and Action, 1780–1850.* 2 vols. Wisconsin: U of Wisconsin P, 1964.
- *Death by Migration: Europe's Encounter with the Tropical World in the Nineteenth Century.* Cambridge: Cambridge UP, 1989.

Curtius, Earnest Robert. *European Literature and Latin Middle Age.* Trans. Willard R. Trask. New York: Pantheon, 1953.

Cuvier, Georges. *The Animal Kingdom, Arranged according to Its Organization, Serving as a Foundation for the Natural History of Animals, and an Introduction to Comparative Anatomy.* 4 vols. London: Henderson, 1834.

– *Essay on the Theory of the Earth, with Mineralogical Notes, and an Account of Cuvier's Geological Discoveries, by Professor Jameson.* Trans. Robert Kerr. Notes supplied by Robert Jameson. 3rd ed. Edinburgh: Blackwood, 1817.

Dacre, Charlotte. *Hours of Solitude.* Ed. Donald H. Reiman. New York: Garland, 1978.

Darwin, Erasmus. *The Loves of the Plants 1789.* Rpt. of *The Botanic Garden, Part II. Containing* The Loves of the Plants, A Poem. With Philosophical Notes. Lichfield: Johnson, 1789. Oxford: Woodstock, 1991.

– *The Poetical Works of Erasmus Darwin. With Philosophical Notes and Plates in Three Volumes.* 3 vols. London: Johnson, 1806. Rpt. Tokyo: Hon-No-Tomo, 1997.

Davie, Donald. 'Shelley's Urbanity.' *English Romantic Poets: Modern Essays in Criticism.* Ed. M.H. Abrams. New York: Oxford UP, 1960. 307–25.

Davies, Damian Walford, and Lynda Pratt, eds. *Wales and the Romantic Imagination.* Cardiff: U of Wales P, 2007.

Davies, Gordon L. *The Earth in Decay: A History of British Geomorphology 1578–1878.* London: MacDonald, 1969.

Dawson, P. M. S. *The Unacknowledged Legislator: Shelley and Politics.* Oxford: Oxford UP, 1980.

De Almeida, Hermione, and George H. Gilpin. *Indian Renaissance: British Romantic Art and the Prospect of India.* Aldershot: Ashgate, 2005.

De Beer, Gavin. *Early Travellers in the Alps.* 1930. London: Sidgwick, 1966.

– *Speaking of Switzerland.* London: Eyre, 1952.

De Luca, V.A. 'The Style of Millennial Announcement in *Prometheus Unbound.*' *Keats-Shelley Journal* 28 (1979): 78–101.

De Man, Paul. *The Rhetoric of Romanticism.* New York: Columbia UP, 1984.

Denon, Vivant. *Travels in Upper and Lower Egypt, in Company with Several Divisions of the French Army, during the Campaigns of General Bonaparte in That Country.* Trans. Arthur Aikin. 3 vols. London: Longman, 1803. New York: Arno, 1973.

De Quincey, Thomas. *Confessions of an English Opium Eater.* Ed. Alethea Hayter. London: Penguin, 1972.

Di Marco, Luis Eugenio. 'The Evolution of Prebisch's Economic Thought.' *International Economics and Development: Essays in Honor of Raúl Prebisch.* Ed. Luis Eugenio Di Marco. New York: Academic, 1972. 3–13.

–, ed. *International Economics and Development: Essays in Honor of Raúl Prebisch.* New York: Academic, 1972.
Dio, Cassius. *Dio's Roman History.* Trans. Earnest Cary. Loeb Classical Library. London: Heinemann, 1927.
Diodorus. *Diodorus of Sicily.* Trans. C.H. Oldfather. 12 vols. Loeb Classical Library. London: Heinemann, 1933–67.
Douce, Francis. *Illustrations of Shakespeare, and of Ancient Manners.* 2 vols. London: Longman, 1807.
Dowden, Edward. *The Life of Percy Bysshe Shelley.* 2 vols. London: Paul, 1886.
Drew, John. *India and the Romantic Imagination.* Delhi: Oxford UP, 1987.
Duerksen, Ronald A. 'Wordsworth and the Austral Retreat in Shelley's "Witch of Atlas."' *Keats-Shelley Journal* 34 (1985): 18–20.
Duff, David. *Romance and Revolution: Shelley and the Politics of a Genre.* Cambridge: Cambridge UP, 1994.
Duffy, Cian. '"One Draught from Snowdon's Ever-Sacred Spring": Shelley's Welsh Sublime.' *Wales and the Romantic Imagination.* Ed. Damian Walford Davies and Lynda Pratt. Cardiff: U of Wales P, 2007. 180–98.
– *Shelley and the Revolutionary Sublime.* Cambridge: Cambridge UP, 2005.
Duffy, Edward. *Rousseau in England: The Context for Shelley's Critique of the Enlightenment.* Berkeley: U of California P, 1979.
Dupin, Charles. *The Commercial Power of Great Britain; Exhibiting a Complete View of the Public Works of This Country.* 2 vols. London: Knight, 1825.
Dupuis, Charles François. *The Origin of All Religious Worship. Translated from the French of Dupuis ... Containing Also a Description of the Zodiac of Denderah.* 1872. New York: Garland, 1984.
Ebbaston, J.R. 'Coleridge's Mariner and the Rights of Man.' *Studies in Romanticism* 11 (1972): 171–206.
Ebel, Johann Gottfried. *Manuel du voyageur en Suisse.* 2nd ed. 4 vols. Zurich: Orell, 1810.
Edgerton, Samuel Y., Jr. 'From Mental Matrix to *Mappamundi* to Christian Empire: The Heritage of Ptolemaic Cartography in the Renaissance.' *Art and Cartography: Six Historical Essays.* Ed. David Woodward. Chicago: U of Chicago P, 1989. 10–50.
Edney, Matthew H. *Mapping an Empire: The Geographical Construction of British India, 1765–1843.* Chicago: U of Chicago P, 1997.
Eliot, T.S. *The Use of Poetry and the Use of Criticism.* London: Faber, 1933.
Embree, Ainslie Thomas. *Charles Grant and British Rule in India.* New York: Columbia UP, 1962.
Encyclopædia Britannica, or a Dictionary of Arts, Sciences and Miscellaneous Literature. 3rd ed. 18 vols. Edinburgh: Bell, 1797.

Encyclopædia Britannica, or a Dictionary of Arts, Sciences and Miscellaneous Literature. Enlarged and improved 5th ed. 20 vols. Edinburgh: Constable, 1817.

Engel, Claire Eliane. *A History of Mountaineering in the Alps.* London: Allen, 1950.

–, comp. *Mont Blanc: An Anthology Compiled by Claire Eliane Engel.* Chicago: McNally, 1965.

The English Hymnal with Tunes. London: Oxford UP, 1906.

Euripides. *The Bacchae.* Trans. Geoffrey S. Kirk. Englewood Cliffs, NJ: Prentice-Hall, 1970.

Evans, Dylan. *An Introductory Dictionary of Lacanian Psychoanalysis.* London: Routledge, 1996.

Everest, Kelvin, ed. *Shelley Revalued: Essays from the Gregynog Conference.* Leicester, UK: Leicester UP, 1983.

Faber, George Stanley. *The Origin of Pagan Idolatry.* 3 vols. 1816. New York: Garland, 1984.

Ferguson, Frances. 'Shelley's *Mont Blanc*: What the Mountain Said.' *Romanticism and Language.* Ed. Arden Reed. Ithaca, NY: Cornell UP, 1984. 202–14.

Flynn, Dennis O., and Arturo Giraldez. 'Path Dependence, Time Lags and the Birth of Globalisation: A Critique of O'Rourke and Williamson.' *European Review of Economic History* 8 (2004): 81–108.

Foersch, N.P. 'Description of the Poison Tree in the Island of Java.' *London Magazine* 1 (Dec. 1783): 511–17.

Foot, Paul. *Red Shelley.* London: Sidgwick, 1980.

Forster, George. *A Journey from Bengal to England, through the Northern Part of India, Kashmire, Afghanistan, and Persia.* 2 vols. London: Faulder, 1798.

Foucault, Michel. *Madness and Civilization: A History of Insanity in the Age of Reason.* Trans. Richard Howard. 1961. New York: Pantheon, 1965.

– 'Of Other Spaces.' Trans. Jay Miskowiec. *Diacritics* 16, no. 1 (1986): 22–7.

– *The Order of Things: An Archaeology of the Human Sciences.* 1966. London: Tavistock, 1970.

Fox, Celina, ed. *London – World City 1800–1840.* New Haven, CT: Yale UP, 1992.

Franklin, Michael J. '"Passion's Empire": Sydney Owenson's "Indian Venture," Phoenicianism, Orinetalism, and Binarim.' *Studies in Romanticism* 45 (2006): 181–97.

–, ed. *Romantic Representations of British India.* London: Routledge, 2006.

Fregosi, Paul. *Dreams of Empire: Napoleon and the First World War 1792–1815.* London: Hutchinson, 1989.

Friedman, John Block. *The Monstrous Races in Medieval Art and Thought.* Cambridge, MA: Harvard UP, 1981.

Frosch, Thomas R. *Shelley and the Romantic Imagination: A Psychological Study.* Newark: U of Delaware P, 2007.
Frye, Northrop, ed. *Romanticism Reconsidered.* New York: Columbia UP, 1963.
– *A Study of English Romanticism.* Sussex, UK: Harvester, 1968.
Fulford, Tim, Debbie Lee, and Peter J. Kitson. *Literature, Science and Exploration in the Romantic Era: Bodies of Knowledge.* Cambridge: Cambridge UP, 2004.
Fulford, Tim, and Peter J. Kitson, ed. *Romanticism and Colonialism: Writing and Empire, 1780–1830.* Cambridge: Cambridge UP, 1998.
Fuseli, Henry. *Henry Fuseli 1741–1825.* Ed. Gert Schiff. London: Tate Gallery, 1975.
– *Johann Heinrich Fuseli 1741–1825.* Ed. Gert Schiff. 2 vols. Zurich: Berichthaus, 1973.
Gallagher, John. *The Decline, Revival and Fall of the British Empire: The Ford Lectures and Other Essays.* Ed. Anil Seal. Cambridge: Cambridge UP, 1982.
Gallagher, John, and Ronald Robinson. 'The Imperialism of Free Trade.' *The Decline, Revival and Fall of the British Empire: The Ford Lectures and Other Essays.* Ed. Anil Seal. Cambridge: Cambridge UP, 1982. 1–18.
Gandhi, Leela. *Postcolonial Theory: A Critical Introduction.* New York: Columbia UP, 1998.
Gardner, Brian. *The Quest for Timbuctoo.* London: Cassell, 1968.
Gilbert, Allan H. *A Geographical Dictionary of Milton.* Ithaca, NY: Cornell UP, 1919.
Gilroy, Amanda. *Romantic Geographies: Discourses of Travel, 1775–1844.* Manchester: Manchester UP, 2000.
Glacken, Clarence J. *Traces on the Rhodian Shore: Nature and Culture in Western Thought from Ancient Times to the End of the Eighteenth Century.* Berkeley: U of California P, 1967.
Godwin, William. *Collected Novels and Memoirs of William Godwin.* Ed. Mark Philp. Vol. 1. London: Pickering, 1992. 8 vols.
– *Enquiry concerning Political Justice and Its Influence on General Virtue and Happiness.* Ed. Isaac Kramnick. London: Penguin, 1976.
Gole, Susan. *India within the Ganges.* New Delhi: Jayaprints, 1983.
– *Indian Maps and Plans: From Earliest Times to the Advent of European Surveys.* New Delhi: Manohar, 1989.
– *A Series of Early Printed Maps of India in Facsimile.* New Delhi: Jayaprints, 1980.
Gosling, William Gilbert. *Labrador: Its Discovery, Exploration and Development.* Toronto: Musso, 1910.

Goss, John. *The Mapmaker's Art: A History of Cartography.* London: Studio, 1993.
Gould, Stephen Jay. *Time's Arrow Time's Cycle: Myth and Metaphor in the Discovery of Geological Time.* Cambridge, MA: Harvard UP, 1987.
Grabo, Carl. *The Magic Plant: The Growth of Shelley's Thought.* Chapel Hill: U of North Carolina P, 1936.
– *The Meaning of 'The Witch of Atlas.'* 1935. New York: Russell, 1971.
– *A Newton among Poets: Shelley's Use of Science in* Prometheus Unbound. Chapel Hill: U of North Carolina P, 1930.
Gregory, Derek. *Geographical Imaginations.* Oxford: Blackwell, 1994.
Grosrichard, Alain. *The Sultan's Court: European Fantasies of the East.* Trans. Liz Heron. London: Verso, 1998. Trans. of *Structure du Sérail: la fiction du despotisme asiatique dans l'occident classique.* Paris: Seuil, 1979.
Grove, Richard H. *Ecology, Climate and Empire: Colonialism and Global Environmental History, 1400–1940.* Cambridge: White Horse, 1997.
– *Green Imperialism: Colonial Expansion, Tropical Island Edens and the Origins of Environmentalism, 1600–1860.* Cambridge: Cambridge UP, 1995.
Haggard, H. Rider. *She, a History of Adventure.* London: Nash, 1886.
Hakluyt, Richard. *Hakluyt's Collection of the Early Voyages, Travels, and Discoveries, of the English Nation: A New Edition.* 5 vols. London: Evans, 1810–12.
Hallam, A. *Great Geological Controversies.* 2nd ed. Oxford: Oxford UP, 1989.
Haller, William. *The Early Life of Robert Southey 1774–1803.* New York: Columbia UP, 1917.
Hallett, Robin. *The Penetration of Africa: European Enterprise and Exploration Principally in Northern and Western Africa up to 1830.* London: Routledge, 1965.
Hamilton, Alexander. Rev. of *Dissertations and Miscellaneous Pieces relating to the History and Antiquities, the Arts, Sciences, and Literature of Asia,* by Sir William Jones and others. *Monthly Review* 23 (1797): 408–14.
Harley, J.B. 'Maps, Knowledge, and Power.' *The Iconography of Landscape: Essays on the Symbolic Representation, Design and Use of Past Environments.* Ed. Denis Cosgrove and Stephen Daniels. Cambridge: Cambridge UP, 1988. 277–312.
Harrington-Austin, Eleanor J. *Shelley and the Development of English Imperialism: British India and England.* Lewiston, NY: Mellon, 1999.
Harvey, David. 'Geographical Knowledges / Political Powers.' *Proceedings of the British Academy* 122 (2004): 87–115.
Hastings, Warren. 'Letter to Nathaniel Smith.' *The British Discovery of Hinduism in the Eighteenth Century.* Ed. P.J. Marshall. Cambridge: Cambridge UP, 1970. 184–91.

Hechter, Michael. *Internal Colonialism: The Celtic Fringe in British National Development, 1536–1966*. Berkeley: U of California P, 1975.
Hein, Wolfgang-Hagen, ed. *Alexander von Humboldt: Life and Work*. Trans. John Cunning. Ingelheim am Rhein: Sohn, 1987.
– 'The American Expedition and its Evaluation.' *Alexander von Humboldt: Life and Work*. Ed. Wolfgang-Hagen Hein. Trans. John Cunning. Ingelheim am Rhein: Sohn, 1987. 56–108.
– 'Humboldt and Goethe.' *Alexander von Humboldt: Life and Work*. Ed. Wolfgang-Hagen Hein. Trans. John Cunning. Ingelheim am Rhein: Sohn, 1987. 46–55.
Hemans, Felicia. *Felicia Hemans: Selected Poems, Prose, and Letters*. Ed. Gary Kelly. Peterborough, ON: Broadview, 2002.
Henriques, Fernando. *Children of Caliban: Miscegenation*. London: Secker, 1974.
Heringman, Noah. *Romantic Rocks, Aesthetic Geology*. Ithaca, NY: Cornell UP, 2004.
Herodianus. *Herodian*. Trans. C.R. Whittaker. 2 vols. Loeb Classical Library. London: Heinemann, 1969–70.
Herodotus. *Herodotus*. Trans. A.D. Godley. 4 vols. Loeb Classical Library. London: Heinemann, 1920–38.
Hill, David. *Turner in the Alps: The Journey through France and Switzerland in 1802*. London: Philip, 1992.
Hippocrates. 'Airs Waters Places.' *Hippocrates*. Trans. W.H.S. Jones. Vol. 1. Loeb Classical Library. London: Heinemann, 1923. 4 vols. 1923–31. 65–137.
Rev. of *Historical Account of Discoveries and Travels in Africa*, by Hugh Murray. *Quarterly Review* 17 (1817): 299–338.
Hoare, Richard Colt. *The Journeys of Sir Richard Colt Hoare through Wales and England 1793–1810*. Ed. M.W. Thompson. Gloucester, UK: Sutton, 1983.
Hobsbawm, E.J. *The Age of Empire 1875–1914*. New York: Pantheon, 1987.
Hobsbawm, E.J., and Terence Ranger, ed. *The Invention of Tradition*. Cambridge: Cambridge UP, 1983.
Hodges, William. *Travels in India, during the Years 1780, 1781, 1782, and 1783*. London: Edwards, 1793.
Hogg, Thomas Jefferson. *The Life of Percy Bysshe Shelley*. 2 vols. London: Moxon, 1858.
Hogle, Jerrold E. 'Metaphor and Metamorphosis in Shelley's "The Witch of Atlas."' *Studies in Romanticism* 19 (1980): 327–53.
– *Shelley's Process: Radical Transference and the Development of His Major Works*. Oxford: Oxford UP, 1984.
Holmes, Richard. *Shelley: The Pursuit*. London: Penguin, 1974.

Holy Bible: Authorized King James Version. Ed. C.I. Scofield. New York: Oxford UP, 1967.

Horneman, Frederick. *The Journal of Frederick Horneman's Travels, from Cairo to Mourzouk, the Capital of the Kingdom of Fezzan, in Africa, in the Years 1797–8.* London: Bulmer, 1802.

Hough, Richard. *Captain James Cook: A Biography.* New York: Norton, 1995.

Hughes, D.J. 'Kindling and Dwindling: The Poetic Process in Shelley.' *Keats-Shelley Journal* 13 (1964): 13–28.

– 'Potentiality in *Prometheus Unbound*.' *Studies in Romanticism* 2 (1962–63): 107–26.

– 'Prometheus Made Capable Poet in Act One of *Prometheus Unbound*.' *Studies in Romanticism* 17 (1978): 3–11.

Humboldt, Alexander von. *Personal Narrative of Travels to the Equinoctial Regions of the New Continent, during the Years 1799–1804 by Alexander de Humboldt, and Aimé Bonpland.* Trans. Helen Maria Williams. 7 vols. London: Longman, 1814–29. Originally published as *Voyage aux régions équinoxiales du nouveau continent.* 11 vols. Paris: Schoell, 1814.

Hume, David. *A Treatise of Human Nature.* Ed. A.D. Lindsay. 2 vols. London: Dent, 1911.

Hungerford, Edward B. *Shores of Darkness.* New York: Columbia UP, 1941.

Hunt, Leigh. *The Autobiography of Leigh Hunt.* Ed. J.E. Morpurgo. London: Cresset, 1949.

Hutton, James. *Theory of the Earth with Proofs and Illustrations.* 2 vols. 1795. Weinhelm: Engelmann, 1959.

Hyam, Ronald. *Britain's Imperial Century 1815–1914: A Study of Empire and Expansion.* London: Batsford, 1976.

– *Empire and Sexuality: The British Experience.* Manchester: Manchester UP, 1990.

Isomaki, Richard. 'Interpretation and Value in "Mont Blanc" and "Hymn to Intellectual Beauty."' *Studies in Romanticism* 30 (1991): 57–69.

Jackson, James Grey. *An Account of the Empire of Morocco, and the Districts of Suse and Tafilelt; Complied from Miscellaneous Observations Made during a Long Residence in, and Various Journies through, These Countries. To Which Is Added an Account of Shipwrecks on the Western Coast of Africa, and an Interesting Account of Timbuctoo, the Great Emporium of Central Africa.* 3rd ed. 1814. London: Cass, 1968.

– *An Account of Timbuctoo and Housa, Territories in the Interior of Africa, by El Hage Abd Salam Shabeeny: With Notes, Critical and Explanatory. To Which is Added, Letters Descriptive of Travels through West and South Barbary, and across the Mountains of Atlas; Also, Fragments, Notes, and Anecdotes; Specimens of the Arabic Epistolary Style, &c. &c.* London: Longman, 1820.

– 'Hints concerning the Colonization of Africa.' *Edinburgh Magazine* 4 (1819): 652–4.
Jackson, J.R. de J. *Poetry of the Romantic Period*. London: Routledge, 1980. Vol. 4 of *The Routledge History of English Poetry*. 4 vols. 1977–81.
Jobson, Richard. *The Golden Trade: London 1623*. New York: Da Capo, 1968.
Jones, William, Sir. *The Works of Sir William Jones*. 6 vols. London: Robinson, 1799.
Kabbani, Rana. *Europe's Myths of Orient: Devise and Rule*. London: Macmillan, 1986.
Keach, William. 'Obstinate Questionings: The Immortality Ode and *Alastor*.' *Wordsworth Circle* 12 (1981): 36–44.
– 'A Regency Prophecy and the End of Anna Barbauld's Career.' *Studies in Romanticism* 33 (1994): 569–77.
– *Shelley's Style*. New York: Methuen, 1984.
Keate, George. *The Alps: A Poem*. London: Dodsley, 1763.
Keats, John. *John Keats: Complete Poems*. Ed. Jack Stillinger. Cambridge, MA: Belknap, 1978.
Kelly, Christopher, Roger D. Masters, and Peter G. Stillman. The Editors' Introduction. *Jean-Jacques Rousseau: The Confessions and Correspondence, Including the Letters to Malesherbes*. Vol. 5 of *The Collected Writings of Rousseau*. Ed. Christopher Kelly, Roger D. Masters, and Peter G. Stillman. Trans. Christopher Kelly. Hanover, NH: UP of New England, 1995. xvii–xxxiv.
Kidwai, Abdur Raheem. *Orientalism in Lord Byron's 'Turkish Tales': The Giaour (1813), The Bride of Abydos (1813), The Corsair (1814) and The Siege of Corinth (1816)*. Lampeter, UK: Mellen, 1995.
King-Hale, Desmond. *Erasmus Darwin*. London: Macmillan, 1963.
– *Erasmus Darwin and the Romantic Poets*. London: Macmillan, 1986.
Kipling, Rudyard. *Kim*. Ed. Edward Said. London: Penguin, 2000.
Kitson, Peter. J. Introduction. *Theory of Race*. Ed. Peter J. Kitson. London: Pickering, 1999. vii–xxxii.
–, ed. *Theory of Race*. London: Pickering, 1999. Vol. 8 of *Slavery, Abolition and Emancipation: Writings in the British Romantic Period*. 8 vols. 1999.
Knight, G. Wilson. The *Starlit Dome: Studies in the Poetry of Vision*. London: Methuen, 1959.
Kolodny, Annette. *The Lay of the Land: Metaphors as Experience and History in American Life and Letters*. Chapel Hill: U of North Carolina P, 1975.
Kraidy, Marwan M. *Hybridity: or the Cultural Logic of Globalization*. Philadelphia: Temple UP, 2005.

Kroeber, Karl. 'Experience as History: Shelley's Venice, Turner's Carthage.' *ELH* 41 (1974): 321–39.
Landor, Walter Savage. *The Complete Works of Walter Savage Landor*. Ed. Stephen Wheeler. Vol. 13. London: Chapman, 1933. 16 vols. 1927–36.
Lane, Christopher, ed. *The Psychoanalysis of Race*. New York: Columbia UP, 1998.
– 'The Psychoanalysis of Race: An Introduction.' *The Psychoanalysis of Race*. Ed. Christopher Lane. New York: Columbia UP, 1998. 1–37.
Lawrence, William. *Lectures on Physiology, Zoology, and the Natural History of Man, Delivered at the Royal College of Surgeons*. 1819. Salem, MA: Foote, 1828.
Leask, Nigel. *British Romantic Writers and the East: Anxieties of Empire*. Cambridge: Cambridge UP, 1992.
– *Curiosity and the Aesthetics of Travel Writing, 1770–1840: From an Antique Land*. Oxford: Oxford UP, 2002.
– 'Mont Blanc's Mysterious Voice: Shelley and Huttonian Earth Science.' *The Third Culture: Literature and Science*. Ed. Elinor S. Shaffer. Berlin: Walter de Gruyter, 1998. 182–203.
Leavis, F.R. *Revaluation: Tradition and Development in English Poetry*. 1936. New York: Penguin, 1978.
Lee, Debbie. 'Mapping the Interior: African Cartography and Shelley's *The Witch of Atlas*.' *European Romantic Review* 8 (1997): 169–84.
– *Slavery and the Romantic Imagination*. Philadelphia: U of Pennsylvania P, 2002.
Lefkowitz, Mary R., and Guy MacLean Rogers, eds. *Black Athena Revisited*. Chapel Hill: U of North Carolina P, 1996.
Leighton, Angela. *Shelley and the Sublime: an Interpretation of the Major Poems*. Cambridge: Cambridge UP, 1984.
Lemprière, John. *A Classical Dictionary; Containing a Copious Account of All the Proper Names Mentioned in Ancient Authors; with the Value of Coins, Weights, and Measures, Used among the Greeks and Romans; and a Chronological Table*. 6th American Edition. New York: Duyckinck, 1827.
Leo, Johannes. *Geographical Historie of Africa. London 1600*. New York: Da Capo, 1969.
Levinas, Emmanuel. 'The Trace of the Other.' *Deconstruction in Context: Literature and Philosophy*. Ed. Mark C. Taylor. Chicago: U of Chicago P, 1986. 345–59.
Lew, Joseph. 'The Necessary Orientalist? *The Giaour* and Nineteenth-Century Imperialist Misogyny.' *Romanticism, Race, and Imperial Culture, 1780–1834*. Ed. Alan Richardson and Sonia Hofkosh. Bloomington: Indiana UP, 1996. 173–202.

Long, Edward. *The History of Jamaica, or General Survey of the Ancient and Modern State of That Island: With Reflections on Its Situation, Inhabitants, Climate, Products, Commerce, Laws and Government*. 3 vols. 1774. London: Cass, 1970.

Louis, W. Roger, ed. *Imperialism: The Robinson and Gallagher Controversy*. New York: New Viewpoints, 1976.

Lowe, Lisa. *Critical Terrains: French and British Orientalisms*. Ithaca, NY: Cornell UP, 1991.

Ludden, David. 'Oriental Empiricism: Transformation of Colonial Knowledge.' *Orientalism and the Postcolonial Predicament: Perspectives on South Asia*. Ed. Carol A. Breckenridge and Peter van der Veer. Philadelphia: U of Pennsylvania P, 1993. 230–78.

Lyell, Charles. *Principles of Geology*. 3 vols. 1830–3. Chicago: U of Chicago P, 1990–1.

Macaulay, Rose. *Pleasure of Ruins*. 1953. New York: Walker, 1966.

Macaulay, Thomas Babington. *Critical and Historical Essays Contributed to 'The Edinburgh Review.'* New ed. London: Longman, 1870.

– *Selected Writings*. Ed. John Clive and Thomas Pinney. Chicago: U of Chicago P, 1972.

Mackenzie, John. *Orientalism: History, Theory and the Arts*. Manchester: Manchester UP, 1995.

Maddox, Donald L. 'Shelley's *Alastor* and the Legacy of Rousseau.' *Studies in Romanticism* 9 (1970): 82–98.

Majeed, Javed. *Ungoverned Imaginings: James Mill's* The History of British India *and Orientalism*. Oxford: Clarendon, 1992.

Makdisi, Saree. *Romantic Imperialism: Universal Empire and the Culture of Modernity*. Cambridge: Cambridge UP, 1998.

Mani, Lata, and Ruth Frankenberg. 'The Challenge of *Orientalism*.' *Economy and Society* 44 (1985): 174–92.

Manuel, Frank E. *The Eighteenth Century Confronts the Gods*. Cambridge, MA: Harvard UP, 1959.

Marshall, P.J., ed. *The British Discovery of Hinduism in the Eighteenth Century*. Cambridge: Cambridge UP, 1970.

– Introduction. *The British Discovery of Hinduism in the Eighteenth Century*. Ed. P.J. Marshall. Cambridge: Cambridge UP, 1970. 1–44.

Marshall, P.J., and Glyndwr Williams. *The Great Map of Mankind: Perceptions of New Worlds in the Age of Enlightenment*. Cambridge, MA: Harvard UP, 1982.

Mason, J.C. *The Moravian Church and the Missionary Awakening in England 1760–1800*. Woodbridge, Suffolk: Boydel, 2001.

Matthews, G.M. 'On Shelley's *The Triumph of Life*.' *Studia Neophilologica*. 34 (1962): 104–34.

- 'A Volcano's Voice in Shelley.' *ELH* 24 (1957): 191–228.
Maurice, Thomas. *Indian Antiquities: or Dissertations, Relative to the Ancient Geographical Divisions, the Pure System of Primeval Theology ... and the Various and Profound Literature, of Hindostan.* 7 vols. London: Richardson, 1793–1800.
Mazzeo, Tilar J. 'The Strains of Empire: Shelley and the Music of India.' *Romantic Representations of British India.* Ed. Michael J. Franklin. London: Routledge, 2006. 180–96.
McClintock, Anne. *Imperial Leather: Race, Gender and Sexuality in the Colonial Contest.* London: Routledge, 1995.
McGann, Jerome J. 'The Secret of an Elder Day: Shelley after *Hellas*.' *Keats-Shelley Journal* 15 (1966): 25–41.
- 'Shelley's Veils: A Thousand Images of Loveliness.' *Romantic and Victorian: Studies in Memory of William H. Marshall.* Ed. W. Paul Elledge and Richard L. Hoffman. Rutherford, NJ: Fairleigh Dickinson UP, 1971. 195–218.
Medwin, Thomas. *The Life of Percy Bysshe Shelley.* Ed. H. Buxton Forman. London: Oxford UP, 1913.
Melzer, Arthur M. *The Natural Goodness of Man: On the System of Rousseau's Thought.* Chicago: U of Chicago P, 1990
Mill, James. *The History of British India: Abridged and with an Introd. by William Thomas.* Chicago: U of Chicago P, 1975.
Mill, John Stuart. *Essays on Ethics, Religion and Society.* Ed. John. M. Robinson. Vol. 10 of *Collected Works of John Stuart Mill.* Toronto: U of Toronto P, 1969.
- *On Liberty and Other Essays.* Ed. John Gray. Oxford: Oxford UP, 1991.
- *Writings on India.* Ed. John M. Robinson, Martin Moir, and Zawahir Moir. Vol. 30 of *Collected Works of John Stuart Mill.* Toronto: U of Toronto P, 1990.
Miller, Christopher L. *Blank Darkness: Africanist Discourse in French.* Chicago: U of Chicago P, 1985.
Miller, Christopher R. 'Shelley's Uncertain Heaven.' *ELH* 72 (2005): 577–603.
Miller, David Philip. 'Joseph Banks, Empire, and "Centers of Calculation" in Late Hanoverian London.' *Visions of Empire: Voyages, Botany, and Representations of Nature.* Ed. David Philip Miller and Peter Hanns Reill. Cambridge: Cambridge UP, 1996. 21–37.
Miller, David Philip, and Peter Hanns Reill, ed. *Visions of Empire: Voyages, Botany, and Representations of Nature.* Cambridge: Cambridge UP, 1996.
Milton, John. *Paradise Lost.* Ed. Scott Elledge. New York: Norton, 1975.
- *Complete Shorter Poems.* Ed. John Carey. London: Longman, 1971.
- *Poems upon Several Occasions, English, Italian, and Latin with Translations.* By

John Milton ... With Notes Critical and Explanatory, and Other Illustrations. By Thomas Warton. London: Dodsley, 1785.
Monk, Samuel. *The Sublime: A Study of Critical Theories in Eighteenth-Century England*. New York: MLA, 1935.
Montesquieu, Charles de Secondat. *The Spirit of the Laws*. Trans. and ed. Anne Cohler, Basia Miller, and Harold Stone. Cambridge: Cambridge UP, 1989.
Moor, Edward. *The Hindu Pantheon*. 1810. New York: Garland, 1984.
Moore, Thomas. *The Epicurean, a Tale. With Vignette Illustrations by J.M.W. Turner, Esq. R.A. And Alciphron, a Poem*. London: Simpkin, 1839.
– *Lalla Rookh, an Oriental Romance*. 17th ed. London: Longman, 1832,
Moore-Gilbert, Bart. Introduction. *Writing India 1757–1990: The Literature of British India*. Ed. Bart Moore-Gilbert. Manchester: Manchester UP, 1996. 1–29.
– *Postcolonial Theory: Contexts, Practices, Politics*. London: Verso, 1997.
–, ed. *Writing India 1757–1990: The Literature of British India*. Manchester: Manchester UP, 1996.
Moretti, Franco. *Atlas of the European Novel 1800–1900*. London: Verso, 1998.
Morgan, Prys. 'From a Death to a View: The Hunt for the Welsh Past in the Romantic Period.' *The Invention of Tradition*. Ed. E.J. Hobsbawm and Terence Ranger. Cambridge: Cambridge UP, 1983. 43–100.
Morton, Timothy, ed. *The Cambridge Companion to Shelley*. Cambridge: Cambridge UP, 2006.
– 'Nature and Culture.' *The Cambridge Companion to Shelley*. Ed. Timothy Morton. Cambridge: Cambridge UP, 2006. 185–207.
– *Shelley and the Revolution in Taste: The Body and the Natural World*. Cambridge: Cambridge UP, 1994.
– 'Shelley's Green Desert.' *Studies in Romanticism* 35 (1996): 408–30.
Mueschke, Paul, and Earl L. Griggs. 'Wordsworth as Prototype of the Poet in Shelley's "Alastor."' *PMLA* 49 (1934): 229–45.
Murray, Hugh. *Historical Account of Discoveries and Travels in Africa, from the Earliest Ages to the Present Time; Including the Substance of the Late Dr. Leyden's Work on That Subject*. 2nd ed. 2 vols. Edinburgh: Constable, 1818.
Myer, Valerie Grosvenor. 'Sacred River from Switzerland?' *Notes and Queries* 42 (1995): 176–7.
Nicolson, Marjorie Hope. *Mountain Gloom and Mountain Glory: The Development of the Aesthetics of the Infinite*. Ithaca, NJ: Cornell UP, 1959.
Nonnos. *Dionysiaca*. Trans. W.H.D. Rouse. 3 vols. Loeb Classical Library. London: Heinemann, 1940–2.
Norwich, Oscar I. *Maps of Africa: An Illustrated and Annotated Carto-Bibliography*. Johannesburg: Donker, 1983.

O'Brien, Karen. 'Poetry against Empire: Milton to Shelley.' *Proceedings of the British Academy* 117 (2002): 269–96.
Oerlemans, Onno. *Romanticism and the Materiality of Nature*. Toronto: U of Toronto P, 2002.
O'Neill, Michael. *The Human Mind's Imaginings: Conflict and Achievement in Shelley's Poetry*. Oxford: Clarendon, 1989.
Osterhammel, Jürgen, and Niels P. Petersson. *Globalization: A Short History*. Trans. Dona Geyer. Princeton, NJ: Princeton UP, 2005. Trans. of *Geschichte der Globalisierung. Dimensionen, Prozesse, Epochen*. Munich: Verlag, 2003.
Owenson, Sydney. *The Missionary: An Indian Tale, by Miss Owenson*. 4th ed. 3 vols. London: Stokedale, 1811.
Paine, Thomas. *Political Writings*. Ed. Bruce Kuklick. Cambridge: Cambridge UP, 1989.
Park, Mungo. *Travels in the Interior Districts of Africa: Performed in the Years 1795, 1796, and 1797. With an Account of a Subsequent Mission to That Country in 1805. By Mungo Park, Surgeon. To Which is Added an Account of the Life of Mr. Park*. New edition. 2 vols. Vol. 1. *Travels in 1795, 1796, and 1797 with an Appendix, Containing Geographical Illustrations of Africa by Major Rennell*. Vol. 2. *The Journal of a Mission to the Interior of Africa in the Year 1805. To Which is Prefixed an Account of the Life of Mr. Park*. London: Murray, 1815–16.
Parkinson, James. *Organic Remains of a Former World: An Examination of the Mineralized Remains of the Vegetables and Animals of the Antediluvian World*. 3 vols. London: Sherwood, 1808–20.
Parry, Benita. 'Problems in Current Theories of Colonial Discourse.' *Oxford Literary Review* 9 (1987): 27–58.
Peacock, Thomas Love. *The Works of Thomas Love Peacock*. Ed. H.F.B. Brett-Smith and C.E. Jones. 10 vols. London: Constable, 1924–34.
Peck, Walter Edwin. *Shelley: His Life and Work*. 2 vols. London: Benn, 1927.
Peterfreund, Stuart. *Shelley among Others: The Play of the Intertext and the Idea of Language*. Baltimore: Johns Hopkins UP, 2002.
Pickering, Samuel F., Jr. *John Locke and Children's Books in Eighteenth-Century England*. Knoxville: U of Tennessee P, 1981.
Pierce, John B. '"Mont Blanc" and *Prometheus Unbound*: Shelley's Use of the Rhetoric of Silence.' *Keats-Shelley Journal* 38 (1989): 103–26.
Pieterse, Jan Nederveen. 'Globalization as Hybridization.' *Globalization: Analytical Perspectives*. Ed. Roland Robertson and Katheleen E. White. London: Routledge, 2003. 265–90.
Pinkerton, John, ed. *A General Collection of the Best and Most Interesting Voyages and Travels in All Parts of the World*. 17 vols. London: Longman, 1808–14.

- *Modern Geography. A Description of the Empires, Kingdoms, States, and Colonies; with the Oceans, Seas, and Isles; in All Parts of the World: Including the Most Recent Discoveries, and Political Alternations*. 3 vols. London: Cadell, 1807.
Pirie, David B., ed. *The Romantic Period*. London: Penguin, 1994. Vol. 5 of *The Penguin History of Literature*. 10 vols. 1987–94.
Plato. *Timaeus and Critias*. Trans. Desmond Lee. London: Penguin, 1965.
- *Works of Plato, viz. His Fifty-Five Dialogues, and Twelve Epistles, Translated from the Greek*. Trans. Thomas Taylor. 5 vols. London: Jeffrey, 1804.
Playfair, John. *Illustrations of the Huttonian Theory of the Earth*. 1802. Intro. George W. White. New York: Dover, 1956.
Pliny. *Natural History*. Trans. H. Rackham. Vol. 2. Loeb Classical Library. London: Heinemann, 1942. 10 vols. 1938–62.
Plutarch. *Plutarch's Moralia*. Trans. Harold Cherniss and William C. Helmbold. Vol. 12. Loeb Classical Library. London: Heinemann, 1976. 15 vols. to date. 1927–.
Porter, Dennis. *Haunted Journeys: Desire and Transgression in European Travel Writing*. Princeton, NJ: Princeton UP, 1991.
- 'Orientalism and its Problems.' Ed. Francis Baker et al. *Politics of Theory: Proceedings of the Essex Conference of the Sociology of Literature July 1982*. Colchester: U of Essex P, 1983. 179–93.
Porter, Roy. *Doctor of Society: Thomas Beddoes and the Sick Trade in Late-Enlightenment England*. London: Routledge, 1992.
- *The Making of Geology: Earth Science in Britain 1660–1815*. Cambridge: Cambridge UP, 1977.
Pottle, Frederick A. 'The Case of Shelley.' *English Romantic Poets: Modern Essays in Criticism*. Ed. M.H. Abrams. New York: Oxford UP, 1960. 289–306.
Pratt, Lynda, ed. *Robert Southey and the Contexts of English Romanticism*. Aldershot: Ashgate, 2006.
Pratt, Mary Louise. *Imperial Eyes: Travel Writing and Transculturation*. London: Routledge, 1992.
Pulos, C.E. *The Deep Truth: A Study of Shelley's Scepticism*. Lincoln: U of Nebraska P, 1962.
Purchas, Samuel. *Hakluytus Posthumus or Purchas His Pilgrimes*. Vols. 5–7. Glasgow: Maclehose, 1905. 20 vols. 1905–7.
Raben, Joseph. 'Shelley the Dionysian.' *Shelley Revalued: Essays from the Gregynog Conference*. Ed. Kelvin Everest. Leicester, UK: Leicester UP, 1983. 21–36.
- 'Shelley's *Prometheus Unbound*: Why the Indian Caucasus?' *Keats-Shelley Journal* 12 (1963): 95–106.

Raffles, Thomas Stamford. *The History of Java*. 2 vols. London: Black, 1817. Rpt. Kuala Lumpur: Oxford UP, 1965.
Raj, Kapil. 'When Human Travellers Become Instruments: The Indo-British Exploration of Central Asia in the Nineteenth Century.' *Instruments, Travel and Science: Itineraries of Precision from the Seventeenth Century to the Twentieth Century*. Ed. Marie-Noële Bourget, Christian Licoppe, and H. Otto Sibum. London: Routledge, 2002. 156–88.
Rajan, Balachandra. *Under Western Eyes: India from Milton to Macaulay*. Oxford: Oxford UP, 1999.
Rajan, Tilottama. *The Dark Interpreter: The Discourse of Romanticism*. Ithaca, NY: Cornell UP, 1980.
– *The Supplement of Reading: Figures of Understanding in Romantic Theory and Practice*. Ithaca, NY: Cornell, UP, 1990.
Raleigh, Walter. *The History of the World*. London: Burre, 1614.
Ramage, Edwin S. 'Perspectives Ancient and Modern.' *Atlantis, Fact or Fiction?* Ed. Edwin S. Ramage. Bloomington: Indiana UP, 1978. 3–45.
Ramond de Carbonnières, Louis Françis Élisabeth. 'Observations on the Glacieres, and the Glaciers, by M. Ramond.' *A Tour in Switzerland; or, a View of the Present State of the Governments and Manners of Those Cantons: With Comparative Sketches of the Present State of Paris*. By Helen Maria Williams. 2nd ed. Vol. 2. London: Robinson, 1798. 279–352.
Randel, Fred V. '*Frankenstein*, Feminism, and the Intertextuality of Mountains.' *Studies in Romanticism* 24 (1985): 515–32.
– 'The Mountaintops of English Romanticism.' *Texas Studies in Literature and Language* 23 (1981): 294–323.
Rees, Abraham. *The Cyclopaedia; or Universal Dictionary of Arts, Sciences, and Literature*. 39 vols and 6 vols of plates. London: Longman, 1819–20.
Reeves, W.P. 'Shakespeare's Queen Mab.' *Modern Language Notes* 17 (1902): 20–7.
Reiman, Donald H. *Percy Bysshe Shelley*. Rev. ed. New York: Twayne, 1990.
– 'Structure, Symbol, and Theme in *Lines Written among the Euganean Hills*.' *PMLA* 77 (1962): 404–13.
Rennell, James. *The Geographical System of Herodotus, Examined; and Explained, by a Comparison with Those of Other Ancient Authors, and with Modern Geography*. London: Bulmer, 1800.
– *James Rennell's Memoir of a Map of Hindustan or the Mughal Empire*. Ed. Brahmadeva Prasad Ambashthya. Delhi: N.V., 1975.
– *Memoir of a Map of Hindoostan; or the Mogul's Empire: With an Examination of Some Positions in the Former System of Indian Geography; and Some Illustra-*

tions of the Present One: And a Complete Index of Names to the Map. London: Faden, 1783.
– Memoir of a Map of Hindoostan; or the Mogul Empire: With an Introduction, Illustrative of the Geography and Present Division of That Country. 2nd ed. London: Bulmer, 1792.
Renwick, W.L. English Literature 1789–1815. Vol. 9 of The Oxford History of English Literature. Oxford: Clarendon, 1963. 17 vols. 1947–86.
Richardson, Alan. 'Escape from the Seraglio: Cultural Transvestism in Don Juan.' Reading Byron: Essays Selected from Hofstra University's Byron Bicentennial Conference. Ed. Alice Levine and Robert N. Keane. New York: Garland, 1993. 175–85.
Richardson, Alan, and Sonia Hofkosh, eds. Romanticism, Race, and Imperial Culture, 1780–1834. Bloomington: Indiana UP, 1996.
Richardson, Donna. 'An Anatomy of Solitude: Shelley's Response of Radical Skepticism in Alastor.' Studies in Romanticism 31 (1992): 171–95.
Rigby, Brian. 'Volney's Rationalist Apocalypse: "Les Ruines ou Meditations sur les Revolutions des Empires."' 1789: Reading Writing Revolution. Ed. Francis Baker et al. Colchester: U of Essex P, 1982. 22–37.
Robertson, Roland, and Katheleen E. White. 'Globalization: An Overview.' Globalization: Analytical Perspectives. Ed. Roland Robertson and Katheleen E. White. London: Routledge, 2003. 1–44.
Robertson, Roland, and Katheleen E. White, ed. Globalization: Analytical Perspectives. London: Routledge, 2003.
Robinson, Charles E. Shelley and Byron: The Snake and Eagle Wreathed in Fight. Baltimore: Johns Hopkins UP, 1976.
– 'The Shelley Circle and Coleridge's The Friend.' English Language Notes 8 (1970–1): 269–74.
Robinson, Julian. 'The Impact of the Orient on European Thought, 1770–1850.' Renaissance and Modern Studies 31 (1987): 102–33.
Rogers, Neville. Shelley at Work: A Critical Inquiry. Oxford: Clarendon, 1956.
Rose, Gillian. Feminism and Geography: The Limits of Geographical Knowledge. Minneapolis: U of Minnesota P, 1993.
Rose, H.J. Mythological Introduction. Dionysiaca. By Nonnos. Trans. W.H.D. Rouse. 3 vols. Loeb Classical Library. London: Heinemann, 1940–2. 1: x–xix.
Rossington, Michael. 'Shelley and the Orient.' The Keats-Shelley Review 6 (1991): 18–36.
Rousseau, Jean-Jacques. The Collected Writings of Rousseau. Ed. Roger D. Masters and Christopher Kelly. 12 vols. to date. Hanover, NH: UP of New England, 1990–.

Rupke, Nicolaas. *The Great Chain of History: William Buckland and the English School of Geology (1814–1849)*. Oxford: Clarendon, 1983.

Russell, Alexander. *Natural History of Aleppo. Containing a Description of the City, and the Principal Natural Productions in Its Neighbourhood. Together with an Account of the Climate, Inhabitants, and Diseases; Particularly of the Plague.* 2nd ed. 2 vols. London: Robinson, 1794.

Ruston, Sharon. *Shelley and Vitality*. Basingstoke: Macmillan, 2005.

Said, Edward W. *Culture and Imperialism*. New York: Knopf, 1993.

– *Orientalism*. New York: Vintage, 1979.

– 'Representing the Colonized: Anthropology's Interlocutors.' *Critical Inquiry*. 15, no. 2 (1989): 205–25.

Sargent, Frederick, II. *Hippocratic Heritage: A History of Ideas about Weather and Human Health*. New York: Pergamon, 1982.

Saussure, Horace Benedict de. 'An Account of the Attempts That Have Been Made to Attain the Summit of Mont Blanc. Written in the Year 1786.' *A General Collection of the Best and Most Interesting Voyages and Travels in All Parts of the World*. Ed. John Pinkerton. Vol. 4. London: Longman, 1809. 677–709.

Schwab, Raymond. *The Oriental Renaissance: Europe's Rediscovery of India and the East, 1680–1880*. Trans. Gene Patterson-Black and Victor Reinking. New York: Columbia UP, 1984.

Scrivener, Michael Henry. *Radical Shelley: The Philosophical Anarchism and Utopian Thought of Percy Bysshe Shelley*. Princeton, NJ: Princeton UP, 1982.

Shaffer, E. S. *'Kubla Khan' and the Fall of Jerusalem: The Mythological School in Biblical Criticism and Secular Literature 1770–1880*. Cambridge: Cambridge UP, 1975.

–, ed. *The Third Culture: Literature and Science*. Berlin: Walter de Gruyter, 1998.

Shakespeare, William. *Romeo and Juliet*. Ed. Brian Gibbons. London: Methuen, 1980.

Shaw, Edward Pease. *Jacques Cazotte (1719–1792)*. Cambridge, MA: Harvard UP, 1942.

Shelley, Mary. *Frankenstein or the Modern Prometheus: The 1818 text* Ed. Marilyn Butler. Oxford: Oxford UP, 1994.

– *Journals of Mary Shelley 1814–1844*. Ed. Paula R. Feldman and Diana Scott-Kilvert. Baltimore: Johns Hopkins UP, 1987.

– *The Last Man*. Ed. Hugh J. Luke, Jr. Lincoln: U of Nebraska P, 1993.

– *The Letters of Mary Wollstonecraft Shelley*. Ed. Betty T. Bennett. 3 vols. Baltimore: Johns Hopkins UP, 1980–8.

Shelley, Mary, and Percy Bysshe Shelley. *History of a Six Weeks' Tour 1817*. 1817. Ed. Jonathan Wordsworth. Oxford: Woodstock, 1989.

Shelley, Percy Bysshe. *The Complete Poetical Works of Shelley*. Ed. George Edward Woodberry. Boston: Mifflin, 1901.
- *The Complete Poetry of Percy Bysshe Shelley*. Ed. Donald H. Reiman and Neil Fraistat. 2 vols. to date. Baltimore: Johns Hopkins UP, 2000–.
- *The Complete Works of Percy Bysshe Shelley*. Ed. Roger Ingpen and Walter E. Peck. 10 vols. London: Benn, 1926–30.
- *The Esdaile Notebook: A Volume of Early Poems by Percy Bysshe Shelley*. Ed. Kenneth Neill Cameron. New York: Knopf, 1964.
- *The Geneva Notebook of Percy Bysshe Shelley: Bodleian MS. Shelley adds. e.16 and MS. Shelley adds. c.4, Folio 63, 65, 71 and 72*. Transcribed and edited by Michael Erkelenz. New York: Garland, 1992. Vol. 11 of *The Bodleian Shelley Manuscripts*. 21 vols. 1986–95.
- *The 'Julian and Maddalo' Draft Notebook: Bodleian MS. Shelley adds. e. 11*. Transcribed and edited by Steven E. Jones. New York: Garland, 1990. Vol. 15 of *The Bodleian Shelley Manuscripts*. 21 vols. 1986–95.
- *The Letters of Percy Bysshe Shelley*. Ed. Frederick. L. Jones. 2 vols. Oxford: Clarendon, 1964.
- *Note Books of Percy Bysshe Shelley, from the Originals in the Library of W.K. Bixby, Described, Transcribed, and Edited, with a Full Commentary by H. Buxton Forman, C.B*. Ed. H. Buxton Forman. 3 vols. Boston: Bibliophile Society, 1911.
- *The Poems of Shelley*. Ed. Geoffrey Matthews and Kelvin Everest. 2 vols. to date. London: Longman, 1989–.
- *The Prose Works of Percy Bysshe Shelley*. Ed. E.B. Murray. Vol. 1. Oxford: Clarendon, 1993.
- *Queen Mab 1813*. Ed. Jonathan Wordsworth. Oxford: Woodstock, 1990.
- *Shelley: Poetical Works*. Ed. Thomas Hutchinson. Corr. G.M. Matthews. Oxford: Oxford UP, 1983.
- *Shelley's 1819–1821 Huntington Notebook: A Facsimile of Huntington MS. HM 2176*. Ed. Mary A. Quinn. New York: Garland, 1994. Vol. 6 of *The Manuscripts of the Younger Romantics: Shelley*. 7 vols. 1985–96.
- *Shelley's Pisan Winter Notebook (1820–1822): A Facsimile of Bodleian MS Shelley adds. e.8*. Transcribed and edited by Carlene A. Adamson. New York: Garland, 1992. Vol. 6 of *The Bodleian Shelley Manuscripts*. 21 vols. 1986–95.
- *Shelley's Poetry and Prose*. Ed. Donald H. Reiman and Neil Fraistat. 2nd ed. New York: Norton, 2002.
- *Shelley's* Prometheus Unbound: *A Variorum Edition*. Ed. Lawrence John Zillman. Seattle: U of Washington P, 1959.

- *Shelley's Prose: The Trumpet of a Prophecy*. Ed. David Lee Clark. Albuquerque: U of New Mexico P, 1954.
- *Shelley's 'The Triumph of Life': A Critical Study*. Ed. Donald H. Reiman. 1965. Rpt. New York: Octagon, 1979.

Sikes, Wirt. *British Goblins: Welsh Folk-Lore, Fairy Mythology, Legends and Traditions*. London: Low, 1880.

Smith, Adam. *An Inquiry into the Nature and Causes of the Wealth of Nations*. 1776. (The Glasgow edition of *The Works and Correspondence of Adam Smith*.) Ed. R.H. Campbell and A.S. Skinner. 2 vols. 1976. Rpt. based on the 6th ed. 1979. Corrected version. Oxford: Oxford UP, 1979.

Soja, Edward W. *Postmodern Geographies: The Reassertion of Space in Critical Social Theory*. London: Verso, 1989.

Southey, Robert. *The Life and Correspondence of Robert Southey*. Ed. Charles Cuthbert Southey. 2nd ed. 6 vols. London: Longman, 1850.

- *The Poetical Works of Robert Southey, Collected by Himself*. 10 vols. London: Longman, 1838.

Spadafora, David. *The Idea of Progress in Eighteenth-Century England*. New Haven, CT: Yale UP, 1990.

Spenser, Edmund. *The Faerie Queen*. Ed. A.C. Hamilton. London: Longman, 1977.

Sperry, Stuart. *Shelley's Major Verse: The Narrative and Dramatic Poetry*. Cambridge, MA: Harvard UP, 1988.

Spivak, Gayatri Chakravorty. 'Can the Subaltern Speak?' *Marxism and the Interpretation of Culture*. Ed. Cary Nelson and Lawrence Grossberg. Urbana: U of Illinois P, 1988. 271–313.

- 'The Rani of Sirmur.' *Europe and Its Others: Proceedings of the Essex Conference of the Sociology of Literature*. Ed. Francis Barker, et al. Vol. 1. Colchester, UK: U of Essex P, 1985. 128–51. 2 vols.
- *The Spivak Reader: Selected Works of Gayatri Chakravorty Spivak*. Ed. Donna Landry and Gerald MacLean. London: Routledge, 1996.
- 'Three Women's Texts and a Critique of Imperialism.' *Critical Inquiry* 12 (1985): 243–61.

Stafford, Barbara Maria. *Voyage into Substance: Art, Science, Nature, and the Illustrated Travel Account, 1760–1840*. Cambridge, MA: MIT P, 1984.

Stafford, Fiona A. *The Last of the Race: The Growth of a Myth from Milton to Darwin*. Oxford: Clarendon, 1994.

Stark, H.A. *Hostages to India, or the Early Life-Story of the Anglo-Indian Race*. Calcutta: Calcutta Fine Art Cottage, 1926.

Stefoff, Rebecca. *The British Library Companion to Maps and Mapmaking*. London: British Library, 1995.
Stepan, Nancy. 'Biological Degeneration: Races and Proper Places.' *Degeneration: The Dark Side of Progress*. Ed. J. Edward Chamberlin and Sander L. Gilman. New York: Columbia UP, 1985. 97–120.
– *The Idea of Race in Science: Great Britain 1800–1960*. London: Macmillan, 1982.
Stillinger, Jack. *Romantic Complexity: Keats, Coleridge, and Wordsworth*. Urbana: U of Illinois P, 2006.
Strabo. *The Geography of Strabo*. Trans. Horace Leonard Jones. Loeb Classical Library. 8 vols. London: Heinemann, 1917–33.
Suleri, Sara. *The Rhetoric of English India*. Chicago: U of Chicago P, 1992.
Swaminathan, N. 'Possible Indian Influence on Shelley.' *Keats-Shelley Memorial Bulletin* 9 (1958): 30–45.
Tetreault, Ronald. *The Poetry of Life: Shelley and Literary Form*. Toronto: U of Toronto P, 1987.
– 'Shelley and Byron Encounter the Sublime: Switzerland, 1816.' *Revue des Langues Vivantes* 41 (1975): 145–55.
– 'Shelley among the Chartists.' *English Studies in Canada* 16 (1990): 279–95.
– 'Shelley at the Opera.' *ELH* 48 (1981): 144–71.
– 'Shelley's Folio Plato.' *Keats-Shelley Journal* 30 (1981): 17–21.
Thomson, John. *A New General Atlas, Consisting of a Series of Geographical Designs, on Various Projections, Exhibiting the Form and Component Parts of the Globe; and a Collection of Maps and Charts, Delineating the Natural and Political Divisions of the Empires, Kingdoms, and States in the World*. Edinburgh: Ramsay, 1817.
Tooke, Andrew. *The Pantheon, Representing the Fabulous History of the Heathen Gods and Most Illustrious Heroes*. 1698. 31st ed. London: Johnson, 1803.
Trench, Richard. *Arabian Travellers: The Early Adventurers, the Romantics, the Opportunists, and the Twentieth-Century Travellers Drawn by a Fascination for the Arabian Peninsula*. London: Macmillan, 1986.
Trumpener, Katie. *Bardic Nationalism: The Romantic Novel and the British Empire*. Princeton, NJ: Princeton UP, 1997.
Trusler, John. *The Habitable World Described, or the Present State of the People in All Parts of the Globe, from North to South*. Vol. 1. London, 1788. 20 vols. 1788–97.
Tuan, Yi-Fu. *Landscapes of Fear*. Minneapolis: U of Minnesota P, 1979.
Tuveson, Ernest Lee. *Millennium and Utopia: A Study in the Background of the Idea of Progress*. 1949. Glouchester, MA: Smith, 1972.
Tytler, James. *A New and Concise System of Geography: Containing a Particular

Account of the Empires, Kingdoms, States, Provinces, and Islands, in the Known World. Edinburgh: Hill, 1788.

United Brethren in Christ. *A Brief Account of the Mission Established among the Esquimaux Indians, on the Coast of Labrador by the Church of the Brethren, or Unitas Fratrum.* London: Brethren's Society for the Furtherance of the Gospel, 1774.

Valentia, George Annesley, Viscount. *Voyages and Travels to India, Ceylon, the Red Sea, Abyssinia, and Egypt, in the Years 1802, 1803, 1804, 1805, and 1806.* 4 vols. London: Rivington, 1811. New Delhi: Asian Educational, 1994.

Vidal-Naquet, Pierre. 'Atlantis and the Nations.' Trans. Janet Lloyd. *Critical Inquiry* 18 (1992): 300–26.

–, ed. *The Harper Atlas of World History.* Rev. ed. New York: Collins, 1992.

Vitaliano, Dorothy B. 'Geomythology: The Impact of Geologic Events on History and Legend with Special Reference to Atlantis.' *Journal of the Folklore Institute* 5 (1968): 5–30.

Volney, C.F. *The Ruins, or, Meditation on the Revolutions of Empire: and The Law of Nature.* Baltimore: Black Classic, 1991.

Voltaire, François-Marie Arouet. *Méanges.* Ed. Jacques von den Heuval. Bibliothéque de la Pléiade. Paris: Gallimard, 1961.

Wallace, Jennifer. *Shelley and Greece: Rethinking Romantic Hellenism.* Basingstoke, UK: Macmillan, 1997.

Wallerstein, Immanuel. *Capitalist Agriculture and the Origins of the European World Economy in the Sixteenth Century.* New York: Academic P, 1974.

– *The Essential Wallerstein.* New York: New P, 2000.

– *Mercantilism and the Consolidation of the European World Economy, 1600–1750.* New York: Academic P, 1980.

– 'The Rise and Future Demise of the World Capitalist System.' *Comparative Studies in Society and History* 16 (1974): 387–415. Rpt. in *Globalization: Analytical Perspectives.* Ed. Roland Robertson and Kathleen E. White. London: Routledge, 2003. 57–85.

– *The Second Era of Great Expansion of the Capitalist World-Economy, 1730–1840s.* New York: Academic P, 1989.

– *World-Systems Analysis: An Introduction.* Durham, NC: Duke UP, 2004.

Walsh, Thomas. *Journals of the Late Campaign in Egypt: Including Descriptions of That Country, and of Gibraltar, Minorca, Malta, Marmorice, and Macri; with an Appendix; Containing Official Papers and Documents.* London: Cadell, 1803.

Wang, Orrin N. 'Disfiguring Moments: History in Paul de Man's "Shelley Disfigured" and Percy Bysshe Shelley's "The Triumph of Life."' *ELH* 58 (1991): 633–55.

Wasserman, Earl R. *Shelley: A Critical Reading*. Baltimore: Johns Hopkins UP, 1971.
- *The Subtler Language: Critical Readings of Neoclassic and Romantic Poems*. Baltimore: Johns Hopkins UP, 1959.
Webb, Timothy. *Shelley: A Voice Not Understood*. Manchester: Manchester UP, 1977.
- 'Shelley and the Religion of Joy.' *Studies in Romanticism* 15 (1976): 357–82.
- 'The Unascended Heaven: Negatives in *Prometheus Unbound*.' *Shelley Revalued: Essays from the Gregynog Conference*. Ed. Kelvin Everest. Leicester, UK: Leicester UP, 1983. 37–62.
- *The Violet in the Crucible: Shelley and Translation*. Oxford: Clarendon, 1976.
Weinberg, Alan M. *Shelley's Italian Experience*. London: Macmillan, 1991.
Weisman, Karen A. *Imageless Truths: Shelley's Poetic Fictions*. Philadelphia: U of Pennsylvania P, 1994.
Whalley, Thomas Sedgwick. *Mont Blanc: An Irregular Lyric Poem*. London: Baldwin, 1788.
White, Gilbert. *A Naturalist's Calendar, with Observations in Various Branches of Natural History; Extracted from the Papers of the Late Rev. Gilbert White*. London: White, 1795.
White, N.I. *Shelley*. 2 vols. New York: Knopf. 1940.
Whiteley, W.H. 'The Establishment of the Moravian Mission in Labrador and British Policy, 1763–83.' *Canadian Historical Review* 45 (1964): 29–50.
Wilford, Francis. 'An Essay on the Sacred Isles in the West, with Other Essays Connected with That Work.' *Asiatic Researches* 8 (1809): 245–375.
- 'On Mount Caucasus.' *Asiatic Researches* 6 (1801): 455–536.
Williams, Gwyn A. *Madoc: The Making of a Myth*. London: Methuen, 1979.
Williams, Helen Maria. Preface. *Personal Narrative of Travels to the Equinoctial Regions of the New Continent, during the Years 1799–1804 by Alexander de Humboldt, and Aimé Bonpland*. By Alexander von Humboldt. Trans. Helen Maria Williams. 7 vols. London: Longman, 1814–29. Vol. 1. v–xii.
- *A Tour in Switzerland; or, a View of the Present State of the Governments and Manners of Those Cantons: With Comparative Sketches of the Present State of Paris*. 2nd ed. 2 vols. London: Robinson, 1798.
Wilson, Milton. *Shelley's Later Poetry: A Study of His Prophetic Imagination*. New York: Columbia UP, 1959.
Windham, William. *An Account of the Glacieres or Ice Alps in Savoy: In Two Letters, One from an English Gentleman to his Friend at Geneva, the Other from Peter Martel*. London: Meadows, 1744.
Wood, Robert. *The Ruins of Palmyra: Otherwise Tedmor in the Desert*. London: n.p., 1753.

Woodman, Ross Greig. 'The Androgyne in *Prometheus Unbound.*' *Studies in Romanticism* 20 (1981): 225–47.
- *The Apocalyptic Vision in the Poetry of Shelley.* Toronto: U of Toronto P, 1964.
Wordsworth, William. *The Poetical Works of William Wordsworth.* Ed. E. de Selincourt and Helen Darbishire. Rev. Helen Darbishire. 5 vols. Oxford: Oxford UP, 1952–9.
- *The Prelude: 1799, 1805, 1850.* Ed. Jonathan Wordsworth, M.H. Abrams, and Stephen Gill. New York: Norton, 1979.
Wyatt, John. *Wordsworth and the Geologists.* Cambridge: Cambridge UP, 1995.
Yeats, W.B. *Essays and Introductions.* London: Macmillan, 1961.
Young, Robert J.C. *Colonial Desire: Hybridity in Theory, Culture, and Race.* London: Routledge, 1995.
- *White Mythologies: Writing History and the West.* London: Routledge, 1990.
Young, W. Introduction. *The Journal of Frederick Horneman's Travels, from Cairo to Mourzouk, the Capital of the Kingdom of Fezzan in Africa, in the Years 1797–8.* By Frederick Horneman. London: Bulmer, 1802. i–xiii.

Index

Abrams, M.H., 93
Aeolian harp, 73
Aeschylus, 110. See also *Prometheus Unbound* (Aeschylus)
African Association, 152, 154, 155, 196–7n1
African Institution, 165
Ahriman, 89, 90–2, 103, 105; Zoroastrian god of darkness, 89, 92, 97
'Alastor' (Shelley), 7, 15, 86, 121, 122, 123, 154; geographic terms used in, 67–8; geography of, 69–70, 80, 83, 104, 119, 192; hybridity in, 117; imperialism and, 59, 81–2; narrator and Poet of, 54–6; not Romantic explorer, 62, 72; 'Petra,' 75; Poet as quester, 60; Poet's death, 80, 138; Poet's inward gaze, 63, 78, 133, 174; Poet's route in, 56, 60, 64, 75–9, 81, 164, 169, 172; Poet's sexual desire, 73–5; ruins in, 62; veiled maid and Asia, 130; veiled maid and Queen Mab, 31; veiled maid and 'The Witch of Atlas,' 153; veiled maid as Oriental other, 81; veiled maid as a Spirit, 79–80, 163; veiled maid as West and East, 73–4, 82; veiled maid encounter scene with Poet, 70–3
Alexander the Great, 112, 118–19, 172; and 'Alastor,' 56, 66–8, 75–7
Alps, 83, 182. See also Mont Blanc
Andes, 34, 51
Annesley, James, 191
Antelope (HMS), 188
anthropocentrism, 39
anti-colonialism, 9, 13, 47. See also colonialism/imperialism
Aornos, 75
Archimedes, 29
Arrian, Lucius Flavius: *Anabasis Alexandri*, 118–19
Arveiron (river), 86, 103–4, 208n35
Asia (in *Prometheus Unbound*), 108, 118, 134–5, 153, 158; as active quester, 123–4; and 'Alastor,' 74; background to, 115–17; and boat in 'The Witch of Atlas,' 164, 179; and colonialism, 191; as 'contagion of good,' 114; in Demogorgon's cave, 127–8, 138; dream of Prometheus, 122–3; her boat, 164, 179; and hybridity, 145–6; as

Mother, 130, 174; mountaintop experience of, 125–6, 210n14; as remembered, 120–1; as space for Europe and East, 142–4; and theatre (open/universal), 142–3; and 'The Witch of Atlas,' 153; as universal love, 130–4, 191; withdraws with Prometheus, 129
Asiatic Society of Bengal, 55, 58, 64, 202n16
atheistic and radical (Shelley), 28–9, 92, 97, 139–40, 206n22
Atlantis, 135–7, 211nn24–5, 28
Atlas Mountains/Mount Atlas, 144, 151–63, 175, 177, 214n18

Bailly, Jean Sylvain, 136
Baker, Carlos, 153
Bakhtin, Mikhail, 14, 48–9
Banier, Antoine: *The Mythology and Fables of the Ancients*, 115
Banks, Joseph, 41, 186–7, 196–7n1, 216n3
Barbauld, Anna: 'Eighteen Hundred and Eleven,' 33, 34
bardic tradition, 26–7
Barrell, John, 4, 11, 27, 30, 63, 132
Baudet, Henri, 57–8, 129–30
Beckford, William: *Vathek*, 65, 92, 141
Beddoes, Thomas; *Alexander's Expedition*, 66, 203n22
Beljame, Al, 76
Bell's New Pantheon, 115, 119, 130
Bentham, Jeremy, 8–9, 195n6
Berkeley, George, 93, 206–7n22
Bernier, François, 67–8
Bewell, Alan, 15, 41, 85, 191–2, 198n14
Bhabha, Homi K., 11, 14, 15, 129, 163, 196n13

Blackstone, Bernard, 61
Blake, William, 136–7, 211n28
Bloom, Harold, 56, 150, 163
Blumenbach, Johann Friedrich, 112, 146–7, 212n1; 'On the Natural Variety of Mankind,' 146, 209n5; *Short System of Comparative Anatomy*, 149
Bourrit, Marc-Théodore, 84
Bracknell circle of radical thinkers, 31, 199n23, 213n10
Brantlinger, Patrick, 15, 16
British Empire: and Africa, 214nn22–5, 215nn26–30; as context to 'Alastor,' 59–60; and decentring in Romantic geography, 48, 59; in India, 57–9; and interracial marriage, 146, 212nn3, 5, 212–13n6; and Labrador, 186–8; power of, 20; Romantic poets and, 5. *See also* colonialism/imperialism
Bruce, James, 61; *The Travels to Discover the Source of the Nile*, 62
Buckland, William, 197n2
Buffon, Georges-Louis Leclerc, 97, 114, 196–7n1; *Époques de la nature*, 88
Burke, Edmund, 3, 57, 179–80; *A Philosophical Enquiry into the Origin of Our Ideas of the Sublime and the Beautiful*, 70
Burnet, Thomas, 83
Butler, Marilyn, 8, 16, 178, 210n18
Byron, George Gordon, 100–1; 'Cain,' 141; *Childe Harold's Pilgrimage*, 91, 182; *Don Juan*, 9–10, 149–50, 166, 178; *Manfred*, 91–2, 95, 107

Caernarvonshire, 23, 24, 26
Cambridge Companion to Shelley (Morton), 17
Cameron, Kenneth Neil, 23, 92, 197n7, 213–14n15
Carbonnières, Ramond de, 89–90
Cartwright, George, 186–8; *A Journal of Transactions and Events* 187; *Labrador: A Poetical Epistle*, 187–8
Cazotte, Jacques, 203–4n29; *Continuation*, 72–3, 153, 154
centre–periphery hegemony: and bardic tradition, 27; and colonialism, 13, 15; and marginal space, 48; and progress of civilization, 34; in Romantic geography, 5–6, 17, 45–6; and semi- peripheries, 30, 196n10; and Shelley's Metropolis as Pandemonium, 19–21; and Shelley's metropolis in the margin, 38; and South America, 196n10. *See also* cities; marginal space
Chamonix, 83–4, 86–7, 89, 91, 94, 100–1, 104–6, 205n11, 207–8n30
Chernaik, Judith, 178
children: as audience for *Queen Mab*, 28–9, 198–9n16; as hybrid spirits, 144, 145, 149–50, 191; encountered in Geneva, 100–1, 107
Chimborazo, 51
Christianity: and Abyssinia, 63; and colonialism, 43; and India, 57–9, 67, 202n10; and Labrador Indians, 186–8; map of, 61; and 'Mont Blanc,' 91, 97, 102, 107; overseas missions and, 46, 200n33; and *Prometheus Unbound*, 113, 124; and *Queen Mab*, 29, 48; and race, 171; and religious difference ('Alastor'), 73; and slavery, 149. *See also* God

cities: absent in 'The Witch of Atlas,' 172; of death, 108; in 'Mont Blanc,' 99; and Mount Atlas, 160–1; as mourning woman, 210n18; in *Prometheus Unbound*, 135–8; in *Queen Mab*, 20–1, 35–40, 49, 59, 62, 136; Rome as city of, 173; in 'The Witch of Atlas,' 175

Clairmont, Claire, 86
Colbert, Benjamin, 17, 87, 101, 107
Coleridge, Samuel Taylor, 22; and 'Alastor,' 55; Alph (river), 104; conversation poems of, 93; 'Frost at Midnight,' 40; 'Hymn Before Sun-Rise,' 91, 92, 97, 182, 206n20; 'Kubla Khan,' 63, 103, 104, 208n34; *Lyrical Ballads*, 117; *Marginalia*, 5; 'Rime of the Ancyent Marinere,' 4; 'The Rime of the Ancient Mariner,' 61, 114, 169, 172, 202n15
Colley, Linda, 15
colonialism/imperialism: and Apollo in 'The Witch of Atlas,' 157, 158; Bible as hybrid text of, 163; and cartographers, 160; and contamination of Power, 183–4, 191–4; dividing up the globe, 13; and explorers, 50, 56, 66, 156, 167–8, 215n30; geography of, 177; and globalization, 193–4; inconsistent attitudes toward, 8–11, 15–18, 181–2; and interracial marriage, 146–50, 212nn3, 5, 212–13n6; Labrador in context of,

185; and language of despotism, 129; and liberating imagination, 178; and marginal space, 48; and masculine gaze, 154; and naturalists and surgeons, 41, 55; and the Other, 198n15; and poetic imagination, 5–6; and 'poison-tree' metaphor, 42–3, 45; and postcolonialism, 4–5; and quester as explorer, 169; and Romantic geography, 82, 192–4; in Romantic world view, 3, 4, 46–8; contrasting views of Shelley and Southey, 113–14. *See also* British Empire

Colwell, Frederic S., 137, 151, 211–12n29

Conant, Martha Pike, 153–4, 203–4n29

Conrad, Joseph: *Heart of Darkness*, 148, 169, 180

'contagion of good' (Shelley), 113–14, 117

Cook, James, 54, 169, 186, 196–7n1

Cooke, G.A., 24

Coxe, William, 84–5, 89, 205nn6, 12

critical theory, 4–5, 11–12

Croker, John Wilson, 33

Curran, Stuart, 15–16, 34, 112

Curtius, Quintius, 75

Cuvier, Georges, 153, 196–7n1, 212n30; *The Animal Kingdom*, 153; *Essay on the Theory of the Earth*, 139–41

Darwin, Erasmus, 199n18; *The Botanic Garden*, 28; *The Loves of the Plants*, 42, 200n32; *Temple of Nature*, 28, 140

de Man, Paul, 185, 190

Demogorgon *(Prometheus Unbound)*, 108, 123, 127–9, 132, 138, 142–3; background to, 115–17; and internalized geography, 134; as Jupiter's fatal child, 145, 176, 191, 194; source for, 209n6; volcanic power of, 134, 211n22

Denon, Vivant, 61

De Quincey, Thomas, 27, 43, 114, 132–3; *Confessions of an Opium Eater*, 89, 176; mental landscape of, 171

disease imagery: and colonialism, 42–3; 'contagion of good,' 113–14, 117; in 'Mont Blanc,' 100–1, 194; and power, 191–2; in *Prometheus Unbound*, 7, 49, 122, 123, 131–2, 211n20. See also *Queen Mab* (Shelley)

domestic space, 28, 30

Duerksen, Roland A., 164–5

Duffy, Cian, 17, 32, 125

Duffy, Edward, 185

Dupin, Charles, 20

Dupuis, Charles François, 215n33; *Origine de tous les cultes*, 171

East India Company, 8, 16, 41, 47, 57, 59, 65, 146, 202nn10, 17; and interracial marriage, 146, 212nn3, 5

East India Company College, 58

Eden, 68, 110, 114, 135, 137

Egypt, 156, 167, 170–2, 176–7, 215n32, 215–16n34

Eliot, T.S., 150

empire. *See* colonialism/imperialism

Encyclopædia Britannica, 146–7, 155, 156, 162–3, 171

Engel, Claire Eliane, 100
environmentalism, 41
epipsyches: and antitypes of foreign lands, 80; Asia and Prometheus, 116, 121, 123; and geography, 192; and mirrors, 71, 209n9; in 'On Love,' 71, 163 (and otherness, 30–1, 82, 95; in 'The Triumph of Life,' 193; in 'The Witch of Atlas,' 163, 174. *See also* mirror
Ethiopia, 62; as Abyssinia, 63–4, 99; as location of Mount Atlas, 153
Etna, 84, 97
Euripides, 115, 203n23; *Bacchae*, 119
Everest, Kelvin, 36, 68, 75, 197n7

Faber, George Stanley, 136
Ferguson, Frances, 107
Forster, George, 61, 66, 67–8, 75, 77, 203n21, 204n32
Fraistat, Neil, 36, 76, 86–7, 162
France: and Switzerland, 22; and universal revolution, 34; and war with England, 20, 86, 188. *See also* Rousseau, Jean-Jacques; *individual places*
French Revolution, 33, 100, 102, 182, 185
Friedman, John Block, 160
Fuseli, Henry, 199n19

Gallagher, John, 13
Gandhi, Leela, 6
Gay-Lussac, Josef-Louis, 51
gender (as masculine/feminine): in 'Alastor,' 59–60, 63–4, 70–3, 95; androgyny in 'The Witch of Atlas,' 162–3; in colonialism, 154; *Frankenstein*, 208n38; in 'Mont Blanc,' 94, 97, 105, 106; in *Prometheus Unbound*, 116–17, 120, 121, 125, 127, 130–1, 142; role in *Queen Mab*, 28–9, 33, 48–9; in 'The Witch of Atlas,' 151, 155, 177, 179, 180
Genesis, 140
geography: of Africa in 'The Witch of Atlas,' 177; in 'Alastor,' 69–70, 75–9; and exploration of Africa, 155–7; and hybridity, 14; internalized in *Prometheus Unbound*, 134–5; mapping of Labrador, 186; mapping of the globe ('Alastor'), 51, 64, 75; and power in maps, 61; in relationship with the self and others, 11; in the Romantic imagination, 12–13; in 'The Witch of Atlas,' 151–2, 168, 170. *See also* Romantic geography
geopolitical imaginings: and ambivalence of colonialism, 10–11, 13; and 'an alteritist fallacy,' 12; and centre–periphery hegemony, 192; and cosmopolitan dialogue, 116; England as hell, 68; and faith in human creative power, 124; in gender and geography, 70; and hybridity, 15; and mapping, 61, 64–5; of the margins, 110; and mythical Welsh figures, 38; in *Queen Mab* landscapes, 29–30, 33, 35, 50, 99, 124; in repositioning of Prometheus, 111; as subject of book, 5–8, 17; sublime and radical politics, 32; in 'The Witch of Atlas,' 151; through Mont Blanc experience, 92–3, 98–102, 106, 108; veiled maid as East and West ('Alastor'),

73–4. *See also* mountains; Romantic imagination; ruins
George IV, 21, 148
Georgian Caucasus, 77–8, 118–19, 138, 204n34
giaour, 65, 202n13
globalization, 3, 7, 9–10, 13, 193–4, 196n12
God: benevolent plan of, 100, 103; Christian, 49, 91–2; and confusing mixture of gods, 91–2, 94, 97; miracle of God's creation, 86; existence of creator-God, 32, 86, 88, 90, 97; nature without, 32; and poetic imagination, 69; Wordsworth's disappointment in 'Mont Blanc,' 207–8n30; and Zoroastrian god of darkness, 89
Godwin, William, 25, 111, 190
Goethe, Johann Wolfgang von, 51, 201n1
Grabo, Carl, 140, 151–2
Greek art, 137, 142–3
Grosrichard, Alain, 11, 195–6n8

Haggard, H. Rider: *She,* 180
Hakluyt, Richard, 214n22
Harley, J.B., 61
Harrington-Austin, Eleanor J., 16–17
Hastings, Warren, 57
Haven, Jens, 187
Heber, Reginald: 'From Greenland's Icy Mountains,' 114
Hemans, Felicia, 26
Heringman, Noah, 12
Herodotus, 156, 170–1
heterotopicality, 12, 196n9
Hindoo-Kho. *See* Indian Caucasus

Hippocratic philosophy, 41, 44, 200n31
Hoare, Richard Colt, 23–4
Hodges, William; 201n3; *Travels in India,* 66–7
Hogg, Thomas Jefferson, 55, 166
Hogle, Jerrold, 151
Horneman, Frederick, 165, 214n24
Humboldt, Alexander von, 47, 62, 200–1n34, 201n1, 205n7; 'Ideas for a Geography of Plants,' 51; *Personal Narratives of Travels,* 46–7, 54, 55–6
Hume, David, 93, 207n24
Hutton, James, 88, 97, 205n7, 206n15
Hyam, Ronald, 146
hybridity: in 'Alastor,' 117; as androgyny, 162–3; and colonialism, 191; of East and West at Mont Blanc, 89, 91, 126–7; and English Bible, 163; of love and poetic imagination, 176–7; of the Minotaur, 148; of plants, 146–7, 213n7; in *Prometheus Unbound,* 117, 126–7, 129–30, 137, 143–4, 145–6; of race, 144, 146–50, 153, 212nn1–3, 5, 212–13n6, 217n12; and Romantic geography, 192–3; the term, 14–15; in 'The Witch of Atlas,' 158–9, 169–70; in 'The Witch of Atlas' (of geography), 170–7; in 'The Witch of Atlas' (of the Witch), 177–80

idealism: and ideal mirror of self, 71; and imperialism, 8, 10; as 'beautiful idealisms' in *Prometheus Unbound,* 129, 142,

193; role of Romantic, 17; and visionary improvement, 50
identity, 196n13, 215n32; Eastern, 129, 152; hybrid, 14, 163, 169, 180; national, 32; and psychoanalysis, 11
imagination. *See* geopolitical imaginings
imperialism. *See* colonialism/imperialism
India, Shelley's interest in, 55, 56–7, 181–2
Indian Caucasus, 108; in 'Alastor,' 56, 64, 67–8, 74, 77–80, 82, 204n33; and Caf (mythological), 136, 209n7; connection to Prometheus, 110–12, 114; as cradle of civilization, 83, 85, 118; historic context of, 111–12; in *Prometheus Unbound*, 117–20, 124, 126–7, 130, 134–6, 174
Ireland, 21, 27

Jackson, James Grey, 154, 156, 160, 215n30
Jobson, Richard, 214n22; *The Golden Trade*, 165
Johnson, Samuel, 63
Jones, William, 57, 58, 59, 64–5, 85, 111, 114–15, 201n7; 'A Hymn to Lacshmí,' 130; 'On the Gods of Greece, Italy, and India,' 114–15
Justel, Henri, 83

Kashmir (vale of), 56, 58–60, 67–9, 74–5, 79, 116–19, 121–4, 132, 203n21
Keates, George: *The Alps: A Poem*, 85
Keats, John, 71; 'Hyperion: A Fragment,' 116, 130, 136; *Lamia*, 177–8
Keswick, 19–20, 23, 37, 62, 99, 101

Kidwai, Abdur Raheem, 16
Kipling, Rudyard: *Kim*, 180
Knight, G. Wilson, 152

Labrador (and Newfoundland), 185–9, 192, 193, 216nn2–3
Lacan, Jacques, 11
Lake District (England), 4, 89, 152
Lake Geneva, 100–1, 104, 182, 208n36
Lake Mareotis (Mariout), 170–1
Lake Moeris (Birket-Qarun), 170–2
Landor, Walter Savage: *Gebir*, 16, 80–1, 183
Lawrence, William, 149, 199n23, 213nn10–11; *Lectures on Physiology, Zoology, and the Natural History of Man*, 149
Leask, Nigel, 4, 11, 15, 16, 59–60, 71, 112, 116–17, 169
Lee, Debbie, 4–5, 151, 167
Lemprière, John, 129, 160; *Classical Dictionary*, 115
Levina, Emmanuel, 5
Lew, Joseph, 150
Lisbon Earthquake, 97, 207n26
literary criticism, 4–5, 11–12
London: compared to Mount Atlas, 160–1; and the ideal city, 20–1; and the 'poison-tree' metaphor, 42, 45–6, 99, 200n32; as Shelley's 'populous city,' 40, 49
love, defining of, 9–10
Lowe, Lisa, 11–12, 196n9
Lucretius, Carus Titus, 29
Lyell, Charles, 95–6

Mackenzie, John, 15
Madocks, William Alexander, 23–4, 25, 26, 50, 197nn8, 9, 198n14

Makdisi, Saree, 13, 16, 60, 76
marginal space, 48, 110, 116, 117–18, 126; in Africa, 154, 158–9; and hybridity, 180, 192–3. *See also* centre–periphery hegemony
Martel, Peter, 84, 205n4
Matthews, Geoffrey, 36, 68, 75, 197n7
Maurice, Thomas: *Indian Antiquities*, 68, 124
Mazzeo, Tilar J., 73
McGann, Jerome, 92
Melzer, Arthur, 190
Mill, James: *History of British India*, 58, 181
Mill, J.S., 8–9, 16, 147
Milton, John, 112; 'L'Allegro,' 22; *Paradise Lost*, 3, 20–1, 48, 49
mimicry, 129, 163
mirror: in 'Alastor,' 70, 78–9, 133, 163; and epipsyche, 71, 79–80, 209n9; in *Queen Mab*, 24. *See also* epipsyches
Montagne des Eschelles, 109
Mont Blanc: glaciers of, 88–91, 126, 134; history of, 83–6; social and political implications of, 106
'Mont Blanc' (Shelley): 'At Pont Pellisier,' 87; colonialism and, 182; context of writing of, 86–91, 206n13; descriptive-meditative mode of, 93; and experience of the glaciers, 89–92, 126, 185; and geological past, 141, 197n7; humanizing geography in, 92–3; Necessity in, 89, 105, 108, 119; Power on, 94, 96–7, 104–6, 116, 126–7, 130, 134; and *Prometheus Unbound*, 109, 133–4, 142; Ravine of Arve, 93–6, 102; Romantic geography of, 96–8, 192; at the summit, 105–8; 'vast caves' in, 103; voice of, 98–100, 128; 'witch Poesy,' 95, 103, 151
Monte San Pellegrino, 144, 157
Moor, Edward: *The Hindu Pantheon*, 57
Moore, Thomas, 153; *The Epicurian, a Tale*, 153, 213n13; *Lalla Rookh*, 68
Moravian missionaries, 186–7, 216n3; Unitus Fratrum, 185.
mountains, 22, 34; experienced as malevolent, 92; and experience of glaciers, 89–90, 91, 103, 106, 126, 134, 185, 204–5n3; geological experience of, 95–6; mountaintop experiences, 85, 91, 108, 110, 119–20, 125–6, 130, 193, 210n14; in 'The Witch of Atlas,' 153. *See also* geopolitical imaginings; *individual mountains*
Mount Ararat, 110
Mount Atlas. *See* Atlas Mountains
Mount Meru (Indian mythology), 111, 118, 126
Mount Vesuvius, 97, 126, 133, 134
Murray, Hugh: *Historical Account of Discoveries and Travels in Africa*, 155

Napoleon, 17, 41, 58, 59, 100, 136, 171–2, 176–7, 215n33
nature: in 'Alastor,' 55; as human habitat, 20, 86; and human-made disease, 42, 100–1; with science and myth, 27; without God, 32, 97
Necessity (idea of), 89, 105, 108, 115, 119, 197n7; as Spirit of Nature, 32

Newfoundland and Labrador. *See* Labrador (and Newfoundland)
Newton, John Frank, 31, 199n23
Niger (HMS), 187
Niger (river), 156, 165–7, 214nn21–2
Nile (river), 158, 166–7, 169, 170–7, 179, 192, 214n16, 215n31
noble savage, 80
Nonnos, Ponepolitanus: *Dionysiaca*, 119, 203n23
Nott, Josiah, 147

O'Brien, Karen, 194
Oerlemans, Onno, 12
Ollier, Charles, 150
opera, 142
Orientalism: and 'Alastor,' 56, 59, 63; and British India, 57–9; countering Said's view of, 65, 67, 82; and gendered oppositions, 116; origins of modern, 9; and psychoanalysis, 11–12; in 'The Witch of Atlas,' 177–8. *See also* Said, Edward
Owenson, Sydney, 121; Hilarion and Luxima *(Missionary)*, 69–70, 71, 72, 153, 183; *The Missionary*, 58–9, 63, 67, 68, 80, 116, 128, 130, 202n13

Paine, Thomas, 29
Palliser, Hugh, 186–8
Palmyra, 30–6, 60, 156, 199n22, 210–11n18
Park, Mungo, 154, 165, 172, 214nn21, 25, 215nn26, 29; *Joliba* (schooner), 166, 168
Parkinson, James, 212n30; *Organic Remains of a Former World*, 139–40

Peacock, Thomas Love, 8–9, 86, 181, 198n10; *Ahrimanes*, 92; 'The Four Ages of Poetry,' 8; *Headlong Hall*, 24; Shelley's *Letters*, 9, 89, 100–2, 106–7, 133
Peterfreund, Stuart, 185
Peterloo Massacre, 184
'Pious Clause' in Charter Act of 1813, 58, 202n10
Plato, 135, 136–7
Playfair, John, 95, 206n15
political poems, 40. *See also* geopolitical imaginings; Shelley, Percy Bysshe
Pompeii, 126
Portuguese empire, 3
postcolonialism, 4–5, 6–7, 10–12, 14–18, 193
Pratt, Mary Louise, 12, 15, 47, 48
progress: of civilization (*translatio imperii*), 34, 37, 47, 60; and human responsibility, 43; against the idea of, 48; and improvement, 50
Prometheus: and Ahasuerus, 49; as confined in India, 118; Shelley's and condemnation of, 31, 110; Promethean fire-bringer, 110, 133. See also *Prometheus Unbound*
Prometheus Bound (Aeschylus), 109–11, 115, 116, 117–18, 138, 142, 143, 209n2
Prometheus Unbound (Shelley): and 'Alastor,' 78; and biblical history, 114–15; Cave and Temple of Prometheus in, 137–8, 143–4, 158; and colonialism/imperialism, 7–8, 10, 129; cosmogony of, 139–41; the Curse as relinquished, 7, 49–50, 120–1, 128–9, 131–2; foreign characters in, 115 (*see also*

Asia [in *Prometheus Unbound*]; Demogorgon [*Prometheus Unbound*]); geographic context to, 109–18; geography internalized, 134–5; geography of, 192–3; idealisms as plural in, 142, 193; Spirit of the Earth, 45, 130–1, 133, 138, 144, 174; and travels in 'Alastor,' 75; unborn child of, 145–6
psychoanalytical studies, 11, 27, 195n8

Queen Mab (Shelley), 199n20; and Ahasuerus, 49; choice of title of, 28; and colonialism, 8; context to, 25; disease metaphor in, 42–4, 132; fairy queen, choice of, 27–9, 33, 48, 199n19; fairy queen origins, 26; geography of, 29–30, 34, 51, 68, 116–17, 170, 192; human-made disease in, 100–1; and the Metropolis, 6, 35, 37–8, 40, 59, 62, 99, 136, 141; 'poison-tree' metaphor in, 42, 44, 45–6, 99, 200n32; Power in, 191; printing of, 28; Promethean fire-bringer in, 110; pyramids in, 44, 173; ruins in, 29–30, 32–3, 35–7, 41, 44–5, 48, 60; tyrannical institutions of, 90; utopian landscape in, 46–9, 124, 130; 'wonders of the human world,' 161

Raben, Joseph, 112, 153
race, 144, 146–50, 153, 193, 209n5, 212n2, 212–13n6, 213nn8–9; in cultural and literary studies, 11–12; and Egypt, 171, 215n32
Rajan, Balachandra, 73, 121

Raleigh, Walter: *The History of the World*, 68, 110
Rees, Abraham, 111–12
Reiman, Donald H., 36, 76, 86–7, 162, 185
Rennell, James, 61, 155; *Bengal Atlas*, 65–6, 72; *Memoir of a Map of Hindoostan*, 65–6, 203n19; 'The Countries, Situated between the Source of the Ganges and the Caspian Sea' (map), 75; *The Geographical System of Herodotus*, 156, 171, 172, 203n21
Ristons, Joseph, 31
Robertson, William: *An Historical Disquisition*, 57
Robinson, Charles, 208n34
Robinson, Ronald, 13
Romantic geography: of 'Alastor,' 76, 77, 80, 82; and centre–periphery hegemony, 45–6; and colonial landscapes, 192, 194; and colonial vocabulary, 47–8; and the ideal city, 21; of Mont Blanc, 85–6, 91; of 'Mont Blanc,' 104; mountains in, 22; and notion of ideal place, 38–9; in *Prometheus Unbound*, 133–5; Shelley a case study for, 15–16; in 'The Triumph of Life,' 185–9; in 'The Witch of Atlas,' 178, 180; and use of hybridity, 15, 192–3; use of term, 5–8, 192–3; of Wales and Middle East, 30; and West's invasion of the East, 59, 192. *See also* geography
Romantic imagination: in 'Alastor,' 55–6; and the East, 63; in (un)making of empire, 5. *See also* geopolitical imaginings
Romantic lyric, 93; in 'Mont Blanc,'

108; in *Prometheus Unbound,* 141–2

Rome, 118, 173

Rousseau, Jean-Jacques, 182, 186; *The Confessions,* 189, 190; *Discours sur les sciences et les arts,* 216–17n10; *First Discourses,* 31, 197n4; on Prometheus, 31,121; on sciences and the arts, 21; *Second Discourse,* 3, 31, 37; Shelley's engagement with, 7, 182; *Social Contract,* 10; and 'The Triumph of Life,' 182–6, 189–94; vision of Vincennes, 189–90, 216–17n10

ruins, 199n22; absent in 'The Witch of Atlas,' 173; in 'Alastor,' 60, 61–2, 75–6; as contact zones, 48; of historical cities, 141; as retrievable, 36–7, 41, 44–5; as site of revolutionary thought, 32–3; as world in decay, 29–30, 35

Ruston, Sharon, 122, 149

Said, Edward: *Orientalism,* 4, 9, 11, 15, 27, 58, 59, 65, 195n8. *See also* Orientalism

Santo Domingo, 146

Saussure, Horace Benedict de, 84–5, 205nn7, 10; and Mont Blanc, 105–6; *Voyage dans les Alps,* 97

Savoy, 100, 103, 109, 205n11

Schwab, Reymond, 58, 59

science and geology, 205nn5, 7; accessing Egypt, 171–2; discoveries in, 19–20, 196–7n1, 197n2; and glaciers, 88; and improvement, 25, 27, 50; on interracial marriage and hybridity, 149, 212n1, 212–13n6, 213nn7–11, 217n12; mapping of India, 65–7, 202n17; and Mont Blanc, 84–6, 102, 107–8; of mountains, 95–6, 97–8; and opening Africa, 166; poetry and, 6, 8, 10, 16, 39; and Prometheus, 31; in *Prometheus Unbound,* 128, 138–41; in 'The Witch of Atlas,' 168; in travel narratives, 54, 56; as weapon, 25

Scotland: bardic tradition of, 27; in Romantic geography, 21

Shakespeare, William, 199n19; *Romeo and Juliet,* 26, 28–9

Shelley, Mary, 73, 86–7, 109–10, 141, 150, 182, 183, 207n23; *Frankenstein,* 168, 190, 208n38; *History of a Six Weeks' Tour,* 86–7, 94; *The Last Man,* 114

Shelley, Percy Bysshe, 197n5; on education of poetic imagination, 6–7; first child of, 199n20; optimism/pessimism, 181; on poetry and social good, 118; as quester, 181–2; books purchased and or read by, 72, 110, 111, 128, 182, 199n18, 216–17n10

– Works: 'An Address, to the Irish People,' 60; *The Assassins,* 138; 'The Cloud,' 157; *A Defence of Poetry,* 8–9, 9–11, 113–14, 118, 162, 175–6, 182; 'The Devil's Walk,' 40; 'England in 1819,' 40; 'Evening: Ponte Al Mare, Pisa,' 174; 'Henry and Louisa,' 157; *History of a Six Weeks' Tour,* 86; 'Hymn to Intellectual Beauty,' 94; 'Hymn to Mercury,' 178; 'Letter to Maria Gisborne,' 151, 161; 'The Mask of Anarchy,' 40, 184; 'To the Nile,' 167; 'Notes on Sculptures,' 143; 'Ode to Liberty,' 173, 174; 'Ode to

the West Wind,' 48, 73; 'Oedipus Tyrannus or Swellfoot the Tyrant,' 40, 148; 'On Leaving London for Wales,' 21–3, 25–6, 29–30, 34–5, 40, 43–4, 50, 106; 'On Love,' 71, 163; 'Ozymandias,' 32, 44; 'Peter Bell the Third,' 20, 155, 213–14n15; 'A Philosophical View of Reform,' 16, 113–14; 'A Refutation of Deism,' 6, 7, 32, 206n22; *The Revolt of Islam*, 39, 108, 110, 116–17, 124, 130, 133, 141; 'The Sensitive Plant,' 148; 'To the Republicans of North America,' 34; *A Vindication of Natural Diet*, 31; 'Zeinab and Kathema,' 56, 58, 60, 68, 74, 79, 116. See also 'Alastor' (Shelley); 'Mont Blanc' (Shelley); *Prometheus Unbound* (Shelley); 'The Triumph of Life' (Shelley); 'The Witch of Atlas' (Shelley)
Shelley scholarship, 15–17
Sheppard, John: *Letters Descriptive of a Tour*, 101
Shuckborough, George, 84
slavery, 4, 149, 150, 154, 177
Smith, Adam, 3, 5
Snowdonia, 22–4, 26, 29, 125, 198n9, 210n16
Southey, Robert, 112–13; and 'Alastor,' 55; *The Curse of Kehama*, 57, 58; *Joan of Arc*, 48; *Madoc*, 26, 27, 28, 36, 46; *Thalaba*, 29, 73
Spanish Empire, 3, 34, 46–7, 200–1n34
Spenser, Edmund, 161
Sperry, Stuart, 108
Spivak, Gayatri, 27, 198n15
Stafford, Barbara, 12
Stanley of Alderley, Lady, 89

St Helena, 41
sublime, the: in 'Alastor,' 55, 73–4; and the Alps, 83; and Burke, 70; and the city, 21; at Mont Blanc, 89, 96; and radical politics, 32; as source of evil (Mont Blanc), 99
Suleri, Sara, 12, 70, 179, 180
Switzerland, 22, 88, 100–1, 205n12

Tan-yr-allt (house in Wales), 25, 27, 29, 40, 199n21
Taylor, Thomas, 135, 136
Tetreault, Ronald, 142
Thomson, John: 'A Comparative View of the Heights of the Principal Mountains' (illustration), 52–3; *A New General Atlas*, 51, 155–6
Timbuctoo, 164–6, 168, 177, 214n21
Tooke, Andrew: *Pantheon*, 115
travellers and tourists: experience of glaciers, 89–90; experience of sublime in the Alps, 83; exploring Africa, 152, 154, 155–7, 164–9, 178, 214nn22–5, 215nn26–9; and the Grand Tour, 17, 32, 86; as hired by governments, 47, 61, 200–1n34; to India, 55–6, 215–16n34; and landscape of *Queen Mab*, 31; as narrator, 54; in the Romantic imagination, 12–13; Shelley's criticism of, 101–2, 106; and travel writing, 61, 69, 87, 205n12
Treath Mawr, 23–6
Tremadoc, 23–7, 50, 197n5, 198n14
'The Triumph of Life' (Shelley): and colonialism, 7, 9, 182, 184, 193–4; context to geography of, 185–8; on European responsibility,

190–1; and Owenson's Luxima, 69; pessimism of, 181; Promethean fire-bringer in, 110; and *Queen Mab*, 31, 39–40, 50; Romantic geography in, 185–9; Rousseau in, 7, 182–6, 189–94, 216n7; two kinds of power in, 183, 191–2

upas tree (poison tree), 42–3, 99, 200n32
utopia, 29, 43, 44–5; and imperialism, 8; in *Prometheus Unbound*, 129; in *Queen Mab*, 46–9, 50, 130

Valentia, George Annesley, 146, 212n5
vegetarianism, 31, 40, 110, 199–200n23, 200n30
Victoria (queen and lake), 169, 213n11, 215n31
Vidal-Naquet, Pierre, 135
Vincennes, 189–90
volcanic eruptions, 97, 133, 134, 207n27
Volney, Constantin: *Ruins*, 30, 33–4, 61, 200n26
Voltaire, 29, 207n26

Wales: embankment at Tremadoc, 23–5, 40, 50, 197n8, 198nn9, 11; mountains of, 22; as place of hope, 40; as place of revolutionary actions, 29; Prince Madoc and Mab, 7, 26–7, 27–9, 38, 46, 48, 116, 198nn13–14, 199n19; in Romantic geography, 21; Shelley in, 197n5
Wallerstein, Immanuel, 13, 30, 196n10
Walsh, Thomas, 176

Warton, Thomas, 22
Wasserman, Earl R., 54, 78, 93, 207n27
Webb, Timothy, 143, 152
Weinberg, Alan M., 112
Weisman, Karen, 129
Western invasion of the East: and 'Alastor,' 75–7, 80–2, 192; and Owenson's *The Missionary*, 67; and *Prometheus Unbound*, 118–19, 132; and Shelley's Romantic geography, 59, 192; and 'Zeinab and Kathema,' 59
Whalley, Thomas Sedgwick: *Mont Blanc: An Irregular Lyric Poem*, 85
White, Gilbert, 148
Wilford, Francis, 110–11, 118, 126, 136, 137, 211n26
Williams, Helen Maria, 47, 54, 55–6, 62, 89
Windham, William, 83–4, 89, 90, 101, 204–5n3, 205n4
'The Witch of Atlas' (Shelley): as an explorer, 155; Apollo in, 157–8, 161, 164, 168–70, 175, 177, 179, 183; and colonialism, 150, 191; composing of, 212n32; context to, 144, 148–50; the Garamantes, 156, 160, 165; geography of, 192; and Haidée in *Don Juan*, 158–9, 163; irony of, 177–8, 180; magic boat of, 164–9; mapping of Southern Hemisphere in, 151; mountains in, 156–7; Mount Atlas in, 159–61; on the Nile, 170–7; and Owenson's Luxima, 183–4; as poetry, 175–6; as a Power, 158, 175; 'sexless bee' of, 162–3
Wood, Robert, 199n22

Wordsworth, William: 87, 91, 101; and narrator in 'Alastor,' 54–5; *Descriptive Sketches*, 89, 91, 99–100, 210n16; *The Excursion*, 63, 80; 'Intimations of Immortality from Recollections of Early Childhood,' 74; *Lyrical Ballads*, 117; 'The Pass of Kirkstone,' 20; *Peter Bell*, 154–5, 164, 167, 213–14n15, 214n21; *The Prelude*, 3, 4, 20–1, 99, 160–1, 207–8n30, 210n16; 'Ruth,' 152–3; 'The Brothers,' 4; 'There was a Boy,' 78; 'Thought of a Briton on the Subjugation of Switzerland,' 22; 'Three years she grew in sun and shower,' 152–3; 'Tintern Abbey,' 93

Yeats, W.B., 173
Young, Robert, 147
Young, W.: *The Journal of Frederick Horneman's Travels*, 165

www.ingramcontent.com/pod-product-compliance
Lightning Source LLC
Chambersburg PA
CBHW030309080526
44584CB00012B/503